EQUALITY LAW IN
AN ENLARGED EUROPEAN UNION

European Union equality and anti-discrimination law was revolutionised by the incorporation of Article 13 into the EC Treaty, adding new anti-discrimination grounds and new possibilities. This comprehensive volume provides a fresh approach to Article 13 and its directives; it adopts a contextual framework to equality and anti-discrimination law in the European Union. Part I deals with the evolution of Article 13, demographic and social change and the interrelationship between European equality law and human rights. Part II contains expert essays on each of the Article 13 anti-discrimination grounds: sex, racial or ethnic origin, religion or belief, disability, age and sexual orientation, with common themes weaving throughout. This book will be of interest to everyone concerned with combating discrimination, academics, NGOs, lawyers, human resource professionals, employers, employees, research students and many others in the European Union and beyond.

HELEN MEENAN holds the Jean Monnet Chair at Kingston University. Her research interests include age discrimination, human rights, elder law, European company law and European social policy.

EQUALITY LAW IN
AN ENLARGED EUROPEAN
UNION

Understanding the
Article 13 Directives

Editor

HELEN MEENAN

CAMBRIDGE
UNIVERSITY PRESS

CAMBRIDGE UNIVERSITY PRESS
Cambridge, New York, Melbourne, Madrid, Cape Town, Singapore, São Paulo

Cambridge University Press
The Edinburgh Building, Cambridge CB2 8RU, UK

Published in the United States of America by Cambridge University Press, New York

www.cambridge.org
Information on this title: www.cambridge.org/9780521865302

© Cambridge University Press 2007

First published 2007

Printed in the United Kingdom at the University Press, Cambridge

A catalogue record for this book is available from the British Library

ISBN 978-0-521-86530-2 hardback

CONTENTS

PREFACE

Few terms in law and philosophy have had as long a life and as important a role in modern history as the idea of equality (SA Lakoff, Harvard University Press, 1964). This is visible in the history of equality in the European Union, which has striven to keep up with the diversity of its peoples, despite a slow start. Since the founding Treaties were signed in the 1950s, European equality law has become far more complex. Theories, themes and definitions of equality and discrimination have developed over time and have been greatly influenced by cases brought by ordinary people. Equality and anti-discrimination are areas of European law that directly serve the individual. They are therefore of interest to us all. Combating discrimination and promoting and achieving equality have become prominent, important and challenging issues in European life.

European enlargement into a Union of twenty-five diverse Member States in 2004, was a historic turning point of political, legal and social significance and a 'reunification' of such magnitude that perhaps it cannot be appreciated fully, except in retrospect. It contrasts dramatically with the original European (Economic) Community of six geographically close Member States. This most ambitious enlargement, which incorporated new regions, new peoples, new languages, new opportunities and new fears within the Union, has also influenced the recent dynamism in European equality law and simultaneously presents a variety of challenges for the European equality matrix. The Nice Treaty and the provisional Constitutional Treaty for the European Union (now overtaken by the draft Reform Treaty) attempted to provide for the socio-political-legal and institutional implications of such a large and diverse European Union.

The original European (Economic) Community Treaty did not cater for, nor was it intended to cater for the many characteristics of a static nature, such as race, and a non-static nature, such as age, inherent in each individual and the multifarious ways they interact with each other. Significantly though it enshrined the principle that men and women

vii

should receive equal pay for equal work and the principle of free movement of workers within the Community, without discrimination on grounds of nationality. These founding principles have developed in rich and varied ways. More recent EU anti-discrimination grounds breathe with their memory and their development through the case law of the European Court of Justice and secondary legislation.

The concrete emergence of a broader equality culture can be seen, above all, in the Treaty of Amsterdam's amendment of the EC Treaty in 1999, with the inclusion of Article 13. The proclamation of the EU Charter of Fundamental Rights in 2000, and the recent cautious expansion of European non-discrimination law into the provision of goods and services, support the idea of a new equality era. Following the most recent enlargements, the European equality matrix must now rise to meet two challenges: (1) cater for the rich diversity brought about by the addition and integration of new EU Member States; and (2) ensure the workability of the Article 13 Directives, which represent a major positive change for the individual even in most, older Member States. Yet these new grounds are predictable and possibly conservative. Their addition may be seen in retrospect as an important point on the journey but far from the end of the road.

We now live in a newly enlarged European Union, increasingly 'united in diversity' so European equality law requires a different and deeper academic scrutiny at this point in time. The authors have chosen the self-selecting subject of Article 13 EC and its grounds of sex, racial or ethnic origin, religion or belief, disability, age and sexual orientation which may be protected from discrimination thereunder, as a discreet and logical focus for this book. However, they have adopted a unique contextual and thematic approach to their work. They deal with all of the Article 13 grounds in a single academic book, as they have much in common by virtue of their cohabitation in this important provision and the family of resulting Directives. Surprisingly, this approach is rarely taken outside the realm of the textbook. The authors also examine these grounds against a contextual background with Article 13 providing the first and most immediate context for them all. The contextual and thematic approaches aim to achieve distinctive insights and perspectives on these non-discrimination grounds. They also seek to make a striking contribution to the present body of mainly journal literature on Article 13. The authors are faced in the first place with the uniqueness of each Article 13 ground as a human characteristic. In the second place, these grounds share many common and similar provisions within the Article 13 legislation. However, very distinct legal exceptions and provisions exist within this legislation for some of their number namely, disability, race, sex, age and religion or belief. Intersections between these grounds and issues of multiple identity and multiple discrimination only serve to make their scrutiny more interesting and more complex.

Thus the authors have constructed this book around three important endeavours: (1) to locate and examine each Article 13 ground within its Directive and as a component of an integrated approach to combating discrimination and promoting equality, so that differences among them and any exceptions and special provisions for them may be better understood; (2) to set this understanding against three carefully chosen and salient contexts, the history and evolution of Article 13 EC, European Human Rights and demographic and social change; and (3) to address certain common issues, questions and themes including, human rights, access to justice and the effects of enlargement on each ground, which help to bind the chapters together. This solidly constructed approach aims to achieve a certain level of coherence among the diverse authorship and grounds, yet its outcomes will doubtless also illuminate areas where grounds can only be converged so far. The emergent conclusions both convergent and divergent will be one of the main strengths of this book, which will reveal fresh insights and make a meaningful and timely contribution to the existing body of literature in this field.

The structure of this book is designed to support a strong and judiciously constructed contextual approach. Part I contains the context-setting chapters and Part II contains a chapter on each of the grounds in Article 13 EC. This book also brings together a *de novo* international group of authors with a rich command of their subject. Many of the authors are members of the European Network of Experts on non-discrimination and the European Networks of Experts on disability and equality between men and women, among many other high profile committees.

The starting point for this volume was a private workshop, which enabled the authors to set about writing with a shared vision. The resulting approach nonetheless aims to preserve the freshness and passion of the authors, to connect the authors and their chapters in all their diversity and generate stimulating thoughts and conclusions. Whether we have fulfilled our mission in this rewarding enterprise I will leave to you, the reader, to decide.

Helen Meenan
July 2007

ACKNOWLEDGEMENTS

This book has been a personal goal for some years, so to reach this point is very sweet. There are many deserving of thanks. The effective starting point can be traced to a discussion with Adam Tyson (Head of Unit E2, Social Protection and Social Inclusion and Policy Co-ordination, DG Employment, Social Affairs and Equal Opportunities, European Commission). I would like to thank Adam most sincerely for his helpful thoughts on this and on previous occasions.

There is a great debt owed to each of my co-authors without whom there would simply be no book. I have been enormously fortunate to have secured some of the most celebrated experts in European anti-discrimination and equality law who have contributed so much to this field both through their writing and their participation in various networks of independent experts at EU level. I am very grateful to Professors Gerard Quinn, Christopher McCrudden (also for his kind assistance at the book proposal stage), Ann Numhauser-Henning and Barry Fitzpatrick for their contributions. I am also very grateful to Robin Allen QC who joined this project with enormous grace and to my colleague Professor Gwyneth Pitt, who must additionally be thanked for granting me invaluable research leave to realise this book. Our remaining co-authors Professor Mark Bell (also a member of various European networks of independent experts), Dr Israel Doron and not least Dr Haris Kountouros are due a special acknowledgement for their enthusiasm and support throughout. Everyone should work with them at least once.

I would also like to thank our colleague Professor Lisa Waddington, Maastricht University, whose early solidarity with this project helped to get it off the ground. Considerable thanks are due to Finola O'Sullivan, Richard Woodham, Wendy Gater, Cheryl Prophett and Sinead Moloney at Cambridge University Press (CUP); to Finola for agreeing to publish this book and for her great patience and understanding. I hope her faith has been well placed. It is important also to acknowledge the constructive comments of CUP's anonymous reviewers which helped to shape this volume. I would also like to thank my colleagues at Kingston University especially Graeme Broadbent, Nicola Aries and Phil Harris.

Edited volumes can present unique challenges and although more personal thanks by the editor may not be the norm I have no choice but to make further acknowledgements. Above all, they are to my husband, John, for his unstinting support and encouragement and to our young son, Sander, whose tremendous love makes everything worthwhile. I would like also to remember many other relatives and friends, too numerous to mention here. It is my sincere wish that I have not omitted anyone and that this book will prove useful and stimulating to the very wide range of people involved in this most human field.

Helen Meenan
July 2007

Robin Allen QC became a barrister in 1974 and a Queen's Counsel in 1995. He works nationally and throughout Europe as an advocate and adviser specialising in equality and non-discrimination law. He has appeared in many of the leading discrimination cases in the UK and ECJ, and has lectured on Article 13 EC and directives made under it to judges and jurists from all the Member States and candidate countries. He has worked with the European Commission and all the Equality Commissions in the UK. He is a special adviser to the Disability Rights Commission and a consultant to Age Concern. He is Head of Cloisters Barristers' Chambers, a Recorder, a Bencher of Middle Temple and a former Chair of the Employment Law Bar Association.

Professor Mark Bell Centre for European Law and Integration, University of Leicester. He is a member of the European Commission's Network of Lawyers in the Non-Discrimination Field and on the editorial board of the *European Anti-Discrimination Law Review.*

Dr Israel Doron LLB (1989) Hebrew University of Jerusalem, Israel; LLM (1994) Washington College of Law, US; D Jur (2000) Osgoode Hall Law School, Toronto, Canada; Advocate (1991) the Israeli Bar Association, is a Senior Lecturer at the Faculty of Welfare and Health Studies, and at the Faculty of Law, Haifa University, Haifa, Israel. He specialises in elder law, social policy and ageing and senior's rights.

He is the author of 'The Fifth Commandment: Issues in Law and Aging' (in Hebrew) and of numerous articles in international journals and is active in various non-governmental organisations, and one of the founders of the Israeli NGO: The Law in the Service of the Elderly.

Professor Barry Fitzpatrick's academic career includes lectureships in polytechnics and universities in Preston, Leicester and Newcastle upon Tyne before becoming Professor of Law at the University of Ulster from 1995–2002. During that time, he was Jean Monnet Professor of

European Law (1998–2002) and Head of the Law School (2001–2002). He was Head of Legal Policy and Advice at the Equality Commission for Northern Ireland from 2002–2005. Much of his professional work has centred upon issues of EU sex equality law and now the wider EU equality law agenda. Most recently he has been closely involved in EU equality training programmes with Maastricht University and the European Disability Forum. He has also acted as UK National Expert in a European Commission funded project mapping non-employment equality law across the EU. He is now an employment and equality law consultant (www.barryfitzpatrickconsulting.co.uk).

Dr Haris Kountouros has specialised in European Labour Law. From 1999 to 2004 he was a Visiting Lecturer in European Law at King's College London. He has also taught Legal Theory at London Metropolitan University and has given a number of lectures on European Employment Law at Kingston University. His published work concentrates on EU law, labour law and related themes.

Professor Christopher McCrudden LLB (1974, first class honours), Queen's University, Belfast; LLM from Yale (1995); D Phil from Oxford University (1981); holds an honorary LLD from Queen's University, Belfast (2006). He is a Fellow and Tutor in Law, at Lincoln College, Oxford; Professor of Human Rights Law at the University of Oxford; non-practising Barrister-at-Law (Gray's Inn; Bar of Northern Ireland); Overseas Affiliated Professor of Law at the University of Michigan Law School. He is a member of editorial boards of several journals, including *European Public Law*, the *Oxford Journal of Legal Studies*, the *International Journal of Discrimination and the Law*, and the *Journal of International Economic Law*, as well as being co-editor of the Cambridge University Press *Law in Context* series. Public service: UK member of the European Commission's Expert Network on the Application of the Gender Equality Directives; scientific director of the European Commission's Network of Experts on Non-Discrimination, member of the Procurement Board for Northern Ireland. His published work spans among others, equality and non-discrimination law, international, European and comparative human rights, public procurement and international law.

Helen Meenan has held the Jean Monnet Chair in European Law at Kingston University since 1998. She read law at University College Dublin (BCL), European Business Law at the University of Amsterdam (LLM) and started her working life as a solicitor of the Irish Courts. Helen has worked as a consultant to TAEN (the Age and Employment Network) and Age Concern England and speaks and publishes nationally and internationally on all aspects of age discrimination. She has also lectured to judges and jurists from all EU Member States (JHMeenan@tiscali.co.uk).

Professor Ann Numhauser-Henning, LLD, is professor of Civil Law at the Law Faculty, Lund University, Sweden and has been the head of the Norma Research Programme since its start in 1996. She is currently also the Pro-Vice-Chancellor of Lund University. She has written widely on labour law, especially employment law and non-discrimination law. A more recent field of research is social security in a European integration perspective. She is a member of the European Commission's Network of Legal Experts on Equal Treatment between Men and Women; the Commission's Network on Non-Discrimination and the Commission's Network on Training and Reporting on European Social Security.

Professor Gwyneth Pitt is Professor of Law at Kingston University. She previously taught at the Universities of Nottingham, Leeds and Huddersfield, specialising in employment, discrimination and commercial law. Gwyneth is the author of a number of books and articles on employment and discrimination law. She is a member of the editorial committee of the *Industrial Law Journal*.

Professor Gerard Quinn is a professor of law at the National University of Ireland (Galway). He specialises in international and comparative disability law. He is a member of the Irish Human Rights Commission and a former First Vice President of the European Committee of Social Rights (Council of Europe's European Social Charter). He is a member of the scientific board of the EU Network on Discrimination Law. He is a former official at the European Commission and a former Director of Research of the Law Reform Commission of Ireland. His 'Study on the Current Use and Future Potential of UN Human Rights Instruments in the Field of Disability' which he co-directed was published by the Office of the United Nations High Commissioner for Human Rights in 2002. He led the delegation of Rehabilitation International to the UN Working Group, which drafted the initial text of the recently agreed UN Treaty on the Human Rights of Persons with Disabilities. His current research focuses on the UN disability treaty and on internet accessibility for persons with disabilities. He is a barrister-at-law (King's Inns) and graduate of Harvard Law School. His first child has a disability.

LIST OF ABBREVIATIONS

AC	Law Reports: Appeal Cases
ACAS	Advisory Conciliation and Arbitration Service
ADA	Americans with Disabilities Act
ADEA	Age Discrimination in Employment Act
A-G	Advocate General
ART	Article
AUT	Association of University Teachers
BME	Black and Ethnic Minorities
CBI	Confederation of British Industry
CD(E)	Cahiers de Droit (Européen)
CEDAW	Convention on the Elimination of All Forms of Discrimination against Women
CEE	Central and Eastern Europe
CEEP	Centre Européen des Entreprises à Participation Publique
CETS	Council of Europe Treaty Series
CMLR	Common Market Law Reports
CMLRev	*Common Market Law Review*
DDA	Disability Discrimination Act
DG	Directorate-General
DRC	Disability Rights Commission
DTI	Department of Trade and Industry
EC Treaty	European Community Treaty
EC	European Community
ECHR	European Convention for the Protection of Human Rights and Fundamental Freedoms
ECJ	European Court of Justice
ECRE	European Council on Refugees and Exiles
ECtHR	European Court of Human Rights
EEA	European Economic Area
EEC	European Economic Community
EES	European Employment Strategy

EHRLR	*European Human Rights Law Review*
EHRR	*European Human Rights Reports*
EIDHR	European Initiative for Democracy and Human Rights
ELRev	*European Law Review*
ENAR	European Network Against Racism
EOC	Equal Opportunities Commission
ESC	European Social Charter
ETD	Equal Treatment Directive
ETS	European Treaty Series
ETUC	European Trades Union Congress
ETUI	European Trade Union Institute
EU	European Union
EUCFR	European Union Charter of Fundamental Rights
EUI	European University Institute
EUMap	EU Monitoring and Advocacy Program
EUMC	European Union Monitoring Centre on Racism and Xenophobia
EWHC	High Court (England and Wales)
EYPD	European Year of Young Persons with Disabilities
FET	Fair Employment Tribunal
FRA	Fundamental Rights Agency
GDP	Gross Domestic Product
GOQ	Genuine Occupational Qualification
GOR	Genuine Occupational Requirement
HLG	High Level Group
HRLJ	*Human Rights Law Journal*
ICCPR	International Covenant of Civil and Political Rights
ICERD	International Convention Against All Forms of Racial Discrimination
ICLQ	*International Comparative Law Quarterly*
ICR	*Industrial Cases Reports*
IJDL	*International Journal of Discrimination and the Law*
ILGA	International Gay and Lesbian Association
ILJ	*Industrial Law Journal*
ILO	International Labour Organisation
IRLR	*Industrial Relations Law Reports*
JPE	*Journal of Political Economy*
KB	Law Reports: Kings Bench
LGB	Lesbian Gay Bisexual
LTR	Long Term Resident

MJ	*Maastricht Journal of European and Comparative Law*
NBER	National Bureau of Economic Research
NGO	Non-Governmental Organisation
NIACE	National Institute of Adult Continuing Education
OECD	Organisation for Economic Cooperation and Development
OJ	*Official Journal (of European Community)*
OMC	Open Method of Co-ordination
PRIAE	Policy Research Institute on Ageing and Ethnicity
QB	Law Reports: Queens Bench
RAXEN	European Racism and Xenophobia Information Network
RED	Race Equality Directive
SCR	Supreme Court Reports (Canada)
SI	Statutory Instrument
SO	Sexual Orientation
TCN	Third Country National
TEU	Treaty on European Union
UDHR	Universal Declaration of Human Rights
UKHL	House of Lords (UK)
UN	United Nations
UNICE	Union des Confédérations de l'Industrie et des Employeurs d'Europe
UNTS	United Nations Treaty series
US	United States
WEBJCLI	*Web Journal of Current Legal Issues*

TABLE OF CASES

PART I

1

Introduction

HELEN MEENAN[*]

Part I

This volume is compiled at a remarkable time in the history of equality and anti-discrimination law in the European Union (EU). The EU has already achieved the expansion of its anti-discrimination grounds from just two[1] under the E(E)C Treaty to seven following the Amsterdam Treaty,[2] which incorporated Article 13 into the EC Treaty (EC). Article 13.1 EC empowers the Council to 'take appropriate action to combat discrimination based on sex, racial or ethnic origin, religion or belief, disability, age or sexual orientation'. The first two Article 13 Directives, the Race Directive and the Employment Equality Directive[3] are six years old at the time of writing and their implementation dates have all expired. The intriguing third such Directive, the Equal Treatment Directive between men and women in access to and supply of goods and services is already two years old.[4] The European Court of Justice (ECJ) has delivered some early judgments on this newly expanded body of equality and anti-discrimination law. But we do not yet have the full measure of the challenges presented by the new anti-discrimination grounds. Nor do we have the full measure of diversity arising from combinations of protected grounds, much less the ability of the Article 13 Directives to deal with them. There is also the increased diversity introduced to the EU by the accession of ten new Member States in 2004, two new Member States in 2007 and future enlargements of the Union to consider.

[*] I am indebted to Dr Haris Kountouros, Frances Meenan, Barrister, Dublin and Nicola Aries, Kingston University, for their helpful comments on an earlier draft.
[1] Sex and nationality which will be discussed below.   [2] 1957 and 1997, respectively.
[3] Council Directive 2000/43/EC of 29 June 2000 implementing the principle of equal treatment between persons irrespective of racial or ethnic origin [2000] OJ L180, pp. 22–6 and Council Directive 2000/78/EC of 27 November 2000 establishing a general framework for equal treatment in employment and occupation [2000] OJ L303, p. 16.
[4] Council Directive 2004/113/EC [2004] OJ L373, p. 37.

The prospect of the 2004 enlargement was a major impetus for the timing and the importance of the Article 13 package of measures.[5] Enlargement also reveals European equality law as a vehicle for new approaches working alongside the Article 13 Directives, which enable targeted responses to the needs of particular groups, as in the case of the Roma.[6] Crucially, this includes the recommendation that 'any measure seeking to promote the integration of the Roma/Gypsy minority should be devised with the active participation of representatives of this group'.[7] However, at present it cannot be assumed that similar approaches will automatically spill over to other groups. At the moment the key question is where will EU equality and anti-discrimination law go from here?

From a 'hierarchy of equality' to inter-sectionality

A substantial body of literature developed rapidly on Article 13 EC. In the early stages there was much commentary and analysis on the so-called legislative hierarchy among the anti-discrimination grounds.[8] This volume acknowledges that the hierarchy argument *on its own* may not be the most effective platform on which to argue for a levelling up of protection or a dismantling of (negative) differences in treatment. There is also an inherent uncertainty in the idea that where one ground leads the way, others may yet follow. In any event, some commentators argue

---

[5] M. Bell, 'Article 13 EC: The European Commission's Anti-discrimination Proposals', (2000) 29 *ILJ* pp. 79–84 at p. 84 and E. Ellis, *EU Anti-Discrimination Law* (Oxford University Press, 2005) at p. 29.

[6] In-depth study by the European Commission 'The Situation of Roma in an Enlarged European Union' (Brussels, 2004). The Inter-Service Group established by the European Commission co-ordinates the policies and programmes dealing with Roma issues, *European Commission, Equality and Non-discrimination Annual Report, 2005* at pp. 25–36. By mid-2006, the EU had already targeted € 100 million for Roma issues. Note the recommendation by the EU Network of Independent Experts in Fundamental Rights *Report on the Situation of Fundamental Rights in the European Union for 2003*, at p. 103, which recommended the adoption of a Directive to encourage the integration of Roma. This has been repeated by the EU Network of Independent Experts on Fundamental Rights *Thematic Comment No.3 The Protection of Minorities in the European Union*, 25 April 2005, at pp. 52 and 64. Note also the European Commission website on the Roma http://ec.europa.eu/ employment_social/fundamental_rights/roma/index_en.htm.

[7] *Thematic Comment No. 3*, ibid., at p. 64.

[8] For an overview see, Mark Bell for the European Commission, *Critical Review of academic literature relating to the EU directives to combat discrimination* (Brussels, 2004) at pp. 12–14. See also Lisa Waddington 'Article 13 EC: Setting Priorities in the Proposal for a Horizontal Employment Directive', (2000) 29 *ILJ*, pp. 176–81 and Mark Bell, 'Article 13 EC: the European Commission's Anti-discrimination Proposals', (2000) 29 *ILJ* pp. 79–84 at p. 80.

that differences between the equality grounds may require and justify specific responses.[9] To date however, it can be said that a ground-specific approach has taken the individual grounds and the Article 13 family as a whole only so far. Indeed a sectoral approach goes against legislative and institutional developments in some EU Member States. In addition to a single piece of comprehensive equality legislation there now or shortly will exist a single body to be charged with the promotion of all protected grounds of equality (and even human rights) in some Member States.[10]

Multiple discrimination is slowly emerging as a key issue at EU level, which will also help to nudge stakeholders away from a purely single ground focus.[11] One theme to emerge from this book is that approaches based on inter-sectionality and human rights should now supplant the hierarchy argument as a means of moving towards a level playing field for all grounds, insofar as this is possible. An intersectional analysis approach to multiple discrimination also makes way for an understanding of a specific type of discrimination resulting from the interaction of anti-discrimination grounds.[12] In this volume the terms inter-sectional discrimination and multiple discrimination are used in the broadest possible senses. Case law long prior to the incorporation of Article 13 EC demonstrated that age limits could trigger sex discrimination.[13] So the idea of intersecting grounds of discrimination in the EU is far from new. Inter-sectionality and multiple discrimination perspectives would give us new ways of thinking about the anti-discrimination grounds and any subgroups they may contain and for devising strategies to tackle their anti-discrimination and equality needs. It may also be time to take a more expanded approach to anti-discrimination which arguably Article 21 European Charter of Fundamental Rights (EUCFR) might help to achieve with its non-exhaustive formulation.

[9] For example, M. Bell and L. Waddington, 'Reflecting on inequalities in European equality law', *European Law Review*, 28 (2003) pp. 349–69 and Barry Fitzpatrick in this volume.

[10] European Commission, *Equality and non-discrimination Annual Report, 2005* (European Communities, Luxembourg, 2005) at pp. 22–4.

[11] On 6 May 2006, the European Commission issued a call for tender (Invitation to tender VT/2006/01) for a study to promote understanding of the causes and effects of multiple discrimination in the EU. This study will include recommendations on how to tackle multiple discrimination.

[12] Timo Makkonen, Institute for Human Rights, Abo Akademi University, Research paper, *Multiple, Compound and Intersectional Discrimination: Bringing the Experiences of the Most Marginalized to the Fore*, April 2002, at pp. 10–11, www.abo.fi/institut/imr/norfa/timo.pdf. Note also Kimberle Crenshaw, 'Mapping the margins: Intersectionality, identity politics and violence against women of color', (1991) 43 *Stanford Labor Review*, Vol. 6, pp. 1241–99.

[13] For example, Case 152/84 *Marshall* v. *Southampton Area Health Authority* [1986] ECR 723.

The goals of this volume

This volume adopts three considered approaches to European equality and anti-discrimination law. Firstly, and of paramount importance, it provides an expert essay on each ground contained in Article 13. Secondly, it adopts a contextual approach. In Part I it lays out a number of important contexts against which the grounds in Part II are examined. This will also act as a reminder that while much has been achieved, more work may be required in light of the various (changing) contexts within which equality and non-discrimination law is applied and must respond. Thirdly, to greater and lesser extents, the individual authors additionally aim to take the following broad issues into account in the assessment of their subject: to include the 2004 enlargement, human rights aspects (including the relevance of the EUCFR and the Constitutional Treaty now overtaken by the proposed Reform Treaty), inter-sectionality and multiple discrimination, gender and age dimensions, access to justice and particular strategies required to combat discrimination and promote equality. The overarching aim is simple: to see what insights can be drawn from a collective and contextual assessment of sex, racial or ethnic origin, religion or belief, disability, age and sexual orientation within this framework, at this important juncture following transposition.

A time of change

The time of writing is also remarkable, as many potentially significant projects are only just underway. The Gender Institute[14] and Fundamental Rights Agency[15] are in the early stages of development. We do not yet know how they will impact on and interact with older EU institutions, existing extra-institutional bodies such as the EU's various networks of independent experts, not to mention national bodies concerned with promoting equality and human rights and the world beyond EU borders.[16] These institutional developments are symptomatic of a major drive towards a stronger fundamental rights edifice for the EU but this was stalled by the

---

[14] European Commission Press Release 3 March 2006 'Commission to tackle gender inequality with new roadmap and ε50 million gender institute.' Commission Proposal for a Regulation Establishing a European Institute for Gender Equality COM(2005) 81 final.

[15] Proposal for a Council Regulation establishing a European Union Agency for Fundamental Rights COM(2005) 280 final.

[16] However, the Proposal states 'The Network of independent experts could be one of the information networks animated by the Agency' and 'The Agency shall co-operate with other Community and Union bodies to ensure mutual support in the accomplishment of their respective tasks, and in particular to avoid duplication of work'.

non-ratification of the Constitutional Treaty in at least five ways. (1) The EU Charter does not have binding legal force. Although it is also true that the underpinning provisions that had binding force before the Charter was adopted will continue to do so[17] and that the Charter remains a source of rights and interpretation. (2) The EU cannot accede to the ECHR or its protocols. (3) The potential of the Union's objective in Article I-3(3) ('[the Union] shall combat . . . discrimination') for anti-discrimination in general remains unexplored. (4) The loss of the general mainstreaming provision in Article III-3 for the Article 13 grounds is considerable.[18] (5) The Constitution would have also elevated equality to one of five values on which the Union is founded.[19] This is not to mention innovations such as, Article I-44 on observance of the principle of democratic equality of citizens by the EU institutions, bodies, offices and agencies. In chapter 3, McCrudden and Kountouros will consider the relevance of the proposed Reform Treaty, 2007 for equality and the EUCFR.

In the meantime, the European Commission has published its first report[20] (to be repeated every five years) to the European Parliament and Council on the Member States application of the Race Directive, with a report on the Employment Directive expected to follow. This report indicates that the three key characteristics of the Directive have proven effective: it applies to all persons, beyond the field of employment and requires the Member States to establish an equality body to promote equal treatment on grounds of racial or ethnic origin. This third feature has proven particularly successful, as victims are more likely to approach an NGO or equality body rather than the courts, for fear of victimisation and issues of cost.[21] At this stage the Roma are the group most represented in complaints.

These reports should include proposals to revise and update the Directives, if necessary.[22] However, there were mixed signals from the European Commission for some time. On his first day at work, Vladimir Spidla, European Commissioner for Employment, Social Affairs and Equal Opportunities, announced that a feasibility study on flanking measures to complement the legal framework would be produced on

---

[17] Personal communication with J.-P. Jacque, Director, Legal Service of the Council of the European Union.

[18] Despite existing mainstreaming provisions for isolated grounds.   [19] Article 1–2.

[20] Commission Communication, 'The application of Directive 2000/43/EC of 29 June 2000 implementing the principle of equal treatment between persons irrespective of racial or ethnic origin', COM(2006) 643 final.

[21] Ibid. at p. 4.   [22] Article 19.1 EED and Article 17 RD.

all grounds and that he would work on a new legal framework for equality.[23] The results of the feasibility study were due at the time of writing and a 'framework strategy for non-discrimination and equal opportunities for all' was adopted.[24] The Framework Strategy aimed to ensure full implementation of the Directives and to support back-up measures for their application and compliance. However, it may have contributed to opposing messages: 1) in light of the differences in level and scope of protection among the anti-discrimination grounds the Commission 'does not intend at this stage to present new legislative proposals'; and 2) the Commission's feasibility study 'will examine national provisions that go beyond Community requirements and will take stock of the advantages and disadvantages of such measures'. Thus the introduction of new grounds and the extension of goods and services legislation to additional grounds, appeared to be off the agenda. The Commission confirmed that it did not see a need to bring forward legislative proposals in respect of the Race Directive. There was no case law from the ECJ on race or ethnic origin and there was a lack of experience with implementation of the Directive at that time.[25]

Securing full implementation of the Article 13 Directives and the possible adoption of appropriate back-up measures focused on bedding down (and improving) what was already in place. Thus it appeared that we were without a second track: a new vision, a new phase or a new direction for the European fight against discrimination. However, *the European Year of Equal Opportunities for All 2007* provided a fresh impetus. In July 2007, the Commission announced that it would propose new initiatives to prevent and combat discrimination outside the labour market for gender, religion or belief, disability, age or sexual orientation[26] and it announced a public consultation on anti-discrimination measures. There is also considerable potential for the ECJ to highlight any limitations of the *acquis communautaire*.[27]

---

[23] Conference, *Equality in a future Europe 'A Social Europe It is time for action'*, 22/23 November 2004 at p. 3.

[24] Commission Communication, 'Non-discrimination and equal opportunities for all – A framework strategy', COM(2005) 224 final.

[25] Communication, ibid. at p. 8.

[26] Decision No 771/2006/EC of the European Parliament and of the Council establishing the European Year of Equal Opportunities for All (2007) – towards a just society [2006] OJ L146, pp. 1–7. Commission's Annual Policy Strategy 2008 COM(2007) 65 final.

[27] Case 249/96 *Grant* v. *Southwest Trains Ltd* [1998] ECR I-621, would be a past example.

Ongoing racial and religious tensions in the EU and beyond

This volume also emerges following a period of worrying tensions, unrest and human rights concerns within the EU and among neighbouring countries in the period 2005–6. The race riots in France, Belgium and Berlin in late 2005 that were triggered by the deaths of two black teenagers, accidentally electrocuted while trying to hide from the police in Paris, are particularly worrying.[28] These riots were of a different order to the incidents of racist violence that were factors in the impetus and speed of the adoption of the Race Directive. Mark Bell in his contribution to this volume outlines those particular factors and discusses the EU's stalled attempts, following the Amsterdam Treaty, to make specific racist activities punishable by criminal law in all Member States.

The more recent race problems have their roots in a combination of poverty, discrimination and harassment experienced by France's North and black African communities extending well beyond the field of employment.[29] Early 2006 also saw demonstrations in the Middle East and European countries against caricatures of the prophet Muhammed printed in a Danish newspaper and reprinted in newspapers in a number of EU and non-EU countries.[30] The cartoons, which were regarded as blasphemous by Muslims, brought freedom of expression into direct conflict with religious beliefs.[31]

McCrudden and Kountouros, in this volume, ask whether the restrictions on freedom that anti-discrimination law represents are unjustified in human rights terms. They believe that 'We are increasingly likely to see, in both European theoretical literature and in litigation, challenges to anti-discrimination law from the perspective of freedom of association, privacy, freedom of speech, the right to property, and freedom of religion, as well as freedom of contract.' They suggest that complex

---

[28] J. Sturcke 'France braced for 12th night of riots', *The Guardian*, 7 November, 2005. G. Murray 'Understanding the riots in France', 18 January 2006, available at www.irr.org.uk/2006/january/ha000016.html.

[29] Ibid.

[30] L. Harding and K. Wilsher 'Anger as papers reprint cartoons of Muhammed', *The Guardian*, 2 February 2006, available at www.guardian.co.uk/print/0,,5389526-110633,00.html. K. Wilsher, L. Harding and N. Watt, 'European elite scrambles to defuse furore over caricatures of Muhammad', *The Guardian*, 3 February 2006.

[31] Anti-semitic incidents also persist within in the EU see inter alia, EUMC Working Paper, 'Antsemitism Summary overview of the situation in the European Union 2001–2005', May 2006.

legal questions will arise. Gwyneth Pitt discusses the collision between freedom of expression and freedom of religion and Mark Bell discusses the challenges of balancing freedom of expression with combating racism.[32] While these points are well made, it is also good to remember that the EC has developed a number of tools to promote human rights and equality, both internally and externally. These include the EC's unique human rights clause contained in its bilateral agreements with third countries[33] and the recent embedding of equality criteria in EC public procurement legislation.[34]

Close to EU borders, the rise of racial hate crimes and xenophobia together with an increasingly negative attitude to human rights NGOs in Russia, also help to characterise these times.[35] These selected issues confirm that this is no time for complacency in the fight against discrimination and the quest for human rights and equality in facing the challenges of simply living together in a modern, urban and globalised world. These issues have deep and complex roots and it is worth asking whether there is a role for EU anti-discrimination and equality law in tackling or preventing the underlying causes of such flash points when they occur within EU borders. To what extent are the Article 13 Directives equipped for such a role? Tailored research is required to find the answer. There are also more pervasive and overarching concerns. What are the implications of demographic ageing for working and living in the EU and for EU anti-discrimination and equality law? The EU has already started to prioritise the former[36] but arguably the latter lags behind notwithstanding the age strand of the Employment Directive and greater efforts in this direction could also help characterise a new era. This is all apart from discussions on the grounds of nationality and national minorities (often linked to race) both of which are absent from Article 13.1 EC and the Race Directive, moreover nationality is also absent from Article 21.1

---

[32] In this volume.

[33] Note the discussion of equality clauses by McCrudden and Kountouros in this volume.

[34] In, for example, Directive 2004/17/EC of the European Parliament and of the Council of 31 March 2004 co-ordinating the procurement procedures of entities operating in the water, energy, transport and postal services sectors.

[35] NCJS 'Number of ethnic and nationalistic crimes grows fast in Russia', *Pravda*, 19 January 2005; *Time Europe Magazine* 'From Russia with Hate', 11 April 2005; N. Paton-Walsh 'Moscow asks court to close civil rights group', *The Guardian*, 28 January 2006.

[36] Note Article 143 EC: 'The Commission shall draw up a report each year on progress in achieving the objectives of Article 136, including the demographic situation in the Community . . . The European Parliament may invite the Commission to draw up reports on particular problems concerning the social situation.'

of the EUCFR. It will be shown below that nationality remains a complex issue within the EU.

This volume must start with some analysis of an important context within which the Article 13 Directives were adopted and continue to operate – the existing rich body of sex and nationality discrimination law. It is well known that these fields have contributed to the development of the Article 13 Directives.

Part II – From simple beginnings

Equality and non-discrimination in all their embodiments stand out as areas of EU law that directly and unashamedly benefit the individual. Their development has been unpredictable, lacking in uniformity, sometimes timid and at other times daring. It pays tribute to the living qualities of EU law and the dynamic interplay between the Member States and the Community institutions, occasionally involving the individual as litigant. This interplay has evolved to provide a growing space for representative bodies concerned with diverse interests to be heard at a national level.[37] Today's rich landscape belies the now remarkable fact that only two grounds benefited from equality or non-discrimination in the E(E)C Treaty, 1957. Article 119 E(E)C Treaty (now Article 141 EC as amended) required Member States to ensure 'the application of the principle that men and women should receive equal pay for equal work'. The E(E)C Treaty contained no general principle of non-discrimination on grounds of sex,[38] contributing towards an initially lower status than nationality. Simply put, the principle of equal pay for men and women was included in the Treaty to deal with the competition concerns largely of one Member State.[39] While Article 7 E(E)C (now Article 12 EC) provided that 'Within the scope of application of this Treaty, and without prejudice to any special provisions contained therein, any discrimination on grounds of nationality shall be prohibited.' By contrast, nationality discrimination was prohibited throughout the entire scope of the Treaty[40]

---

[37] Note Articles 9.2 and Article 14 EED.

[38] S. Prechal and N. Burrows, *Gender Discrimination Law of the European Community* (Dartmouth, 1990) at p. 10.

[39] France.

[40] But this scope can also be viewed restrictively. See Sacha Prechal: 'Then there was the general prohibition of discrimination on grounds of nationality, but this applied only within the scope of application of the EEC Treaty' in 'Equality of treatment, Non-discrimination and social policy: achievements in three themes', (2004) 41 *Common Market Law Review*, p. 533.

and was specifically enunciated in Part II of the E(E)C Treaty, in important fundamental rights such as the free movement of persons, freedom
of establishment and freedom to provide services.[41] Article 13 EC is closer
in many respects to former Article 7 than the former Article 119 E(E)C,
in having the potential to cover a greater breadth of Community activity.
The fact that Article 13 includes sex among its grounds is necessary given
the still limited, though expanded, scope of Article 141 EC.

The initial limited reference to sex equality in the E(E)C Treaty spawned
a vast body of legislation, the emergence of new legal concepts and the
gradual introduction of new tools[42] for achieving equality. Developments
in respect of both sex and nationality have influenced and may continue
to influence the new grounds, which in turn have influenced sex equality.
However, it is difficult to detect much evidence of any Article 13 grounds
influencing the development of EC nationality discrimination law just
yet. It will be shown that the sex *acquis communautaire* has arguably
converged with the new Article 13 grounds in many respects but non-
discrimination on grounds of nationality generally occupies a place quite
apart and is currently stalled as an equality and non-discrimination issue,
by comparison. Perhaps this reflects the view put forward by Advocate-
General Capotorti almost thirty years ago that 'Nationality is a ground
of discrimination quite different from that of sex.'[43] Today it can be seen
that sex and ethnicity (if not also sex and nationality) interact in ways
that are particularly detrimental to women in particular.[44]

The goals of non-discrimination and equality: from market integration to human rights

The development of European equality law is arguably a metaphor for the
evolution of the EU itself and its current state of responsiveness to human
capital. This is apparent from the stated and hidden goals of the equality
principle, at any given time. However, the ECJ has recorded organic shifts
in the goal of this principle in key cases over the years. In *Defrenne* v.
Sabena the ECJ acknowledged that Article 119 (now Article 141 EC) contained a social objective for the first time, referring to a 'double aim, which

---

[41] Now contained principally in Articles 39, 43 and 49 ECT .
[42] Such as mainstreaming, see inter alia, Jo Shaw, 'Mainstreaming Equality and Diversity in
European Union Law and Policy', (2005) 58 *Current Legal Problems*, pp. 255–312.
[43] In his Opinion in Case 149/77 *Defrenne* v. *Sabena* [1978] ECR 1364.
[44] Sandra Fredman, 'Double trouble: multiple discrimination and EU law', in European
Network of Legal Experts in the Non-Discrimination Field, *European Anti-Discrimination
Law Review*, Issue No. 2, October 2005 (European Commission, 2005) p. 13–18, at p. 15.
'The Situation of Roma in an Enlarged Union', ibid. at pp. 33–5. European Commission,
Report on equality between women and men, 2005 at pp. 5, 6 and 8.

is at once economic and social'.[45] The ECJ reversed the order of this double aim in *Deutsche Telekom AG* v. *Lili Schroeder*, declaring that the 'economic aim pursued by Article 119 of the Treaty . . . is secondary to the social aim pursued by the same provision, which constitutes the expression of a fundamental human right'.[46] From a relatively early stage the right not to be discriminated against on grounds of sex was accorded the status of a fundamental personal human right and the Court declared it part of the general principles of European law.[47]

The Court has more recently in *Hill and Stapleton* v. *Revenue Commissioners*, assigned a further and infinitely more novel aim to this principle, stating 'Community policy in this area is to encourage and, if possible, adapt working conditions to family responsibilities'.[48] This judicially declared aim may well have unintended positive consequences for other Article 13 grounds. It is to be hoped that the Court will remain consistently open to acknowledging and responding to the human realities of modern (working) life, especially contexts such as demographic ageing and the linked issue of elder care.

By contrast, the Article 13 Directives have three identifiable goals from the outset: economic, social and (fundamental) human rights, in no stated order.[49] Gerard Quinn in his chapter on disability argues that the human rights rationale of the Employment Directive is the dominant rationale of that instrument.[50] This point of view is in harmony with the present era, which is marked by the parallel rich, if incomplete, development of human rights in EC law. The shift away from a principally economic goal for the Community principles of equality and non-discrimination has been particularly pronounced in the phase since the incorporation of Article 13 EC. This has led to the acknowledgement that these principles are no longer primarily related to market integration and have become 'objectives in their own right'.[51] Indeed, Robin Allen QC in his contribution to this volume states: 'The introduction of Article 13 can be seen to have been

---

[45] Above n. 43, at paras. 9, 10 and 12.   [46] Case C-50/96, [2000] ECR I-743 at para. 57.

[47] *Defrenne* v. *Sabena* Case (Defrenne III) 149/77, paras. 26–7.

[48] Case 243/95, [1998] ECR I-3739, para. 42. The development of social policy in the EC can be traced back to the early 1970s' note, Council Resolution initiating the Social Action Programme of 21 January 1974. This aimed at full and better employment and 'to attempt to reconcile the family aspirations of all concerned with their professional aspirations'.

[49] See, for example, Recitals 1, 4, 6, 7, 8, 9 and 11.

[50] In this volume. Recent terminology now refers to a rights-based approach to equality, see Colm O'Cinneide's report for the European Network of Independent Experts in the non-discrimination field, 'Age Discrimination and European Law' (European Commission, 2005) at p. 11 and Sandra Fredman 'Equality: A New generation?' (2001) 30 *ILJ*, p. 145.

[51] S. Prechal 'Equality of Treatment' (2004), p. 538 and Lisa Waddington 'The Expanding Role of the Equality Principle in European Union Law', European University Institute, Florence,

a point at which the Community, building on its experience in the field of sex discrimination, decisively adopted a human rights approach to equality.'

Equality: towards an autonomous right?

The Court of Justice has played an invaluable role in expanding the principles of non-discrimination and equality in relation to sex. It originally developed the scope of non-discrimination on grounds of sex to cover pay in a broad sense, including occupational pensions.[52] However, *Defrenne* v. *Sabena (No.3)*[53] saw two almost opposing developments that can best be understood in the context of the Community and the Member States in the late 1970s. On the one hand, it declared that the elimination of discrimination based on sex is a fundamental personal human right and a general principle of Community law.[54] On the other hand, the Community had not at the relevant time 'assumed any responsibility for supervising and guaranteeing the observance of the principle of equality between men and women in working conditions other than remuneration'.[55] The adoption of Directive 76/207 on equal treatment in access to employment, vocational training and promotion and working conditions (the Equal Treatment Directive) saw the legislative expansion of the principle of equal treatment for men and women to cover areas other than pay.[56] It also contained three exceptions to the principle of equal treatment for occupational activities, pregnancy and maternity and positive action.[57] This Directive was built on a formal concept of equality.[58] The evolution of positive action through the case law of the Court to its ultimate current expression in substantive equality terms, in Article 141.4 EC is traced below. Meanwhile, attempts to broaden the EC principles of non-discrimination and equality to embrace other grounds failed.

Advocates-General made a real effort to expand the principle of equality to cover 'arbitrary grounds' not specifically mentioned in the EC

Robert Schumann Centre Policy Paper (2003/04) available at www.iue.it/RSCAS?e-texts/CR2003-04.pdf at p. 11.

[52] *Bilka-Kaufhaus* and Case C-262/88 *Barber* v. *Guardian Royal Exchange Assurance Group* [1990] ECR I-1889.

[53] Above n. 47.   [54] Paras. 26–7.   [55] Para. 30.

[56] OJ 1976 L39/40, and Directive 2002/73/EC amending Council Directive 76/207/EEC on the implementation of the principle of equal treatment for men and women as regards access to employment, vocational training and promotion and working conditions OJ 2002 L269/15.

[57] Article 2.2, 2.3 and 2.4.

[58] Note Article 2.4 on positive action and Craig and De Búrca, *EU Law Text, Cases and Materials* (3rd edn, Oxford University Press, 2003) at pp. 886–9.

Treaty or already individually pronounced as general principles in *Grant* v. *Southwest Trains* and *P* v. *S and Cornwall County Council*.[59] They variously declared 'the principle of equality prohibits unequal treatment of individuals based on certain distinguishing factors, and these specifically include sex' and 'The rights and duties which result from Community law apply to all without discrimination.'[60] The Court chose not to adopt an expanded equality principle on these occasions. In tantalising fashion, the Court in *D and Sweden* v. *Council* later appeared to accept a principle of equal treatment regardless of sexual orientation, while deciding against the claim on other grounds.[61] In *Grant*, the Court felt constrained rather than empowered by the incoming Article 13 EC. It is clear that in *Grant* and *P* v. *S* the Court chose not to develop an autonomous right or principle of equality or non-discrimination. The adoption of Article 13 EC and Directives thereunder meant that any responsibility for the expansion of these principles to embrace the grounds named therein was firmly placed in the hands of the legislature at that time. This at first would seem to partly fulfil Lisa Waddington's prophecy in 2003 that 'In addition to the Charter, which devotes a complete Chapter to equality, Article 13 EC and the directives based thereon, are now driving forward the recognition of the equality and non-discrimination principle in EU law, rather than the Court's case law.'[62] However, she had expressed the view previously that the incorporation of Article 13 'combined with the existing provisions in numerous Member State constitutions and international instruments, may therefore open up the way for expansion by the ECJ of the general principle of equality/non-discrimination'.[63]

The recent judgment in *Mangold* v. *Rudiger Helm*,[64] which concerned German rules on fixed term contracts for older workers, viewed in isolation may signal a greater willingness to rely upon and declare general principles of non-discrimination and equality. As discussed by a number of writers in this volume, *Mangold* has significance for grounds beyond age. The Court declared that the principle of non-discrimination on grounds of age was (already) a general principle of European law and that the source of the general principle of non-discrimination for the various

---

[59] See the Opinions of Advocate-General Elmer in *Grant* and Advocate-General Tesauro in Case C-13/94 *P* v. *S and Cornwall County Council* [1996] ECR I-2143. Note also Lisa Waddington, 'The Expanding Role', pp. 19–22.

[60] In *P* v. *S* and *Grant*, respectively.

[61] Para. 47. Note Lisa Waddington 'The Expanding Role', p. 21.

[62] Lisa Waddington 'The Expanding Role', p. 22.

[63] Lisa Waddington 'Testing the Limits of the EC Treaty Article on Non-discrimination', (1999) 28 *ILJ* p. 133 at pp. 149–50.

[64] Case C-144/04 [2005] ECR I-9981.

grounds in the Employment Directive was international Treaties and the constitutional traditions of the Member States.[65] Barry Fitzpatrick in his chapter on sexual orientation remarks that following *Mangold* it is clear that all equal treatment principles manifested in the two Directives are equally fundamental.[66]

This renewed reliance on the traditional sources of general principles in European law appeared to indicate a renewed confidence of the Court in its role as the creator and guardian of these principles and the new framing of equality instruments. The Equal Treatment Directive *puts into effect* the principle of equal treatment for men and women in conditions of employment. While the Employment Equality Directive *lays down a general framework for combating discrimination* in employment and occupation, a difference seized upon by the Court when it declared in *Mangold* that 'above all, Directive 2000/78 does not itself lay down the principle of equal treatment in employment and occupation'.[67]

One question presents itself though, why do general principles of non-discrimination on the grounds listed in the Employment Directive already exist in European Law today when they did not at the time of the *Grant* case?[68] The ECJ in *Chacon Navas* appears to have heeded Advocate-General Geelhoed's call for 'a more restrained interpretation and application of Directive 2000/78 than adopted by the Court in *Mangold*'.[69] In *Chacon Navas* the ECJ declined to rely on 'fundamental rights' to extend the scope of the Employment Directive by analogy or addition to the existing grounds named therein.[70] Thus echoing its approach to fundamental rights and the non-extension of a Treaty provision in *Grant*.[71]

The evolution of equality and non-discrimination into an autonomous human rights standard is the subject of a growing debate.[72] Such a development would provide protection to a wider range of persons and would invite special protection when there are competing interests at play.[73] On the one hand, Prechal reminds us that Article 13 and the Charter

---

[65] Paras. 74 and 75.   [66] In this volume.   [67] At para. 74.
[68] Note, Anthony Arnull, 'Out with the old . . .', (2006) *ELRev* 31(1) 1–2 at p. 2.
[69] Case 13/05, Judgment of 16 March 2006 at paras. 56 and 53.
[70] Paras. 56–57.   [71] Para. 45.
[72] Here discussed primarily in the sense of not being tied to a particular ground or characteristic. But note McCrudden and Kountouros in this volume who discuss the right to equality and non-discrimination as an 'autonomous principle', 'that is a human right that is of value independently of the economic or social benefits it may bring'.
[73] S. Prechal, 'Equality of Treatment' (2004), at p. 7.

are inherently limited by the competence of the EU, which prevents equality and non-discrimination becoming an 'entirely autonomous and all-embracing human right'.[74] On the other hand, McCrudden and Kountouros in this volume, see the Article 13 Directives as 'a significant step towards the development of an autonomous principle of equal treatment in the Community legal order'. But they too highlight additional impediments to this process and warn of the tensions that may occur when equality conflicts with the protection of other human rights. Ultimately, they predict a more refined evolution of the equality and non-discrimination principle into 'one that draws on but is not wholly anchored in human rights instruments'.

Prechal and Burrows, writing in 1990, stated that the rationale for the Community was to provide a better standard of living for everyone and 'As part of this aim there is the desire to enhance working and living conditions for the benefit of individuals and the society to which they belong. The abolition of discrimination and the achievement of equality is to serve this end; these are not goals in themselves.'[75] Today, 'equality between men and women' is one of the principal objectives of the Community.[76] Moreover, EC equality instruments can now be said to have a human rights goal and this goal together with a richer human rights culture is drawing us closer to the idea of an autonomous principle of equality. They also have some advantages over discrimination provisions in other systems.[77] They are generally addressed, as in the Article 13 Directives, to both public and private parties. They also cover a broad range of grounds and have the potential in time to expand protection for all Article 13 grounds beyond employment. Despite any shortcomings, the Article 13 Directives and the EC principles of equality and non-discrimination result in real shelter for the individual in his everyday life. Moreover, they will continue to reach vast numbers of people.[78] An autonomous equality principle could additionally ensure a distinct dynamism to the EU's equality regime and would help to enhance the EU's human rights image both internally and externally.

---

[74] Ibid. at 8.   [75] Above n. 38 at p. 319.   [76] Article 2 EC.

[77] Referring principally to the ECHR and the European Social Charter. Olivier De Schutter predicts that the ESC 'may become of rising importance', in influencing the development of anti-discrimination law in the EU, in Report for the European Network of Independent experts in the non-discrimination field, *The Prohibition of Discrimination under European Human Rights Law Relevance for EU Racial and Employment Equality Directives* (European Commission, Belgium, 2005) at p. 6.

[78] See Ellis, *EU Anti-Discrimination Law*, at p. 29.

Part III – Influential early developments

Indirect discrimination

In the early days, the E(E)C Treaty and European legislation lacked numerous elements that today are viewed with great importance and are now commonplace: the concept of indirect discrimination, tools permitting substantive equality, broad legislative competence, broad personal scope. Throughout this journey the equal treatment standard has been central (though not the exclusive standard) to Article 141[79] and now Article 13 EC. This section will discuss the development of select key concepts of EC equality and anti-discrimination law developed and elaborated in the spheres of the prohibition of sex and nationality discrimination before the Amsterdam Treaty. Arguably the first major milestone in European anti-discrimination law was the development of the concept of indirect discrimination.[80] Many notable commentators now view indirect discrimination as an important tool for dismantling systemic discrimination and credit it with attempting to achieve substantive equality.[81] Sacha Prechal ascribes the effects based approach and the 'taking into account the social, cultural, economic or other *de facto* realities' aspect of indirect discrimination as marking a shift from formal to substantive equality.[82] However, she and others also point to weaknesses with this concept as a tool for tackling structural or institutional discrimination (in the context of the gender pay gap), believing it can only be dismantled by additional instruments at Community and national level or in collective agreements.[83] Other commentators typically recommend positive action or positive duties as suitable approaches to these problems.[84]

The ECJ originally developed indirect discrimination in relation to nationality discrimination and the free movement of persons in *Sotgiu*

---

[79] Note the discussion of the equal treatment standard in Article 119 E(E)C and the sex equality Directives in Prechal and Burrows, at pp. 319–21.

[80] Note that Council Directive 75/117/EEC on the approximation of the laws of the Member States to the application of the principle of equal pay for men and women, 1975 OJ L45/19 at Article 1, merely refers to the principle of equal pay as meaning 'the elimination of all discrimination on grounds of sex'. However, the ECJ in *Defrenne* v. *Sabena II* at para. 60 refers to the intention behind the adoption of this Directive to encourage the proper implementation at national level 'in order, in particular, to eliminate indirect forms of discrimination'.

[81] Craig and De Búrca, *EU Law Text*, p. 852, Ellis, *EU Anti-Discrimination Law*, p. 188.

[82] S. Prechal, 'Equality of Treatment', (2004) p. 537.

[83] Ibid. at 539. Note also Craig and De Búrca, *EU Law Text*, p. 862.

[84] Hepple *et al.*, *Equality: A New Framework* (Hart Publishing, 2000) and S. Fredman and S. Spencer (eds.) *Age as an Equality Issue*, (Hart Publishing, 2003).

v. *Deutsche Bundespost*.[85] The application of a residence requirement in Germany was regarded by the ECJ in the circumstances as being 'tanatamount, as regards . . . practical effect, to discrimination on the grounds of nationality, such as is prohibited by the Treaty and the Regulation'.[86] Notably, the ECJ opened the door for objective justification in this case.[87] The seeds for indirect sex discrimination can be traced from at least an early Resolution of 1961 requiring Member States to outlaw both direct and indirect discrimination in pay between men and women by 31 December 1964.[88] Then in *Defrenne* v. *Sabena II* the ECJ drew a distinction for the purposes of Article 119 E(E)C, between on the one hand, 'direct and overt discrimination which may be identified solely with the aid of the criteria based on equal work and equal pay' referred to in that Article. It referred on the other hand to 'indirect and disguised discrimination which can only be identified by reference to more explicit implementing provisions of a Community or national law character'.[89]

This approach to indirect discrimination was maintained for a time[90] with the later case of *Jenkins* v. *Kingsgate (Clothing Productions) Ltd*[91] marking the real birth of indirect sex discrimination in European law. The Court decided that if a considerably smaller number of women than of men was able to work the minimum number of hours to qualify for the full-time rate of hourly pay that would be contrary to Article 119.[92] In *Bilka-Kaufhaus GmbH* v. *Karin Weber von Hartz*[93] the ECJ set out the test for justifying indirect sex discrimination. It was for the national court to decide whether the employer's measures respond to a 'real need on the part of the undertaking', are 'appropriate' to achieve the objectives and are 'necessary'.[94] The language of objective justification for indirect discrimination in the Article 13 Directives (and objective justification of direct age discrimination under Article 6 Employment Directive) differs only in that a 'real need' has been supplanted by a 'legitimate aim'.

---

[85] Case 152/73, [1974] ECR 153.

[86] At para. 11. Article 7.1 Regulation 1612/68 states that 'A worker who is a national of a Member State may not, in the territory of another Member State, be treated differently from national workers by reason of his nationality.'

[87] Para. 12.

[88] Resolution concerning the harmonisation of rates of pay of men and women, 30 December 1961. This Resolution responded to the poor implementation by some Member States, by the time limit imposed by Art. 119, *Defrenne* v. *Sabena II*, at paras. 46–8.

[89] Para. 18.   [90] Case 129/79 *Macarthys Ltd* v. *Smith* [1980] ECR 1275.

[91] Case 96/80, [1981] ECR 911.   [92] Para. 13.

[93] Case 170/84, [1986] ECR 1607. Prechal and Burrows, *Gender Discrimination Law* at pp. 19–20, argue that in *Bilka* the ECJ seemed to return to the formulation of indirect discrimination it had laid down in *Sotgiu*.

[94] Para. 36.

Indirect nationality discrimination took a different route to indirect sex discrimination in the free movement case, *O'Flynn* v. *Adjudication Officer*, where the ECJ appeared to set a lower bar for establishing discrimination than it had for sex discrimination, one that did not require complicated statistical evidence.[95] It decided that 'a provision of national law must be regarded as indirectly discriminatory if it is intrinsically liable to affect migrant workers more than national workers and if there is a consequent risk that it will place the former at a particular disadvantage'.[96] This understanding of indirect discrimination found favour in the influential Vienna conference on Article 13 in 1998.[97] It is now reflected in all three Article 13 Directives whose language on indirect discrimination, speaks of putting persons at a 'a particular disadvantage' rather than 'a considerably smaller number' being able to comply.

The Burden of Proof Directive in 1997[98] defined indirect sex discrimination as a provision, criterion or practice disadvantaging 'a substantially higher proportion of the members of one sex unless that provision, criterion or practice is appropriate and necessary and can be justified by objective factors unrelated to sex'.[99] Importantly, this was redefined on the occasion of amending the Equal Treatment Directive in 2002,[100] to bring it into line with the definition of indirect discrimination in the Race Directive and the Employment Equality Directive. This development is a concrete example of Christopher McCrudden's remarks on the mutual influence of gender and the Article 13 grounds and his prediction that 'there is likely to be a continuing significant legislative symbiosis between all the Article 13 grounds into the future'.[101] However, this book will reveal that this effect though significant may be naturally self-limiting at a certain point in time. The process of legislative symbiosis may never reach total *harmonisation* among the whole family of Article 13 grounds. Such a development may be undesirable due to the individual pathologies of the various grounds and the (differing) equality needs of each one. Though the slow emergence of awareness of subgroups and the issue of multiple

---

[95] Case 237/94 [1996] ECR I-2417.

[96] Ibid. at paras. 20–21. Note also Case C-278/94 *Commission* v. *Belgium* [1996] ECR I-4307 and Case C-35/97 *Commission* v. *France* [1998] ECR.

[97] See Robin Allen QC 'Article 13 and the search for equality in Europe: overview', Conference documentation *Article 13 Anti-discrimination: the way forward*, Vienna, 3–4 December 1998 at p. 18.

[98] Directive 97/80/EC on the burden of proof in cases of discrimination based on sex [1998] OJ L14/6.

[99] Article 2.2.   [100] Ibid.

[101] 'Theorising European Equality Law', in Costello and Barry (eds.) *Equality in Diversity* (Ashfield Publications, 2003) at pp. 13–15.

discrimination could indicate that as far as possible, greater legislative harmony is the only way to ensure justice for these special interests.

Direct discrimination

Unlike indirect discrimination, the prohibition on direct discrimination benefited from being easily discerned in the original E(E)C Treaty in respect of sex and nationality. As stated above, the ECJ in *Defrenne v. Sabena II* drew a simple distinction between 'direct and overt discrimination' on the one hand and 'indirect and covert discrimination' on the other. The Court later modified this terminology, which allowed for the fact that direct discrimination could also be disguised.[102] In the interim, the EC legislature adopted the Equal Treatment Directive in 1976 which defined the principle of equal treatment as: 'there shall be no discrimination whatsoever on grounds of sex either directly or indirectly.'[103] This is now reflected in the Race and Employment Directives.[104] Direct discrimination, in relation to the free movement of persons,[105] involves the prohibition of different treatment on grounds of nationality and the abolition of any discrimination based on nationality.[106] In relation to the Race and Employment Directives it is where one person is treated less favourably than another person. However, it has long been recognised in European law that discrimination may also involve treating differently situated persons in the same way.[107] It remains to be seen how this particular meaning will come into play in respect of the new grounds in Article 13 EC.

Positive action

The simplicity of the term positive action belies the variety of forms it may take and the variety of actors who may undertake it, which are often related to each other.[108] Within EC law positive action is *permitted*

---

[102] Case 69/80 *Worringham v. Lloyds Bank Ltd.*   [103] Article 2.1, Council Directive 76/207.

[104] Explanatory Memorandum accompanying the proposal for a Council Directive establishing a General Framework for Equal Treatment in Employment and Occupation, COM(1999) 565 final at p. 8.

[105] Article 7.1, Regulation 1612/68.   [106] Article 39.2 ECT.

[107] ECJ in Case C-279/93 *Finanzamt Köln-Altstadt v. Schumacker* [1995] ECR I-225, at para. 30, stated that 'discrimination can arise only through the application of different rules to comparable situations or the application of the same rule to different situations'. Note also the discussion of the principle of equality in Takis Tridimas, *The General Principles of EU Law* (2nd edn. Oxford University Press, 2006) at pp. 61–2.

[108] For a thorough discussion of positive action in the EU, Cathryn Costello 'Positive Action', in *Equality in Diversity*, pp. 176–212.

at national level and Member States are free to choose the form that it takes. However, the mainstreaming of gender equality into all Community activities and policies, is seen in terms of the related concept of a 'positive duty' at EU level.[109] One of the most significant contributions of the ECJ to sex discrimination law has been in the field of positive action, which was not referred to by the E(E)C Treaty until Article 141.4 was inserted by the Treaty of Amsterdam.[110] Article 141.4 is crafted in substantive law terms with the aim of 'ensuring full equality in practice'. It allows Member States to maintain or adopt 'measures providing for specific advantages in order to make it easier for the under-represented sex to pursue a vocational activity or prevent or compensate for disadvantages in professional careers'. What is now referred to as positive action first appeared in EC legislation (though not using this term) in Article 2.4 of the Equal Treatment Directive of 1976 (ETD).[111] The Directive at that time was without prejudice to national measures 'to promote equal opportunity for men and women, in particular by removing existing inequalities which affect women's opportunities'.[112]

The ECJ's contribution to positive action was initially inauspicious in the *Kalanke* judgment but its clear, if cautious understanding of the role of Article 2.4 ETD and an acknowledgement of the social situation of women were already emerging.[113] The aim of a national measure in favour of women was seen as 'improving their ability to compete on the labour market and to pursue a career on an equal footing with men'.[114] In *Marschall* the ECJ, faced with a similar German scheme, acknowledged 'the mere fact that a male candidate and a female candidate are equally qualified does not mean that they have the same chances' thus indicating a deeper understanding of the situation of men and women in the workplace.[115] The Court was able to differentiate this case from *Kalanke*.[116] In *Badeck* the ECJ ruled that a range of positive action rules that gave priority to women were compatible with the ETD, the key being that they did not give automatic or unconditional priority to women.[117] It seems

---

[109] Sandra Fredman, 'The Age of Equality', in *Age as an Equality Issue*, p. 62.

[110] This amendment is said to be in reaction to the *Kalanke* judgment discussed below, see among others S. Prechal, 'Equality of Treatment' (2004), p. 4.

[111] Ibid.   [112] Article 2.4.

[113] Case C-450/93 *Kalanke* v. *Freie Hansestadt Bremen* [1995] ECR I-3051 at para. 18.

[114] Para. 19 and 21.

[115] Case C-409/95 *Hellmut Marschall* v. *Land Nordrhein Westfalen* [1997] ECR I-6363.

[116] On the basis of a saving clause.

[117] Case C-158/97 *Badeck* v. *Landesanwalt beim Sttatsgerichtshof des Landes Hessen* [1999] ECR I-1875 at para. 28.

likely that this approach will also apply to the new anti-discrimination grounds.[118] The Court's shift to a substantive equality understanding is clear in *Badeck* where it states: 'Such criteria . . . are manifestly intended to lead to an equality which is substantive rather than formal, by reducing the inequalities which may occur in practice in social life.'[119] The ECJ confirmed the substantive equality role of these criteria in *Abrahamsson*.[120]

There are subtle differences between the positive action provisions for sex compared with race and the remaining Article 13 grounds. Article 141.4 contains additional elements 'in order to make it easier for the under-represented sex to pursue a vocational activity or . . . in professional careers'. Article 2.8 of the amended ETD, now aligns the Directive with Article 141.4 EC. The limits of Article 141.4 remain unclear because, as Evelyn Ellis points out, the ECJ has not given a comprehensive definition of positive action but case law would indicate that positive discrimination is not allowed under this provision.[121] Articles 5 and 7, of the Race and Employment Equality Directives respectively, provide 'With a view to ensuring full equality in practice, the principle of equal treatment shall not prevent any Member State from maintaining or adopting specific measures to prevent or compensate for disadvantages.' These differences in terminology may stand in the way of achieving full equality in practice for subgroups. The interests of older female workers may be better served by positive action under Article 141.4 or the amended ETD than the positive action permitted for older workers by Article 6.1.a, Employment Directive, or even the horizontal positive action provision contained in Article 7 of that instrument. The fact that positive action is governed at national rather than Community level may be an impediment to its efficacy. While the national level is undoubtedly crucial, older women, for example, appear to be a group with particular needs on a Europe-wide basis and perhaps a coherent approach is also required to dismantle properly the quite considerable barriers they face.[122] In any event, positive

---

[118] Miguel Paoires Maduiro, 'The European Court of Justice and Anti-discrimination Law', in *European Anti-Discrimination Law Review, Issue 2* (European Commission, 2005), pp. 21–6 at p. 25.

[119] Para. 32. Note also para. 31 where the ECJ includes as appropriate criteria in the assessment of a candidate 'capabilities and experience which have been acquired by carrying out family work are to be taken into account in so far as they are of importance for the suitability, performance and capability of candidates'.

[120] Case C-407/98 *Abrahamsson* v. *Fogelqvist* [2000] ECR I-5539.

[121] Evelyn Ellis *EU Anti-Discrimination Law* at pp. 297 and 311.

[122] Costello, 'Positive Action', at p. 212, seems to suggest that it is not enough to allow positive action at a national level and that genuine policy choices are required.

action under EU law has its critics[123] and is destined to have an image problem for as long as indirect discrimination is seen as the principal tool for tackling barriers to equality.

One objection to positive action is that it is susceptible to an accusation of discrimination against the other (sex).[124] Another objection is that it 'privileges group rights over individual rights'.[125] However, it is credited with achieving significant improvements in jurisdictions where it has been used.[126] The inadequacies of law on its own to achieve change have received much attention and the cry for wider measures to complement legal approaches is escalating all the time.[127] It seems clear that the largely anti-discrimination model represented in the Article 13 Directives is based (primarily) on a 'traditional model which, sees the discrimination as a set of individual acts of prejudice, and the role of the law as being to establish who is at fault and to require compensation'.[128] While Cathryn Costello sees 'room for much positive action even in an individual rights based system of equality law'.[129]

EC sex equality and nationality anti-discrimination law have and will continue to influence the interpretation and shaping of the legal framework for the Article 13 grounds.[130] New approaches to the Article 13 grounds have already been suggested, which take their inspiration from initiatives in the Member States and other jurisdictions, admittedly sometimes with their bases in national sex discrimination law. Thus Fredman suggests that 'positive duties are the most appropriate way for public authorities to advance age equality' and that they are 'particularly well suited to the promotion of social inclusion'.[131] The amended ETD requires that the Member States 'in accordance with national law, collective agreements, or practice, encourage employers to promote equal treatment for men and women in the workplace in a planned and systemic way'.[132] A similar provision requires the Member States to encourage employers and those responsible for access to vocational training to take measures

[123] For example, Ellis *EU Anti-Discrimination Law* at pp. 308–9.   [124] Ibid.

[125] Costello, 'Positive Action', at p. 209.

[126] Hepple *et al.*, *Equality: A New Framework*.

[127] For example, Prechal and Burrows, *Gender Discrimination Law* at p. 321; Ellis *EU Anti-Discrimination Law* at p. 115. Note also the Commission's Communication of 1 June 2005, 'A Framework Strategy', announcing a feasibility study on new approaches to complement the legal framework.

[128] Fredman, 'The Age of Equality', ibid at p. 61.   [129] Costello, 'Positive Action', at p. 212.

[130] Note Ellis *EU Discrimination Law*, at p. 209 predicts a consistency of interpretation between the Employment, Race and Equal Treatment Directives.

[131] *Age as an Equality Issue*, at p. 63.   [132] Article 8(b)3.

to prevent all forms of discrimination on grounds of sex, in particular harassment and sexual harassment in the workplace.[133] Thus an obligation is placed on Member States to *encourage* employers and others to prevent discrimination on grounds of sex and promote equal treatment for men and women. This obligation falls short of a positive duty in the sense intended by Fredman and others or as exists in some Member States but could be a small step in that direction.[134]

The more recent Directive 2004/113 on Equal Treatment between men and women in access to and supply of goods and services contains an interesting provision on dialogue with 'relevant stakeholders' which exhorts the Member States to encourage such dialogue 'with a view to promoting equal treatment'.[135] This contrasts with the corresponding provisions in the Employment Directive. These require Member States to take adequate measures 'to promote dialogue between the social partners with a view to fostering equal treatment' and to encourage dialogue with appropriate NGOs.[136] It also contrasts with the Race Directive, which contains two provisions, one governing social dialogue in similar terms but 'between the two sides of industry' and another concerning dialogue with NGOs, which is closer but not identical.[137]

The involvement of 'relevant stakeholders' would seem to be both appropriate and necessary for the identification and design of any measures to complement the legislative and policy frameworks for all EC anti-discrimination grounds. This approach has already been used successfully in Ireland to help achieve equality for older people.[138] Insofar as the term 'relevant stakeholders' in Directive 2004/113 is quite broad and thus likely to include groups covered by the legislation this is to be welcomed. It faintly echoes the recent public sector duty for disability in the United Kingdom, which requires public authorities to promote disability equality inter alia by involving disabled service users in the development of their disability equality schemes.[139] These approaches have much to

---

[133] Article 2.5.

[134] Note the public authorities' duty to eliminate discrimination and promote equality in the UK, under ss. 76A, 76B, 76C of the Sex Discrimination Act 1975, s. 71 of the Race Relations Act 1976 and ss. 49A and 49D of the Disability Discrimination Act (DDA) 1995.

[135] Article 11.   [136] Article 13 and Article 14.   [137] Articles 11 and 12.

[138] The Equality Authority Report *Implementing Equality for Older People* (Dublin, 2002) which was drawn up in partnership with older people, also made recommendations which fed into the amendment of the Employment Equality Act 1998.

[139] Section 49A of the DDA 1995 as amended by DDA 2005. See also Catherine Casserley, 'The disability equality duty for the public sector and its legal context', Disability Rights Commission, *Legal Bulletin*, Issue 9, May 2006 at pp. 5–12.

recommend them throughout the EU and beyond their specific target groups.

Part IV – Nationality

The deceptively simple prohibition against discrimination on grounds of nationality contained in Article 12 EC is at the core of European integration, underpinning basic freedoms, achieving the single European market and in its role as a general principle. The importance of this principle was renewed in light of the enlargement of the EU on 1 May 2004, which introduced ten new Member States and nearly 75 million people bringing the population of the EU close to 460 million.[140] Initial fears of an influx of migrants have been unfounded so far[141] but EC rules on free movement of workers will remain necessary to ensure the mobility and integration of these new EU citizens after the expiration of any transitional arrangements. This largest enlargement also brings increased diversity to the EU including new ethnic minorities and new national minorities.

A key concern even prior to the 2004 enlargement was the often close relationship between race, religious or ethnic minority discrimination on the one hand and nationality discrimination on the other. This led to some criticism of the omission of nationality as a ground of discrimination from Article 13 and its Directives and to calls to remove the exemption for treatment based on nationality from the Race Directive.[142] This exemption reads: 'This Directive does not cover differences in treatment based on nationality and is without prejudice to provisions and conditions relating to the entry into and residence of third-country nationals and stateless persons in the territory of Member States, and to any treatment which arises from the legal status of the third-country nationals and stateless persons concerned.'[143] It is observed that the Race Directive thus fails to address 'the complexity of how individuals experience discrimination'[144] and in respect of the Employment Directive that

---

[140] Eurostat.

[141] Press Release European Commission, Employment, Social Affairs and Equal Opportunities 8/2/2006 *Free Movement of workers since the 2004 enlargement had a positive effect.*

[142] European Network Against Racism (ENAR) *Council Directive implementing the principle of equal treatment between persons irrespective of racial or ethnic origin, 2000/43/EC Five year report on the application of the Directive: Overview of ENAR's initial assessment,* October 2005, at p. 4.

[143] Article 3.2, Race Directive and Employment Equality Directive. Note Paul Skidmore, below at pp. 127–8.

[144] ENAR.

'multiple and overlapping discrimination is therefore unlikely to be recognised adequately'.[145] Nationality is also excluded from Article 21.1 EUCFR.[146] However, Article 12 EC has some advantages over Article 13; for example, it possesses direct effect.[147] But in as much as Article 13 supplemented sex equality under Article 141, it is possible to argue that Article 13 ideally ought to include nationality or national origin in some way. This is not to ignore fears of mass migration and the social and economic implications if these were realised.

Nationality as a tool of classification

Nationality creates a de facto classification for people within EU borders. So far it is a concept that is decided according to the national law of the Member State in question.[148] It leads above all to the right to free movement for EU workers without discrimination based on nationality primarily in relation to employment. To be a national of a Member State is also the sole condition for European citizenship: 'Every person holding the nationality of a Member State shall be a citizen of the Union.'[149][150] However, this clear statement is not the reality for certain categories of nationals in some Member States.[151] A particular subcategorisation under Member State law can deny them European citizenship.[152]

The combined effect of the Amsterdam and Maastricht Treaties has resulted in a basic categorisation of people in the EC Treaty as citizens, nationals of other Member States and Third Country Nationals (TCNs). Moreover, it has been strenuously argued elsewhere that the EUCFR is

---

[145] Paul Skidmore 'EC Framework Directive on Equal Treatment in Employment: Towards a Comprehensive Community Anti-Discrimination Policy?' (2001) 30 *ILJ* 1, pp. 126–32 at p. 128.

[146] However, it is contained in the more narrowly constrained Article 21.2. Membership of a national minority is included in Article 21.1. Given that Article 14 ECHR is one of the main sources for Article 21.1, the omission of national origin therein is regrettable.

[147] Note Mark Bell's discussion in 'The New Article 13 EC Treaty: A Sound Basis for European Anti-Discrimination Law?' (1999) 6 *Maastricht Journal of European and Comparative Law*, pp. 5–24 at p. 10.

[148] 'Declaration (No.2) on nationality of a Member State', attached to the Maastricht Treaty.

[149] Article 17.1 ECT. Note the rewording in Article I-8(1) Treaty establishing a Consitution for Europe.

[150] Article 8(1).

[151] Gerard-Rene de Groot 'Towards a European Nationality Law', *Electronic Journal of Comparative Law*, 8.3 (2004) at s. 3, available at www.ejcl.org/83/art83-4.html.

[152] Ibid. at pp. 4–8.

built on this division between citizens and others.[153] This distinction helps to highlight gaps in protection from discrimination in the Article 13 Directives, resulting inter alia from the exemption in Article 3.2 therein. Paul Skidmore observes: 'It appears that only Community nationals are intended to receive protection against discrimination on grounds of nationality.'[154] At least three groups stand to be affected by the current exclusion of nationality and national origin from Article 13 EC and Article 21.1 EUCFR. They are: (1) TCNs; (2) EU nationals affected by the EC's approach to reverse discrimination[155] whereby a national may be treated less favourably than an EU migrant worker; and (3) nationals from other EU Member States.

Third country nationals (TCNs)

Many TCNs fall within ethnic or religious minorities, suffer race discrimination, social exclusion and are particularly vulnerable to nationality discrimination, which can sometimes be difficult to disentangle from other forms.[156] Even viewed from the perspective of TCNs alone, Article 21.1 EUCFR ought to contain the additional grounds of national origin and nationality. This provision is a direct general prohibition with broader application than Article 13.[157] Article 21.2 EUCFR states that 'Within the scope of application of the Constitution and without prejudice to any of its specific provisions, any discrimination on grounds of nationality shall be prohibited.' Any future inclusion of nationality in Article 21.1 would be of special importance for TCNs as the wording of Article 21.2 does not appear to include them. The exclusion of nationality from Article 13 arguably harms TCNs more than nationals of the Member States who are in any event covered by Article 12 EC and related provisions. However, some TCNs may now enjoy rights of residence and limited rights of movement within the EU which go some way to improving their situation.

---

[153] Siobhain McInerney 'The Charter of Fundamental Rights of the European Union and the Case of Race Discrimination' (2000) 27 *ELRev* 4, 483–91 at pp. 483–4.

[154] Above n. 145.

[155] Although as Niamh Nic Shuibhnein, 'Article 13 EC and non-discrimination on grounds of nationality: Missing in action?' in Costello and Barry (eds.) above n. 101 pp. 269–93, at p. 290, notes, over the years the number of issues that are purely internal to Member States has reduced and the recent case law of the ECJ varies on the issue of a Community link.

[156] Siobhain McInerney, 'The Charter of Fundamental Rights', p. 485 and Steve Peers 'Implementing Equality? The Directive on Long Term Resident Third Country Nationals', (2004), 29(4) *ELRev*, pp. 437–60 at p. 437.

[157] See Lenaerts and De Smijter, 'A Bill of Rights for the European Union' (2001) 38 *CMLR* 273 at 283–4.

The Third Country Nationals Directive (TCN Directive)

Prior to the TCN Directive, TCNs were regarded as a particularly disadvantaged and vulnerable group within the EU.[158] However, this clear term belies the diversity within this group[159] which, goes well beyond long-term residents (LTRs). Since the European Council in Tampere in 1999, TCNs who are long-term residents and reside legally in the EU have emerged as worthy of 'fair treatment'.[160] In 2003, Council Directive 2003/109/EC concerning the status of third-country nationals who are long-term residents (TCN Directive) was adopted in light inter alia of the Tampere Conclusions.[161] This Directive provides a mechanism whereby TCNs who have been 'legally and continuously' resident in a Member State for five years may acquire permanent long-term resident status there. This status entitles them to equal treatment with nationals across a range of activities including access to employment and access to goods and services.[162] One of the Directive's strongest features is the right for a long-term resident to reside in a second Member State for a period of more than three months. In general, LTRs will enjoy equal treatment with nationals in the second state in the same way as in the first Member State.[163] The TCN Directive also provides for the acquisition of LTR status in the second Member State.[164] However, the TCN Directive is equally interesting for those who fall outside its scope including refugees.[165] It does not apply to the United Kingdom, Ireland[166] and Denmark.[167]

Nationality and the 'European Year of Equal Opportunities for All'

The omission of nationality from Article 13 ECT was clearly a conscious one directed primarily against TCNs. Reliance on the prohibition of nationality discrimination in the EC Treaty will, if anything be more important in an enlarged and enlarging EU.[168] For this and other

---

[158] Paul Skidmore, 'EC Framework Directive', p. 128 and Siobhain McInerney, 'The Charter of Fundamental Rights', at p. 486.

[159] Nic Shuibhne 'Missing on Action?' at pp. 277–8.

[160] Tampere European Council, 15 and 16 October 1999, Presidency Conclusions at para. II.1.

[161] [2004] OJ L16. Recital (1) of the preamble also echoes Article 61 EC which includes safeguarding the rights of TCNs as a goal of an area of freedom, security and justice.

[162] Articles 8.1 and 4.1.   [163] Article 21.

[164] Article 23 but this is subject to Articles 3, 4, 5 and 6.   [165] Article 3.2.

[166] Recital 25.

[167] Note Protocol on the position of the United Kingdom and Ireland and Protocol on the position of Denmark attached to the EC Treaty.

[168] Bulgaria and Romania joined the EU in 2007.

reasons, it is remarkable that The European Year of Equal Opportunities for All is concerned with a purely Article 13 vision of equal opportunities. The preamble to the 'Decision of the European Parliament and of the Council establishing the European Year of Equal Opportunities for All (2007) – towards a just society'[169] states that European legislation on equal treatment and non-discrimination covers all persons in the EU. However, there is no specific reference to nationality in this document. Moreover, Article 1, which sets out the objectives of the European Year, states that 'The European Year will highlight the message that all people are entitled to equal treatment, irrespective of their sex, racial or ethnic origin, religion or belief, disability, age, or sexual orientation. The European Year will make groups that are at risk of discrimination more aware of their rights.'[170] The European Year will highlight the positive contribution of people with these same characteristics,[171] thus ignoring the past and ongoing contribution of migrant workers from other EU Member States to the labour market.[172] The sidestepping of nationality in debates and strategies concerning the future of non-discrimination and equality in the EU is also evident from the European Commission's Green Paper *Equality and non-discrimination in an enlarged Union*, 2004[173] and *Communication Non-discrimination and equal opportunities – A Framework Strategy*, 2005.[174] However, the Green Paper did list membership of a national minority as one of seven grounds covered by Article 21 of the Charter asking whether it should stimulate debates on any of these grounds.[175]

The Article 13 grounds appear to dominate the EU's equality and anti-discrimination agenda for now.[176] The hierarchy argument previously applied liberally to the Article 13 grounds would perhaps be more appropriate to describe the place of nationality among the EU's modern anti-discrimination priorities. It would however, be more helpful to ensure that nationality is included in research into multiple discrimination. It is also crucial to conduct research into the scale of nationality discrimination *per se* in the EU before any future enlargements take place, as enlargement

---

[169] Decision No. 771/2006/EC of the European Parliament and of the Council [2006] OJ L146.

[170] Article 1(a).   [171] Article 1(c).

[172] See Press Release European Commission 8/2/2006.   [173] COM(2004) 379 final.

[174] COM(2005) 224 final.   [175] At p. 23.

[176] See the Green Paper at pp. 6–7. Note however, the important role of the *O'Flynn* case above.

is an important stimulus for anti-discrimination thinking and measures. Mark Bell has expressed the powerful view that Article 12 may be of more assistance than Article 13 EC as: 'it does not expressly limit its potential to discrimination based on EU nationality.'[177] However, this remains to be seen.

Nationals from other Member States

For the purposes of this chapter only the right to free movement of workers shall be discussed. This is apart from but linked to the rights of residence pertaining to EU citizens in Directive 2004/38 (Citizen's Rights Directive). Strictly speaking, three elements are necessary to avail of the right to free movement of workers in Article 39.2 EC, amplified by Regulation 1612/68. The individual must be a worker, he must possess the nationality of a Member State and he must have activated his right by moving to another Member State in search of work or to take up employment. It is generally true that the ECJ has always demonstrated a generous approach towards the definition of a migrant worker, the traditional principal beneficiary of the right to non-discrimination on grounds of nationality. This generosity may be facilitated by the fact that the *worker* enjoys a unique position in EC non-discrimination law – it is provided for in the Treaty but developed by the ECJ as a Community concept.[178]

The ECJ's broad early interpretation of *work* covered by the free move-ment rules endures today: 'effective and genuine activities, to the exclusion of activities on such a small scale as to be regarded as purely marginal or ancillary'.[179] Its three-part interpretation of a *worker* in *Lawrie-Blum* also continues in use: 'The essential feature of an employment relationship, however, is that for a certain period of time a person performs services for and under the direction of another person in return for which he receives remuneration.'[180] The Court's approach to the free movement rules arguably reached a new plane in *Meeusen* in respect of the definition of a worker and social advantages for descendants of workers.[181] The term

---

[177] Mark Bell, 'The new Article 13 EC Treaty', p. 22.
[178] Case 75/63 *Hoekstra (nee Unger)* v. *Bestuur der Bedrijfsvereniging Voor Detailhandel en Ambachten* [1964] ECR 177.
[179] Case 53/81 *Levin* v. *Staatssecretaris van Justitie* [1982] ECR 1035 at para. 17.
[180] Case 66/85 *Lawrie-Blum* v. *Land Baden-Wurttemberg* [1986] ECR 2121, at para. 17.
[181] Case C-337/97 *CPM Meeusen* v. *Hoofddirectie van de Informatie Beheer Groep* [1999] ECR I-3289.

'worker' was found to embrace a part-time employee who was related by marriage to the director and sole shareholder of a company. Of particular interest in this case was the fact that neither the Belgian husband and wife resided in the state of employment, the Netherlands.

The ECJ's broad interpretation of the term 'social advantages' in Article 7.2, Regulation 1612/68 as amended,[182] has produced benefits for a worker and his heterosexual cohabitee,[183] and children.[184] However, it is the interpretation of children's independent rights that has shown the Court at its most benevolent.[185] In particular where children's carers have been permitted to stay in the EU in the absence of the carer having the status of a Community worker or possessing the nationality of a Member State, to care for minor children.[186] Thus demonstrating humanity towards both child and carer. The Citizen's Rights Directive now captures a shift whereby some rights are available by virtue of EU Citizenship rather than worker status, subject to certain conditions.[187] Takis Tridimas observes that 'the advent of Union citizenship has bred a new generation of rights . . . Article 12 . . . has been transformed from a tool of economic integration to an instrument of citizen empowerment'.[188]

Much amplification of the material and personal scope of antidiscrimination provisions in the EC Treaty was provided relatively soon by the legislature starting with the Equal Pay Directive in 1975[189] for sex discrimination and Regulation 1612/68 on freedom of movement for workers.[190] However, these are very different instruments. The former is quite narrow in scope and may be regarded (together with the Equal Treatment Directive) as a distant forerunner of the Article 13 Directives. While Regulation 1612/68 sets out detailed rights for the migrant worker and his family, it did not outlaw victimisation, contain a requirement to enable claims to be pursued by judicial process or a requirement that effective means are available to ensure the principle of non-discrimination is

---

[182] By Directive 2004/38/EC on the right of citizens of the Union and their family to move and reside freely within the territory of the Member States, [2004] OJ L158/77.

[183] Case 59/85 *Netherlands* v. *Reed* [1986] ECR 1283.

[184] Case 316/85 *Centre public d'aide sociale de Courcelles* v. *Lebon* [1987] ECR 2811.

[185] Case C-7/94 *Landesamt fur Ausbildungsforderung Nordrhein-Westfalen* v. *Lubor Gaal* [1996] ECR I-1031.

[186] Case C-413/99 *Baumbast and R* [2002] ECR I-7091 and Case C-200/02 *Chen and Zhu* [2004] ECR I-9923. The *Chen* case, however, relied on a combination of the child's status as an EU citizen and her rights under Article 18(1) EC and a general right of residence which has now been supplanted by Directive 2004/38.

[187] For example Article 6.1.   [188] Above no. 107, at p. 61.   [189] Ibid.

[190] [1968] OJ (Sp. Ed.) L257/2 at p. 475.

observed. The Citizen's Rights Directive redresses only one of these.[191] It requires Member States to lay down effective and proportionate sanctions for breach of national implementing law.[192] Importantly, however, Article 24 on equal treatment, contains the basic principle that 'all Union citizens shall enjoy equal treatment with the nationals of that Member State within the scope of the Treaty'.[193] Thus rectifying the sporadic provision for equal treatment in free movement legislation[194] and providing a clear point of convergence with sex and the other Article 13 grounds.[195] Regulation 1612/68 was remarkable for spawning a trend in free movement of persons in the EU, which can be traced to the Citizen's Rights Directive and is even evident in the TCN Directive. This refers to coverage of the worker's family, which is not mentioned in the EC Treaty.[196]

A Member State's own nationals: the rule against wholly internal situations

Nationals of an EU Member State cannot rely on EC law on the free movement of workers where their situation is 'wholly internal' to their own Member State. A national would need to demonstrate a Community dimension to his situation that so far is best achieved through movement to and a period of work in another Member State.[197] The inability of an EU citizen in his own Member State to rely on EC free-movement provisions, for example to bring parents from a third country to live with him,[198] is often understood as a Member State treating their own nationals less favourably than nationals from other Member States.[199]

---

[191] Article 31 on procedural safeguards only requires access to judicial or administrative redress in respect of decisions taken on the basis of public policy, public security or public health, updating Directive 64/221/EEC.

[192] Article 36.

[193] Article 36.2 contains two important derogations. The host State is not required to provide social assistance during the first three months of residence or any longer period for the self-employed or job-seekers. Nor is it obliged to give study grants to students before they acquire the right to permanent residence.

[194] For example, in relation to free movement of persons, those contained in Article 7, Regulation 1612/68 and Article 8, Directive 64/221.

[195] For sex, note the clear early attempt to implement the equal treatment principle by means of Directive 76/207/EEC (the ETD).

[196] Note Craig and De Búrca, *EU Law Text* at p. 734.

[197] Case C-370/90. *R v. Immigration Appeal Tribunal, ex p. Secretary of State for the Home Department* [1992] ECR I-4265.

[198] Cases 35 & 36/82 *Morson and Jhanjan v. Netherlands* [1982] ECR 3732.

[199] Or in terms of reverse discrimination.

In the *Uecker* and *Jacquet* cases,[200] the national court questioned 'whether the fundamental principles of a Community moving towards European Union' did not allow a rule that would infringe Article 48(2) EC (now Article 39.2) to be applied by a Member State to its own nationals and their spouses from non-EC countries.[201] This line of thinking was not adopted by the ECJ. However, it seemed likely that if and when the Constitution for the European Union would have been ratified there would have been considerably more scope for arguments of this kind.[202] While the concept of citizenship has assisted in the free movement of persons, the ECJ has signalled that it is unlikely to assist nationals of a Member State in an internal situation.[203] Until now nationals seeking to overcome the wholly internal rule faced a tough and often insuperable barrier in the phrase 'in the territory of another Member State' which peppers Regulation 1612/68, and is also found in the Citizen's Rights Directive.[204]

At present, the inclusion of nationality in Article 13 ECT and its Directives would seem the most certain way of combating less favourable treatment of nationals in their own Member State. This may remain politically unacceptable to the Member States. However, rights that apply to situations that are wholly internal to a Member State were not unknown in the EU even prior to Article 13 EC, for example Article 141 EC. Waddington expresses some of the complexities as follows: 'the right to equal treatment when exercising free movement is simply a rather strange right which does not fit easily into a constitutional framework. The principle does not apply to internal situations.'[205] Nationality remains firmly outside the Article 13 equality family despite any role in influencing the Article 13 Directives. This raises a number of questions: ought sex and the other Article 13 grounds influence the development of nationality discrimination in the EU or bring nationality within their fold, in any respect? Is the present situation sustainable in light of those for whom a combination of their nationality and other identities causes discrimination? While these questions arguably require tailored research to resolve them, it is important to recall that other influences bear on the principle of non-discrimination

---

[200] Cases C-64/96 & 65/96 *Land Nordrhein-Westfalen* v. *Uecker and Jacquet* v. *Land Nordrhein-Westfalen* [1997] ECR I-3171.

[201] Paras. 22–3.

[202] Note the remarks of Nic Shuibhne, 'Missing in Action' at p. 290 and Preamble, Treaty Establishing a Constitution for Europe, which will now be replaced by the Reform Treaty if it is agreed and ratified by all EU Member States.

[203] *Uecker and Jacquet*, Para. 23.   [204] See, for instance, Article 7.

[205] Lisa Waddington 'The Expanding Role', at p. 9.

on grounds of nationality, such as the concept of EU citizenship, however, this status is not open to all persons. The Article 13 Directives will
benefit from existing understanding of non-discrimination and equality
law acquired mainly, though not exclusively, in the field of sex equality. Though it cannot be automatically assumed at this point that all the
existing common concepts and machinery will be adequate to combat
discrimination or achieve equality for the diversity represented by the
new grounds and combinations of protected grounds.

The adoption of the Part-Time Work Directive and Fixed-Term Work
Directive in the late 1990s[205a] are also an interesting part of the EU anti-
discrimination story. They are built on the application of the principle of
non-discrimination. But unlike the Article 13 Directives, they are related
to the characteristics of the work rather than the personal characteristics of the employee and they do not incorporate a ban on indirect
discrimination.[206] These Directives may well support the argument that
equality and non-discrimination 'have become objectives in their own
right'.[207]

In the remainder of Part I which now follows, Robin Allen QC discusses
the evolution of Article 13 EC and its current contexts and critically analyses missed opportunities and strengths of Article 13 and its Directives. Among the points he raises, is the issue of discrimination by
association or on account of perceived grounds which were not con-
sciously brought within the scope of the Article 13 Directives. While
it seems likely that the Court of Justice will interpret the Race and
Employment Equality Directives to prohibit this form of discrimination, he advises that this must await definitive interpretation. Christopher McCrudden and Haris Kountouros then provide a compelling analysis of the various evolving human rights and equality contexts in which
the Article 13 Directives were adopted. They also consider EU equality law in light of the proposed Reform Treaty. Finally, Israel Doron
describes and analyses the impact of demographic and social change on
society and on the individual as an important context for EU equality
law.

[205a] Council Directive 97/81 concerning the framework agreement on part-time work [1998]
OJ L14/9 and Council Directive 1999/70 concerning the framework agreement on fixed-
term work [1999] OJ L175/43.
[206] Although it must be acknowledged that these forms of work are frequently dominated by
women, see Ann Numhauser-Henning's discussion in this volume.
[207] Lisa Waddington, 'The Expanding Role', at p. 11.

Part II contains a chapter on each of the six anti-discrimination grounds contained in Article 13 EC. Ann Numhauser-Henning scrutinises the contribution of sex equality law to the drafting of the Article 13 Directives and the influence in turn of the Article 13 Directives on the development of European sex equality law. She asks: 'Will multiple non-discrimination grounds reinforce a formal equality approach as the common denominator or, on the contrary, draw our attention to the obvious need for proactive measures?' This question will be revisited in the concluding chapter. Mark Bell's analysis of EU anti-racism strategy reveals that progress in this field is very unbalanced particularly from the perspective of measures such as mainstreaming and institutional commitment. He is not alone in questioning the choice to isolate race in its own Directive.[208] Gwyneth Pitt anticipates many definitional issues in relation to 'religion or belief'. She also explores whether the Race Directive ought to include religion as an ascribed characteristic in addition to the protection of 'religion or belief' in the Employment Equality Directive. Gerard Quinn captures the international and EU trend away from paternalism to basic rights for all in the field of disability and focuses on the unique role of reasonable accommodation. He emphasises the part that proxies or stereotypes play particularly in disability discrimination and discusses the special susceptibility of disability to discrimination on grounds of perception or association.

In the chapter on age, I highlight the tremendous heterogeneity of older people and people in any particular age group and argue that the chronological age approach of Article 6 of the Employment Directive arguably ignores this important reality. While there is some kernel of truth that age impacts on functional capacity this is so highly individualised as to demand an individual rather than a general response. Issues such as current age limits and mandatory retirement ages may also be out of step with key contexts such as the Lisbon agenda and population ageing which has added decades to human longevity. Finally, Barry Fitzpatrick considers that different (and particularly newer) anti-discrimination grounds may require both an integrated and differentiated approach to deal with their particular issues and controversies. He demonstrates this through an analysis of sexual orientation within each provision of the Employment Directive. He argues that the Directive contains many elements that can be built upon to create the necessary proactive environment for sexual orientation. But in other respects it may not go far enough for the particular

---

[208] Note also Robin Allen in this volume.

access to justice issues facing this ground. The concluding chapter reflects on common themes throughout this volume and the road ahead. Above all it is clear that the incorporation of Article 13 EC and the adoption of its Directives, while enormously important in themselves, are merely the beginning of the modern era in EU anti-discrimination and equality law.

2

Article 13 EC, evolution and current contexts

ROBIN ALLEN QC

Introduction

Amongst the most exciting of the new possibilities in the Amsterdam Treaty[1] is the provision enabling European legislation to be made in relation to equality and non-discrimination.[2] This provision is contained in Article 13 EC, which as then agreed,[3] stated:

> Without prejudice to the other provisions of this Treaty and within the limits of the powers conferred by it upon the Community, the Council, acting unanimously on a proposal from the Commission and after consulting the European Parliament, may take appropriate action to combat discrimination based on sex, racial or ethnic origin, religion or belief, disability, age or sexual orientation.

It was clear from the outset that action under Article 13 depended for its content on proposals from the European Commission. As soon as the Amsterdam Treaty was agreed the Commission began to mull this over. There was time to do this. Although the Amsterdam Treaty was signed by the high representatives on 2 October 1997 it required ratification by each Member State to come into effect. This was not concluded until 1 May 1999,[4] and the hiatus provided a useful opportunity for some preliminary consideration as to the effect that would be given to it. For this purpose

---

[1] OJ C340, 10/11/1997.

[2] For a discussion of the background to the drafting of this provision see E. Guild, 'The European Union and Article 13 of the Treaty Establishing the European Community', in G. Moon (ed.), *Race Discrimination, Developing and Using a New Legal Framework* (Hart and JUSTICE, 2000) and M. Bell, *Anti-discrimination Law and the European Union (Oxford Studies in European Law*, Oxford University Press, 2002).

[3] An additional sub-article was added by the Treaty of Nice, see below.

[4] By Article 14 it did not come into force until the first day of the second month following that in which the instrument of ratification is deposited by the last signatory state to fulfil the formality of ratification.

the Commission held a major conference over 3 and 4 December 1998 to discuss what could and should be done with Article 13.

Before this conference it had been suggested that at least one Directive should be made at an early stage but the form and content of that Directive was not then settled.[5] In this respect, the venue for the first major Commission conference could not have been more apt. In the second half of 1998, the Presidency had moved to Austria, where the rise of Jörg Haider's Austrian Freedom Party with its ultra-nationalist platform, was already causing great consternation across European capitals. So when the conference took place in the city of Vienna, and was run with the co-operation of the Austrian Federal Ministries for Labour, Health and Social Affairs, and for Justice, race and ethnicity discrimination was very much on the political agenda. All participants were keen to discuss how this should be addressed. But this was not the only issue, since the chosen title of the conference was 'Anti-Discrimination: the way forward'. It was a central question to be debated whether *more* than just race and ethnicity should be addressed in the first stage, or whether a limited approach should be taken. Related to this was a question as to the most desirable scope of any new provision.

History, of course, reveals that the more comprehensive approach was indeed taken: proposals for two Directives swiftly followed and these soon became law.[6] The Vienna conference was seen by all as the first big step in giving effect to Article 13. The fight for such an Article which had been fought for with such determination had to be converted into real action at Community level.

The next part of this chapter explores how the debate was started at Vienna, while following parts discuss the evolution and current context of the debate on the use of Article 13 EC. Some of the events of that conference[7] and its significance are discussed from a perspective allowed only by the passage of time.

In some respects the seven years since the conference might seem quite a long time for reflection, but in the context of the *acquis* this is not so. After all the second of the two Directives made in 2000 under Article 13

---

[5] The British Presidency had held an initial conference in Oxford in early 1998.

[6] The two proposals made at the Vienna Conference became Council Directive 2000/43/EC of 29 June 2000 implementing the principle of equal treatment between persons irrespective of racial or ethnic origin and Council Directive 2000/78/EC of 27 November 2000 establishing a general framework for equal treatment in employment and occupation.

[7] For the full report of the Conference see 'Article 13, Anti-Discrimination: the Way Forward' (Europaforum Wien, 1999).

EC permitted Member States until 2 December 2006 to implement its provisions in relation to age and disability.[8] Moreover, at present Article 13 EC has only been cited in very few Opinions[9] and Judgments of the Court of Justice,[10] and the Directives have barely featured at all. Of course, the *thinking* around non-discrimination and equality has developed enormously and this is dealt with elsewhere in this book.

It was my privilege to be invited by the European Commission to give the keynote speech to the Vienna Conference.[11] The speech was written with the express purpose of setting out the legal context within which the participants might address the possibilities for action under Article 13 EC.[12] In one sense it is therefore a statement of the starting point from which life was breathed into Article 13. That is one reason why it has been incorporated into the second part of this chapter. A second reason is that it provides a marker by which to measure the developments which have since occurred in the evolution and use of Article 13.

The Vienna Conference Keynote Address

Article 13 and the search for equality in Europe: an overview

Introduction

It is my task to address the main areas of discrimination which will be in scope under Article 13, to consider the possibilities it offers, to give some thoughts for the future and to share some personal reflections. The invitation to undertake that task was one that I accepted with great pleasure because Article 13 promises so much. I know how eagerly its implementation has been awaited. I very much hope that what I have to say will help to animate the discussions that are to follow.

Until now, the human right not to suffer discrimination has been seen by many citizens and third country nationals as having only secondary

---

[8] See Art 18 of Council Directive 2000/78/EC.

[9] See Cases C-186/01 *Dory*, C-117/01 *K. B.* and C-227/04 P *Lindorfer* v. *Council*. A reference has also been made by a Spanish Court in Case C-411/05 *Félix Palacios de la Villa* v. *Cortefiel Servicios SA, José María Sanz Corral and Martin Tebar Less* in relation to mandatory retirement ages, and by an Employment Tribunal in Great Britain in Case No. 2303745/2005 *Coleman* v. *Attridge Law*.

[10] See Cases C-186/01 *Dory*, C-144/04 *Mangold* and C-13/05 *Sonia Chacón Navas* v. *Eurest Colectividades SA*.

[11] Written on the 16 November 1998.

[12] The footnotes have been renumbered and in a few places there have been some minor corrections to the text.

importance and being only weakly enforceable. In many areas it has been limited in scope or even non-existent in municipal legislation; though there are also undoubtedly examples of good practice.[13] In those Member States with proactive official equality organisations the wish for more effective and obvious results remains as strong as ever. I know this to be true of the United Kingdom[14] and I believe it to be true of other countries. At an important conference in Utrecht[15] this summer I heard something similar about Austria. One participant said that even after 20 years' work the effects of the Austrian Equal Treatment Commission on the position of women in society were still unclear.[16] So the task of giving effect to the aspirations contained in Article 13 is by no means to be underestimated.

I propose to start by outlining the international human rights context for action under this Article.

The human rights context

Article 14 of the European Convention of Human Rights[17] states:

> The enjoyment of the rights and freedoms set forth in this Convention shall be enjoyed without discrimination on any ground such as sex, race, colour, language, religion, political or other opinion, national or social origin, association with a minority, property, birth or other status.

However, that Article does not provide a free-standing right not to be discriminated against. It only operates with the other provisions of the Convention. It has been accurately described as having an 'accessory nature'[18] and 'no independent existence'.[19] Moreover, even when presented with a complaint under Article 14, the European Court of Human Rights has

---

[13] For instance, the Dutch Equal Treatment Commission (*Commissie Gelijke Behandeling*) deals with unequal treatment involving religion, personal conviction and views, political orientation, race, gender, nationality, sexual preference, marital status and duration of employment. It plainly takes active steps in all these areas: see its Annual Report 1997.

[14] See, e.g. the introduction by Sir Herman Ouseley to 'Reform of the Race Relations Act 1976' (Commission for Racial Equality, 1998).

[15] The International Conference on Comparative Non-Discrimination Law, Universiteit Utrecht, 22–4 June 1998, jointly organised by the Dutch Equal Treatment Commission and the School of Human Rights Research.

[16] Paper given to the Utrecht Conference, 'The Austrian Equal Treatment Commission as an Instrument of Equality Law Enforcement', by Anna Sporrer, Chair of the Equal Treatment Commission (Private Sector) of Austria.

[17] Hereafter the ECHR.

[18] See 'Law and Practice of the European Convention on Human Rights and the European Social Charter' by Gomien, Harris and Zwaak (Council of Europe, 1996), p. 346.

[19] See, e.g., the *Belgian Linguistics Case* (1979–1980) 1 EHRR 578, para 9, and *Airey* v. *Ireland* (1979–1980) 2 EHRR 305, para 30.

often failed or declined to consider what is the impact of Article 14.[20] As a result, the jurisprudence of the Human Rights Court on this Article is limited. For instance, in a recent discrimination case brought against the UK concerning the proper conduct of discrimination litigation in Northern Ireland, the Human Rights Court declined even to consider whether there had been a breach of Article 14.[21] Nevertheless this is an Article which the Community must take seriously.[22]

There is also Article 26 of the United Nations International Covenant of Civil and Political Rights (ICCPR):[23]

> All persons are equal before the law and are entitled without any discrim-
> ination to the equal protection of the law. In this respect the law shall
> prohibit any discrimination and guarantee to all persons equal and effec-
> tive protection against discrimination on any ground such as race, colour,
> sex, language, religion, political or other opinion, national or social origin,
> property, birth or other status

This Article *does* provide a free-standing right to non-discrimination. Its enforcement is through the Human Rights Committee of the United Nations and its impact has proved to be fairly limited,[24] although some Member States have incorporated it into their municipal law.[25]

There is now an increasing awareness at international level of the need for a strong protection of the right not to suffer discrimination. In the Council of Europe, recognising the weakness of Article 14 of the European Convention on Human Rights, the Minister's Deputies have instructed the Steering Committee on Human Rights to draft an additional protocol, or protocols, to the ECHR broadening in a general fashion the field of application of Article 14. While the nature of that protocol is still under debate, action cannot be delayed indefinitely. The steering committee is required to report to the Ministers by the end of next year. There is hope

---

[20] See Gomien, Harris and Zwaak, p. 349.

[21] See *Tinnelly and Sons Ltd. and others and McElduff and others* v. *UK* Case No 62/1997/846/1052–1053 Judgment 10.7.98.

[22] See, for instance, Case C-260/89 *ERT* [1991] ECR I-2925, and also Art 6 (formerly F) and 49 (formerly O) of the Treaty of European Union as amended by the Amsterdam Treaty, as examples of the central place of the convention in the Community.

[23] Referred to below as the ICCPR.

[24] See Lord Lester of Herne Hill QC and Joseph 'Obligations of Non-discrimination' in Haris and Joseph (eds.) *The International Covenant on Civil and Political Rights and United Kingdom Law* (Clarendon Press, 1995).

[25] For instance, the Netherlands by Act of 24 November 1978.

of action in the Council of Europe to run in parallel with action within the Community.

The Belfast Agreement[26] made earlier this year between the United Kingdom and the Republic of Eire and the political parties in Northern Ireland is also significant. Its central theme is the principle of non-discrimination.

So, in the wider international context, the implementation of Article 13 is keenly awaited. This is also true of Europe. Let me take just three specific examples where the need for its implementation has been highlighted recently within the Community:

- In *Grant* v. *South-West Trains Ltd.*[27] the Court of Justice decided that the Equal Pay and Equal Treatment Directives[28] could not be extended to protect two lesbian women. However, the Court pointed out that the future implementation of legislation under Article 13 could provide equivalent protection.[29]
- The Starting Line Group (whose important work I consider further below) has emphasised how:

  > Up till now efforts to combat racism, xenophobia, anti-Semitism, and religious hatred and intolerance have been constrained by lack of competence in the Union's institutions. The new Article 13 marks the first time that racial and religious discrimination have been mentioned in the treaty... After ratification, it will be possible to draft and pass a Community directive, establishing a common standard of protection for citizens throughout the Union and requiring member states within a time limit to pass their own legislation enforcing this standard.[30]

- Finally a '*Comité des Sages*'[31] has very recently said that:

  > A European Union which fails to protect and promote human rights consistently and effectively will betray Europe's shared values and its long-standing commitment to them. However, the Union's existing policies in

---

[26] See 'The Belfast Agreement: An Agreement reached at the Multi Party Talks on Northern Ireland' Cm 3883: in particular pp. 16–18 'Rights, Safeguards and Equal Opportunity'.
[27] Case C-249/96.   [28] Directive 75/117/EEC and Directive 76/207/EEC.
[29] See in particular paras. 47 and 48
[30] See 'Proposals for Legislative Measures to Combat Racism and to Promote Equal Rights in the European Union', Isabelle Chopin and Jan Niessen (eds.) (Commission for Racial Equality, 1998) p. 16.
[31] Judge Antonio Cassese, Mme Catherine Lalumière, Professor Peter Leuprecht, and Mrs Mary Robinson. See 'Leading by Example; A Human Rights Agenda for the European Union for the Year 2000' (Academy of European Law, European University Institute, Florence, 1998). I refer to this document below as 'the Agenda'.

this area are no longer adequate. They were made by and for the Europe of yesterday; they are not sufficient for the Europe of tomorrow. The strong rhetoric of the Union is not matched by the reality. There is an urgent need for a human rights policy which is coherent, balanced, substantive and professional.[32]

With that exhortation very much in mind, I turn now to make some observations on the constituent parts of the Article.

The relationship with the other parts of the treaty

Without prejudice to the other provisions of this Treaty . . .

This phrase would seem to mean that other provisions of the Treaty (TEC) are not to be constrained by Article 13. It has been pointed out by Mark Bell[33] and others that there are other provisions of the TEC that provide scope for action to prevent discrimination. The social powers of the TEC in Articles 131–146 mainly relate to employment but certainly contain some possibilities for action. In particular it has been suggested that Article 137(1) allows for the adoption of directives on 'integration of persons excluded from the labour market' and would therefore permit directives on race discrimination at work. If this is so then it brings into question the proper way in which to legislate. Under these social provisions the European Parliament has a more important role and qualified majority voting is possible.[34] Thus the legal base for action needs to be considered very carefully.

The limits of the Article

. . . within the limits of the powers conferred by [the Treaty] *upon the Community . . .*

This point is re-enforced by the next part of the Article. The word 'powers' is very important here. It can be interpreted in a variety of ways: broadly permitting far reaching action, or narrowly permitting much more limited action. Bell concludes that:

---

[32] Ibid. para. 2

[33] I wish to acknowledge my debt to Mark Bell of the European University Institute whose paper to the Justice Seminar at London 22 October 1998 has helped me enormously with the issues arising under Article 13 in particular in respect of competence. His paper is to be published as 'The new Article 13 EC Treaty: a sound basis for European anti-discrimination law?' in the *Maastricht Journal of European and Comparative Law.*

[34] See Art 137(2) EC.

Article 13 is slightly less broad in its field of application than Article 12. The implication is that Article 13 may be relied upon to prohibit discrimination within those areas for which the Community already has competence.[35]

In my view this is an issue about political will. Since Article 13 requires unanimity in Council it seems unlikely that the resulting legislation could be subject to an effective challenge on the basis that it goes beyond the limits of the powers conferred by the Treaty. It is of primary significance that Article 13 is to be found within that part of the TEC which is headed 'Principles' and that it relates so closely to other international human rights norms. Moreover, Article 13 asserts the basic concept of equal treatment in a very wide range of areas.

Certainly I am confident that Article 13 permits action beyond the field of employment. As Article 13 includes discrimination on grounds of sex it must have in mind legislation outside that field as there can be no doubt that the Community already has the necessary powers to deal with discrimination on grounds of sex in employment.

Education and housing have been suggested by Bell and others as being in scope. Education is specifically dealt with under the TEC by Chapter 3 Title X1.[36] It is less obvious how housing could be brought within the scope of Article 13, though it is obviously connected with issues relating to the free movement of workers and is a prime cause, as well as an effect, of social exclusion which is dealt with in Article 137(2).

I consider that there are other important areas where there can be discrimination particularly in access to goods and services. It should be noted that Article 1 of the draft Starting Line Directive concerning the Elimination of Racial and Religious Discrimination identifies[37] as in scope: professional activities; access to jobs or posts, dismissals, and other working conditions; social security, health and welfare benefits, education, vocational guidance and training; housing; the provision of goods facilities and services; the exercise of functions by any public body; and participation in political, economic, social, cultural, and religious life or any other public field.

---

[35] Bell refers also to the similar opinion of R. Whittle in 'Disability Discrimination and the Amsterdam Treaty' (1998) *European Law Review* 23, pp. 50, 53.

[36] Formerly Title VIII.

[37] Proposals for Legislative Measures to Combat Racism and to Promote Equal Rights in the European Union, p. 26.

Action to combat discrimination

. . . appropriate action to combat discrimination . . .

It is perhaps on this aspect of Article 13 that this section will concentrate most. If the action that is taken is weak or ineffectual there will be a sense of alienation between those who have hoped for so much and the political process which will have delivered too little. Here I want to emphasise some points about the different ways in which discrimination can occur so as to help this conference focus on what action is appropriate at Community level.

• **The Court of Justice and the concept of discrimination**   When we consider what is meant by appropriate action to combat discrimination we do not start with a blank piece of paper. The Community has already learnt much about what is appropriate action from the way in which it has provided protection from discrimination, both in relation to equal pay and sex discrimination, and in the exercise of free movement rights.[38]

The concept of discrimination used by the Court of Justice (which accords with the jurisprudence of the Human Rights Court[39]) is found in propositions such as the following:

> comparable situations are not to be treated differently and . . . different situations are not to be treated alike . . .[40]
>
> or
>
> discrimination can arise only through the application of different rules to comparable situations or the application of the same rule to different situations.[41]

It is well established that discrimination may be justifiable on objective grounds.[42] It is worth noting here that the Human Rights Court considers some kinds of direct discrimination as being particularly suspect and therefore less likely to be justified. Discrimination which is exclusively on the grounds of sex or race will rarely be compatible with the ECHR.[43]

---

[38] For a very substantial overview of the law see D. Martin, 'Discriminations, entraves et raisons impérieuses dans la traité CE: trois concepts en quête d'identité'.

[39] See, e.g., *Belgian Linguistics* (1986) 1 EHRR 252, para. 10.

[40] E.g. Case 203/86 *Kingdom of Spain* v. *Council of the European Communities* [1988] ECR 4563, para. 25.

[41] See, e.g., Case C-279/93 *Finanzamt Koeln-altstadt* v. *Roland Schumacker* [1995] ECR I-225.

[42] Case 170/84 *Bilka-Kaufhaus GmbH* v. *Karin Weber von Hartz* [1986] ECR 1607.

[43] See *Schmidt* v. *Germany* (1994) 18 EHRR 513 and *Belgian Linguistics* supra.

However, a problem arises when legislating under Article 13, because the Court of Justice has not been consistent in the way that it approaches indirect or disguised discrimination. In my view, this problem must be addressed because it is this type of discrimination which is both the most difficult to identify and the most important to eradicate.

In cases involving the free movement of workers the test for indirect discrimination was stated thus in O'Flynn v. Adjudication Officer:[44]

> A provision of national law must be regarded as indirectly discriminatory if it is intrinsically liable to affect migrant workers more than national workers and if there is a consequent risk that it will place the former at a particular disadvantage. It is not necessary to find that the provision in question does in practice affect a substantially higher proportion of migrant workers. It is sufficient that it is liable to have such an effect.

This 'intrinsically liable' test does not call for elaborate statistical evidence. It is almost intuitive – the risk of particular disadvantage is enough. This contrasts sharply with some of the jurisprudence of the Court of Justice in the field of sex discrimination and equal pay. Here a more statistical or even formulaic approach has been developed. The origin of this approach can be found in Jenkins v. Kingsgate Clothing Productions.[45] The Court of Justice ruled that if the impugned requirement affected 'a considerably smaller proportion of women' it was necessary to examine whether there was any objective justification.[46] Thereafter, the Court has sometimes referred to numbers rather than proportions.[47] This approach can be seen in numerous subsequent cases and has led to detailed statistical considerations in cases of sex discrimination and equal pay.[48] It has also led to the Directive on the burden of proof in cases of discrimination based on sex[49] defining indirect discrimination as occurring:

---

[44] Case C-237/94 [1996] ECR I-2417, paras. 20 and 21; see also Case C-278/94 Commission v. Belgium [1996] ECR I-4307 and Case 35/97 Commission v. France Judgment 24 September 1998.

[45] Case 96/80 [1981] ECR 911, initially in the Opinion of Advocate General Jean Pierre Warner.

[46] See para. 13.

[47] See, e.g., Case C-102/88 M. L. Ruzius-Wilbrink v. Bestuur van de Bedrijfsvereniging voor Overheidsdienste [1989] 4311.

[48] See, e.g., the approach taken in Case C-127/92 Enderby v. Frenchay Health Authority [1993] ECR I-5535, paras. 16 et seq.

[49] Directive 97/80/EC.

> Where an apparently neutral provision, criterion, or practice disadvantages a substantially higher proportion of the numbers of one sex unless that provision criterion or practice is appropriate and necessary and can be justified by objective factors unrelated to sex.[50]

Yet adequate statistics are not always available. Is it to be said that such cases must fail even where it is quite clear that a provision, criterion or practice is liable to disadvantage the protected group? There may simply be too few persons in a firm who are affected by the provision in question to provide adequate statistics,[51] or where the provision, criterion or practice has only just been introduced, there may have been inadequate time for statistics to be collected.[52]

In my view, there is no good reason to treat indirect sex discrimination less favourably than indirect discrimination in the exercise of free movement rights.[53] Accordingly, in this respect I consider that the draft directive proposed by the Starting Line Group does not go far enough. In my view, the *O'Flynn* approach is necessary to secure appropriate action to combat discrimination.

● **Situations of particular disadvantage**   It is important to bear in mind that the focus in assessing whether there has been discrimination will differ according to the protected group in question. In most cases it is rightly assumed that a person in the protected group is equally competent to undertake a particular task as a person outside it. Thus it will normally be assumed that a female is as competent as a male to undertake any task. On the other hand, in some circumstances we recognise from the beginning that a person suffers a particular disadvantage.

For instance, when a woman is pregnant there comes a time when she is not as able to work. At that stage it is inappropriate to compare her with a man. She must have a protected status and her inability to carry out a job should not be compared with that of, for instance, an ill

---

[50] Article 2(2).

[51] For an example of this dilemma see *London Underground* v. *Edwards (2)* [1998] IRLR 664. In that case the Court of Appeal of England and Wales concluded that a requirement to work flexible hours which adversely affected only one woman out of twenty-two, and none out of 2,023, was indirectly discriminatory, but only after locating the statistics in a wider social context.

[52] This is one of the issues that has arisen in *R.* v. *Secretary of State for Employment ex parte Seymour Smith*, currently before the Court of Justice.

[53] I have discussed this point further in 'Equal Treatment, Social Advantages and Obstacles: in Search of Coherence in Freedom and Dignity' in E. Guild (ed.), *The Legal Framework and Social Consequences of Free Movement of Persons in the European Union* (Kluwer, 1998).

man.[54] It is now well understood that in asking whether there has been discrimination against a pregnant woman it will be inappropriate to carry out a comparison. Acting to the detriment of the pregnant woman is direct discrimination.[55]

Article 13 concerns another situation of particular disadvantage – disability. Where treatment disadvantages a person because of the disability the key question must be whether there has been a proper attempt to provide for the disabled person in order to minimise or reduce the disadvantage that otherwise would be suffered by that person.[56] The focus of the inquiry is on the nature of the disability and not on the ability of the person. This is not to equate pregnancy with disability. The key point is that for some groups special treatment is essential to ensure that there is no discrimination. It is impermissible to argue on behalf of a man or able-bodied person that they were disadvantaged by the failure to provide them with the special treatment that was necessary for the pregnant woman or disabled person.

It may be that as we consider the situations of the protected groups that other special situations will emerge as important and relevant. For instance, in considering discrimination against the old or young it may be that a similar approach should be taken.

• **Equality before and under the law; equal protection and equal benefit of the law; affirmative action**   The text of Article 26 ICCPR reminds us that action under Article 13 should aim to secure both equal protection before the law and equality under the law. Both of these aspects of equality are important and both need to be addressed. Equal benefit of the law is also necessary.[57] Also the key issue of positive discrimination or affirmative action must be addressed here.

Equal treatment by itself may not be enough if it does not lead to an equality of outcomes. The present effect of past disadvantage, in, for instance, education, social or immigration status, may mean that equal treatment will or may lead to unequal outcomes. This is not just a point about indirect or disguised discrimination but about the need to remedy

---

[54] See, e.g., C-32/93 *Webb* v. *EMO* Case [1994] I-3567, para. 24.
[55] Case C-179/88 *Handels- og Kontorfunktionærnes Forbund i Danmark, acting on behalf of Hertz* v. *Dansk Arbejdsgiverforening acting on behalf of Aldi Marked K/S* [1990] ECR I-3979 ('Hertz'), para. 13 and C-421/92 *Habermann-Beltermann* [1994] ECR I-1657, para. 15.
[56] In the UK the Disability Discrimination Act 1995 differs markedly in its approach to the definition of discrimination from the Race Relations Act 1976 or the Sex Discrimination Act 1975.
[57] Compare s. 15(1) of the Canadian Charter of Rights and Freedoms.

past disadvantage. For instance, in decisions about recruitment, minimum educational attainment rules may be readily justified. However, if in one region all the best educational establishments are run by the churches, there will be a structural disadvantage for Muslim children. It is therefore not enough to look at discrimination solely from the point of equality before the law. This accords with international human rights norms. In interpreting Article 26 ICCPR the UN Human Rights Committee[58] has stressed the need for states to take affirmative action to diminish or eliminate conditions which cause or help to perpetuate discrimination prohibited by the Covenant. It is also an approach which is consistent with other major constitutional documents which expressly permit affirmative action.[59]

Nevertheless it is clear from the US experience that affirmative action raises many further problems. Perhaps the right way forward is to adopt the approach of the Indian Supreme Court that a measure of affirmative action must 'contain [within] itself the seed of its termination'.[60] It may be that affirmative action should also be limited to particular issues such as training. Certainly, time limiting affirmative action ensures that it is focused and more acceptable to those who cannot take the benefit of the action.

The need for affirmative action is one which has already been discussed both in the Court of Justice in *Kalamke* v. *Freie Hansestadt Bremen*[61] and *Marschall* v. *Land Nordrhein-Westfalen*[62] and at Community level in Commission proposals for an amendment to the Equal Treatment Directive.[63] In my view, this is an area where it is most obvious that a European approach is essential. Affirmative action is about social coherence in the fullest sense. It seeks to give an equalised stake in the future to groups which have very different and unequal social attributes and histories.

● **Subsidiarity**   Legislation under Article 13 must comply with the principle of subsidiarity[64] in particular as set out in the Protocol to the Amsterdam Treaty on the application of the principles of subsidiarity

---

[58] General Comment 18/37 of 1989.
[59] See for instance section 15(2) of the Canadian Charter of Rights and Freedoms and Articles 15(3) and (4) of the Indian Constitution and Article 4 of the United Nations Convention on the Elimination of All Forms of Discrimination Against Women.
[60] See *Indra Sawhey* v. *Union of India* 80 AIR SC 477 1993.
[61] Case C-450/93 [1995] ECR I-3051.   [62] Case C-409/95 [1997] ECR I-6363.
[63] Case C-179/88 OJ 1996 C 179, p. 8. See also the amendment to TEC Article 141 (ex 119) made by the Amsterdam Treaty.
[64] See Article 5 EC.

and proportionality.[65] Legislation under Article 13 must enable Member States to take the action that is appropriate to their situation within a framework set by the Community as a whole.

> For Community action to be justified, both aspects of the subsidiarity principle shall be met: the objectives of the proposed action cannot be sufficiently achieved by Member States' action in the framework of their national constitutional system and can therefore be better achieved by action on the part of the Community.[66]

The Protocol provides a three point guidance on when Community action will be justified:

- 'the issue under consideration has transnational aspects which cannot be satisfactorily regulated by action by Member States';

An example of a situation where this might apply is in relation to age discrimination. It is well known that the age profile of Europe is changing rapidly. However, very few European countries have specific legislation which protects older workers, and where it does exist such legislation is said often to be flouted.[67] In another area, the Amsterdam Treaty might be cited for its recognition of the problem of cross-border racism and xenophobia.[68]

- 'actions by Member States alone or lack of Community action would conflict with the requirements of the Treaty (such as the need to correct distortion of competition or avoid disguised restrictions on trade or strengthen economic and social cohesion) or would otherwise significantly damage Member States' interests';

Here social cohesion is likely to be the key issue. This conference will add to the evidence that is available.[69] One recent study[70] of racially motivated crime[71] in three major European cities has made this need for action at Community level very clear. The authors stated that:

---

[65] OJ C 340, 10/11/1997, p. 105.   [66] See Art. 5 of Protocol 30 to the Treaty.
[67] *European Industrial Relations Review* 247 (August 1994), pp. 13–16.
[68] See the new Art. 29 (Formerly Art. K1) of the TEU.
[69] See the Agenda already referred to.
[70] J. Chirico, A. Das and C. Smith, *Racially Motivated Crime – Responses in three European Cities: Frankfurt Lyons and Rome*, Dummett, A. (ed.) (Commission for Racial Equality, 1997).
[71] See also R. Oakley, 'Report on Racial Violence and Harassment in Europe', by (1993) Strasbarg: (Council of Europe ref: MG-CR (91) 3 rev. 2; Council of Europe, 23 September 1992, and the Report Consultative Commission on Racism and Xenophobia for the Cannes European Council (Kahn Commission) SN 2129/95).

> Many of the interviewees [in Frankfurt] expressed the view that an increased
> European dialogue would help all policy actors to improve their policies
> and procedures[72] [and] . . . racism . . . is widespread across Europe and
> to combat it effectively . . . structures . . . [are needed] . . . that transcend
> national bodies, because in electoral campaigns at national level the parties
> of the extreme right exploit the issue[73]

Also, there can be no doubt that competition can be distorted by discrimination. It was no accident that the original treaty contained the equal
pay provisions in Article 119.[74] The Commission has already pointed out
that: 'The Union must act to provide a guarantee for all people against the
fear of discrimination if it is to make a reality of free movement within
the single market.'[75]

- 'action at Community level would produce clear benefits by reason of its
  scale or effects compared with action at the level of the Member States'.

In my view there are some very obvious reasons why action at Community level would have effects which would produce comparatively greater
benefits than those achievable within Member States alone. The creation
of a uniform base of rights to non-discrimination would certainly facilitate the deepening of the concept of European Citizenship, assist other
countries that wish to become members of the Community to know what
are the basic standards of the Community in these important areas, and
discourage social migration within the Community because certain states
secured the rights in Article 13 more or less effectively.

● **Five conditions for effective legislation against discrimination**   In
my view there are five essential conditions for real equality under the rule
of law.

Individual rights and remedies   Effective anti-discrimination laws must
give a victim a right to an effective personal remedy against the person
or body who has perpetrated the discrimination. The Court of Justice
has already declared the need for adequate individual remedies, which
'guarantee real and effective judicial protection and have a real deterrent
effect on the employer', in *Helen Marshall* v. *Southampton and South-West
Hampshire Area Health Authority*.[76] This need is equally true of all the

---

[72] Per A. Das at p. 139.   [73] Per J. Chirico at p. 139.   [74] Now Art. 141.
[75] See 'European Social Policy – A way forward for the Union' Com (94) Final 333, 27/7/94,
Ch. VI, para. 27.
[76] Case C-271/91[1993] ECR I-4367, para. 24.

other grounds set out in Article 13. This implies proper access to the Courts and equality of arms before the Courts.[77] Some states have Commissions which help with the preparation and funding of discrimination cases; others will have to consider what assistance is necessary to make sure that such individual rights are real.

Criminal sanctions   Some discriminatory acts are so grave that the state must invoke the criminal process against the perpetrators. There are three main reasons for this.

Firstly, often the victim will be too alienated or feel too weak or frightened to seek an individual remedy. In those circumstances the state cannot stand by and permit the wrongful act to occur and perhaps to re-occur. Secondly, the state exercising the democratic will of the people, and the courts as guardians of human rights, must mark disapproval of grave acts of discrimination, especially those involving violence or grave oppression. Thirdly, and more particularly, public order can be quickly undermined by racist or other discriminatory attacks, or by vigilante action or retaliation provoked by acts of discrimination. Only through an effective criminal process will that be prevented.

Accordingly, an effective code of criminal laws, an adequately resourced and motivated system of criminal investigation and a suitable judicial process giving proportionate sentences are all essential.

Information and training   The scope and principle of equal treatment and the need for objective justification for differential treatment is not naturally part of the public discourse. Experience shows that merely giving rights to individual remedies and creating mechanisms for state enforcement will not be enough. The principle of equal treatment needs to be fully understood and accepted as desirable for society, ensuring that decisions are taken on an objective basis thereby promoting stability and social coherence. The more effective the system of public information is the less need there will be for either of the previous two remedies.

There are two general levels for such public information: information to the adult public and education to those of school age as a core curriculum issue. Additionally, more detailed training and information will be necessary for judges, the police and other social actors. I want to emphasise particularly the need for education and training of the police and the judiciary. Neither group can be assumed to understand what Article

[77] See *Airey* v. *Ireland* (1979–1980) 2 EHRR 305.

13 means. Experience in my country teaches me that ensuring that such education is effective is a long and slow process.[78] I do not suggest that the education should be delivered at Community level, but that the need for it is recognised and encouraged through Community action.

Mainstreaming   All social actors have a responsibility to ensure that their policies are formulated with a due regard to the importance of all equality issues. Unless this responsibility is taken very seriously the effectiveness of any legislation under Article 13 will be much reduced. The importance of mainstreaming was most notably recognised at an international level in relation to the position of women at the Fourth United Nations World Conference on Women.[79] Mainstreaming has already been taken up by the Community in its Fourth Medium-term Community Action Programme on Equal Opportunities for Men and Women (1996 to 2000).[80] It has also been recognised that its implications go further than just gender issues: for instance, the European Parliament called for a similar policy in relation to disability matters in accordance with UN Standard Rules on Equalisation of Opportunities for Persons with Disabilities.[81] The Amsterdam Treaty included the following declaration: 'In drawing up measures under Article 100a the institutions of the Community shall take account of the needs of persons with a disability.'[82]

So, in my opinion, an assessment of the impact on all equality issues is a necessary precondition for the proper formulation of all laws, rules, and policies, by all social actors. Mainstreaming should not just be limited to governmental organisations, though of course they must take a lead in this.

Monitoring   Without continual monitoring of the situation of those classes of persons who are in the scope of the anti-discrimination

---

[78] It was only very recently that the Judicial Studies Board, which is responsible for the train-ing of judges in England and Wales, created an Equal Treatment Advisory Committee. There has been some excellent work done by Her Majesty's Inspectorate of Constabulary (for instance the Thematic Inspection on Police, Community and Race Relations 1996/7 entitled 'Winning the Race – Policing Plural Communities') and the Home Office. How-ever, this work has not been universally welcomed. I expect that this is a problem that will be common to many Member States.

[79] See 'Platform for Action and the Beijing Declaration – the Report of the Fourth World Conference on Women, Beijing China 4–15 September 1995' (United Nations Department of Public Information, 1996) in particular para. 204.

[80] Council Decision 95/593/EC, [1995] OJ L335, 30/12/1995, pp. 37–43.

[81] Resolution on the rights of disabled people OJ C020, 20/01/1997, p. 389.

[82] Declaration 22, OJ C340, 10/11/1997, p. 135.

provisions, the four previously mentioned conditions will be only partly and incompletely achieved. It is essential that the effect of laws and policies are monitored. It is essential that workplace practices and commercial polices are monitored. There is increasing experience of the importance of monitoring. In Northern Ireland it has proved an invaluable tool in securing tolerance of religious and political diversity in the workplace.[83] The argument for wider monitoring is perhaps most fully made out in the recitals to the Council Regulation establishing a European Monitoring Centre on Racism and Xenophobia.[84]

Whatever legislation is proposed under Article 13 it must be set in a framework which will meet these five conditions.

The protected grounds

I wish to add only a few further remarks about discrimination in relation to the grounds which Article 13 protects.

Sex A key question for this conference will be what areas of sex discrimination outside employment require protection. The Equal Treatment Directive has already been interpreted to provide protection to transsexuals in *P* v. *S and Cornwall County Council*.[85] However, discrimination against transsexuals goes much further than just employment. Here the case law of the Human Rights Court has not yet been helpful,[86] although there was a strong dissenting opinion that holds out hope for the future.[87] Distinctions between post- and pre-operative transsexuals have no place in any modern legislation on sex discrimination.

Racial or ethnic origin Here I can do no better than to refer to the Starting Line proposals on which I have already commented. The need for such action is now very widely appreciated. Obviously the task is to consider the way in which these proposals meet the needs of the Community.[88] A

---

[83] In Northern Ireland the Fair Employment (Northern Ireland) Acts 1976 and 1989 which prohibit religious and political discrimination in the employment field impose detailed and effective monitoring requirements on firms. For a useful guide to these Acts see the *Fair Employment Handbook*, C. McCrudden (ed.) (Industrial Relations Services, 1995).

[84] No. 1035/97 of 2 June 1997, OJ L151, 10/06/1997, pp. 1–7.

[85] Case C-13/94 [1996] ECR I-2143.

[86] See the recent judgment of the Human Rights Court in *Sheffield and Horsham* v. *UK*.

[87] See in particular the dissenting judgment of Judge van Dijk at para. 3.

[88] See Prof. C. Gearty 'The Internal and External "Other" in the Union Legal Order: Racism, Religious Intolerance and Xenophobia in Europe' in ch. 10 of P. Alston (ed.) *The European Union and Human Rights* (Oxford University Press, 1999).

particular aspect for consideration will be the position of third country nationals.[89]

Religion or belief   The Court of Justice has already decided in principle that examinations for the Community's civil service which were held on Saturday were discriminatory against Jews.[90] This should provide a starting point for a wider consideration of religious discrimination both at work and in education. It should be noted also that the connection between religion and belief echoes Article 9 ECHR. It is right that the Starting Line proposals should also consider them together because there is a very close relationship between racial and religious discrimination. The ECHR jurisprudence has conspicuously avoided giving a definitive ruling on what constitutes a religion[91] and it is probably as well not to seek a definitive answer. A particularly difficult question is the extent to which protection in respect of religion and belief should be given. Should an employer be prevented from implementing any rule at all that has a discriminatory effect, such as working on Friday,[92] Saturday or Sunday? Or is it sufficient to require that such a rule is objectively justified? In the Netherlands, discrimination of this kind in the workplace has been taken very seriously[93] and this experience may be of particular relevance.

I would like to add a few comments in respect of discrimination on grounds of belief, because this could also include political opinion. The jurisprudence of the ECHR already provides strong protection in this field under Article 10.[94] It is surely important that the Community do not take too restricted a view as to what discrimination on the grounds of belief is within any legislation under Article 13.

Disability   The disabled sometimes feel that they are an invisible part of the Community. It is now well recognised that this is quite incompatible

---

[89] See also the Starting Line 'Draft Directive on Third Country Nationals' in 'Proposals for Legislative Measures to Combat Racism and to Promote Equal Rights in the European Union', p. 37.

[90] Case 130/75 *Prais* v. *EC Council* [1976] ECR 1589.

[91] See *X and the Church of Scientology* v. *Sweden* No. 7805/77 or *Chappell* v. *UK* No.12587/86.

[92] The Human Rights Commission rejected a complaint by a Moslem teacher that he had been denied his rights under Art. 9 ECHR when his employer would not let him attend prayers on Fridays: *X* v. *UK* 8160/78, Dec 12.3.81 DR 22, p. 27.

[93] See the Dutch High Court decision of 30 March 1984, Nederlands Jurisprudentie 1985 no 350; and see Dr. B. C. Labuschaigne 'Religious Freedom and Newly Established Religions in Dutch Law' *Netherlands International Law Review* XLIV: 2 (1997).

[94] See, e.g., *Vogt* v. *Germany* [1996] 21 EHRR 205.

with a comprehensive approach to social cohesion. Nevertheless legislating for the disabled raises difficult questions about who is in scope. Is mental disability to be treated in the same way as physical disability? Are those with hay fever to receive the same protection as those with diabetes? Are those with myopia in need of the same protection as those with schizophrenia? What is the right approach to disability through addiction to alcohol, tobacco or other drugs? These are difficult questions that have been approached in some countries in their municipal legislation. Perhaps a key question is whether to propose a unified approach to the meaning of disability.[95]

Age   There is much work to be done in respect of age discrimination. In the employment field a recent survey[96] of eleven European countries identified five sets of discriminatory measures which particularly affect older persons: loss of employment, discrimination in recruitment, exclusion from special unemployment measures, exclusion from training and discrimination at retirement. The US has had long experience of age discrimination legislation which will provide a useful source for comparison. In the UK, the Government has just proposed a voluntary Code of Practice in relation to age discrimination, while accepting that legislation may be necessary in the future. I personally doubt whether such an approach is likely to be effective.

Sexual orientation   The need for action in relation to sexual orientation has already been mentioned.[97] The case law of the Human Rights Court shows that discrimination against homosexuals can be contrary to the Convention[98] but it does not treat discrimination, by the more favourable treatment of married persons or heterosexual couples than homosexual couples, as a breach of Article 14.[99] There is an expectation that this may change, with the abolition of the European Commission on Human Rights.[100] It is essential that the Community addresses the rights

---

[95] The World Health Organisation has an International Classification of Diseases to which reference might be made.

[96] 'Age discrimination against older workers in the European Community' (Eurolink Age, 1993).

[97] See Case C 249/96 *Grant* supra.

[98] See, e.g., *Dudgeon* v. *UK* [1981] 4 EHRR 149; see also the report of the *Commission in Sutherland* v. *UK* Application No. 25186/94.

[99] *S* v. *UK* No. 11716/85 47 DR 274, and *B* v. *UK* No. 16106/90 64 DR 278.

[100] See the powerful arguments advanced in 'A case for Equality' by Peter Duffy QC in the Stonewall Lecture reported at [1998] 2 EHRR 134.

of homosexual couples from a human rights perspective in a way similar to that taken by the Court of Justice in respect of transsexuals in *P* v. *S and Cornwall County Council.*[101]

Conclusions

Article 13 has real potential to meet the expectations to which I have referred. As the Community moves into the next millennium, it will be of the greatest importance, in creating a Union truly founded on human rights. It brings the principle of non-discrimination closer than ever before to those who are in need of protection from discrimination. Although the Article is one which empowers further action by the Community, its adoption, is of itself, a significant political fact. It has created an expectation that action will be taken. Despite the need for unanimity it will surely be impossible for no action to be taken under this provision. The challenge is to take *effective* action. I look forward to working towards the achievement of this goal.

The 'sleeping giant' awakes

There followed five further short lectures which discussed some of the possibilities for action,[102] followed by the usual workshops. Other participants at the Conference discussed whether different kinds of Community initiatives might be appropriate such as awareness training activities and exchanges of experience. All considered the extent to which radical action rather than incremental steps were appropriate. In a memorable phrase, in one of the workshops, former judge of the Court of Justice, Manfred Zuleeg, described Article 13 as a 'sleeping giant' and stated that it was the task of the Conference and by implication the Commission, to wake it up and demonstrate its strength. It was a challenge which was welcomed by all who attended and one which the Commission has continued to address with energy and commitment.

---

[101] Case C-13/94 [1996] ECR I-2143.

[102] The other speakers and their topics were A. Heymann-Doat, 'Motives of Discrimination, Discriminatory practices and means to combat them', B. Niven, 'Combating discrimination – What types of Community Action?', W. Okresek, 'Article 13 and the legal environment – an instrument for the fight against discrimination', G. Shaw, 'Balancing legislative standards and voluntary action: experience from the business sector' and M. Zuleeg, 'The content of Article 13 of the Treaty establishing the European Community as a amended by the Treaty of Amsterdam'.

Thus there was loud applause when, at the conclusion of the conference, Commissioner Padraig O'Flynn announced that the Commission would indeed immediately bring forward two draft directives: the first would be wide ranging in scope and based on race; the other would provide a framework for equality in relation to all the other grounds contained in Article 13, save sex, but would be limited to the employment context.[103] These were the first steps of the giant, but more were to come. Specific aspects of the giant's waking life are discussed in other chapters of this book, yet one or two are worth mentioning here.

Firstly, the Conference contributed significantly to a developing political impetus for immediate action and within record time the directives became law as Directive 2000/43/EC of 29 June 2000 implementing the principle of equal treatment between persons irrespective of racial or ethnic origin ('the Race Directive') and Directive 2000/78/EC of 27 November 2000 establishing a general framework for equal treatment in employment and occupation ('the Employment Framework Directive'). This impetus has continued but not in an entirely uniform way. Most states have taken some steps to implement these Directives but enforcement proceedings in the Court of Justice have had to been taken by the Commission under Article 226 EC against Austria, Germany, Luxembourg and Finland,[104] and it is understood that the implementation by other countries has been criticised by the Commission.

Secondly, this legislative programme has been the precursor to other important acts of the organs of the Community, ranging from action by the Commission to Council Resolutions. The first and most important was a decision to have a Community Action Programme in relation to combating discrimination.[105] This Programme has been hugely influential in the dissemination, across old and new Member States, of the ideas contained within Article 13 and developed in the Vienna Conference. A first review of the Programme took place in the Green Paper published in 2004.[106] This led to some changes in the way in which the Commission has worked. The Programme is now coming to an end and is being evaluated[107] and a further Green Paper is expected to be published to propose

---

[103] See the Report of the Conference, pp. 60–3.
[104] See http://ec.europa.eu/employment_social/fundamental_rights/legis/lginfringe_en.htm.
[105] Council Decision of 27 November 2000 establishing a Community action programme to combat discrimination (2001 to 2006) (2000/750/EC).
[106] See http://ec.europa.eu/employment_social/fundamental_rights/pdf/ pubst/grpap04_en. pdf.
[107] See http://ec.europa.eu/employment_social/fundamental_rights/ policy/aneval/eval_en. htm.

the next steps in the autumn of 2006. There is no doubt that there is more to be done and already there have been calls for more and deeper legislation in relation to the protected grounds.[108] One important sign of that is the decision that 2007 be designated European Year of Equal Opportunities for All.

In the field of sex discrimination, the Union has utilised Articles 13 and 141 EC, to amend the Equal Treatment Directive[109] to bring sex discrimination broadly into line with the provisions of the Employment Equality Directive.[110] Further provision has been made to outlaw discrimination on grounds of sex outside the employment field.[111]

Various Council resolutions have been passed by reference to Article 13; for instance, the Council, relying on Article 13, passed a Resolution of 15 July 2003 on promoting the employment and social integration of people with disabilities.[112] This called on Member States, among other things, to promote greater co-operation with all bodies concerned with people with disabilities; to promote the full integration and participation of people with disabilities in all aspects of society; to continue efforts to remove barriers to the integration and participation of people with disabilities in the labour market; to pursue efforts to make lifelong learning more accessible to people with disabilities; to remove barriers impeding the participation of people with disabilities in social life and, in particular, in working life, and prevent the setting up of new barriers through the promotion of design for all; and to mainstream disability issues when drafting future national action plans relating to social exclusion and poverty.

Article 13 has also not stood still. Thus in the Treaty of Nice a second paragraph was added to permit decision-making under Article 13 by qualified majority voting pursuant to Article 251, in relation to certain kinds of incentive measures to support action taken by Member States in

---

[108] See, for instance, the suggestion for a Directive in relation to age discrimination in relation to goods facilities and services, put forward by Age Concern and other age related organisations across Europe: www.ace.org.uk/AgeConcern/Documents/Age_Directive_one_Goods_Facilities_and_services_final1.pdf.

[109] Council Directive 76/207/EEC.

[110] See Directive 2002/73/EC of the European Parliament and of the Council of 23 September 2002 amending Council Directive 76/207/EEC on the implementation of the principle of equal treatment for men and women as regards access to employment, vocational training and promotion, and working conditions.

[111] See Council Directive 2004/113/EC of 13 December 2004 implementing the principle of equal treatment between men and women in the access to and supply of goods and services.

[112] See Council Resolution of 15 July 2003 on promoting the employment and social integration of people with disabilities (2003/C 175/01).

order to contribute to the achievement of the objectives in the main text of Article 13. The possibility of such decisions being taken on a less than unanimous basis underlines the importance of the objectives of Article 13 as a key element of the social policy of the Union.

Finally, it should also be noted that the draft constitution of the European Union intended to transpose Article 13 to Article III-124, which was set out in Title II of Part III of the proposed Constitution under the general heading 'Non-discrimination and Citizenship',[113] and the Charter of Fundamental Rights of the European Union 2000[114] contains extensive reference to equality rights in Chapter III. At the time of the Vienna Conference neither the proposal for a Constitution[115] nor a Charter[116] had been formulated within the Union.

Outside the Union there have been developments in relation to equality and non-discrimination. The most important development has been the agreement by the Council of Europe on a text for a twelfth Protocol to the ECHR. The text was intended to supplement Article 14 ECHR by removing its limitations as merely an accessory right. There has been a realisation that a free-standing right, somewhat akin to Article 26 of the ICCPR, was needed in the European context.[117] The essence[118] of Protocol 12 is in Article 1:

1. The enjoyment of any right set forth by law shall be secured without discrimination on any ground such as sex, race, colour, language, religion, political or other opinion, national or social origin, association with a national minority, property, birth or other status.

---

[113] See http://eur-lex.europa.eu/LexUriServ/site/en/oj/2004/c-310/c-31020041216en0055 G85.pdf.

[114] [2000] OJ C 364/1.

[115] The proposal for constitution followed the Declaration on the Future of the Union made by the Council in 2000 in Nice.

[116] The proposal for a Charter came from the Cologne European Council of the 3–4 June 1999.

[117] The explanatory memorandum to the Protocol is at www.humanrights.coe.int/Prot12/ Protocol%2012%20and% 20Exp%20Rep.htm#EXPLANATORY%20REPORT.

[118] It should be noted that the Recitals to the Protocol add that 'Having regard to the fundamental principle according to which all persons are equal before the law and are entitled to the equal protection of the law; Being resolved to take further steps to promote the equality of all persons through the collective enforcement of a general prohibition of discrimination by means of the Convention for the Protection of Human Rights and Fundamental Freedoms signed at Rome on 4 November 1950 (hereinafter referred to as "the Convention"); Reaffirming that the principle of non-discrimination does not prevent States Parties from taking measures in order to promote full and effective equality, provided that there is an objective and reasonable justification for those measures.'

2. No one shall be discriminated against by any public authority on any ground such as those mentioned in paragraph 1.

As yet the utility of Protocol 12 has not really been tested. It only came into force on 1 April 2005 when it was ratified by a tenth state. As of July 2006 there were fourteen ratifications but of these only the Netherlands of the main Member States of the European Union had ratified it. There is as yet no jurisprudence of the European Court of Human Rights on its application.

Commentary

The conference was an undoubted success in providing an important opportunity for contributions from many different experts. Yet it is now appropriate to consider some of the aspects of the development of equality and non-discrimination law which it anticipated well and to consider some of the problems which the conference either underestimated or did not foresee.[119]

The five conditions

Broadly the five conditions that I posited for effective legislation against discrimination have been met in the two Directives which followed the Vienna conference. Yet there are some important lacunae which should be noted.

Firstly, while both Directives require effective sanctions neither expressly states that criminal sanctions may be necessary. However, in the period in between, in which I have discussed these issues with judges and jurists from every Member State and candidate country, I have *not* heard that a lack of criminal sanctions has been a problem. The necessary criminal laws seem to be there; the issue is the willingness to invoke criminal law when it is necessary to secure compliance with the principle of equal treatment.

In part this may reflect the lack of efficient enforcement mechanisms in the hands of equality bodies. While the Race Directive required such a body to be set up in each Member State, the Employment Equality Directive did not. This was a real missed opportunity which was fortunately avoided in the re-enactment of the Equal Treatment Directive.

It must be acknowledged that the Commission has worked hard in relation to information and training through the Action Programme. This

---

[119] For these the author must take at least a fair share of blame!

activity has not always been transposed into the Member States though perhaps paradoxically the new Member States, who have been required to demonstrate their compliance with the principle of equal treatment, have in some cases done best in this respect.

Much still needs to be done in relation to the mainstreaming of these ideas. This depends very much on adequate monitoring and here too there was perhaps a missed point. Implementation of the Directives has pointed out the difficulties that exist in relation to the uniform collection of data in relation to these protected grounds across Europe. While in the UK there is a happy familiarity with the process of data collection through the means of a census or otherwise, many, indeed possibly most, European countries are not so at ease. This is a particular legacy of the worst parts of their common history through the twentieth century, firstly, in the World Wars and, secondly, through the era of communist states. The Commission has, however, worked hard to address the issues of data collection. In a very important conference in Helsinki in December 2004 these issues were addressed and proposals formulated, but much more needs to be done.[120] The pursuit of equality depends on good data.

Scope

A good deal of the time at the conference was taken up with discussions about the material scope of Article 13 EC. The possibilities for action seemed so large that there was a real concern as to the extent to which the material scope of the EC Treaty was itself a limiting factor. In practice, however, this has not proved to be a major concern. In this respect the skill of the Commission in choosing to lead with the proposal for the extensive Race Directive may come to be seen as critical. Had the Commission led with a comprehensive Directive covering all the grounds in Article 13 and extending to the full extent of the scope of the Race Directive it seems certain that arguments would have raged as to the limitations to the material scope of Article 13.[121] On the other hand, leading with only a proposal for a far-ranging Race Directive might equally have drawn extensive criticism.

---

[120] The papers are available at http://ec.europa.eu/employment_social/ fundamental_rights/ events/helsinki04_en.htm.

[121] While the Commission has commenced proceedings against several Member States for failure to fully transpose these two Directives, it is not understood that in any case has a plea been entered that either Directive exceeded the permitted material scope of the source power in Art. 13.

In the event, no Member State felt able to argue that the ultimate scope of the Race Directive covering the wide range from employment, vocational matters, social protection, social advantages, education and housing, went too far.[122] This is probably one of the most important points to take out of the conference, since it was always possible that a more restrictive view of the possibilities envisaged by the Member States when articulating and agreeing Article 13 EC at Amsterdam would prevail. In particular it must be remembered that health is an area in which Member States have been concerned to maintain a degree of autonomy.[123] Likewise it is noteworthy that that Council Directive 2004/113/EC of 13 December 2004 implementing the principle of equal treatment between men and women in the access to and supply of goods and services was implemented without extending to education. Perhaps this was because a separate approach to the education of boys and girls is too entrenched for European legislation. Yet in the context of equality any separate provision should always be subject to the closest scrutiny. Separateness has long been a cloak for different and less favourable.

The definition of disability

One issue which concerned me at the Vienna conference was the concept of disability. Though raised in the keynote speech it was not given a closed definition in the Employment Equality Directive.

This point was picked up by a Spanish Court which made the first reference to the Court of Justice in a case concerning the transposition: C-13/05 *Sonia Chacón Navas* v. *Eurest Colectividades SA*. The judgment of the Court is particularly interesting though not perhaps as informative as might be hoped. The Court ruled that:

> It follows from the need for uniform application of Community law and the principle of equality that the terms of a provision of Community law which makes no express reference to the law of the Member States for the purpose of determining its meaning and scope must normally be given an autonomous and uniform interpretation throughout the Community, having regard to the context of the provision and the objective pursued by the legislation in question.[124]

---

[122] See Race Directive Art. 3.

[123] See, e.g., Art. 152 EC, and see also Case C-372/04 *The Queen (on the application of Yvonne Watts)* v. *Bedford Primary Care Trust, and the Secretary of State for Health.*

[124] See para. 40.

It pointed out that since disability and sickness were not to be equated and since sickness was not used, mere sickness did not give rise to protection under the Employment Equality Directive.

The question posed to the Court of Justice related to rudimentary facts, so the more difficult question whether any particular state of ill-health amounted to disability was not addressed. It did not need to be. Much work is currently underway under the auspices of the United Nations and it seems likely that if a common worldwide definition of disability is adopted the Court would be likely to adapt its interpretation of the autonomous meaning to that definition. At present this issue remains unresolved.

Associative and perceived grounds

Although there was a good deal of discussion as to the way in which discrimination can occur, it is much to be regretted that discrimination on *associative* or *perceived* grounds was not discussed. When a person suffers less favourable treatment not because they are themselves black or disabled, but because they *associate* with persons of minority ethnic origin or care for disabled persons, it would seem that they are as much in need of protection. This was not specifically discussed. In the UK at least the first of these two examples is considered highly controversial.[125] Indeed, the UK has taken an inconsistent approach permitting perceived discrimination in some but not all cases. By contrast, it was a conscious decision not to define the concept of disability more closely[126] and this has led to an early reference to the Court of Justice.

It seems likely that those who receive adverse treatment because they are *perceived* as gay, or disabled or having some other protected status would be considered by the Court of Justice to be in scope, but this too must await a definitive interpretation.

---

[125] The UK expressly rejected the recommendation of the Parliamentary Pre-legislative Scrutiny Committee on this point when deciding how to incorporate the Employment Equality Directive into UK law, however, a reference has now been made in relation to this by the Employment Tribunal in Case C-303/06; *Coleman* v. *Attridge Law* Case No. 2303745/2005 the questions asked include questions as to whether in the context of the prohibition of discrimination on grounds of disability, the Employment Equality Directive only protects from direct discrimination and harassment persons who are themselves disabled, and if not whether it protects employees who, though they are not themselves disabled, are treated less favourably or harassed on the ground of having a disabled son for whom they care.

[126] It is important to recall that the Amsterdam Treaty contained its own Declaration Regarding Persons with a Disability.

This may yet prove to be a major issue across Europe though in some countries, such as the Republic of Ireland,[127] appropriate implementation to secure that such discrimination is in scope, has been made. It seems likely that the Court of Justice will in due course interpret the two Directives as prohibiting such discrimination but this cannot yet be guaranteed.

Indirect discrimination

One of the major differences between the two Directives made in 2000 and the *acquis* in relation to sex discrimination lay in the definition of indirect discrimination. As the keynote speech has pointed out there were real difficulties of application and effectiveness in the existing jurisprudence. The definition in the Directives takes a much more practical approach, permitting reliance on statistics but not requiring them.[128] Thus, taking the Race Directive, by Article 2(2)(b) indirect discrimination is said to occur:

> where an apparently neutral provision, criterion or practice would put persons of a racial or ethnic origin at a particular disadvantage compared with other persons, unless that provision criterion or practice is objectively justified by a legitimate aim and the means of achieving that aim are appropriate and necessary.

This is a really important development and ought to enable much more recourse to be made to the concept of indirect discrimination as a tool for analysing situations for compliance with the principle of equal treatment.

Harassment

Another major issue at the time was racial and sexual harassment. To an extent this was protected in some civil law countries through criminal provisions more effectively than in common law countries. Racial harassment was specifically discussed in the context of the experience across the different Member States. All were concerned to see effective protection. In 1992 the European Commission had issued a Recommendation and Code of Practice on the protection of the dignity of men and women at work[129] which encouraged a more proactive response to such harassment. When they came to be enacted both the Race and the Employment Framework

---

[127] The Irish Legislation can be found at www.equality.ie/index.asp?locID = 60&docID = -1.
[128] See Recital 15 to each Directive.
[129] See Commission Recommendation 92/131/EEC.

Directives contained strong provisions in relation to harassment which are based on the protection of the key human rights concept of dignity.[130] Thus the Race Directive states that:

> Harassment shall be deemed to be a form of discrimination . . . when unwanted conduct related to racial or ethnic origin takes place with the purpose or effect of violating the dignity of a person and of creating an intimidating, hostile, degrading, humiliating or offensive environment.[131]

In retrospect it is perhaps surprising that not more was made of the contribution of the concept of dignity to the development of these ideas.[132] However, if that was an omission it is one which is being made good. The importance of dignity across the European Union can be seen quite clearly in the Charter of Fundamental Rights of the European Union which devotes the whole of its first Chapter to dignity,[133] in the conjunction of equality and dignity as core values in Article I-2 of the draft Constitution,[134] and in recent case law of the Court of Justice holding that the Court must 'ensure that the fundamental right to human dignity and integrity is observed'.[135]

Comparable situations

The Vienna conference probably took too much for granted in respect of the issue of comparability. The two Article 13 Directives made after the conference are based squarely on the equal treatment principle but it is a principle which is not always easy to apply. It is becoming an increasingly vexed question of when the principle requires that it is appropriate to treat two persons as being in an analogous or comparable situation, and when not.

---

[130] See, e.g., the United Nations Declaration of Human Rights. Respect for human dignity is also a key part of common constitutional traditions across Europe.

[131] See Art. 2(3) Directive 2000/43/EC implementing the principle of equal treatment between persons irrespective of racial or ethnic origin. The Employment Equality Directive contains a similar text.

[132] Both the French and German Constitutions have strong dignity provisions: see the Preamble and Art. 1 of the French Constitution of 4 October 1958, and Art. 1 of the German Basic Law.

[133] http://europa.eu.int/scadplus/constitution/objectives_en.htm.

[134] http://europa.eu.int/constitution/en/ptoc2_en.htm#a3.

[135] See Case C-377/98 Netherlands v. the European Parliament, and the Council of the European Union, Judgment 9 October 2001, at [70].

At present there is no single explicit set of principles by which to determine whether two persons are in a comparable position so that equal treatment is entailed. Comparisons can be established generically at the level of legislation and must be established more specifically in individual cases. So there are two aspects to this problem: what are the principles by which to decide generically whether a comparison should be made, and how should specific questions about comparability be addressed? This deficit has a direct social cost leading to more litigation and less certainty. It is regrettable that more work was not done on this issue at the outset. As it is, the Court of Justice has addressed it on a rather piecemeal and unsatisfactory basis.[136]

Positive action

The conference was perfectly clear that positive action was essential in some cases. Although the jurisprudence under the Equal Treatment Directive was brought to the attention of the participants not much progress was made in discussing just how much should be done. It is therefore particularly noteworthy that in her closing contribution to the Vienna conference, Lore Hostasch, the Austrian Minister for Labour Health and Social Affairs reiterated, with emphasis, the point that equal treatment by itself may not be enough if it does not lead to equality of outcomes.[137]

Ultimately, the two Article 13 Directives took the safe course of adopting almost completely the text of the amendment to Article 119 of the EC Treaty as it was when transposed to Article 141.[138] The key concept utilised in the two Directives is 'full equality in practice'. At present it seems that the Court of Justice will permit this concept to provide at least a small step change in the possibilities for securing a more substantive equality. Thus the Court has recently contemplated permitting steps to be taken to eradicate historic disadvantage so as to secure a more profound equality of opportunity.[139] In retrospect, Vienna was perhaps a missed opportunity to look more deeply and harder at the reasons why the principle of equal treatment can sometimes seem an arid rule of mere formal justice. While

---

[136] See, e.g., Cases C-356/98 and C-466/00 *Kaba* v. *Home Secretary* (1) and (2), and Case C-19/02 *Hlozek* v. *Roche Austria Gesellschaft mbH*.

[137] See Conference Report p. 66.

[138] See Art. 5 of the Race Directive and Art. 7 of the Employment Framework Directive.

[139] See Case C-319/03 *Serge Briheche* v. *Ministre de l'Intérieur, Ministre de l'Éducation Nationale and Ministre de la Justice*. See in particular the Advocate-General's Opinion for a review of the possibilities that are presented by this concept.

I commented that it was not enough to look at discrimination solely from the point of view of equality before the law, the conference did not adequately address the challenge that this comment posed.

The next step in a social Europe must be to address deep-seated inequalities arising from past disadvantages. In this context the response to demographic change will be key. The Commission has stated that by 2009 across Europe there will be more persons in the last cohort of working life than in the first. The implications of this have been extensively discussed in its Green Paper 'Confronting Demographic change: a new solidarity between generations'.[140] In essence the loss of productive capacity can only be addressed by more immigration, longer working or more family friendly working. Each of these demands a sound equality framework to provide the necessary solution. So it seems inevitable that for this if no other reason the Commission will have to revisit how rights for and action to secure substantive equality can be achieved.

Conflict of rights

Neither the Vienna conference nor the two Directives addressed generically the question of how and by what principles should conflicts of rights between competing equality claims be resolved. Article 4 of the Employment Equality Directive makes a passing reference to the kinds of conflict that can arise between religious affairs and other protected grounds, but its text is a study in ambiguity.[141] Indeed, it is known that the relevant text was added at a late stage in the discussions to secure agreement but not to resolve the problems that can arise on a general basis.

These problems are occurring increasingly and it may be anticipated that with the development of new grounds of protection from discrimination such conflicts will become more frequent. Religion and sex provide particularly fertile grounds but others have also arisen. At present it is not at all clear how, that is to say by what mechanism or juridical principle, such disputes should be resolved.[142] It is regrettable that more work was not done on developing a principle akin to the Canadian concept of

---

[140] Brussels 16.3.2005, COM(2005) 94 final.

[141] The relationship between age rules and sex discrimination may prove to be the most difficult in the future but this relationship, while recognised as existing (see *Price* v. *Civil Service Commission* [1978] ICR 27), is only now beginning to lead to more developed case law, see, e.g., Case C-187/00 *Kutz-Bauer* v. *Freie und Hansestadt Hamburg* [2003] ECR I-2741.

[142] It is only in Art. 4(2) Directive 2000/78/EC establishing a general framework for equal treatment in employment and occupation that we find any attempt to offer a

reasonable adjustment, by which the rights of one protected group might be moderated when in conflict with those of another. Either the European legislator or domestic legislature will have to address them or else judges will have to cope on a case-by-case basis.[143] This point links closely with the issue of intersectional discrimination.

Intersectional discrimination

This is a contrasting problem that was also not properly addressed in either the Vienna conference or the Directives. It concerns the proper way to address discrimination arising on combined or multiple grounds. This issue is one which is now increasingly apparent as requiring special consideration.[144] The separate existence of the Race and Employment Equality Directive may well come to be seen as anachronistic as multiple ground discrimination demands greater action.

Some obvious examples of this can be cited. Thus it is widely recognised that Roma women are often in a state of particular disadvantage, and youth and ethnicity can also be specific markers for disadvantage. Moreover it is obvious that direct age discrimination can be indirect sex discrimination. Issues which will have to be addressed either by the Community legislator

resolution of a possible conflict of right between religion and other matters addressed: '2. Member states may maintain national legislation in force at the date of adoption of this Directive or provide for future legislation incorporating national practices existing at the date of adoption of this Directive pursuant to which, in the case of occupational activities within churches and other public or private organisations the ethos of which is based on religion or belief, a difference of treatment based on a person's religion or belief shall not constitute discrimination where, by reason of the nature of these activities or of the context in which they are carried out, a person's religion or belief constitute a genuine, legitimate and justified occupational requirement, having regard to the organisation's ethos. This difference of treatment shall be implemented taking account of Member States' constitutional provisions and principles, as well as the general principles of Community law, and should not justify discrimination on another ground.'

Provided that its provisions are otherwise complied with, this Directive shall thus not prejudice the right of churches and other public or private organisations, the ethos of which is based on religion or belief, acting in conformity with national constitutions and laws, to require individuals working for them to act in good faith and with loyalty to the organisation's ethos.

[143] For an example of the kinds of difficulties that can occur see *O'Neill* v. *Governors of St. Thomas More Roman Catholic Voluntarily Aided Upper School* [1997] ICR 33.

[144] See, e.g., S. Hannett, 'Equality at the Intersections: the Legislative and Judicial Failure to Tackle Multiple Discrimination' *Oxford Journal of Legal Studies* (2003) 23, p. 65. Note also that the Equal Opportunities Commission has recently launched an investigation into the position of ethnic minority women at work. See 'Moving on up? ethnic minority women at work' at www.eoc.org.uk/Default.aspx?page = 17696&lang = en.

or the Court of Justice will also include what is the proper approach to objective justification where two grounds are present in the same factual situation. A good example of this was brought to light when I was arguing for the Equal Opportunities Commission that length of service pay increments were prima facie indirectly discriminatory against women and required to be justified.[145] The UK pointed out that such pay systems would also be potentially indirect age discrimination and that there were different European rules for the justification of age discrimination.[146] The UK argued that two rules for justifying the same pay system made little sense.

The Commission seems likely to discuss the possibility for a different approach to legislation to deal with this point. Thus a non-discrimination Directive which addressed all aspects of goods, facilities and services or all aspects of employment might be proposed. In many ways this should be welcomed but it is important to post a note of caution too. At the stage when there are still serious problems about transposition of the existing Article 13 Directives this might be a bridge too far. Moreover, the legislative process for such harmonisation is likely to be lengthy and difficult. Experience from the UK shows that the goal of a single Equality Act while highly desired is still difficult to reach.

Concluding points

The introduction of Article 13 can be seen to have been a point at which the Community, building on its experience in the field of sex discrimination, decisively adopted a human rights approach to equality. Social Europe required social cohesion, not exclusion, and Article 13 provides a key mechanism by which important contributions can be made to this end. It has given rise to a huge exercise, organised by the Commission, of dissemination and training to judges and NGOs. It has provided a basis for discussions with the new Member States when they were merely candidate countries as to the steps that they have taken in preparation for accession to the EC Treaty. It has therefore operated at a normative level even before it has been litigated in the Court of Justice. It has already proved that it is indeed worthy of its place at the beginning of the Treaty in Part One, under the rubric 'Principles', since it states clearly that non-discrimination

---

[145] Case 17/05 *Cadman* v. *Health and Safety Executive* argued in the Grand Chamber of the European Court of Justice 8 March 2006.
[146] See Art. 6 of the Framework Directive.

is indeed a principle of the Treaty. In due course it seems likely that the Equality Provisions of the Charter of Fundamental Rights of the European Union 2000 which are more extensive might lead to a further development of Article 13. However, it must always be remembered that it was Article 13 which took the critical step in enabling policy and legislation to be adopted on a Europe-wide basis in relation to discrimination.

3

Human rights and European equality law

CHRISTOPHER McCRUDDEN AND HARIS KOUNTOUROS*

Introduction

This chapter provides an analysis of the evolving human rights and equality contexts within which the European Union (EU) equality and non-discrimination Directives were developed and continue to operate.[1] Part I sets out a theoretical framework for considering the variety of differing conceptions of equality that we shall subsequently identify as operating in European equality and human rights law. We then trace how these differing approaches are seen in the differing areas of EU law in which equality features. Part II sets out the international, regional and domestic human rights law on equality and non-discrimination, which has played and will continue to play an important role in the development of EU human rights and equality law. In Part III we focus on human rights and equality in EU Law more specifically and place human rights in the context of EU values and objectives. The negotiations over treaty amendments between 2004 and 2007 played a vital part in shaping this role. A proposed new Constitutional Treaty bringing together the existing treaties failed to gain sufficient support. Instead, a European Council held in Brussels in June 2007 agreed a mandate for a somewhat less ambitious draft Reform Treaty, but incorporating many features of the proposed Constitutional Treaty, to be agreed by an Intergovernmental Council during 2007. In this context,

---

* We would like to thank several people who commented on earlier drafts: Mark Bell, Mark Freedland, Sandra Fredman, Gerard Quinn, Helen Meenan, and Christine Bell. They are not responsible for any remaining errors.
[1] This chapter concentrates particularly on those adopted under Art. 13 EC: Council Directive 2000/43/EC, implementing the principle of equal treatment between persons irrespective of racial or ethnic origin [2000] OJ L180/22; Council Directive 2000/78/EC, establishing a general framework for equal treatment in employment and occupation [2000] OJ L303/16; Council Directive 2004/113/EC, implementing the principle of equal treatment between men and women in the access to and supply of goods and services [2004] OJ L373/37, hereafter referred to as 'the Race Directive', 'the Employment Framework Directive' and 'the Sex Equality Directive', respectively.

we discuss the role of the Charter of Fundamental Rights in the continuing evolution of rights in the Community legal order. We also consider some notable current and likely future developments in the area of equality and human rights in the Community. In Part IV we turn to consider some more theoretical issues, including the differing conceptions of rights generally, and return to consider the implications of the differing approaches to equality and non-discrimination that are apparent in these differing contexts.

Conceptions of equality and non-discrimination

How should we understand the concept of discrimination in human rights discourse?[2] Equality and non-discrimination are complex concepts, with considerable debate about their meanings and justification. In order to better understand the variety of different ways of understanding anti-discrimination provisions currently operating in the human rights context, and the place of Community law within this context, four categories[3] of, or approaches to, equality and non-discrimination applicable in human rights may usefully be identified.[4] Several caveats are necessary regarding these distinctions. First, the categories are constructed to try to make sense of a sometimes bewildering range of legal material; these categories have received no judicial approval. Second, these categories are not watertight, but porous, with developments in one category influencing approaches in others. Third, in some respects, the principles underlying each category may be in tension with each other, and this may require decisions as to priority between the categories in the case of

---

[2] This section of the chapter draws on previous work by one of the authors. See C. McCrudden, 'Equality and Non-Discrimination', in D. Feldman (ed.), *English Public Law* (Oxford University Press, 2004); and C. McCrudden, 'Theorising European Equality Law', in C. Costello and E. Barry (eds.), *Equality in Diversity* (Irish Centre for European Law, 2003). Other parts of the chapter also draw on the latter source, in particular.

[3] We will use the term 'category', 'approach' and 'meaning' interchangeably in this chapter. No significance should be attached to this.

[4] The first three approaches have echoes in the United States Fourteenth Amendment context where, at the risk of oversimplification, the United States Supreme Court distinguishes those legislative or governmental distinctions where the courts will be more deferential to political judgments (when the so-called 'rational relationship' test is adopted), from those the courts consider they should pay particular attention to where the distinctions are based on 'suspect classifications' (race is the paradigm) or where 'fundamental interests' (such as the right to travel) are at stake (when the so-called 'strict scrutiny' test is adopted). The reason why this example from the US is of some interest is because a similar approach has evolved in the UK, although this is only now becoming clear in retrospect. The fourth meaning does not have any clear equivalent in the US constitutional context, although there are somewhat similar statutory requirements for government contractors.

conflict. Europe has only just begun to explore these tensions. Fourth, this chapter attempts to describe the current approaches to equality and non-discrimination in Europe, rather than to provide a normative analysis of these approaches.

Equality as 'rationality'

The first approach is where the principle of non-discrimination (inter-preted as the limited principle that likes should be treated alike, unless there is an adequate justification for not applying this principle) is a self-standing principle of general application, without specific limitation on the circumstances in which it is applicable (except that it be in the public realm, broadly defined), and without limitation on the grounds on which the difference of treatment is challengeable. In many jurisdictions, this approach to equality is particularly associated with constitutional guarantees.[5] This approach is essentially rationality-based. Under this approach, then, discrimination is merely an example of irrationality, with no greater moral or legal significance than if the government decided to allocate houses only to those with red hair. This approach is often apparent in the interpretation of constitutional provisions guaranteeing non-discrimination in general terms.

However, non-discrimination is often tied to some more specific context. There are, essentially, two methods of limiting the prohibition of discrimination, and they operate both separately and together. One method is where the prohibition of discrimination is limited to particular subject areas, such as employment, or to certain rights, such as freedom of speech. A second approach is where the right to non-discrimination is limited to certain grounds or statuses, such as sex, race, religion, disability, etc. As we shall see, the approach in regional and international human rights instruments often differs on these issues, and no consensus of approaches can be discerned. These two different approaches give rise to important differences in methods, aims and justifications for legal intervention, giving rise to two further approaches of non-discrimination, additional to 'equality as rationality'.

Equality as protective of 'prized public goods'

In a second approach, the non-discrimination principle becomes an adjunct to the protection of particularly prized 'public goods', including

---

[5] See, in general, the Council of Europe's Constitutional Law Bulletin which is a good source of case law on the constitutional principle of equality.

human and other rights. The principle is essentially that such 'prized public goods' should in principle be distributed to everyone without distinction. In the distribution of the 'public good', equals should be treated on a non-discriminatory basis, except where differences can be justified. In this context, the focus is on the distribution of the public good, rather than the characteristics of the recipient. The courts will scrutinise public authorities' (less frequently, private bodies'[6]) actions in a more intense way than under the first approach, when the actions of the public authority give rise to discrimination (defined essentially as treating someone differently) in these circumstances. Under this approach, discrimination is objectionable because it is an unacceptable way of limiting access to the 'prized public good'. We see this approach operating in the context of the interpretation of Article 14 of the European Convention on Human Rights, for example.

Equality as preventing 'status-harms' arising from discrimination on particular grounds

In a third approach to non-discrimination, the focus of attention turns instead to the association between a limited number of particular characteristics (such as race, gender, etc.) and the discrimination suffered by those who have, or who are perceived to have, those characteristics, irrespective of whether the decision might be justified as rational. The courts will scrutinise public authorities' (and others') actions in a more intense way than under the first approach, where the public authorities' actions discriminate against individuals with those particular characteristics. In this context, however, the meaning of discrimination expands beyond the principle that likes should be treated alike to embrace also the principle that unlikes should not be treated alike. This approach is essentially aimed at preventing status-harms arising from discrimination on particular grounds.

The third approach also differs from the second in being less concerned with the importance of the good being allocated, and more concerned with the use of actual or imputed identity in a wide range of situations. In the second approach, the harm to be prevented lies in the arbitrary allocation of something that, in principle, all should have. In the third

---

[6] We leave to one side the extent to which norms applying to states give rise to state responsibility where third parties within the state act contrary to the norm.

approach, the harm lies in the use made of particular statuses to affect the allocation of a wide range of opportunities, which may or may not reach the importance of rights, but where the use of those characteristics is unacceptable in such decisions. In this third approach to non-discrimination, the focus of attention shifts from the importance of the 'public good' (particularly the human right in issue) and turns instead to the association between a limited number of particular characteristics (such as race, gender, etc.) and the discrimination suffered by those who have, or are perceived to have, those characteristics, where the public authorities' actions discriminate against individuals with those particular characteristics. National anti-discrimination legislation illustrates this approach.

In several ways, the third category of discrimination and equality is more complex than the first and second categories discussed previously, and this greater complexity has resulted in the emergence of legal issues that are so far relatively underdeveloped in the context of discussions about the other categories. Unlike under the second approach, it does not apply as a penumbra of all major areas of rights (indeed many fundamental rights are not included within the coverage of anti-discrimination law). In another respect, the approach taken under this third approach is considerably broader in scope, covering both public and private sector actors operating in those areas covered, whereas to a considerable extent the first and second approaches apply largely to the public sector.

Equality as proactive promotion of equality of opportunity between particular groups

In the fourth approach, certain public authorities are placed under a duty actively to take steps to promote greater equality of opportunity (the legal meanings of which are yet to be fully articulated) for particular groups. In that sense, it is a further development of the third ('status-based') approach. However, the concept of 'equality of opportunity' goes beyond any of the concepts of discrimination characteristic of the previous approaches. Under this fourth approach, a public authority to which this duty applies is under a duty to do more than ensure the absence of discrimination from its employment, educational, and other specified functions, but also to act positively to promote equality of opportunity between different groups throughout all its policy-making and in carrying out all its activities.

International and regional human rights law dealing with equality and non-discrimination

These differing approaches are useful in understanding the different ways in which human rights law addresses the issue of discrimination and equality.

Sources of international provisions on equality and non-discrimination

It is notable that many of the international and regional human rights treaty commitments that European states have entered into since the end of the Second World War contain equality and non-discrimination requirements of a broad-based inclusive type. International human rights instruments which contain equality or non-discrimination provisions and which European states have ratified come from three principal sources: (a) Conventions inspired by the principles of equality and non-discrimination of the UN Charter and the Universal Declaration of Human Rights; (b) Council of Europe Conventions; and (c) International Labour Organisation (ILO) Conventions.

To the first category belong the 1966 International Covenant on Economic, Social and Cultural Rights and the 1966 International Covenant on Civil and Political Rights, as well as the 1953 Convention on the Political Rights of Women, the 1966 Convention on the Elimination of All Forms of Racial Discrimination, the 1979 Convention on the Elimination of All Forms of Discrimination Against Women, the 1989 Convention on the Rights of the Child, and the 2007 Convention on the Rights of Persons with Disabilities. To these we should add a number of international Declarations, including the 1959 Declaration on the Rights of the Child, the 1967 Declaration on the Elimination of Discrimination against Women, the 1975 Declaration on the Rights of Disabled Persons, and the 1981 Declaration on the Elimination of All Forms of Intolerance and of Discrimination Based on Religion or Belief. These provisions are likely to be drawn on as sources of argument in the interpretation of EU equality law.[7]

The second category includes the European Convention on Human Rights and Fundamental Freedoms (ECHR), the European Social Charter (1961) and the revised 1996 Charter, the 1995 Framework Convention for the Protection of National Minorities and the 1992 European Charter

---

[7] See, as an example, C. McCrudden, 'National Remedies for Racial Discrimination in European and International Law', in S. Fredman (ed.), *Discrimination and Human Rights* (Oxford University Press, 2001).

for Regional or Minority Languages. Of these, Article 14 ECHR, which lays down the principle of non-discrimination, and the provisions of the European Social Charter, are especially pertinent to the Community's anti-discrimination provisions.[8]

Article 14 ECHR provides that:

> The enjoyment of the rights and freedoms set forth in this Convention shall be secured without discrimination on any ground such as sex, race, colour, language, religion, political or other opinion, national or social origin, association with a national minority, property, birth or other status.

Article 14, however, is not a free-standing right and must be invoked in conjunction with another substantive Convention right (including the rights contained in the Protocols). Additionally, it has been the established practice of the European Court of Human Rights (ECtHR) frequently not to examine a complaint under Article 14 where a separate breach of the substantive Article has been found, unless discriminatory treatment forms a fundamental aspect of the case.[9] However, Protocol 12, which was adopted in June 2000 and came into force on 1 April 2005 for those states that have ratified it, creates a free-standing anti-discrimination provision. Article 1 of Protocol 12 provides:

1. The enjoyment of the rights and freedoms set forth *by law*[10] shall be secured without discrimination on any ground such as sex, race, colour, language, religion, political or other opinion, national or social origin, association with a national minority, property, birth or other status.
2. No one shall be discriminated against by any public authority on any ground such as those mentioned in paragraph 1.

Ratification of Protocol 12 by EU Member States has so far been limited. By June 2007, only Cyprus, Finland, Luxembourg, the Netherlands, and Romania had ratified the Protocol. Eight Member States – Bulgaria, Denmark, France, Malta, Lithuania, Poland, Sweden and the UK – had not even signed it. Thus, despite its potential significance Protocol 12 has only a limited legal effect on EU countries, at present.

---

[8] We can note in passing, however, that the relationship between equality and the Framework Convention on National Minorities is by no means unproblematic. See, for a case study of the difficulties in one Member State, C. McCrudden, 'Consociationalism, Equality and Minorities in the Northern Ireland Bill of Rights Debate', in J. Morison, K. McEvoy and G. Anthony (eds.), *Judges, Transition and Human Rights Cultures* (Oxford University Press, 2007), 315.

[9] See, for instance, *Dudgeon* v. *UK* (1982) 4 EHRR 149, para. 67. Cf. P. Leach, *Taking a Case to the European Court of Human Rights* (Blackstone, 2001) p. 178.

[10] Emphasis added.

Although less well known than the ECHR, the European Social Charter (ESC) has recently become much more important than it previously was in developing principles applicable to discrimination.[11] The ESC was signed in 1961, but was substantially revised in 1996. It sets out to protect a wide range of social rights in areas such as employment, education, housing, social security and healthcare.[12] The 1961 Charter only referred to non-discrimination in its preamble. The Revised ESC, however, now includes a provision that specifically addresses issues of non-discrimination, in somewhat similar terms to those adopted in Article 14 ECHR.[13] The obligations of EU Member States vary considerably, however.[14] Twenty-seven countries, including all EU Member States (except Estonia, Lithuania, Slovenia), have ratified the original ESC. Twenty-one countries have ratified the Revised ESC, including 15 EU Member States.[15] Some EU states have ratified the 1961 version and not the Revised ESC,[16] whilst others have ratified the Revised ESC and not the 1961 version.[17] In addition, states are not obliged to accept every article within the ESC. As Mark Bell has written, 'despite this rather fragmented picture, the prominence of the ESC has increased in recent years'.[18] In particular, he points to 'the ability of non-governmental organisations and trade unions, amongst

[11] See M. Bell, 'Walking in the Same Direction? The Contribution of the European Social Charter and the European Union to Combating Discrimination', in G. de Búrca and B. de Witte, *Social Rights in Europe* (Oxford University Press, 2005), p. 261 and G. Quinn, 'The European Social Charter and EU Anti-discrimination Law in the Field of Disability: Two Gravitational Fields with One Common Purpose', in de Búrca and de Witte, ibid., p. 279.

[12] More detailed consideration of the content of the Charter and its relevance to discrimination is available: O. de Schutter, 'The prohibition of discrimination under European human rights law – relevance for EU Racial and Employment Equality Directives' Report prepared for the European Network of Independent Experts in the non-discrimination field (European Commission, 2005), available at: http://europa.eu.int/comm/employment_social/fundamental_rights/pdf/legisln/prohib_en.pdf.

[13] Article E states: 'the enjoyment of the rights set forth in this Charter shall be secured without discrimination on any ground such as race, colour, sex, language, religion, political or other opinion, health, association with a national minority, birth or other status.'

[14] For more information on the content of each state's ratification, see: www.coe.int/T/E/Human_Rights/Esc/5_Survey_by_country/.

[15] The EU Member States that have ratified the Revised ESC are: Bulgaria, Belgium, Cyprus, Estonia, Finland, France, Ireland, Italy, Lithuania, Malta, the Netherlands, Portugal, Romania, Slovenia and Sweden.

[16] Austria, Czech Republic, Denmark, Germany, Greece, Hungary, Latvia, Luxembourg, Poland, Slovakia, Spain, and the UK.

[17] Estonia, Lithuania, Slovenia.

[18] M. Bell, 'Combating Discrimination through Collective Complaints under the European Social Charter', (2006) *European Anti-Discrimination Law Review*. Issue 3, p. 13.

other actors, to initiate "collective complaints"' as having led to the production of 'a new body of case-law' on discrimination issues. By January 2006, around one-third of all lodged complaints raised issues of discrimination.[19] *Autism-Europe* v. *France* was a particularly important decision,[20] in which France was held to have breached several provisions of the 1996 Revised ESC, including a finding of unlawful discrimination on the ground of disability, because of the insufficient provision of education for children and adults with autism.[21]

A third source of international provisions on equality and non-discrimination is the ILO. The ILO Constitution, 1919, was one of the first multi-lateral international treaties to recognise the right to equal treatment. The preamble to the ILO Constitution refers to the need for 'recognition of the principle of equal remuneration for work of equal value'. Article 1 of the Declaration of Philadelphia 1944, subsequently incorporated in the Constitution, affirms the principle that 'all human beings, irrespective of race, creed or sex, have the right to pursue both their material well-being and their spiritual development in conditions of freedom and dignity, of economic security and equal opportunity'. Together with the other principles set out in the Declaration, most notably that 'labour is not a commodity', the principle of non-discrimination is intended to be 'fully applicable to all peoples everywhere'.

The elimination of discrimination in employment and occupation remains a key issue for the ILO. Two of the ILO Conventions in this area have been identified by the Organisation's Governing Body as 'fundamental'.[22] These are the Equal Remuneration Convention 1951 (No. 100) and the Discrimination (Employment and Occupation Convention) 1958 (No. 111), both of which have been ratified by all 25 EU Member States. The principle of non-discrimination is also found in Article 1 of the Employment Policy Convention 1964 (No. 122), which is a 'priority'

---

[19] For a list of all lodged complaints and the text of all decisions, see: www.humanrights. coe.int/cseweb/GB/GB3/GB30_list.html/.

[20] Complaint No. 13/2002, 4 November 2003.

[21] The Committee noted the non-exhaustive nature of the list of grounds in Article E and held that disability was implicitly included.

[22] The importance of these Conventions is also reflected by their basic principles being incorporated in the controversial ILO Declaration on Fundamental Principles and Rights at Work, 1998, in which the International Labour Conference declared that 'all Members, even if they have not ratified the Conventions in question, have an obligation arising from the very fact of membership in the Organisation to respect, to promote and to realize, in good faith and in accordance with the Constitution, the principles concerning the fundamental rights which are the subject of those [fundamental] Conventions'.

Convention,[23] while other relevant instruments include Convention No. 156, on Workers with Family Responsibilities, 1981,[24] the Maternity Protection Convention 2000 (No. 183),[25] the Vocational Rehabilitation and Employment (Disabled Persons) Convention 1981 (No. 159),[26] and the Equality of Treatment (Social Security) Convention 1962 (No. 118).[27] In some of these Conventions, like C111 and C159, positive action is expressly permitted.[28]

Finally, the principle of equal treatment is also laid down in ILO Conventions that deal specifically with atypical forms of work, given that discrimination in employment often takes place in this context. Two Conventions in this respect are the Part-time Work Convention 1994 (No. 175),[29] and the Home Work Convention 1996 (No. 177).[30] Often ILO standards are higher than those in equivalent legislation in Community law (where these exist). The Part-time Work Convention, for example, unlike the Directive implementing the Agreement on Part-time work,[31] explicitly provides that pay and social security are covered by the Convention and therefore come under the principle of equal treatment.[32]

EC equality approaches as a contribution to international equality law

It would be misleading to give the impression that the EU is simply a recipient of international and regional human rights developments. It actively contributes to these developments also. The EU has for a number of years pursued an active policy on human rights and democratisation

---

[23] Member States are urged to ratify 'priority' Conventions because of their importance to the functioning of the international labour standards system. C122 has been ratified by all Member States except Bulgaria, Malta and Luxembourg.

[24] C156 has been ratified by Bulgaria, Finland, France, Greece, Lithuania, the Netherlands, Portugal, Slovakia, Slovenia, Spain and Sweden.

[25] C183 has been ratified by Austria, Bulgaria, Cyprus, Hungary, Italy, Lithuania, Romania, and Slovakia.

[26] Preamble, 4th recital and Art. 4. C159 has been ratified by twenty EU Member States. Austria, Bulgaria, Belgium, Estonia, Latvia, Romania, and the UK have not ratified the Convention.

[27] Article 3. C118 has been ratified by Denmark, Finland, France, Germany, Ireland, Italy, the Netherlands and Sweden.

[28] Articles 5(2) and 5, respectively.

[29] C175 has been ratified by Cyprus, Italy, Finland, Luxembourg, the Netherlands, Portugal, Slovenia and Sweden.

[30] C177 has been ratified by Finland, Ireland and the Netherlands.

[31] Council Directive 97/81/EC, concerning the Framework Agreement on part-time work concluded by UNICE, CEEP and the ETUC [1998] OJ L14/9, extended to the UK by Council Directive 98/23/EC [1998] OJ L131/10.

[32] See C175, Arts. 5–7, but cf. Art. 8.

in its external policies. First, the Community has, since the early 1990s, inserted a human rights clause in its bilateral trade and co-operation agreements with third countries. A Council Decision systematised this in May 1995 and more than twenty agreements have been concluded so far. The human rights clause is unique to the Union's bilateral agreements and applies to over 120 countries, stipulating that respect for fundamental human rights and democratic principles as laid down in the Universal Declaration of Human Rights, and therefore including the principle of equality and non-discrimination, underpin the internal and external policies of the parties and constitute an essential element of the agreement.[33]

Second, the Commission funds a broad range of human rights activities in third countries through its European Initiative for Democracy and Human Rights (EIDHR) which currently has a budget of some €120 million per year.[34] The partners eligible for financing are regional and international organisations, NGOs, national, regional and local authorities and official agencies, Community-based organisations and public or private-sector institutes and operators. The EIDHR focuses on four thematic priorities, including the combating of racism and xenophobia and discrimination against minorities and indigenous peoples,[35] and the Commission has to ensure that promotion of gender equality and of children's rights are mainstreamed in all thematic priorities pursued under the EIDHR.[36] While not without its critics, the EIDHR forms a key element in the Union's contribution to the promotion of human rights, democratisation and conflict prevention across the world.

Finally, the Community has been contributing to international human rights law on equality in particular through association with various organisations, such as the United Nations and the ILO. Community law on equality, in particular sex equality, is probably the most advanced of any jurisdiction in the world.[37] The Union played a constructive role in the 1995 Beijing conference on women and continues to be an active

---

[33] For a greater discussion see D. C. Horng, 'The Human Rights Clause in the European Union's External Trade and Development Agreements' (2003) 9 *European Law Journal* 677.

[34] Visit http://europa.eu.int/comm/europeaid/projects/eidhr/eidhr_en.htm.

[35] European Commission, 'The European Union's Role In Promoting Human Rights And Democratisation In Third Countries', COM(2001) 252 final, 8 May 2001, p. 17.

[36] Ibid., p. 15.

[37] Y. Kravaritou, 'Equality Between Men and Women (Article 23)', in B. Bercusson, *European Labour Law and the EU Charter of Fundamental Rights*, Summary Version (ETUI, Brussels, 2002), pp. 39–43, at p. 39.

supporter of the action programme adopted in the conference.[38] The Union has begun making an impact on issues concerning equality other than in relation to gender, for instance by actively participating in the drafting of what became the Convention on the Rights of Persons with Disabilities.[39] The enlargement of the Union and the recent impetus given to the concepts of equality and non-discrimination within the Community legal order may well lead to a more substantial contribution on behalf of the Community to the international development of human rights, especially in relation to equality.

Domestic legal developments

There are also extensive provisions in the domestic law of several European countries dealing with such discrimination that pre-date EU and other initiatives. These provisions usually take one of two forms, with some countries having one form, some the other, and some having both.

The first form that these domestic provisions take is in the form of general *constitutional provisions*. These either prohibit discrimination in general, leaving open the grounds included in the prohibition, or list particular grounds, which nearly always include a prohibition of racial discrimination and sex discrimination. Constitutional provisions on human rights in general are especially important to the Community legal order, since they provide a source from which the Court of Justice recognises human rights as general principles of law, which the Court has said it is bound to protect.[40] But obviously they are also extremely important in the domestic context, not least because they establish part of the legal context in which domestic courts will interpret Community provisions. The second form these domestic provisions take is *specific legislation* prohibiting particular types of discrimination, most notably sex discrimination. Provisions, especially of the second type, have influenced the approach taken by the EU in adopting Directives in the past, and it is likely that in the future these domestic approaches will influence the interpretation of the EU Directives by the ECJ.

Increasingly, however, we can expect that domestic and EU legislation on discrimination will become less and less different, with each influencing the other. EU Directives, including those enacted on the basis of

---

[38] See L. Pavan-Woolfe, 'Statement on Behalf of the European Commission at the 49th Session of the Commission on the Status of Women of the United Nations' (10 March 2005).

[39] Submitted by the Italian Presidency in September 2004. Visit www.un.org/esa/socdev/enable/rights/wgcontrib-EU.htm.

[40] See the discussion that follows in section 1 of part II.

Article 13 EC, require transposition into national law. Implementation of the Employment Framework and Race Directives, for example, has resulted in extensive legislation at the national level. Prior to 2000, most Member States lacked legislation on one or more of the grounds covered by the two Directives. Most Member States transposed the two Directives in good time, if not always fully.[41] However, the Commission launched infringement proceedings against Austria, Finland, Germany and Luxembourg for failure to communicate transposition of either the Race or the Framework Directive, and against Greece regarding the Race Directive.[42] By the end of January 2006, the Court gave judgment in all cases concerning the Race Directive,[43] as well as in the case against Luxembourg concerning the Employment Framework Directive.[44] In all cases it found against the Member State. Though implementation continues to be problematic in some cases,[45] the general pattern of anti-discrimination legislation is increasingly similar throughout the Community in most respects.

This is not universally true, however, since the Directives are minimum standards. In several jurisdictions, some of the actions taken by domestic legislatures go beyond the minimum requirements of the Directives. For example, in some Member States, including Austria, Belgium, Ireland, the Netherlands and Sweden, specialised bodies have been set up and have been entrusted with promoting enforcement of the principle of non-discrimination for grounds covered by the Employment Framework Directive, although this Directive, unlike the Race Directive, does not require the establishment of such bodies.[46] Particularly interesting

---

[41] See 'Developing Anti-Discrimination Law in Europe: The 25 EU Member States Compared', Report for the European Network of Independent Legal Experts in the non-discrimination Field, November 2000 (OOPEC, Luxembourg) at p. 12.

[42] C-320/04 *Commission* v. *Luxembourg* [2004] OJ C 228/33; C-335/04 *Commission* v. *Austria* [2004] OJ C 239/8; C-329/04 *Commission* v. *Germany* [2004] OJ C 239/7; C-327/04 *Commission* v. *Finland* [2004] OJ C 239/7 re. failure to notify transposition of Directive 2000/43/EC; and C-70/05 *Commission* v. *Luxembourg* [2005] OJ C 82/23; C-43/05 *Commission* v. *Germany* [2005] OJ C/82/14; C-99/05 *Commission* v. *Finland* [2005] OJ C 93/21; C-133/05 *Commission* v. *Austria* [2005] OJ C 143/20 re. failure to notify transposition of Directive 2000/78/EC. Judicial proceedings had also been launched against Greece in respect of the Race Directive but the case was later withdrawn.

[43] C-320/04, Judgment 24 February 2005; C-329/04, Judgment 28 April 2005; C-327/04, Judgment 24 February 2005; C-335/04, Judgment 4 May 2005.

[44] C-70/05, Judgment 20 October 2005.

[45] C. Bell *et al.*, *European Anti-Discrimination Law Review*. Legal Bulletin by the European Network of Legal Experts in the Non-Discrimination Field, Issue 1 (OOPEC, Luxembourg, 2005), p. 32.

[46] See K. Waaldijk, 'Conclusion', in K. Waaldijk and M. Bonini-Beraldi (eds.), *Combating Sexual Orientation Discrimination in Employment: Legislation in Fifteen EU Member States*.

are domestic provisions in relation to sanctions, given the considerable scope offered by the Directives. Some examples can serve as good practice. These include provisions found in French, Italian, Dutch and Swedish instruments which stipulate the nullity or voidability of discriminatory dismissals; binding or non-binding opinions of specialised enforcement bodies; and provisions in Portuguese, Italian, French and Austrian instruments which stipulate the exclusion from public procurement contracts or from public subsidies of employers who breach the principle of equal treatment for the grounds covered by the Directives.[47] Domestic anti-discrimination law is thus always likely to remain an important source of inspiration for the development of EU law.

Differing approaches to equality and non-discrimination revisited

Community law operates, therefore, in a wider human and constitutional rights context. This context both affects and is affected by the development of Community equality law. We can see, however, that the approach taken in human and constitutional rights law to equality and discrimination is by no means uniform. Of the differing approaches we sketched out in the first section, we see the first approach frequently being adopted in domestic constitutional law. We see the second approach as characteristic of the European Court of Human Rights' approach to Article 14 ECHR, where Article 14 was regarded as an adjunct to other substantive rights. Although no violation of the substantive right was necessary in order to allow Article 14 to be raised, a substantive right had, at least, to be engaged. This also led to the Court frequently holding that it did not need to consider the discrimination issue in a case further, where violation of the substantive right had been established. We see the third approach developing in the context of the ILO Conventions, with much less emphasis being placed on other substantive rights (the public goods approach) and an emphasis instead on the need to justify distinctions on certain particular grounds such as race and gender. In the *Autism* case, we see the adoption of a

Report of the European Group of Experts on Combating Sexual Orientation Discrimination submitted to the European Commission (November, 2004), p. 604.

[47] See C. Tobler, *Remedies and Sanctions in EC Non-Discrimination Law*. Report by the European Network of Legal Experts in the Non-discrimination Field for the European Commission (OOPEC, Luxembourg, 2005) pp. 25–9. Cf. Waaldijk, ibid., p. 605. A wealth of information about the Equality Directives, including domestic, comparative and synthetic reports can be found at the European Union's Anti-discrimination website at http://europa.eu.int/comm/employment_social/fundamental_rights/public/pubs_en.htm.

'positive obligations' approach to the interpretation of the social rights, and then tying the progressive achievement of the social right in issue to the non-discrimination principle, in a way that comes close to the fourth approach suggested above.

Human rights and equality in Community law

Human rights as general principles of Community law

In the EC legal system, protection of human rights similar to those found in international and domestic instruments was pioneered by the European Court of Justice (ECJ). The ECJ has made it its responsibility to ensure the observance of human rights, which it recognises as 'general principles of Community law'.[48] The Court's – and, as we shall see subsequently, the Community's – particular approach to human rights reflects three factors: (i) there were no express provisions on human rights in the Treaty of Rome; (ii) the ECHR does not form an integral part of the Community legal order's foundational document either; and (iii) Community institutions, particularly the Court and the Commission, wish to preserve the primacy and autonomy of Community law. What prompted the Court to seek to be seen to protect human rights in the first place was the tension between the process of economic integration, as bolstered by the doctrines of direct effect and supremacy, and the perception by domestic constitutional courts that domestic, constitutionally protected rights might be undermined by this process.[49] The pivotal moment was the German constitutional court's *Solange I* decision, in 1974, which threatened to bring about a breakdown in the co-operation between national courts and the ECJ.[50] The Court responded by reassuring domestic courts that EC institutions were also bound by human rights principles. According to the ECJ, rights guaranteed by the ECHR and by 'constitutional traditions common to the Member States' are the sources of these principles that

---

[48] Two early landmark rulings are Case 29/69 *Stauder* v. *City of Ulm* [1969] ECR 419 and Case 11/70 *Internationale Handelsgesellschaft* [1970] ECR 1125. More generally, see, inter alia, Case C-260/89 *ERT* [1991] ECR I-2925; Case C-274/99 P *Connolly* v. *Commission* [2001] ECR I-1611; Case C-94/00 *Roquette Frères* [2002] ECR I-9011; Case C-112/00 *Schmidberger* [2003] ECR I-5659; Case C-36/02 *Omega* [2004] ECR I-9609.

[49] L. Betten and N. Grief, *EU Law and Human Rights* (Longman, 1998), p. 58.

[50] *Internationale Handelsgesellschaft mbH* v. *Einfuhr- und Vorratsstelle fur Getreide und Futtermittel* [1974] 2 CMLR 540. Cf. *Frotini* v. *Ministero delle Finanze* [1974] 2 CMLR 372. See also *Brunner* v. *TEU* [1994] 1 CMLR 57.

bind all Community institutions. Through interpretation, these include the right to non-discrimination.[51]

Political support for this approach first came in the form of a joint declaration by the Commission, the Council and the Parliament in 1977,[52] and then in the preamble to the Single European Act 1986.[53] The first 'hard law' reference to human rights in the Treaty came as late as in 1992 with the Treaty of Maastricht. Article F of the Treaty on European Union (TEU) committed the Union to 'respect fundamental human rights as guaranteed by the [ECHR] and by the constitutional traditions common to the Member States, as general principles of Community law'. This provision was maintained in subsequent revisions of the Treaty and is now Article 6(2) TEU (the Nice Treaty). The proposed Constitutional Treaty also retained the essence of this provision and formulated it in a rather more emphatic wording. Draft Article I-9(3) stated that 'Fundamental rights, as guaranteed by the European Convention for the Protection of Human Rights and Fundamental Freedoms and as they result from the constitutional traditions common to the Member States, shall constitute general principles of the Union's law.' The Reform Treaty would include the same provision in a new Article 6 TEU.

As general principles of Community law, human rights provide an interpretative framework and also form part of the principles of judicial review.[54] Hence, Community institutions and Member States when interpreting, applying or derogating from Community law must ensure that their actions respect such human rights. In addition, Community legislation that is incompatible with human rights may be declared null and void – though the Court is normally very reluctant to annul general legislative acts and the procedural obstacles, particularly for non-privileged applicants, are substantial.[55] Domestic legislation that falls within the scope of Community law can also be challenged on the ground that it breaches fundamental rights recognised as general principles of Community law. There is, however, considerable uncertainty as to the exact boundaries of the sphere of action within which Member States can be held to account by the Court for their observance of human rights, and

[51] See, for instance, Case 4/73 *Nold* v. *Commission* [1974] ECR 491.
[52] [1977] OJ C 103/1.   [53] SEA 1986, Preamble, 3rd recital.   [54] Article 230 EC.
[55] Cf. Craig and de Búrca, *EU Law. Text, Cases and Materials* (3rd edn., Oxford University Press, 2003), p. 332. A greater chance for success exists for administrative acts, such as acts by the Commission in the field of competition or in staff cases. See, for instance, Case C-191/98P *Tzoanos* v. *Commission* [1999] ECR I-8223; Case C-252/97 *N* v. *Commission* [1998] ECR I-4871; Case C-404/92 *P X* v. *Commission* [1994] ECR I-4737.

concerns about the weight the Court gives respectively to economic rights and human rights where they conflict.[56]

The significance, for the operation of the equality Directives, of recognising equality as a general principle can be seen in the decision of the ECJ in *Mangold*,[57] which involved the issue, inter alia, of the application of the Framework Directive's prohibition of age discrimination in Germany. A major problem standing in the way of the application of the Directive appeared to be that the time limit for transposition of the age discrimination provisions of the Directive had not yet passed for Germany. The ECJ, however, did not find this to be an insuperable barrier for two reasons. First, the ECJ based its view on its previous case law, which established a duty on Member States to refrain from taking any measures that would seriously compromise the attainment of the result prescribed by a directive.[58] In support of this argument, the ECJ drew attention to the duty of the Member States which have elected to take advantage of the extended period of transposition, under Article 18 of the Directive, to report to the Commission on the progress made in the area of age discrimination before the transposition date, and to detail what measures of transposition have been taken. The ECJ considered that this provision would become redundant if Member States were able to act in a manner contrary to the aims of the Directive before the date on which transposition was required. Second, and crucially for our purposes,[59] the ECJ stated that the principle of non-discrimination on grounds of age must be regarded as a general principle of Community law (drawing on international human rights instruments, inter alia) and that the application of the general principle of equal treatment, including on the grounds of age, was not conditional on the expiry of the period allowed for the transposition of a directive implementing the principle of non-discrimination in a specific area. The same reasoning would, presumably, apply to discrimination on the basis of the other statuses listed in Article 13 EC.

The Court held that the principle of non-discrimination as a general principle of Community law, on the grounds of age and, by analogy, on the other grounds designated by Community law, meant that 'it

---

[56] Craig and de Búrca, ibid., at 347. For a greater discussion see J. H. H. Weiler, 'Fundamental Rights and Fundamental Boundaries: On the Conflict of Standards and Values in the Protection of Human Rights in the European Legal Space', in J. H. H. Weiler, *The Constitution of Europe* (Cambridge University Press, 1999), pp. 102–29.

[57] Case C-144/04 *Mangold* v. *Rudiger Helm* [2005] ECR I-9981.

[58] Case C-129/96 *Inter-Environnement Wallonie* [1997] ECR I-7411.   [59] Paras. 74–7.

is the responsibility of the national court, hearing a dispute involving the principle of non-discrimination in respect of age, to provide, in a case within its jurisdiction, the legal protection which individuals derive from the rules of Community law and to ensure that those rules are fully effective, setting aside any provision of national law which may conflict with that law'.[60] This seems to imply that, even if the parties to a case may not rely on the provisions of the Directives before national courts, the national court is still obliged to respect the primacy of Community law. This appears to create the possibility of the evolution of a body of EU non-discrimination law through direct application of the general principle of non-discrimination, if the ECJ is prepared to continue in the direction implied by the judgment. What remains unclear, however, is which of the differing approaches to non-discrimination examined above would provide the basis for this development. This would clearly be crucial; basing themselves on the first approach would be likely to result in very different results than if the second or third approaches were used, for example.

Human rights in the context of Community values and objectives

A second EU legal context in which the equality Directives are situated is the expanded role that human rights explicitly now play in the Treaties themselves, and not just as general principles of Community law of the type we considered above. This issue has long been debated in the Community. We can identify, for example, the important role played by a Comité des Sages[61] in 1996 before the Amsterdam Treaty. It is important to bear in mind also two further influential projects which reported on the issues during the latter part of the 1990s, prior to the process of drafting a Charter. The first, arising from a project funded by the Commission at the European University Institute in Florence, resulted in the adoption of a 'human rights agenda' by another Comité des Sages,[62] and the publication of a detailed report by a group led by Professor Alston at the European University Institute in Florence, on which the 'agenda' was based. A further Commission-appointed group, led by Professor Simitis,

---

[60] Para. 77.

[61] For a Europe of Civic and Social Rights: Report by the Comité des Sages chaired by Maria de Lourdes Pintasilgo (1996).

[62] Leading by Example: A Human Rights Agenda for the European Union for the Year 2000: Agenda of the Comité des Sages and Final Project Report (1998) (hereafter, 'Leading by Example').

reported, in 1999, recommending a way forward on the issue.[63] These reports have influenced the development of an approach that has, in turn, led to progressive incorporation of human rights into the Treaties, the drafting of the Charter of Fundamental Rights, and proposals to ratify the ECHR.

Human rights as founding principles and values

The Treaty of Amsterdam, 1997, recognised human rights as part of the principles upon which the Union is founded. More specifically, Article 6(1) TEU states that:

> The Union is founded on the principles of liberty, democracy, respect for human rights and fundamental freedoms, and the rule of law, principles which are common to the Member States.

Respect for the fundamental principles mentioned in Article 6(1) also forms a condition for application for membership in the EU.[64] An additional provision, Article 7 TEU, sets out a procedure whereby the Council may determine the 'existence of a serious and persistent breach' by a Member State of the principles mentioned in Article 6(1), leading to the temporary suspension of the voting rights of that state in the Council.[65] The Nice Treaty amended Article 7 to empower the Council to issue recommendations to a Member State which is 'in clear risk of a serious breach' of the principles mentioned in Article 6(1).[66] In both cases the assent of the European Parliament is required.[67] Following the Treaty of Nice, the ECJ has been granted jurisdiction over the procedural provisions of Article 7.[68] The procedure that is laid down by Article 7 is a political one and needs to be distinguished from the judicial procedures operating in the event of violations of human rights in the application of Community law by the institutions or the Member States. Instead, Article 7 TEU is aimed at preventing infringement of human rights by states in a purely domestic context.[69] The broader intention behind these developments has been

---

[63] Affirming fundamental rights in the European Union: Report of the Expert Group on Fundamental Rights (1999).

[64] Article 49 TEU.   [65] Article 7(2)–(5) TEU.   [66] Article 7(1) TEU.

[67] For this purpose the Parliament must act by a two-thirds majority of the votes cast, representing a majority of its Members. Article 7(6) TEU.

[68] Article 46 TEU.

[69] Cf. Betten and Grief, *EU Law and Human Rights*, p. 135. See also M. Merlingen, C. Muddle and U. Sedelmeier, 'The Right and the Righteous? European Norms, Domestic Politics and Sanctions Against Austria' (2001) 39 *Journal of Common Market Studies*, p. 59.

to show the Union's commitment to fundamental rights and to address long-standing criticisms regarding the absence of Treaty provisions on human rights.

The draft Constitutional Treaty would have enhanced further the status of human rights and, explicitly, equality in the Community legal order. These would have become *values* upon which the Union is founded. More particularly, Article I-2 stated:

> The Union is founded on the values of respect for human dignity, freedom, democracy, equality, the rule of law and respect for human rights, including the rights of persons belonging to minorities. These values are common to the Member States in a society in which pluralism, non-discrimination, tolerance, justice, solidarity and equality between women and men prevail.

The Reform Treaty would include the same provision in a new Article 2 TEU. From the perspective of equality and non-discrimination, the new provision would be a positive development. Although somewhat peculiarly drafted, in that a question arises about the relationship between the different and overlapping concepts set out in the Article, in practice it would be difficult and arguably fruitless to seek to draw too rigid demarcations between the concepts. The procedure laid down in Article 7 TEU would have been preserved in the Constitutional Treaty, in Article I-59, and would have applied also with respect to the values listed in Article I-2. The Reform Treaty would take a similar approach adding equivalent provisions to Article 49 TEU. States that wished to join the Union would also be obliged to respect these values.[70]

Human rights as objectives

It is remarkable that despite the current high level of rhetoric about human rights and equality there is hardly any reference to these in the general statement of the objectives of the Community in the Treaty on European Union or the EC Treaty (Articles 2 TEU and 2 EC). The sole reference relates to the aim to promote 'equality between men and women' which appeared in Article 2 EC following the Amsterdam Treaty. This omission contrasts with the frequent articulation of, and emphasis on, economic objectives, which appear, therefore, to predominate among the general objectives of the Community.

---

[70] Art. 49 TEU.

The Constitutional Treaty would have signaled some positive changes in this regard: Article I-3 would have listed the objectives of the Union; Article I-3(1) would have reinforced Article I-2, discussed above, and provided that 'the Union's aim is to promote peace, its values and the well-being of its peoples'; Article I-3(3) would have preserved the reference to 'equality between men and women' as a specific objective. The same paragraph, however, introduced a novelty and provided further that '[the Union] shall combat . . . discrimination'. The provision did not target a specific form of discrimination; rather any form of discrimination appeared to come under the scope of Article I-3(3), although the very generality of this provision risked diluting its strength in practice. During the drafting process the Working Group on Social Europe had proposed that 'non-discrimination on the basis of racial or ethnic origin, religious or sexual orientation, disability and age' be added as one of the objectives under Article I-3,[71] but this call found no response in the adopted text.

Article I-3(3) would have contained two other references which are relevant to human rights and non-discrimination. First, it would have provided that 'the Union shall . . . promote . . . solidarity between generations'. This is particularly pertinent to the issue of age discrimination, since combating such discrimination is arguably a precondition for achieving solidarity between generations. Second, it would have provided that '[the Union] shall respect its rich cultural and linguistic diversity, and shall ensure that Europe's cultural heritage is safeguarded and enhanced'. Undoubtedly, respect and promotion of cultural and linguistic diversity requires respect and promotion of related rights, while the duty 'to ensure' that Europe's cultural heritage is enhanced may be read as implying a duty of positive action to this end, as well as (possibly) the prohibition of discrimination based on language.[72] Finally, the fourth paragraph of Article I-3 would have set out the objectives in respect of the Union's dealings with the world community, and this included the obligation to contribute to the protection of human rights.[73] The Reform Treaty would adopt an identical approach, by incorporating these provisions in a new Article 3 TEU.

The concept of equality (non-discrimination) also features as a specific policy objective in various guises in existing Community law. First, with regard to nationality, the principle of non-discrimination is laid

---

[71] Final report of Working Group XI on Social Europe, CONV 516/1/03 REV 1, para. 22.

[72] Cf. the 1995 Framework Convention for the Protection of National Minorities and the 1992 European Charter for Regional or Minority Languages.

[73] See also Art. III-242.

down in Article 12 EC and other provisions in the area of fundamental freedoms. These provisions also act as legal bases on which measures to combat such discrimination and promote market integration can be, and have been, enacted.[74] Second, there is the familiar Article 141 EC, which aims to promote equality between men and women. The same provision forms a legal basis for the adoption of relevant measures.[75] Third, under Article 13 EC the Council is empowered to adopt measures to combat discrimination based on sex, racial and ethnic origin, religion or belief, disability, age or sexual orientation.[76] Importantly, however, Article 13 is not self-executing; rather it empowers the Community to bring forward legislation to further the goals set out in the article. The Directives that form a primary focus of this book have been enacted on this legal basis.[77]

Finally, the concept of non-discrimination is relevant to the aim of the Community, set out in Article 136 EC, to promote employment and improve living and working conditions, so as to make possible their harmonisation while improvement is being maintained. The Council in co-decision or consultation with the Parliament, or the social partners, may adopt measures in a range of fields, including 'working conditions' and 'equality between men and women with regard to labour market opportunities and treatment at work'.[78] Two Agreements concluded by the social partners on part-time and fixed-term work have been implemented by Council Directives and establish the principle of equal treatment for these workers engaged in these forms of employment.[79] The Agreements constitute a basic element of the European social model, not only because

---

[74] See Arts. 39, 40, 43, 49, 50 EC. The Reform Treaty would preserve these provisions with some small modifications.

[75] Art. 141(3) EC.

[76] Article 13 EC becomes Art. III-124 in the Constitution, with the difference that where the Council adopts measures rather than merely consulting the Parliament, it will need to obtain its consent.

[77] Council Directive 2000/43/EC [2000] OJ L180/22; Council Directive 2000/78/EC [2000] OJ L303/16; Council Directive 2004/113/EC [2004] OJ L373/37.

[78] Article 137(1)(b) and (i). Both these fields fall under the co-decision procedure. In addition, Art. 140 EC enables the Commission to proceed with a series of actions to encourage co-operation between Member States and facilitate co-ordination of their action in the social policy fields under the Social Chapter.

[79] Council Directive 97/81/EC, concerning the framework agreement on part-time work concluded by UNICE, CEEP and the ETUC [1998] OJ L14/9, as extended to the UK by Council Directive 98/23/EC [1998] OJ L131/10; Council Directive 1999/70/EC, concerning the framework agreement on fixed-term work concluded by ETUC, UNICE and CEEP [1999] OJ L175/43, corrigendum [1999] OJ L244/64.

they seek to improve the working conditions of atypical workers, but also because they are vital to the effort to promote equal treatment between men and women.

The Lisbon strategy and non-discrimination

The basis for the development of non-discrimination policies and rules in the Community is not confined to existing constitutional instruments, such as the EC and EU Treaties. It is also located in political events and initiatives. It has been remarked that the prospect of enlargement 'provided the backdrop, and even to some extent the raison d'être, for the adoption of the [Article 13] measures'.[80] More generally, the development of human rights in the Community order currently takes place against the backdrop of the Lisbon strategy. An extremely ambitious project, the strategy was adopted by the Lisbon European Council in March 2000, and aims to increase economic growth and competitiveness, improve job creation and quality in work and enhance social cohesion within a timeframe of ten years.[81] It is accompanied by a plethora of policy communications, action plans and targets in three main policy areas: economic, employment and social. The combating of discrimination, the development of fundamental rights and the promotion of gender equality form key objectives within the broader social policy aim to enhance social cohesion.[82] Indeed it is quite impossible to understand the continuing evolution of anti-discrimination policies, including the establishment of specialised EU bodies to assist and monitor the implementation of the principle of equal treatment,[83] without appreciating the impetus given to issues of equality by the launch of the strategy. The importance of the strategy for non-discrimination lies primarily with the rationale of the strategy. This acknowledges the positive impact that social policies, including anti-discrimination policies, have on economic growth and competitiveness as well as employment growth.[84] This approach differs markedly from

---

[80] E. Ellis, 'The Principle of Non-Discrimination in the Post-Nice Era', in Arnull and Wincott, *Accountability and Legitimacy in the European Union* (Oxford University Press, 2002), pp. 291–305, at p. 291 and see also pp. 293–5.

[81] European Council, Presidency Conclusions of the Meeting in Lisbon, 23–24 March 2000, para. 5.

[82] European Commission, 'Social Policy Agenda', COM(2000) 379 final, pp. 20–1.

[83] For instance, the European Institute for Gender Equality was conceived within the framework of the Social Policy Agenda.

[84] European Commission Communication, 'Employment and Social Policies: A Framework for Investing in Quality', COM(2001) 313 final. See also D. Fourage, *Costs of Non-Social*

the one that permeated the Treaty of Rome model, where social policies were viewed merely as a product of economic development, rather than a productive factor themselves.

Within the parameters of the new policy reasoning, the development of an environment free from discrimination which allows the flourishing of the productive capabilities of disabled and older people is seen as vital in facilitating the achievement of the strategy's particular objectives to reach, by 2010, a general employment rate of 70 per cent and an employment rate for older workers of 50 per cent (up from, respectively, 63 and 41 per cent, in 2004). Combating discrimination based on age, in particular, is crucial for the Union's effort to promote active ageing, meet the demographic challenge and secure the sustainability of social security systems.[85] In like terms, the elimination of discrimination against women is a precondition to reaching the target of an employment rate for women of 60 per cent, by 2010, and to unleashing Europe's potential for greater economic growth.[86] Effective policies against discrimination based on sex, age and racial or ethnic origin also form part of the strategy's aim to combat poverty and promote social inclusion, given that women, older people, ethnic and racial minorities are particularly vulnerable in these respects.[87] This positive interplay between economic, employment and social policies, which is at the heart of the Lisbon strategy, constitutes therefore at once an objective and the means with which the strategy's aims, including the combating of discrimination and the promotion of equality, can be realised.

Mainstreaming and the European Employment Strategy

'Mainstreaming', especially gender mainstreaming, has also gained much prominence in recent years. According to the Commission, '[gender] mainstreaming is the integration of the gender perspective into every stage of policy processes – design, implementation, monitoring and evaluation – with a view to promoting equality between women and men. It

---

Policy: Towards an Economic Framework of Quality Social Policies – and the Costs of Not Having Them. Report for DG Employment and Social Affairs of the European Commission (Brussels, 2003).

[85] Cf. Economic and Social Committee, 'Opinion on Older Workers' [2001] OJ C14/50; European Commission Green Paper, 'Confronting Demographic Change: A New Solidarity Between the Generations', COM(2005) 94 final.

[86] COM(2000) 379 final, pp. 18–20.

[87] Ibid., pp. 12–13; European Commission, Employment in Europe 2004. Recent Trends and Prospects (OOPEC, Luxembourg, 2004), p. 129.

[also] means assessing how policies impact on the life and position of both women and men – and taking responsibility to readdress them if necessary.'[88] Work on gender mainstreaming began in the mid-1990s, following the UN Women's Conference in Beijing in 1995,[89] and was formalised at institutional level with the Treaty of Amsterdam in 1997. The Amsterdam Treaty added a specific provision, Article 3(2) EC, which provides that 'in all the activities referred to in [Article 3(1) EC] the Community shall aim to eliminate inequalities, and to promote equality, between men and women'. Since 2001, an informal High Level Group on Gender Mainstreaming, consisting of representatives from relevant departments of Member States' governments and chaired by the Commission, meets twice a year in close co-operation with the Presidency in order to offer support to Presidencies in identifying policy areas and topics to address during the meetings of the European Council.[90]

Mainstreaming is most developed in the employment field, in particular within the context of the European Employment Strategy (EES), which is adopted on the basis of Articles 137–138 EC and aims to promote job creation and quality and productivity in work. EES has been described as a 'cyclical process',[91] involving the preparation by the Commission of European Employment Guidelines and their adoption by the Council. Each Member State is required to take these into account in devising and implementing their national employment policies, and to submit 'National Action Plans' to the Commission and the Council describing how it plans to respond. The Council may issue non-binding recommendations to Member States regarding their employment policies. On the basis of experience, new Guidelines are drafted and the process starts again. Issues of equality and non-discrimination have become prominent parts of the strategy. For example, Council Decision 2005/600/EC, setting out guidelines for the employment policies of the Member States for the years 2005–8, emphasises that 'equal opportunities and combating discrimination are essential for progress. Gender mainstreaming and the

---

[88] See European Commission, Gender Mainstreaming, General Overview at http://europa.eu.int/comm/employment_social/gender_equality/gender_mainstreaming/general_overview_en.html.

[89] See European Commission, 'Incorporating Equal Opportunities for Women and Men Into All Community Policies and Activities', COM(1996) 67 final.

[90] Visit http://europa.eu.int/comm/employment_social/gender_equality/gender_mainstreaming/gender/high_level_group_en.html.

[91] M. Zysk, 'Legal responses to the problem of age discrimination in the European Union: does the law fit its purpose' (PhD thesis, EUI, December 2005), p. 44, from which this paragraph draws extensively.

promotion of gender equality should be ensured in all action taken.'[92] How far the EES has been effective in driving Member States on employment equality issues and its relationship to the delivery of human rights is the subject of a lively debate.[93] If applied effectively, mainstreaming, and in particular the approach taken in the EES, would be examples of the fourth approach to equality considered earlier.[94]

Mainstreaming was also addressed in the Constitutional Treaty. Article 3(2) EC would have become Article III-116 and covered the activities referred to in Part III of the Constitution. In addition, however, the Constitutional Treaty would have ushered in a significant development with respect to the other grounds of discrimination. Article III-118 would have provided for the first time that:

> In defining and implementing the policies and activities referred to in this Part, the Union shall aim to combat discrimination based on sex, racial or ethnic origin, religion or belief, disability, age or sexual orientation.[95]

It appears that the Reform Treaty would include equivalent provisions in a Revised EC Treaty, to be renamed the Treaty on the functioning of the Union (TFU). Lombardo has argued that the approach followed in the Constitution-making process, reflected in the adopted provisions, fell short of transforming existing policy paradigms in a manner that prioritises equality objectives among competing concerns.[96] Even so, the importance of the mainstreaming provisions, in particular the extension of mainstreaming to the grounds listed under Article 13 EC, should not be underestimated. The range of areas affected would be considerable. It would include, amongst others, the internal market, economic and monetary policy, employment, social, agricultural, consumer protection and transport policies, and the Union's external policies. The implications could potentially be much more far-reaching than what might initially be imagined, although much would depend on how these mainstreaming

---

[92] Council Decision 2005/600/EC, on Guidelines for the employment policies of the Member States [2005] OJ L205/21, at 23.

[93] See generally, G. de Búrca and B. de Witte (eds.), *Social Rights in Europe* (Oxford University Press, 2005); M. Bell, 'Combating Racial discrimination through the European Employment Strategy', (2004) 6 *Cambridge Yearbook of European Legal Studies*, pp. 52–73.

[94] S. Fredman, 'Transformation or Dilution: Fundamental Rights in the EU Social Space', (2006) 12 *European Law Journal*, pp. 41–60.

[95] See also Art. I-45 of the draft Constitutional Treaty which aimed at promoting democratic accountability: 'in all its activities, the Union shall observe the principle of equality of its citizens, who shall receive equal attention from its institutions, bodies, offices and agencies.'

[96] See E. Lombardo, 'Integrating or Setting the Agenda? Gender Mainstreaming in the European Constitution-Making Process' (2005) 12 *Social Politics*, p. 412.

provisions were implemented. In this respect, it is suggested that a more active implementation would be required than what has so far been achieved under the existing provision (Article 3(2) EC). Arguably, failure on behalf of the Union institutions to meet the mainstreaming objectives when designing and enacting legislation could render adopted acts liable for judicial review before the Court.[97]

The Charter of Fundamental Rights of the European Union and equality

A major development in the area of fundamental rights in the European Union has been the adoption of a Charter of Fundamental Rights in 2000.[98] This holds the potential to contribute to the development of a more rights-oriented system legally, as well as contribute in more symbolic terms to the development of an EU rights-culture.[99] With particular reference to the concept of equality and non-discrimination, the Charter reinforces existing Community provisions and focuses the Union's efforts towards the promotion of equality within a conceptual framework that prioritises broader humanitarian over narrower economic considerations. In considering the implications of the Charter for the future development of European equality law, we are faced, however, with an even more complex difficulty than in dealing with the draft Constitutional Treaty and the proposed Reform Treaty. This is because the Charter has both an independent status, as well as a status as part of the Reform Treaty were it to come into force. We shall need to consider the implications of the Charter if the Reform Treaty were adopted and if it is not. (All references to the specific Titles and Articles, for reasons of convenience, refer to the Constitutional Treaty as this is the text which at the time of writing (June 2007) is closest to that likely to be adopted by the Reform Treaty).

There is a specific Title on equality and three provisions under it make direct reference to equality or non-discrimination.[100] Interestingly, the Charter's provisions reflect all four of the approaches to equality and non-discrimination sketched out in the first part of this chapter.

---

[97] See Art. 230 EC.   [98] [2000] OJ C346/1.

[99] See F. G. Jacobs, 'The EU Charter of Fundamental Rights' in A. Arnull and D. Wincott, *Accountability and Legitimacy in the European Union* (Oxford University Press, 2003), pp. 275–90, at 284–5.

[100] In brackets we have included the Articles' numbers as appearing in Part II of the Constitution. The other four provisions under the Equality Title are Art. 22 (II-82), cultural, religious and linguistic diversity, Art. 24 (II-84), the rights of the child, Art. 25 (II-85), the rights of the elderly, and Art. 26 (II-86), integration of persons with disabilities.

Article 20 (II-80): equality before the law

> Everyone is equal before the law

Article 21 (II-81): non-discrimination

1. Any discrimination based on any ground such as sex, race, colour, ethnic or social origin, genetic features, language, religion or belief, political or any other opinion, membership of a national minority, property, birth, disability, age or sexual orientation shall be prohibited.
2. Within the scope of application of the Constitution and without prejudice to any of its specific provisions, any discrimination on grounds of nationality shall be prohibited.

Article 23 (II-83): equality between men and women

> Equality between women and men must be ensured in all areas, including employment, work and pay.
>
> The principle of equality shall not prevent the maintenance or adoption of measures providing for specific advantages in favour of the underrepresented sex.

The Charter has not displaced existing EU law on fundamental rights, discussed above. This is clear not least from proposal to include in the Reform Treaty a provision which, as noted earlier, would commit the Union to respecting fundamental rights as protected by the ECHR and constitutional provisions common to the Member States. In other words, both the ECHR and domestic constitutions continue to provide a reference point for the determination of rights by the ECJ. In developing its fundamental rights jurisprudence, the Court is likely to be influenced by the contents of the Charter, but not be restricted by it where other rights not currently identified by the Charter appear relevant and important in the future. The Charter, then, should be seen as 'work in progress' rather than the apex of the achievement of human rights in the EU. Union law should be seen to be open to future evolution in ECHR and Member States' domestic human rights law.

The Charter is not presently directly legally binding, and because of this the ECJ has so far refrained from relying on its provisions. However, several Advocates General and the Court of First Instance have seen the Charter as providing the basis for an interpretative framework apart from its status as part of any future Treaty.[101] The Constitutional Treaty would

---

[101] See, for instance, Opinion of Tizzano AG in Case C-173/99 *BECTU* [2001] ECR I-4881, paras. 26–8; Opinion of Jacobs AG in Case C-270/99 P *Z* v. *Parliament* [2001] ECR I-9197, para. 40 and in Case C-50/00 P *Unión de Pequeños Agricultores* [2002] ECR I-6677,

have incorporated the Charter in Part II and recognises its justiciability in general.[102] On the other hand, bowing to political pressure not least from the UK Government, the Convention drafting the Constitutional Treaty inserted some amendments to the horizontal provisions of the Charter (Title VII) that would have had the effect of limiting the justiciability of a number of the rights laid down in the Charter, in particular social rights of the type mostly found in Title IV on 'solidarity'. In general, the horizontal provisions of the Charter are of immense importance for understanding the implications of the Charter and we turn to examine these, as these appear in the Constitutional Treaty, using the numbering appearing there.

First, according to Article II-111(1),[103] 'the provisions of [the] Charter are addressed to the institutions, bodies, offices and agencies of the Union with due regard for the principle of subsidiarity and to the Member States *only when they are implementing Union law*'.[104] As with the scope of responsibility of Member States in respect of human rights in general, there is a debate as to the boundaries within which the Charter's provisions will be binding on Member States. The Explanations to the Charter make explicit reference to the *ERT* judgment,[105] which suggests that Member States are bound by the Charter's provisions even when derogating from Community law (as for instance happens when derogating from the fundamental freedoms).[106]

Second, according to Article II-111(2),[107] the Charter 'does not establish any new power or task for the Union, or modify powers and tasks defined by the Constitution'. There are no EU powers to promote many Charter rights. A most striking example is Article 137(5) EC which excludes Community competence from the area relating to the right of association and the right to strike,[108] yet the freedom of association and

---

para. 39; Opinion of Leger AG in Case C-353/99 P *Council* v. *Hautala* [2001] ECR I-9596, paras. 80–3; Mischo AG in Case C-20/00 *Booker* v. *Aquaculture* [2003] ECR I-7411, para. 126. The Court of First Instance has also relied on the Charter. See, for instance, Case T-54/99 *max.mobil Telekommunikation Service GmbH* v. *Commission* [2002] ECR II-313, para. 57.

[102] See Art. I-9(1).

[103] Article 52(1) in the Charter.   [104] Emphasis added.

[105] Case C-260/89 *ERT* [1991] ECR I-2925 in which the Court held that national rules derogating from Community law must conform with fundamental rights.

[106] See Council of the European Union, *Charter of Fundamental Rights of the European Union. Explanations Relating to the Complete Text of the Charter*, December 2000, p. 73. See also A. J. Menéndez, 'Chartering Europe: Legal Status and Policy Implications of the Charter of Fundamental Rights of the European Union' *JCMS* 49 (2002), p. 471, at p. 480.

[107] Article 51(2) in the Charter.   [108] See Art. III-210(6) replicating Art. 137(5) EC.

the right to take collective action, including strike action, are explicitly guaranteed in Articles 12 and 28 of the Charter.

Third, according to Article II-112(1),[109] any limitation on the exercise of the rights and freedoms recognised by the Charter must be provided for by law, respect the essence of those rights and freedoms, be proportional and necessary to meet objectives of general interest recognised by the Union and the need to protect the rights and freedoms of others. This provision is based on the Court's jurisprudence in the area of fundamental rights, and is a broader exception than provided under the ECHR.[110] In contrast to the ECHR, where limitations are stipulated only in respect of certain rights and freedoms,[111] the EU Charter applies a general limitation provision that appears to limit, in principle, all of the rights recognised. Under the ECHR, limitations on the rights must be 'necessary in a democratic society', in pursuit of particular legitimate objectives and are subject to the principle of proportionality. The scope of objectives that may justify limitation on rights in the ECHR is, therefore, also more limited than in the EU Charter.[112] However, to read the Charter as providing a general limitation to all rights of such a broad scope would be incorrect. Article II-112(3)[113] acts as a safeguard to the level and scope of protection, providing that rights in the EU Charter that 'correspond' to the ECHR must be interpreted in line with the Convention,[114] without prejudice to Union law to provide more extensive protection.

---

[109] Article 52(1) in the Charter.

[110] Joined Cases C-37/02 and C-38/02 *Di Lenardo Adriano Srl* v. *Ministero del Commercio con l'Estero* [2004] ECR I-6911, para. 82. See also, inter alia, Case C-44/94 *Fishermen's Organisations and Others* [1995] ECR I-3115, para. 55; Case C-200/96 *Metronome Musik* [1998] ECR I-1953, para. 21; and Joined Cases C-20/00 and C-64/00 *Booker Aquacultur and Hydro Seafood* [2003] ECR I-7411, para. 68.

[111] See in particular Arts. 8-11 ECHR and Article 1 (right to property) in Protocol 1. The latter right is subject to a broader range of limitations than existing in respect of Arts 8-11.

[112] In theory, the principle of price stability, being a general objective under the proposed Reform Treaty, might justify limitation on the exercise of the Charter's rights.

[113] Art. 52(3) in the Charter.

[114] The 'Explanations' list the articles of the Charter where presently both the meaning and scope are the same as the corresponding articles of the ECHR as well as those whose meaning is the same as the corresponding articles of the ECHR but their scope is wider. See Council of the European Union, *Charter of Fundamental Rights of the European Union. Explanations Relating to the Complete Text of the Charter*, pp. 75–6. It should be noted that the 'Explanations' were given legal status by the Constitutional Convention which revisited the Charter and added a new paragraph to Art. 52. Now, Art. II-112(7) provides that 'the explanations . . . shall be given due regard by the courts of the Union and of the Member States'. See CONV 354/02, pp. 10, 17.

Further, Article II-113[115] provides that the Charter cannot be interpreted 'as restricting or adversely affecting human rights and fundamental freedoms' as recognised by Union law, international agreements concluded by the EU or Member States (including the ECHR) or by domestic constitutions. In addition, Article II-114[116] states that 'nothing in this Charter shall be interpreted as implying any right to engage in any activity or to perform any act aimed at the destruction of any of the rights and freedoms recognised in this Charter or at their limitation to a greater extent than is provided for herein'. The intention of these provisions is to set a minimum floor to the level of protection of the rights recognised by the EU Charter corresponding to that guaranteed by the ECHR as well as to ensure consistency between the two instruments.

A final important issue to be considered relates to what is now Article II-112(5). This provision was inserted by the Constitutional Convention and states that: 'The provisions of this Charter which contain principles may be implemented by legislative and executive acts taken by institutions, bodies, offices and agencies of the Union, and by acts of Member States when they are implementing Union law, in the exercise of their respective powers. *They shall be judicially cognisable only in the interpretation of such acts and in the ruling on their legality*.'[117] Article II-112(5) applies a distinction between subjective rights (*subjektive Rechte, droits subjectifs*) and principles. The latter do not create enforceable rights or positive claims for individuals, but are, rather, guiding principles for Member States or Union action. They may, at most, serve as an aid to interpretation for the courts of legislative or executive acts taken to implement these principles, or as a standard to be applied in judicial review (review of legality) of such legislative or executive acts.

The new provision is ostensibly designed to enhance legal clarity. According to Working Group II, which tabled this provision, the distinction 'is consistent both with case law of the Court of Justice and with the approach of the Member States' constitutional systems to "principles" particularly in the field of social law'.[118] Yet, as Ewing, Collins and McColgan observe, 'the puzzle about this distinction is that the Charter does not appear to draw a sharp distinction in its language between rights and principles'.[119] Indeed, the Convention which drafted the Charter did not follow suggestions made by the House of Lords Select Committee on

[115] Article 53 in the Charter.
[116] Article 54 in the Charter.   [117] Emphasis added.   [118] CONV 354/02, p. 8.
[119] H. Collins, K. D. Ewing and A. McColgan, *Labour Law: Text and Materials* (2nd edn., Hart Publishing, 2005), p. 9. For a critical assessment see S. Prechal, 'Rights v. Principles,

the European Communities to draw a clear distinction within the Charter between those rights which should be justiciable and those which are merely aspirations or objectives.[120] Some provisions, like Article 38 (II-88), which states that 'Union policies shall ensure a high level of consumer protection', are clearly of an aspirational nature. However, the scope of the new provision is broad enough to risk the interpretation of several other rights under the Charter being seen as subject to the Member States. This weakens the Charter's strength and undermines the uniform development of rights in the Community legal order. Of particular concern are the rights under the 'solidarity' and 'equality' Titles.

Brussels European Council and the Charter of Fundamental Rights

We have so far considered the relationship between the Charter and the proposed Constitutional Treaty, which did not come into effect. Understanding the contours of that proposed relationship, however, helps us understand the approach proposed to be adopted under the Reform Treaty. The European Council held in June 2007 agreed a complex set of arrangements regarding the Charter, partly adopting the approach proposed in the Constitutional Treaty, partly not.

First, it was agreed that the version of the Charter as adopted in the 2004 IGC would be re-enacted by the Parliament, the Council and the Commission during 2007 and would be published in the *Official Journal of the European Union*; the text of the Charter would not, however, be included in the Reform Treaty itself. Second, it was agreed that in place of the arrangements adopted in the draft Constitutional Treaty, Article 6 TEU on fundamental rights would be replaced with a new Article which states, in part: 'The Union recognises the rights, freedoms and principles set out in the Charter of Fundamental Rights [as re-enacted] . . . which shall have the same legal value as the Treaties'. Under these provisions, then, the Charter would be given 'legally binding value', as the Presidency Conclusions put it.[121] Third, a Declaration would be agreed by the IGC responsible for adopting the Reform Treaty. This 'declaratory protocol' (our term) would provide that the Charter of Fundamental

Or How to Remove Fundamental Rights From the Jurisdiction of the Courts' in J. W. de Zwaan, J. H. Jans and F. A. Nelissen (eds.), *The European Union: An Ongoing Process of Integration*, (Liber Amicorum Alfred E. Kellermann, 2004), p. 177.

[120] 8th Report, Session 1999–2000, 16 May 2000, paras. 144–6. Cf. B. Hepple, 'The EU Charter of Fundamental Rights' (2001) 30 *Industrial Law Journal* 225, p. 228.

[121] Presidency Conclusions, European Council, Brussels, June 2007, Annex 1, para. 9.

Rights, 'which has legally binding force, confirms the fundamental rights guaranteed by the European Convention on Human Rights and Fundamental Freedoms and as they result from the constitutional traditions common to the Member States', thus explicitly linking the Charter to the reference to human rights as part of the general principles of Union law, discussed above. Fourth, several limits on the scope and operation of the Charter, which were already included in the text of the Charter as a result of the Constitutional Convention's proposals, would be reiterated. The provisions of the Charter 'shall not extend in any way the competences of the Union as defined in the Treaties'. (The 'declaratory protocol' would also make clear that the Charter 'does not extend the field of application of Union law beyond the powers of the Union or establish any new power or task for the Union, or modify powers and tasks as defined by the Treaties'.) The rights, freedoms and principles in the Charter 'shall be interpreted in accordance with the general provisions in Title VII [the horizontal provisions] of the Charter governing its interpretation and application and with due regard to the explanations referred to in the Charter, that set out the sources of those provisions'.

There was, however, considerable unease with this general approach among some delegations, particularly the United Kingdom, Ireland and Poland, each of which negotiated limited escape routes. The most fundamental was that negotiated by the United Kingdom, which succeeded in getting an agreement that an additional Protocol would be attached to the TEU. This was widely interpreted as seeking to prevent the use of the Charter to upset provisions in domestic British labour law, particularly those limiting the right to strike. This new 'UK Protocol' (our term) would include a lengthy list of preambular clauses, listing various aspects of the Charter which the UK government wished to have on record as agreed by the other Member States. The Charter would be applied 'in strict accordance' with the provisions of the new Article 6 and Title VII of the Charter itself. The Charter would be applied and interpreted by the courts of the United Kingdom 'strictly in accordance with the Explanations referred to in that Article'. The Charter contains 'both rights and principles' and 'provisions which are civil and political in character and those which are economic and social in character'. The Charter 'reaffirms the rights, freedoms and principles recognised in the Union and makes those rights more visible, but does not create new rights or principles'. On the other hand, the United Kingdom accepted that the main point of the Protocol would be to 'clarify . . . the application of the Charter in relation to the laws and administrative action of the United Kingdom and of its justiciability within the United Kingdom', that the Protocol was 'without prejudice to the application of the Charter to other Member States', and 'without prejudice to other obligations of the United Kingdom' under the treaties 'and Union law generally'.

In contrast to the relatively lengthy Preamble, there are two brief substantive articles of the Protocol. These would provide, first, that the Charter 'does not extend the ability of the Court of Justice, or any court or tribunal of the United Kingdom, to find that the laws, regulations or administrative provisions, practices or action of the United Kingdom are inconsistent with the fundamental rights, freedoms and principles that it reaffirms'.[122] Second, 'for the avoidance of doubt', the Protocol would provide that 'nothing in [Title IV] of the Charter [the provisions dealing with "solidarity rights", including the right to strike] creates justiciable rights applicable to the United Kingdom except in so far as the United Kingdom has provided for such rights in its national law'.[123] Third, the Protocol would provide that '[t]o the extent that a provision of the Charter refers to national laws and practices, it shall only apply in the United Kingdom to the extent that the rights or principles that it contains are recognised in the law or practices of the United Kingdom'.[124]

Poland and Ireland took somewhat different positions, and reserved their final decision on what to do about the application of the Charter to their countries until the IGC responsible for approving the Reform Treaty, reserving their right to join both the 'declaratory protocol', and the 'UK protocol'. In addition, a Unilateral Declaration by Poland was attached to the Presidency Conclusions, stating that: 'The Charter does not affect in any way the right of Member States to legislate in the sphere of public morality, family law as well as the protection of human dignity and respect for human physical and moral integrity.' This was widely interpreted as Poland's response to its fear that the Charter might be used to interfere with aspects of Poland's social legislation, for example that restricting access to abortion, or limiting the rights of homosexuals in the area of marriage.

Continuing developments on equality and human rights in the European Union

In this section we touch briefly on some other notable future developments in relation to human rights in the European Union that would have a direct impact on discrimination and equality. A first issue concerns the accession

---

[122] Article 1(1).   [123] Article 1(2).   [124] Article 2.

of the Union to the ECHR. The ECJ has held that the Community does not at present have competence to accede to the Convention.[125] This, however, would have changed with the coming into force of the Constitutional Treaty which provided in Article I-9(2) that 'the Union shall accede to the European Convention on Human Rights and Fundamental Freedoms. Such accession shall not affect the Union's competences as defined in the Constitution.' The Reform Treaty would include the same provision in a new Article 6 TEU.

From the point of view of equality one specific issue that is raised by the prospect of accession is whether the existing protections for equality under the *acquis* would be affected. On the positive side, in certain circumstances the judgments by the ECtHR can fill some of the gaps in coverage left by the EC equality legislation.[126] On the other hand, the concept of 'discrimination' under the Convention is more problematic, not least because the approach to discrimination adopted in Article 14 ECHR is a limited one, falling within the second approach discussed earlier. It is not a free-standing right. As Leach remarks, 'the "parasitic" nature of the right is one of the reasons why the Article 14 case law has been limited'.[127] Moreover, it is not entirely clear whether or, if it does, how far the Convention incorporates the notion of 'indirect discrimination'. What is more, especially on the issue of sex discrimination, while EC law only allowed justifications in cases of indirect discrimination, the ECtHR has in the past permitted justifications to be advanced also in cases of direct discrimination, although this may be changing.[128]

However, as we noted above, the EU Charter provides that 'corresponding' rights have the same scope and meaning as laid down in the ECHR but, where more extensive protection has been achieved by Community law, the higher standard prevails.[129] This provision should act as a safeguard with respect to the concept of 'discrimination' and its judicial treatment, at least by the Court of Justice. Yet, there remains the question as to whether in the long term these rather different approaches can co-exist and, if not, which will predominate. If the Union also accedes to Protocol 12, which provides for a self-standing prohibition of discrimination, some of the most important problems with respect to the issue

---

[125] See in this respect Opinion 2/94, *Accession by the Community to the Convention for the Protection of Human Rights and Fundamental Freedoms* [1996] ECR I-1759.

[126] See, inter alia, *Van Raalte* v. *The Netherlands*, no. 20060/92 [1997] ECHR 6 (21 February 1997); *Wessels-Bergervoet* v. *The Netherlands*, no. 34462/97 [2004] 38 EHRR 793 (4 June 2002).

[127] Leach, *Taking a Case to the European Court of Human Rights*, p. 178.

[128] *Timishev* v. *Russia* 13 December 2005, paras. 56–8.

[129] See Art. 52(3), or Art. II-112(3) under the Constitution.

may be avoided. However, Working Group II, which dealt with the issue of accession to the ECHR, did not make any recommendations in respect of the issue of acceding to the Protocols accompanying the Convention. The justification given in its final report was that such a question was 'not of a constitutional nature', implying that it is a political question to be decided by the EU institutions.[130]

A second issue for the future relates to the establishment of new institutions in the Community that have equality issues as part of their mandate, in particular the EU Agency for Fundamental Rights. The political decision for the establishment of a Fundamental Rights Agency (FRA) was made by the Brussels European Council in December 2003.[131] The FRA came into operation on 1 March 2007.[132] The FRA replaces the European Monitoring Centre (EUMC) on Racism and Xenophobia that has operated since 1997.[133] Its objective is 'to provide the relevant institutions, bodies, offices and agencies of the Community and its Member States when implementing Community law with assistance and expertise relating to fundamental rights in order to support them when they take measures or formulate courses of action within their respective spheres of competence to fully respect fundamental rights'.[134] The responsibilities of the Agency include the evaluation of the practical impact of EU policies and measures in the area of fundamental rights and the promotion of respect for rights across the Union. The Agency is also responsible for promoting and co-ordinating dialogue on fundamental rights with civil society and for establishing relevant networks. Raising public awareness of fundamental rights is another responsibility.[135] The FRA should operate independently and its work should avoid duplication with the work of national and international human rights bodies, in particular the Council

---

[130] Final Report of Working Group II, CONV 354/02, p. 11.
[131] European Council, Presidency Conclusions of the Meeting in Brussels, 12–13 December 2003. See, in general, C. McCrudden, 'The Contribution of the EU Fundamental Rights Agency to Combating Discrimination and Promoting Equality', in P. Alston and O. de Schutter (eds.), *Monitoring Fundamental Rights in the EU: the Contribution of the Fundamental Rights Agency* (Hart, 2005).
[132] Established by Council Regulation (EC) No. 168/2007 of 15 February 2007.
[133] Council Regulation 1035/97, establishing a European Monitoring Centre on Racism and Xenophobia [1997] OJ L151/11.
[134] European Commission, 'Proposal for a Council Regulation establishing a European Union Agency for Fundamental Rights', COM(2005) 280 final. See also European Commission, 'The Fundamental Rights Agency: Public Consultation Document', COM(2004) 693 final.
[135] COM(2005) 280 final, draft Art. 4–5.

of Europe and the Institute for Gender Equality.[136] A separate Council declaration provides for the extension of the Agency's advisory remit to cover the areas referred to in Title VI TEU concerning police and judicial co-operation in criminal matters.[137] Our earlier consideration of the differing approaches to equality and non-discrimination highlights the dilemma of whether the pursuit of ground-specific strategies (the third approach) is more effective in practice than pursuing the broad approach of equality as rationality (the first approach). The debate over the transformation of the EUMC into the FRA illustrates this tension, with some expressing scepticism as to whether the broader approach will prove more effective.

Human rights and equality: more theoretical issues

Although there are common elements among all these differing international, regional and EU legal norms and policy initiatives, in that each uses the concepts of equality and non-discrimination, there are also clear differences. One important issue for the future interpretation of the equality Directives is the extent to which the ECJ in particular regards the similarities as more important than the differences, or vice versa. So, where do the differences lie? We have suggested that there are substantial differences in the conceptions of 'equality' and 'non-discrimination' involved. In this last section, we argue that there are also significant differences in the conception of 'rights' involved as well.

There are several important differences in the way in which rights are conceptualised in these different instruments. First, there is the crucial distinction between rights accorded to individuals as citizens, and rights accorded to individuals as individuals. In the former approach, often adopted in domestic constitutional law, rights are protected essentially as aspects of citizenship. The theory frequently advanced to support these rights is based on a loose notion of a social contract between individuals who came together to form the (new) state and agreed to accord each other certain rights. In this category we find political rights, such as the

---

[136] Ibid., draft Arts. 9 and 11(8) and draft Preamble, 15th recital. Cf. Parliamentary Assembly of the Council of Europe, 'Plans to set up a Fundamental Rights Agency of the European Union', Draft Resolution, points 10–12; European Parliament, 'Resolution on the Promotion and Protection of Fundamental Rights: The Role of National and European Institutions, including the Fundamental Rights Agency', 26 May 2005.

[137] Declaration by the Council on Police and Judicial Cooperation in Criminal Matters, adopted at the Justice and Home Affairs Council, 15 February 2007, 6396/07 Add 1.

right to vote, but also economic rights, such as rights relating to social security benefits. The process of European integration, in particular the evolution of the concept of EU citizenship, is having a major impact on the entitlement to these rights, with Community law according access to these rights on the basis of Community citizenship rather than domestic citizenship.[138]

Particularly post-Second World War, a different approach to rights has been developed and this is encountered in various international instruments. This newer approach concentrates on vesting human rights in individuals regardless of their citizenship status. A country that has taken on these human rights obligations will be required to accord these rights to non-citizens within the jurisdiction of the state. The ECHR is an obvious example of this approach. Although this approach typically concerns such rights as the right to life, freedom from torture and degrading treatment, other rights, such as the right to property, may also be accorded to non-citizens. The EU Charter of Fundamental Rights, interestingly, divides rights into those attached to citizens and those attached to all within the jurisdiction, and includes equality rights in the latter category.

In conceptual terms, the Directives adopted on the basis of Article 13 EC belong to the second tradition, since they are inspired by ideas of equality and non-discrimination in a context not linked primarily to the concept of citizenship. The reference to 'persons', rather than 'citizens' reinforces their 'universalist' nature. Citizenship, or more accurately nationality, continues, however, to play a major (if limited) role in the scope and application of the Race and Employment Framework Directives because both Directives 'do not cover difference of treatment based on nationality and [are] without prejudice to provisions and conditions relating to the entry into and residence of third-country nationals and stateless persons on the territory of Member States, and to any treatment which arises from the legal status of the third-country nationals and stateless persons concerned'.[139]

A second important difference in the way rights are conceptualised under the different international, regional and domestic human rights instruments we have examined relates to the role of the state. Under some instruments, most commonly constitutional documents and international, as well as regional, conventions and treaties, rights are accorded against the state, and against the state alone. There are important questions that often arise as to what constitutes 'the state', although private

---

[138] See, for instance, Case C-85/96 *Martinez Sala* v. *Freistaat Bayern* [1998] ECR I-2691.
[139] Article 3(2) in both Directives.

businesses usually fall outside the scope of those bodies obligated to accord human rights protections. Other instruments protecting human rights often take a rather different approach, particularly where the method of protection is ordinary legislation addressing a particular issue. In this case the obligation is frequently placed on public and private bodies alike. The Article 13 Directives adopt the latter approach insofar as they are intended to require Member States to introduce legal obligations for private as well as public persons.[140]

Yet, even where the obligation is placed on the state alone, the position is frequently more complicated as the state is often under an obligation to ensure that violations of rights by private parties are prevented. In the Community legal context, and with regard to the Article 13 Directives in particular, this is manifested by explicit provisions obliging Member States to provide for effective sanctions for breach of the national provisions adopted pursuant to the Directives.[141] It is also seen in the requirements on Member States to ensure that provisions even under private law – such as collective agreements – contrary to the principle of equal treatment are declared null and void or are amended;[142] and, in the case of the Race and the Sex Equality Directives, also by the obligation to establish equality bodies to promote the principle of equal treatment.[143] Ultimately, an EU Member State may be liable for loss or damage caused to an individual where this has resulted from the State's failure to implement correctly Community law.[144] Thus, for example, a Member State might be obliged to pay damages to a homosexual man who has been dismissed because of his sexuality, where domestic rules failed to transpose correctly the Employment Framework Directive so as to make this unlawful.

There is, finally, a third distinction as regards the way in which rights are conceptualised, in particular when applied to the concept of non-discrimination. Essentially this relates to whether the right is seen as (i) a method of delivering particular economic goals, for instance to facilitate market access, or (ii) as a method of delivering particular social policies, for instance social inclusion, or (iii) as a 'human right', where the right is regarded as an end in itself, not simply a means to an end.

[140] The obligation to transpose the Directives into domestic law remains an obligation of the state alone.

[141] Council Directive 2000/43/EC, Art. 15; Directive 2000/78/EC, Art. 17; Directive 2004/113/EC, Art. 14.

[142] Council Directive 2000/43/EC, Art. 14(b); Directive 2000/78/EC, Art. 16(b); Directive 2004/113/EC, Art. 13(b).

[143] Council Directive 2000/43/EC, Art. 13; Directive 2004/113/EC, Art. 12.

[144] Joined Cases C-6 9/90 *Francovich and Bonifaci* v. *Italy* [1991] ECR I-5357.

In the European Community, rights to equality (in respect of pay between men and women) and non-discrimination (in respect of nationality) were originally conceived as legal instruments to ensure the establishment and proper functioning of the common market.[145] Subsequent political and legislative developments reflect broader social considerations, leading to the recognition of new rights in a range of areas, including on gender equality as part of a strategy of building a social dimension to Community policy,[146] especially during the 1970s.[147] Simultaneously, existing rights, such as the right to equal pay, were being remodelled on the basis of both economic *and* social considerations.[148] More widely still, this reflects the evolution of the Community from an economic one to a markedly more encompassing organisation. Within this expanded scope for a broader social discourse, the right to equal treatment was gradually emancipated from the need to be formally legitimated by economic justifications. A parallel development has taken place with other rights – and measures setting out such rights – in the broader social policy area.[149] So, for example, in the context of the Lisbon Strategy, it is important not to lose track of the social value of equality and to guard against an over reliance on the economic benefits that anti-discrimination

---

[145] See especially Arts. 7, 48(2) and 119 EEC (now 12, 39(2) and 141 EC). Implicitly the principle of non-discrimination also appears in Arts. 30, 52 and 59 EEC (now 28, 43 and 49 EC). Cf. G. More, 'The Principle of Equal Treatment: From Market Unifier to Fundamental Right?, in P. Craig and G. de Búrca (eds.), *The Evolution of EU Law* (Oxford University Press, 1999), pp. 517–53, at pp. 521–35; G. de Búrca, 'The Role of Equality in European Community Law', in A. Dashwood and S. O'Leary (eds.), *The Principle of Equal Treatment in EC Law* (Sweet & Maxwell, 1997), pp. 13–34.

[146] The adoption of Council Directive 76/207/EEC, on the implementation of the principle of equal treatment for men and women as regards access to employment, vocational training and promotion, and working conditions [1976] OJ L39/40, is an example. Cf. Council Resolution of 21 January 1974 concerning a Social Action Programme [1974] OJ C13/1.

[147] J. Kenner, *EU Employment Law. From Rome to Amsterdam and Beyond* (Hart Publishing, 2003), pp. 23–69; R. Nielsen and E. Szyszczak, *The Social Dimension of the European Union* (3rd edn., Handelshøjskolens Forlag, 1997), pp. 25–8.

[148] See Case 43/75 *Defrenne* v. *Sabena (No. 2)* [1976] ECR 455.

[149] Compare, for instance, the Preambles to the Acquired Rights Directive and the Collective Redundancies Directive in their original and amended versions twenty or so years later. See Council Directive 77/187/EEC, on the approximation of the laws of the Member States relating to the safeguarding of employees' rights in the event of transfers of undertakings, businesses or parts of undertakings or businesses [1977] OJ L61/26 and cf. Council Directive 98/50/EC [1998] OJ L201/88; and Council Directive 75/129/EEC, on the approximation of the laws of the Member States relating to collective redundancies [1975] OJ L48/29 and cf. Council Directive 98/59/EC [1998] OJ L225/16.

policies entail.[150] It would be unfortunate if the development of equality in this context were made conditional upon it having an economic value.[151]

However, a caveat is needed. Despite the seeming success in recognising and protecting social rights, in particular equality, in Community law, this is a highly contested political terrain. The drafting of the Constitutional Treaty, including the drafting of the values and objectives of the Union, was marked by problems over the inclusion of rights seen as underpinning the European social model.[152] This appears to reflect the continuing difficulties in developing a rights culture in the Union, especially where they intersect with social policy. In turn, this perpetuates the perception that human rights, and social issues more generally, are still not given sufficient importance.[153] Arguably, the rejection of the Constitutional Treaty in France and the Netherlands was, partly, an outcome of this perception.[154] Article 13 EC appears to be part of a yet further development in Community law towards recognising the right to equality and non-discrimination as an 'autonomous principle', that is a human right that is of value independently of the economic or social benefits that it may bring.[155] However, this development is also somewhat hesitant and halting: the limitation of the Employment Framework Directive to employment and occupation, that is, the restriction of the material scope within which the right to non-discrimination can be exercised, shows that the right to equal treatment is still not completely autonomous.[156]

---

[150] Cf. C. McCrudden, 'Thinking About the Discrimination Directives', *European Anti-Discrimination Law Review*, Issue 1 (2005) pp. 17–21, at p. 19.

[151] The Social Policy Agenda and other key policy documents accompanying the Lisbon strategy regard equality as an objective in itself and not only as a means to promote the other particular objectives. See COM(2000) 379 final, p. 14.

[152] A notable flaw regards the considerable delay in establishing a Working Group (XI) to deal with social issues, a fact which had a negative impact on the consideration that was given to these issues in the provisions setting out the values and objectives of the Union.

[153] Cf. K. van der Pijl, 'Lockean Europe?' (2006) 37 *New Left Review*, p. 9; R. Blackburn, 'Capital and Social Europe' (2005) 34 *New Left Review*, p. 87.

[154] Blackburn, ibid., at pp. 87–88; P. Hainsworth, 'France Says No: The 29 May 2005 Referendum on the European Constitution' (2006) 59 *Parliamentary Affairs* 98.

[155] More, 'The Principle of Equal Treatment: From Market Unifier to Fundamental Right?', at p. 547–8. For interesting explorations of the relationship between social and fundamental rights in the EU context, see S. Fredman, 'Transformation or Dilution: Fundamental Rights in the EU Social Space', (2006) 12 *European Law Journal*, p. 41; S. Prechal, 'Equality of Treatment, Non-Discrimination and Social Policy: Achievements in Three Themes', (2004) 41 *Common Market Law Review*, p. 533.

[156] L. Waddington, *The Expanding Role of the Equality Principle in European Union Law* (EUI, 2003), p. 29.

Rather, its protection in Community legislation is still largely determined by the existence of a social and economic nexus. In the EC context, this issue is, in part, also related to the complex question of how far the jurisdiction of the EU extends to non-economic issues; the extension of the scope of the Race Directive is not uncontroversial from this perspective.

Finally, as we have touched on previously, although human rights include equality and non-discrimination, that is not all that human rights provisions protect, and there may be tensions between advancing equality and protecting other rights. The human rights challenge to anti-discrimination law, simply put, raises the question whether the restrictions on freedom that anti-discrimination law represents are unjustified in human rights terms. This is important in setting the intellectual context for a much more sustained consideration of the tensions and conflicts between anti-discrimination law and other rights than has hitherto been the case in the European context, except in the context of debates about affirmative action. We are increasingly likely to see, in both European theoretical literature and in litigation, challenges to anti-discrimination law from the perspective of freedom of association, privacy, freedom of speech, the right to property, and freedom of religion, as well as freedom of contract. The debate about the role that human rights should play in the context of equality, therefore, is an important (and potentially problematic) one for those concerned with equality. Complex legal questions will arise. For example, the freedoms that may come into conflict with equality are all likely to be subject to a justification defence, including protecting 'the rights and freedoms of others'. What weight should be given, in this context, to the fact that equal treatment has been affirmed as a fundamental value of the EU in the *Mangold* case?

Conclusion

This chapter has sought to provide an analysis of the evolving human rights and equality contexts within which the Article 13 Directives were developed and will continue to operate. The basic groundwork for recognising such rights pre-existed Article 13 in international, regional and domestic provisions, the jurisprudence of the ECtHR, and even in some respects within the Community legal order itself through the case law of the Court. But protection in the Member States of the principle of equal treatment for the grounds under Article 13 prior to the Directives was both limited and dissonant. Furthermore, the protection offered by the Court of Justice on human rights in general was often very limited. In the absence of express Community provisions victims of human rights violations, especially of discrimination, have been left without appropriate protection.

A part of the developing story of equality in Community law will lie with the development of human rights in the Community. We should not neglect, therefore, the continuing difficulties of achieving the goal of protecting and promoting fundamental rights across the Union. Tensions between various fundamental rights and between rights and other Community objectives have not disappeared, despite political rhetoric, judicial efforts and legal safeguards. Moreover, the rejection of the Constitutional Treaty by France and the Netherlands and the subsequent complex set of agreements reached by the European Council in June 2007, leaves many questions open in relation to the future of human rights in the Community order, not least because the result appears to be that the EU Charter of Fundamental Rights continues to lack clear, legally binding effect throughout the European Union. The increasingly high profile sought by the Union with respect to human rights in its external relations policies also raises important and difficult issues, involving questions on how far such external policies fit easily with the current uneasy status of the Charter. Arguably, both acceding to the ECHR, including Protocol 12, and giving legally binding effect to the Charter are necessary in order to strengthen the protection of human rights, in particular equality, within the Union and to provide the requisite moral authority to the Union in its efforts to strengthen the protection of human rights globally, although the complex interaction between them will need to be resolved.

However, the enactment of the Article 13 Directives marks a significant step towards the development of an autonomous principle of equal treatment in the Community legal order, while their implementation holds the potential to offer significant protection for the persons coming within their scope. It is important not to narrow the equality discourse to only one, predominantly individualistic and economic-centred, meaning, but to acknowledge the diversity of meanings of the concept and provide appropriate means with which various policy goals related to equality can be advanced.[157] One cross-cutting theme that emerges from our analysis is the complexity that arises when a market integration mechanism

---

[157] Ibid. pp. 18–19.

(in this case the EU) attempts to incorporate conceptions of equality that show promise in shaping, regulating and controlling that market. What we see is how the EU project is an experiment in making human rights real in the market context. This is likely to lead to the evolution of the non-discrimination ideal, one that draws on but is not wholly anchored in human rights instruments but is transformed into an instrument that harnesses and, possibly, tames power across a broad range of market operations. In order to achieve this, it will be important to remember that the promotion of equality does not only require legal provisions, but also requires other economic, social and cultural supporting mechanisms.[158] In other words, the enactment and implementation of the equality Directives is a necessary, but in itself insufficient, step towards the combating of discrimination and the promotion of equality in the richer sense that the Community is currently edging towards.

[158] McCrudden, 'Thinking About the Discrimination Directives', p. 19.

4

Demographic, social change and equality

Demographic ageing will force European society to adapt and European people to change their behaviour. The extent to which these societal and behavioural changes can be brought about in a positive way will depend largely on the choice of policies put forward at European, national and local level.

('Towards a Europe for All Ages', 1999)

Introduction

It is stated that the principles of equal treatment and non-discrimination are at the heart of the European Social Model. According to this view, they represent a cornerstone of the fundamental rights and values that underpin today's European Union.[1] But does equality, in its legal and philosophical sense, have meaning without a human context? Can we discuss these concepts without anchoring the discussion within the lives and experiences of real people in a real world?

This chapter will argue that any discussion on the conceptualisation of equality and non-discrimination in the European Union has to be done within a concrete social context. When discussing and constructing the legal concept of 'equality', one cannot ignore the social context, in general, and the demographic context, in particular.

Equality in the European Union today cannot be understood without realising the unique social revolution that Europe is going through: a demographic revolution. Truly, a dramatic change in the last decade has led to unprecedented ageing in the population of Europe and other developed countries. Because of the developments in science and technology over the past one hundred years, such factors as disease, famine and even complications occurring in as natural a process as childbirth no longer sweep most people away before they reach old age. At present, the proportion of older people in the European population is higher than it has

---

[1] See O. Quintin 'Forward' in *Equality and Non-Discrimination in an Enlarged European Union – Green Paper* (European Commission, Employment and Social Affairs, 2004).

been in human history, and the trend is expected to continue well into the twenty-first century. We find ourselves in the midst of an extraordinary revolution, one that has been unheralded and thus easily ignored, but one that will have the most profound effects on the nature of our lives.[2]

Thus, in this chapter, an attempt will be made to sketch a draft of the European Union's demographic revolution and its socioeconomic consequences. The picture that will be revealed will serve as the necessary background to the deeper legal analysis made in the remaining chapters in this book. This chapter will include four parts: the first part will describe the broad European demographic revolution; the second part will detail the causes and social factors that brought about this demographic revolution; the third part will analyse the social consequences of the ageing revolution; and the fourth and final part will try to connect the ageing revolution to law and equality.

Demographic change and the ageing of Europe

As described by Bloom and Canning (2004), until the early eighteenth century, global population size was relatively static and the lives of the vast majority of people were 'nasty, brutish, and short'. Since then, the size and structure of the global population have undergone extraordinary change.[3] Over three decades have been added to life expectancy, with a further gain of close to two more decades projected for this century. World population has increased by an order of magnitude to over six billion, and is projected to reach nine billion by mid-century.[4]

The ageing of human society has caused the difference. In 1950 there were about 200 million persons aged sixty and over in the world, constituting 8.1 per cent of the global population. By 2050 there will be a ninefold increase and the world's elderly population is projected to be 1.8 billion people, about 20 per cent of the total population. Coupled with the projected increase in global population, ageing is a demographic revolution: the older population aged sixty and over, will quadruple by the year 2050.[5]

---

[2] P. Silverman, 'Introduction' in P. Silverman (ed.), *The Elderly as Modern Pioneers* (Indiana University Press, 1987) pp. 1–16.

[3] D. E. Bloom and D. Canning, *Global Demographic Change: Dimensions and Economic Significance* (NBER Working Paper Series No. 10817, 2004) p. 3.

[4] Ibid.

[5] *Global Demographic Change*, ibid.; see also P. Auer and M. Fortuny, *Ageing of the Labour Force in OECD Countries: Economic and Social Consequences* (Geneva: Employment Paper 2002).

There is no doubt today that global ageing will be a major determinant of long run social and economic development in the European Union.[6] As Borsch-Supan maintains, 'The extent of the demographic change is dramatic and will deeply affect future labour, financial and goods markets. The expected strain on public budgets and especially social security has already received prominent attention, but ageing poses many other economic challenges that threaten productivity and growth if they remain unaddressed.'[7]

Europe is, and is projected to remain, the area of the world most affected by ageing.[8] The proportion of older persons above the age of sixty-five will increase from 15.5 per cent in 2000 to 24.3 per cent in 2030.[9] By 2050, one in every three persons in Europe will be sixty years or above. Southern Europe, with a proportion of older persons above the age of sixty of 22 per cent in 1998, is the world region with the oldest population. By 2050, its proportion of older persons will have reached 39 per cent. Finally, in another perspective of the ageing face of Europe, data shows that in 2000, the country with the largest proportion of old people in the world was Italy (with 18.1 per cent of its population over the age of sixty-five), followed by Greece and Sweden (17.3 per cent), Japan (17 per cent), Spain (16.9 per cent) and Belgium (16.8 per cent), and basically the rest of the European countries down the line.[10]

The number of elderly residents is growing in virtually all countries. Developed nations have relatively high proportions of people aged 65 and over, but the most rapid increases in elderly population are in the developing world. Seventy-seven per cent of the world's net gain of elderly individuals from July 1999 to July 2000 – 615,000 people monthly – occurred in developing countries.[11] The ageing of the European Union has many social faces. For example, ageing is not gender neutral. As described by Kinsella and Phillips,[12] women constitute a majority of the older population in almost every country, and their majority increases with age. The primary reason for many more women than men at older ages, is that men have higher death rates than women at all ages. A precise explanation of

---

[6] K. Kinsella and V. A. Velkoff, *An Aging World: 2001* (US Government Printing Office, 2001).
[7] A. Borsch-Supan, *Global Aging: Issue, Answers, More Questions* (University of Michigan Retirement Research Center, 2004).
[8] European Commission, *The Social Situation of the European Union* (2004).
[9] Kinsella and Velkoff (2001), *An Aging World*, p. 9.   [10] Ibid., p. 10.
[11] See K. Kinsella and D. R. Phillips, 'Global Aging: The Challenges of Success' (2005) 60 *Population Bulletin* 1, pp. 3–40, at p. 8.
[12] Ibid., p. 23.

why women live longer than men still eludes scientists because it involves the complex interplay of biological, social and behavioural conditions. However, empirical data from industrialised countries shows no clear pattern of change and the reality is complex: the gender life expectancy gap is widening in much of Eastern Europe and the former Soviet Union, while it is narrowing in most other countries.[13]

Finally, Europe is not just ageing and becoming more feminine; just as described in 'Towards a Europe for All Ages',[14] the European population will soon stop growing in size.

> It will then gradually start decreasing, though at different times and speeds in different countries and regions. In almost one quarter of European regions the population will already have stopped growing before the end of the century. Soon our societies will have a much larger proportion of older persons and a smaller working age population. The youngest generation, the 0–14 age group, representing 17.6% of the population in 1995, will fall to 15.7% in 2015, a decline of almost 5 millions. The generation 15–29, from which entrants into the labour market are drawn, will decrease even more rapidly (-16%, equivalent to a decline of 13 million).[15]

The causes of demographic change

Demographic change is a complex human phenomenon. While sometimes, within a limited sociogeographic and historic context, it might be easily explained, in most cases it involves a complex web of socioeconomic elements. Thus, current European demographic change is not easily understood. Without pretending to fully explain it, a few of the dominant factors will be detailed as follows.

Increase in life expectancy

Bloom and Canning (2004) describe how improvements in health and the related rise in life expectancy are among the most remarkable demographic changes of the past century.[16] The growing multidisciplinary

---

[13] Ibid., p. 24.

[14] Commission of European Communities, *Towards a Europe for All Ages: – Promoting Prosperity and Intergenerational Solidarity* (Brussels, 1999), p. 7.

[15] Ibid.

[16] *Bloom and Canning*, (2004), *Global Demographic Change*, p. 4. See also R. D. Lee, 'The Demographic Transition: Three Centuries of Fundamental Change', *Journal of Economic Perspectives, 17* (2003), pp. 167–90.

research consensus attributes the gain in human longevity since the 1800s to the interplay of advancements in medicine and sanitation against a backdrop of new modes of familial, social, economic and political organisation (Kinsella and Phillips, 2005, at p. 12). The global reality, for the world as a whole, is that life expectancy more than doubled from around thirty years in 1900 to sixty-five years by 2000.[17] Life expectancy is projected to continue to rise both for men and women.[18]

Decrease in fertility rates

Fertility is another major determinant of a nation's population and the primary driver of the Europe Union's demographic transition.[19] As noted by Sleebos,[20] traditionally, concerns about fertility have focused on 'excess' fertility, mainly in developing countries, and on its implications for natural and environmental resources. However, European Union Members States are confronting a very different problem today: fertility has declined for several decades to levels that are, in most of them, well below those needed to secure generation replacement. This decline started in the late nineteenth century, was widespread throughout Western Europe and seems to have been fairly independent of economic factors.[21]

As a consequence of the declines observed in most European countries, fertility rates have reached levels that are well below those needed to secure generational replacement (roughly 2.1 children per woman). Current levels of fertility — such as those recorded in several countries in Southern and Continental Europe — imply, for given mortality and migration rates, that the population of these countries may shrink to about a third of today's level in as little as one century (see **Figure 1** below).[22]

---

[17] See Table 2, and see also Bloom and Canning, *Global Demographic Change*, p. 3.

[18] Kinsella and Phillips (2005) *Global Aging*, pp. 12 and 13.

[19] Kinsella and Phillips (2005) *Global Aging*, p. 10.

[20] See J. E. Sleebos, *Low Fertility Rates in OECD Countres: Facts and Policy Responses* (OECD Social, Employment and Migration Working Papers, 2003).

[21] Bloom and Canning (2004) *Global Demographic Change*, p. 5.

[22] Figure 1 Trends in total fertility rates in selected OECD countries, 1970–2000, J. Sleebos, 'Low Fertility Rates in OECD Countries: Facts and Policy Responses' (OECD Social, Employment and Migration Working Papers No. 15, DELSA/ELSA/WD/SEM, 2003), p. 15, copyright ECD 2005. For detailed sources see OECD, *Society at a Glance. Social Indicators 2002, Edition* (Paris, 2002): available at www.oecd.org/els/social/indicators.

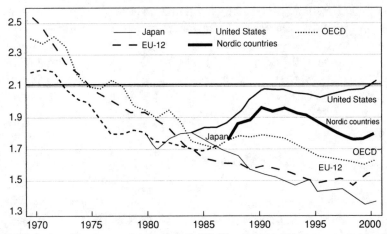

Note: The horizontal line corresponds to the level of total fertility rates needed to assure a constant population.
Source: OECD (2002), *Society at a Glance. Social Indicators 2002*, Paris (www.oecd.org/els/social indicators)

Figure 1. Trends in total fertility rates in selected OECD countries, 1970–2000, Sleebos, J., *Low Fertility Rates in OECD Countries: Facts and Policy Responses*, OECD Social, Employment and Migration Working Papers No. 15, DELSA/ELSA/WD/SEM (2003) 15, © OECD 2005.

Globalisation

The concept of globalisation is as contested as it is popular; as it still bears the birthmarks of its multidisciplinary paternity, it is virtually impossible, amongst the myriad accounts and interpretations, for the would-be synthesiser to discern a simple meaning or referent for the term.[23] The term 'globalisation' is undoubtedly complex, unclear, inexact and ambiguous. The only generally accepted statement that can be made about it, is that there is no consensus as to its exact meaning, content or extent. Nonetheless, though there is no agreement on the meaning of the concept, it is definitely possible to discern a number of trends or processes whose common denominator is related to the decreasing importance of the local and the national in determining the behaviour of the individual.

At the highest level of generalisation, there is something close to a consensus that the concept 'refers both to the compression of the world and the intensification of consciousness of the world as a whole'.[24] It is possible to

[23] I. Clark, *Globalization and International Relations Theory* (Oxford University Press, 1999).
[24] R. Robertson, *Globalization: Social Theory and Global Culture* (Sage, 1992).

derive many varied definitions from this generalised interpretation. One among many is that globalisation is:

> the process of increasing inter-connectedness between societies such that events in one part of the world more and more have effect on people and societies far away. A globalized world is one in which political, economic, cultural and social events become more and more interconnected. In each case, the world seems to be 'shrinking', and people are increasingly aware of this.[25]

In his book *Future Shock*, Alvin Toffler underlines the dramatic significance of technological change to globalisation:

> Never in history has distance meant less. Never have man's relationships with place been more numerous, fragile and temporary . . . Figuratively, we 'use up' places and dispose of them in much the same way that we dispose of Kleenex or beer cans. We are witnessing a historic decline in the significance of place to human life. We are breeding a new race of nomads, and few suspect quite how massive, widespread and significant their migrations are.[26]

Another central trend in this connection is the development of mass communication, and of the technology of transport of data. International journalism, the Internet, telephones, cables, television and satellites have transformed the meaning of the concept 'communication'. They have turned the citizens of the whole world into a single 'audience' which is the target of a great many sources of information. The ability to transfer great quantities of electronic data to remote parts of the world within seconds has brought about a qualitative change in economic, social and political thinking. The development of the Internet, which affords access to information from different lands and cultures, making geographical frontiers almost meaningless or irrelevant, has added another dimension to the process of globalisation.

Globalisation has become a major force in shaping Europe's ageing population. Growing old has itself become relocated within a transnational context, creating new conditions and environments for older people. Within the European Union this has especially been true in the context of the enlargement process. As argued by Estes, Biggs and Phillipson, it has produced 'a distinctive stage in the social history of ageing, with growing tension between nation state-based solutions (and anxieties)

---

[25] J. Baylis and S. Smith (eds.), *The Globalization of world politics* (Oxford University Press, 1997), p. 7.

[26] A. Toffler. *Future Shock* (The Bodley Head, 1970), p. 69.

about growing old and those formulated by global actors and institutions'.[27]

Migration

Compared to life expectancy, fertility rates and globalisation, migration is probably the most complex social phenomenon that has changed its face in the globalised world. Divergence in the population profile of developed and developing countries, with shrinking population in the former and expanding population in several of the latter, and with regions that traditionally had been a source of migration, have all made Europe one of the main regions for receiving the migrants of the world.[28]

The demographer Douglas Massey (2000) argues that, barring some calamity or a radical shift in family planning trends, 'migration will play a greater role than reproduction in determining the strength and tenor of our societies'.[29] This is especially true in Europe, where for many countries immigration (both legal and illegal) has become the main driver of population growth.

In reality the foreign presence in the total population varies widely across European countries. In 2000 it was very large in Luxembourg (37.3 per cent) and in Switzerland (19.3 per cent). In the other traditional immigration countries, the foreign presence ranged from 4 per cent in the UK to 9.3 per cent in Austria. The proportion was close to 9 per cent in Germany and 8.5 per cent in Belgium, as against 5.6 per cent in France and 4.2 per cent in the Netherlands.[30]

To sum up, the long-period data (1960–2000, by region and by country) and cross-sectional (2000, by country) data shows that the migration component makes the larger contribution to total population growth in many OECD countries. This is particularly the case in countries where fertility levels are low (Austria, Germany, Greece, Italy and Spain). These

[27] C. L. Estes, S. Biggs and C. Phillipson, *Social Theory, Social Policy and Ageing* (Open University Press, 2003), p. 102.
[28] See K. F. Zimmermann, *European Labour Mobility: Challenges and Potentials* (Bonn: Institute for the Study of Labor, 2004). It should be noted that international migration statistics are patchy, of varying degrees of reliability and subject to problems of comparability. These difficulties stem largely from the diversity of migration systems and legislation on nationality and naturalisation, which reflect the individual history and circumstances of each country.
[29] D. Massey, 'To study migration today, look to a parallel era'. *The Chronicle of Higher Education* (18 August 2000), p. B4–B5.
[30] See *Trends in International Migration. Annual Report* (OECD, 2003), p. 39.

countries would have seen their total population fall, were it not for an inflow of new immigrants.[31] Looking into the future, especially in light of the 2004 enlargement of the European Union, these migratory trends seem to continue to be on the rise.[32]

Migration is a very complex phenomenon. Within the general migration trends described above, there are some more specific and unique aspects which should be elaborated upon.

Growth in employment-related migration

One of the most significant trends in migration into the European Union in recent years has been the rise in permanent, but especially temporary, migration for employment purposes. Employment-related migration includes both unskilled labour migration, e.g., the substantial flows of southern Europeans, many from rural backgrounds, to the thriving industrial and commercial cities of northern Europe (Salt, 1994),[33] as well as skilled labour migration among the Continent's major financial and commercial cities (Salt, 1993).[34]

In 2000, this trend continued and was accentuated despite the economic slowdown in the second half of the year. It is the result of a combination of several factors involving the intensity of the expansion phase that marked the latter half of the 1990s and the dawn of the twenty-first century, as well as the development of the information technology sector, for which in some countries there is a shortage of skilled and highly skilled workers.

These trends are not uniform, however, and they reflect the effects of migration policies, active or not, implemented by different countries, and sociopolitical developments such as the enlargement of the EU. Some countries explicitly give priority to foreign workers (the UK and Switzerland), while others, such as Canada, seek a more stable distribution amongst categories. A number of other OECD countries, that apply more restrictive policies, give implicit priority to non-selective migration arising from family reunification or requests for asylum (France and the Nordic countries).[35]

A unique labour migration concern arose with the most recent enlargement of the EU in 2004. Enlargement poses concerns of negative

---

[31] Ibid.   [32] See *Trends in International Migration. Annual Report* (OECD, 2003).

[33] J. Salt, *Europe's International Migrants: Data Sources, Patterns and Trends* (Her Majesty's Stationery Office, 1994).

[34] J. Salt, *Migration and Population Change in Europe*. Research Paper 19, UN Institute for Disarmament Research (United Nations Organisation, 1993).

[35] *Trends in International Migration. Annual Report* (OECD, 2003), p. 21.

short-term effects on EU labour markets due to increased labour migration. These concerns are based on income differentials, high unemployment, propensity to migrate and geographical proximity of new Member States. In the short-run, the EU estimates that 70,000 to 150,000 workers will migrate to the EU yearly from the former Central and Eastern European candidate countries alone. According to EU estimates, the long-run migration potential (approximately ten years post-accession) from these countries is calculated at around one per cent of the present EU population. The effects of labour migration will be more pronounced in certain EU Member States, particularly those in closest proximity to the new Member States (Foreign Labor Trends, 2003).[36]

Continued intensification of refugee and asylum-seeker flows

Another important aspect of migration is the population of refugees and asylum seekers. In different EU countries, refugees and asylum seekers do not arrive in quite the same way. Refugees generally arrive within the framework of government programmes negotiated either with specialised international organisations or with countries that are sheltering the refugees. Asylum seekers, on the other hand, most often apply for refugee status (which they do not necessarily obtain) upon arrival at the border, or after they are already inside the potential host country. In addition, EU countries authorise certain persons, for humanitarian reasons, to remain either temporarily or on a more permanent basis.[37]

From the mid-1980s until the early 1990s, applications for asylum rose appreciably, sometimes spectacularly (as in Austria, Germany, the Netherlands, Norway, Sweden, the UK and the US). Faced with an increasing number of asylum seekers, OECD countries reacted by speeding up the processing of applications, and by introducing restrictive measures. Most OECD countries also decided to restrict asylum applications, except for special cases, to persons from countries that have not signed the United Nations Conventions on Refugees and on Human Rights, provided they have not previously passed through a country that is a signatory. In spite of these measures, and after declining generally in the early 1990s, flows of new asylum seekers began rising again in most EU countries from 1997 onwards, due to the effect of numerous regional conflicts.[38]

---

[36] *Foreign Labor Trends: European Union* (US Department of Labor, 2003), pp. 7–8.
[37] *Trends in International Migration. Annual Report* (OECD, 2003), p. 25.
[38] ECRE – Asylum Applications in 35 Industrialised Countries, 1982–2002; and ECRE – Asylum in the European Union: 2002–2003, available at: www.ecre.org.

Migration: a multi-faceted panorama

Along with the traditional refugees and asylum seekers and employment-related migration, some more specific forms of demographic mobility are developing in the shadow of the ageing revolution and EU enlargement. One such interesting development is the phenomenon of retired persons electing to live abroad or migrate to places with warmer climate ('sun belt migration') or closer to other family members.[39] For example, a growing awareness has been developed in recent years to the phenomenon of older retired migrants in the enlarged European Union. Retired British, German and Nordic workers are increasingly engaged in international retirement migration to southern European countries such as Spain, Italy or Greece, creating expatriate communities on places like the Costa Blanca.[40]

This population movement raises considerable theoretical questions regarding the social powers and life-course perspectives that 'push' and 'pull' people from their original place of residence; these are beyond the scope of this chapter but clearly create a whole set of new social and legal challenges.[41]

Another interesting phenomenon of ageing with an international dimension is 'distant caring' or 'long distance caregiving'.[42] This is not simply the case of adult children caring for their ageing parents from a distant city or village. Today, this term, in an international context also refers to adult children who have migrated to European countries, and are obliged to bear the brunt of informal care for ageing parents who remained in the land of their birth. Thus, for example, young Indians who migrated to England are liable to find themselves responsible for their elderly parents who remained in India. Such care, though it may seem impossible,

---

[39] See *Trends in International Migration Annual Report* (OECD, 2003), p. 26; See also A. M. Warnes, 'The international dispersal of pensioners from affluent countries' (2001) 7 *International Journal of Population Geography*,' pp. 373–88.

[40] M. A. Cassado-Diaz, U. Lundh and T. Warnes, *European Dimensions of Retirement Older Migrants in Europe: Projects and Sources* (European Science Foundation: Scientific Network on International Migration in Europe, 2003), avaibable at www.shef.ac.uk/sisa/esf/EW_Bibliography.shtml; M. A. Casado-Diaz, C. Kaiser and A. M. Warnes, 'Northern European retired residents in nine southern European areas: characteristics, motivations and adjustment' (2004) 24 *Ageing and Society*, pp. 353–81.

[41] W. H. Walters, 'Place characteristics and later-life migration', *Research on Aging*, 42(2) (2002), pp. 243–77; C. F. Longino, A. T. Perzynski and E. P. Stoller, (2002), 24(1) *Research on Aging*, pp. 29–49.

[42] See *Miles Away: The Metlife Study of Long-Distance Caregiving*, Westport, CT: Metlife Mature Market Institute.

may embrace a variety of activities ranging from sending money by post, intensive telephonic communication, frequent journeys to India, or even the need for the daughter to return in order to care for the old family member.

A different aspect of distant caring is the reunion of families. In these cases, in order to solve the problems created by distant caring the young members of the family who migrated for economic reasons 'bring' their ageing parents to join them. This 'import' of an ageing population, all of whom are dependent on their children for care and the implementation of their rights, also raises many different issues, and creates an elderly segment of the population with many special social problems, in a country where they are, in effect, complete foreigners.[43]

Socioeconomic consequences

Once we move from the demographic arena into the social realm, things become even more complicated. The effects of the demographic revolution described above, for individuals, firms and governments are far reaching and important. Once again, any attempt to describe fully the social consequences of any demographic change, and especially such a dramatic change as European society has been experiencing since the 1970s, is due to fail. Hence, one can only attempt to point to some of the most prominent social issues arising from this social change, keeping in mind that it is only the tip of the iceberg.

Economic consequences

The dominant academic belief, which was supported by a body of empirical research, has tended to support what has come to be known as the population neutralist view: population growth neither systematically impedes nor promotes economic growth.[44] However, in recent years, new evidence and thinking has emerged, that relates to the importance of population age distribution in the determination of macroeconomic performance and international capital flows.[45] Contrary to the neutralist view, the

---

[43] See R. King, A. M. Warnes, A. M. Williams, 'International Retirement Migration in Europe' (1998) 4 International Journal of Population Geography, pp. 91–111.

[44] Bloom and Canning, (2004), p. 16.

[45] A. Borsch-Supan, A. Ludwig and J. Winter, Aging and International Capital Flows (Cambridge, MA: National Bureau of Economic Research, 2001).

emerging evidence indicates that population does matter to economic growth, with age structure playing a central role.[46]

Hence, as summarised by Borsch-Supan and mentioned above, today's common view is that 'Global aging will be a major determinant of long run economic development in industrial and developing countries. The extent of the demographic changes is dramatic and will deeply affect future labor, financial and goods markets. The expected strain on public budgets and especially social security has already received prominent attention, but the aging poses many other economic challenges that threaten productivity and growth if they remain unaddressed.'[47]

A full analysis of the economic consequences of demographic change is beyond the scope of the chapter thus, only a few examples and directions will be presented. One example is provided by Roseveare et al. (1996) who studied the impact of age-related public expenditures on overall government budget positions and on national savings for twenty countries. Using demographic projections, models were constructed for the evolution of public pension expenditures and contributions, on the assumption that present policies continue. The quantitative analysis suggests that, if no further measures were taken, ageing would have a major impact on government budgets and on national savings in most of the countries considered.[48] For example, OECD projections suggest that the OECD population of working age, following increases of 76 per cent in the past fifty years, will increase by only 4 per cent in the next fifty years. Because of demographic changes, growth of potential gross domestic product (GDP) is projected to decline in Europe, from 2.3 per cent today to 0.5 per cent by 2050.[49]

Because of the greater decline for the population of working age than for total population, income per capita will also decline, relative to what it would otherwise have been. The growth rates of per capita income is also projected to decline from 1.7 per cent today to 1.1 per cent by 2050

[46] G. Carone, D. Costello, N. Diez Guardia, G. Mourre, B. Przywara, A. Salomäki *The economic impact of ageing populations in the EU25 Member States* (European Commission, 2005).

[47] A. Borsch-Supan, *Global Aging: Issue, Answers, More Questions* (University of Michigan Retirement Research Center, 2004).

[48] D. Roseveare, *et al.*, *Ageing populations, pension systems and government budgets: simulations for 20 OECD countries* Economics Department Working Paper No. 168 (OECD, 1996).

[49] See Sleebos, 'Low Fertility Rates in OECD Countries'.

in European countries; and from 1.7 per cent to 1.2 per cent in the US.[50] However, this effect is smaller relative to the reduction in the growth of real GDP.

A different economic concern is raised by the economic accounts of old age migration. Old age migration involves substantial income transfers, producing economic 'winners' and 'losers'.[51] Rising population numbers in retirement communities translate into housing investment, consumer spending and capitation grants. The common estimate is that the scale of income transfers into favoured retirement regions in Europe is likely to be substantial, and has already been sufficient to alter markedly the geography and economics of some parts of southern Europe.[52]

Dependency ratio

The impact of population ageing and demographic transition is clearly expressed in the old-age dependency ratio. The prospective demographic transition in nine OECD countries foresees a large and rapid increase of the old-age dependency ratio.[53] That is, the ratio of people older than sixty-five to those of working age (15–64). This ratio is purely demographic, i.e. it does not take into account labour force participation or benefit dependency.

The rise of dependency ratio does not, in all cases, mean that the old population as a whole, is dependent on transfer payments (pensions) because some are still economically active. However, given the trend towards earlier retirement and the arrival of the baby boom generation at retirement age, old-age dependency is increasing and this trend will continue. The fact that less and less active people have to support more and more inactive people is an issue of major concern especially for the financing of retirement systems.[54]

---

[50] However, despite this decline, per capita GDP in European countries is still projected to double from current levels. See D. Turner, G. Giorno, A. De Serres, A. Vourc'h and P. Richardson, *The Macroeconomic implications of ageing in a global context*, Economics department Working Paper No. 63, (OECD, 1998).

[51] R. King, A. M. Warnes and A. M. Williams, 'International retirement migration in Europe', (1998) 4 *International Journal of Population Geography*, pp. 91–111.

[52] A. M. Williams, R. King and A. M. Warnes, 'A place in the sun: international retirement migration from Northern to Southern Europe', (1997) 4 *European Urban and Regional Studies*, pp. 115–34.

[53] P. Auer, and M. Fortuny, *Ageing of the Labour Force in OECD Countries: Economic and Social Consequences* (ILO – Employment Sector International Labour Office Geneva, 2000), p. 9.

[54] Ibid.

Poverty, pensions and social security in old age

Undoubtedly, the implications of ageing on the pension system is at the heart of current concern in many European countries about future population trends. Beyond the arguments on the relative merits of pay-as-you-go and funded pensions systems, which is not to be discussed here, the pay-as-you-go system is viewed as a fundamental element of intergenerational solidarity and social cohesion.[55]

Under current institutional arrangements, whereby public pensions are financed out of the contributions paid by today's workers, fewer workers supporting a greater number of older retirees (in terms of pensions, caring and health expenditures) will put greater pressures on governments' budgets. As the extra costs of this higher public spending will largely exceed the savings in educational expenditure, higher public deficits and debt will follow. For a 'stylised' country, representative of the OECD average conditions – i.e. a country with a primary government budget surplus of 2.5 per cent of GDP and a public debt of 55 per cent of GDP – the demographic impact of population ageing may increase the governmental primary deficit by 6 per cent of GDP, and double its public debt over the next fifty years.[56]

In the absence of major reforms or sometimes dramatic increases in contribution rates to the European public pension systems, a substantial financing problem will emerge as the number of workers per pensioner falls. If policies remain unchanged, the direct effect of public pension commitments (abstracting from interest payments on accumulated debt) would increase government deficits.[57]

The debate on the public pension system is crucial from an equality and social security point of view. This is so due to the fact that the aged are more susceptible to poverty. As concluded by Tsakloglou:[58] 'On the side of similarities, the results show that, on average, in all EU countries the non-elderly appear to be better-off than the elderly. Even though there are some exceptions to this rule, the elderly have lower mean equivalent expenditure and mean equivalent income than their non-elderly

[55] G. P. Tapinos, *Policy Responses to Population Ageing and Population Decline in France* (UN Secretariat, 2000).
[56] T. Dang, P. Antolin, H. Oxley *Fiscal implications of ageing. Projections of age-related spending*, Economics Department, Working Paper No. 284 (OECD, 2001).
[57] See D. Turner, *et al.*, *The macroeconomic implications of ageing in a global context*, Economics Department Working Paper No. 193 (OECD, 1998).
[58] P. Tsakloglou, 'Elderly and non-elderly in the European Union: A comparison of living standards', *Review of Income and Wealth*, Series 42, No. 3 (1996) pp. 271–91.

compatriots, proportionally more of them are located in the lower half of
the distributions of equivalent consumption expenditure and equivalent
income and/or fall below the poverty line.'[59]

Employment, labour market and labour consequences

Demographic change and the ageing process deeply affect future labour
markets. As described by Borsch-Supan,[60] on a macroeconomic level,
labour is becoming relatively scarce in the ageing countries while capital
becomes relatively more abundant. This precipitates changes in the relative price of labour and will lead to higher capital intensity, and might
generate large international flows of labour, capital and goods from the
faster to the slower ageing countries. On a microeconomic level, the age
composition of the labour force will change, which might affect labour
productivity and employment cycles and patterns.[61]

Beyond these very broad changes, some more age- and gender-specific
changes can be traced in the European labour market, for example in the
field of participation rates and retirement age. Over the past decades, most
European countries have experienced a substantial drop in the average
age at which individuals retire from the labour market. As described in
Auer and Fortuny[62] in 1950, the average effective age of retirement for
males was above sixty-five in all OECD countries except in Belgium and
New Zealand. By 1995, that average had dropped to fifty-nine years, with
striking differences emerging between countries. Only in Iceland and
Japan did men continue to work on average well beyond the age of sixty-
five. Austria, Belgium, Finland, France, Luxembourg and the Netherlands
arrived at effective retirement ages below sixty.[63]

Auer and Fortuny continue to describe how in most OECD countries,
labour force participation rates of older workers (above fifty-five) have
declined considerably with the decline being more marked in Europe
and in the US than in Japan. Labour force participation rates of older
people vary according to gender, education and the state of economic
development of the country. The decline in rates of older workers is

---

[59] Ibid., p. 288.   [60] Borsch-Supan, at note 47, p. 1.

[61] G. P. Tapinos, *Policy Responses to Population Ageing and Population Decline in France* (UN
Department of Economic and Social Affairs, 2000). For other dimensions of labour in
older ages, see H. Meenan, in Chapter 9 of this book.

[62] P. Auer and M. Fortuny, *Ageing of the Labour Force in OECD Countries: Economic and
Social Consequences* (ILO, 2000).

[63] See Auer and Fortuny, ibid., p. 14.

associated with the trend towards earlier retirement, influenced by increasing national per capita income. Longer education, shorter working lives and longer retirement periods are all consequences of increased wealth.

Once again, these trends are not only age related but also gender related. For example, unlike men, female participation rates in the labour force have been increasing, even among older women. Participation rates of older women are especially high in Nordic countries. In Sweden, they have increased continuously since the 1950s and Sweden now has the highest participation rates of older women (around 80 per cent for the group 55–59 and over 50 per cent for the group 60–64). This has partially offset the decline in male labour force participation rates.[64]

Costs of health and long term care

As described by Casey et al.,[65] health care costs have risen rapidly as a share of GDP in many countries. Many, if not most, European countries have introduced measures to control costs and reforming healthcare systems is already a major policy concern. Looking forward, spending is expected to increase further as the share of the elderly increases. This reflects the fact that the per capita consumption of healthcare services by the elderly is three to five times higher than for younger groups. This will affect both 'normal' healthcare (hospital and ambulatory care and pharmaceuticals) and care services for the frail elderly. As seen in **Table 1**, for most European countries, the projections indicate an average increase in health and long-term care spending of around 3–3.5 percentage points of GDP over the 2000–2050 period. Once again, there are wide cross-country differences, ranging from almost 5 per cent in the Netherlands to under 2 per cent in the UK.[66]

Because of the wide range of factors at play, the importance of this increase is particularly difficult to judge. Against this background, the crucial issues for long-term care policies concern the appropriate level of supply of long-term care for the elderly, the most cost-effective pattern of care between hospitals, nursing homes and care in the home and the way in which these services are supplied and financed.[67]

---

[64] Auer and Fortuny, ibid., p. 10.
[65] B. Casey, H. Oxley, E. Whitehouse, P. Antoline, R. Duval and W. Leibfritz, *Policies for an Ageing Society: Recent Measures and Areas for Further Reform*, Economic Department, Working Paper No. 23 (OECD, 2003), p. 9.
[66] Ibid., p. 35.   [67] Ibid., p. 27.

Table 1. *Projections of age-related spending, 2000–2050.[1]*
Levels in per cent of GDP; changes in percentage points

	Total age-related spending		Old-age pensions		'Early retirement' programmes		Healthcare and long-term care		Child/family benefits and education	
	level 2000	change 2000–50	level 2000	change 2000–50	level 2000	change 2000–50	level 2000	change 2000–50[2]	level 2000	change 2000–50
	(1)	(2)	(3)	(4)	(5)	(6)	(7)	(8)	(9)	(10)
Australia	16.7	5.6	3.0	1.6	0.9	0.2	6.8	6.2	6.1	−2.3
Austria[2]	[10.4]	[2.3]	9.5	2.2	:	:	[5.1]	[3.1]	:	:
Belgium	22.1	5.2	8.8	3.3	1.1	0.1	6.2	3.0	6.0	−1.3
Canada	17.9	8.7	5.1	5.8	:	:	6.3	4.2	6.4	−1.3
Czech Republic	23.1	6.9	7.8	6.8	1.8	−0.7	7.5	2.0	6.0	−1.2
Denmark[3]	29.3	5.7	6.1	2.7	4.0	0.2	6.6	2.7	6.3	0.0
Finland	19.4	8.5	8.1	4.8	3.1	−0.1	8.1	3.8	:	:
France[4]	[18.0]	[6.4]	12.1	3.9	:	:	[6.9]	[2.5]	:	:
Germany	[17.5]	[8.1]	11.8	5.0	:	:	[5.7]	[3.1]	:	:
Hungary[5]	7.1	1.6	6.0	1.2	1.2	0.3	:	:	:	:
Italy	[19.7]	[1.9]	14.2	−0.3	:	:	[5.5]	[2.1]	:	:
Japan	13.7	3.0	7.9	0.6	:	:	5.8	2.4	:	:
Korea	3.1	8.5	2.1	8.0	0.3	0.0	0.7	0.5	:	:
Netherlands[6]	19.1	9.9	5.2	4.8	1.2	0.4	7.2	4.8	5.4	0.0
New Zealand	18.7	8.4	4.8	5.7	:	:	6.7	4.0	7.2	−1.3

Norway	17.9	13.4	4.9	8.0	2.4	1.6	5.2	3.2	5.5	0.5
Poland[6]	12.2	−2.6	10.8	−2.5	1.4	−0.1	..	..	..	..
Spain	[15.6]	[10.5]	9.4	8.0	..	..	[6.2]	[2.5]	..	..
Sweden	29.0	3.2	9.2	1.6	1.9	−0.4	8.1	3.2	9.8	−1.2
United Kingdom	15.6	0.2	4.3	−0.7	..	..	5.6	1.7	5.7	−0.9
United States	11.2	5.5	4.4	1.8	0.2	0.3	2.6	4.4	3.9	−1.0
Average of countries above[7]	**21.2**	**5.8**	**7.4**	**3.4**	**1.6**	**0.2**	**5.9**	**3.1**	**6.2**	**−0.9**
Portugal[8]	*15.6*	*4.3*	*8.0*	*4.5*	*2.5*	*−0.4*	..	..	..	..

1. Data for healthcare shown in parenthesis are drawn from EPC (2001). They are the result of an EC exercise using a common methodology for all countries. The projections are based on the same macroeconomic assumptions as in OECD (2001) Table 3.1. These health and long-term care projections assume that costs per capita rise in line with productivity wages. They do not allow for technological change or other non-age-related factors.

2. Total pension spending for Austria includes other age-related spending which does not fall within the definitions in Cols. 3–10. This represents 0.9 per cent of GDP in 2000 and rises by 0.1 percentage point in the period to 2050.

3. Total for Denmark includes other age-related spending not classifiable under the other headings. This represents 6.3 per cent of GDP in 2000 and increases by 0.2 percentage points from 2000 to 2050.

4. For France, the latest available year is 2040.

5. Total includes old-age pension spending and 'early retirement' programmes only.

6. 'Early retirement' programmes only include spending on persons 55+.

7. Sum of column averages. OECD average excludes countries where information is not available and Portugal where the data are less comparable than for other countries.

8. Portugal provided an estimate for total age-related spending but did not provide expenditure for all of the spending components.

Source: OECD, Table 2 fn, B. Casey, H. Oxley, E. Whitehouse et al., *Policies for an Ageing Society: Recent Measures and Areas for Further Reform*, Economic Department Working Papers No. 369, ECO / WKP (2003) 23 © OECD 2003, and EPC (2001).

Family and social consequences regarding care

The ageing of European society has[68] also influenced family ties and responsibilities. As Kinsella and Phillips describe,[69] while some social analysts suggest that vertical family bonds – tying together different generations – have weakened over recent decades, this suggestion has been refuted by research findings in many countries. Indeed, greater longevity actually makes bonds among adults more important than in the past and, while direct contact between generations may have lessened, indirect contacts are as strong as ever.[70]

Within this context, a heated debate has emerged in many countries about the so-called 'decline of the family'. Some sociologists argue the family has been stripped down to its bare essentials: just two generations and two functions (childbearing and financial and emotional support for nuclear family members). Other analysts argue that, while families have changed over the last century, population ageing has actually extended families across generations and expanded their support functions over longer periods.[71]

Finally, it should also be mentioned that in various European countries elder-care has adopted an 'international face', as it has become a field of work for foreign workers. The needs of these workers and the needs of the elderly in European countries have given rise to a global trend in this field, where a significant part of elder-care is actually foreign, replacing the traditional family-based elder-care. These changes have a profound effect on the wellbeing and care of older people.[72]

Politics and intergenerational conflict

The EU's ageing revolution potentially entails political tension and unrest. Possible tensions and shifts in political clout of different generations may lead to political conflicts when larger and healthier groups of elderly

---

[68] Ibid., p. 35.   [69] Kinsella and Phillips (2005), p. 27.

[70] V. L. Bengtson *et al.*, 'Families and Intergenerational Relationships in Aging Societies', (2000) 2 *Hallym International Journal of Aging* 1, pp. 3–10.

[71] For an overview of the sociological approaches towards the ageing family see A. Lowenstein, R. Katz, D. Prilutzkey and D. Mehlhausen-Hasson, 'The intergenerational solidarity paradigm', in S. O. Daatland and K. Herlofson, *Ageing, Intergenerational Relations, Care Systems and Quality of Life* (NOVA – Norwegian Social Research, 2001), pp. 11–30.

[72] B. Ben-Zvi, 'The Globalization of Nursing Care', *Haaretz* (9 September 2002), C2; See also S. Vandergeest, A. Mul, and H. Vermeulen, 'Linkages between migration and the care of frail older people: observation from Greece, Ghana and the Netherlands', (2004) 24 *Ageing and Society*, pp. 431–50.

persons at the top of hierarchical organisations (in firms, governments and bureaucracies), resist the progression and career advancement of younger people.[73] From the opposite direction, the argument will be that the elderly obtain an unfair share of resources compared to the generations which follow them.[74]

These political tensions might represent an 'intergenerational conflict' within the European Union. There is a growing debate in the literature to what extent this conflict mirrors true intergenerational inequalities or opens the possibility of the breakdown of the so-called intergenerational contract.[75] However, as asserted by Vincent, 'The key politics of inter-generational equity is about legitimacy. It is about the loyalty and commitment to different social groupings.'[76] As Phillipson[77] says, 'we should not "offload" the responsibilities for an ageing population to particular generations or cohorts'.

Multiculturalism and social integration

Another important dimension of the increase in migration into the EU, over and above the traditional movements, is an inflow of immigrants whose cultural and linguistic links with the host EU country are weaker. These new populations have serious difficulties in integrating into the labour market and into society as a whole. Even though there is still a strong element of self-selection in migration, the percentage of immigrants whose mother tongue is the same as the official language of the host country is small in most EU countries.

When these foreigners age, as they do in the enlarged European Union these days, a whole new social issue arises. Those young people from various countries who migrated to developed states in the 1950s and 1960s are today old people in these countries (e.g. Japanese women who migrated with their husbands to Britain in the post-1973 period). Because of the ageing of former immigrants in the host countries, the elderly population is changing and becoming much more culturally heterogeneous. As a result, European countries have to cope with problems previously

---

[73] See F. Fukuyama, *The great disruption. Human nature and the reconstitution of social order* (Profile Books, 1999), ch. 2. See also WWR, *Generationally-Aware Policy, Reports to the Government, Summary of the 55th report* (The Hague, 2000).

[74] J. A. Vincent, *Politics, Power and Old Age* (Open University Press, 1999).

[75] Ibid., p. 121.   [76] Ibid.

[77] C. Phillipson, 'Intergenerational conflict and the welfare state: American and British perspectives', in A. Walker (ed.), *The New Generational Contract* (UCL Press, 1996), p. 219.

unknown, particularly in relation to multiculturalism, multiethnicism and the need to establish special cultural-sensitive social services for the aged.[78]

What have law and equality got to do with it?

In 'Towards a Europe for All Ages',[79] the Commission of European Communities asserted that 'demographic ageing will force European society to adapt and European people to change their behaviour. The extent to which these societal and behavioural changes can be brought about in a positive way will depend largely on the choice of policies put forward at European, national and local level.'

Law is a central tool of policy. It is through law that the state maintains cohesion between its departments and agencies and 'pursues concrete objectives of political, ethical, utilitarian or some other kind'.[80] It is impossible to understand the social situation of older people without an understanding and consciousness of their constitutional and legal situation. There is an unbreakable, dynamic link between law and the society within which it exists and which it serves.[81]

Therefore, the study, knowledge and investigation of the law can teach us much about the sociological, historical and cultural background of the society it serves. It reflects power relationships between various social groups, the rise and fall of particular groups as a result of social and political processes, and the interests of each group. In the words of Justice Oliver Wendell Holmes, Jr:

> This abstraction called the Law is a 'magic mirror', [wherein] we see reflected, not only our own lives, but the lives of all men that have been![82]

Following on from Holmes' insight, legal philosophers such as Roscoe Pound and the founders of modern sociology such as Durkheim and

---

[78] See M. Izuhara and H. Shibata, 'Migration and old age: Japanese women growing older in British society', *Journal of Comparative Family Studies*, 32(4) (2001), pp. 571–86; and also PRIAE *Policy Response: Equality and non-discrimination in an enlarged European Union – Green Paper*, submitted to the European Commission, August 2004.

[79] Commission of European Communities, *Towards a Europe for All Ages: – Promoting Prosperity and Intergenerational Solidarity* (Brussels, 1999), p. 8.

[80] M. Weber, *Economy and Society* (University of California Press, 1978), pp. 644–5.

[81] V. Vago, *Law and Society* (4th edn., Prentice-Hall, 1994).

[82] O. W. Holmes, 'The Speeches of Oliver Wendell Holmes', in R. Posner, *The Essential Holmes: Selections From the Letters, Speeches, Judicial Opinions, and Other Writings of Oliver Wendell Holmes, Jr* (University of Chicago Press, 1992).

Weber have discussed the social functions of the law. These scholars, each in his own different way, have maintained that it is impossible to define or relate to the law in isolation from its social, cultural and historical context. It cannot be cut off from its social aspects. Thus, according to some views, the law is:

> a system of social choice, one in which government provides for the allocation of resources, the legitimate use of violence, and the structuring of social relationships.[83]

It is clear that the social change described in the previous parts raises many legal questions: Is the right to an old-age pension valid when the pensioner ceases to be a resident of the mother country and migrates to a foreign land? How is the right to health put into practice, and to what extent does health insurance in the country of emigration cover the cost of health in the host country?[84] Is the migrating pensioner entitled to vote in the country of which he is a citizen when he is living abroad?[85] What is the citizenship status of various groups of retired migrants throughout the European Union with regard to various social entitlements?[86] To what extent do current European social security laws include or exclude migrants?[87]

The answers law gives to these questions and its interaction with real life directly affects social realities. This has been proven again and again. For example, research in the field of retired European migrants demonstrates

---

[83] D. Black, *The Behavior of Law* (Academic Press, 1976).

[84] See E. Mossialos and W. Palm 'The European Court of Justice and the Free Movement of Patients in the European Union', (2003) 56 *International Social Security Review*, pp. 3–29.

[85] The most developed network of agreements among national social security agencies to make payments to their citizens abroad is among the Member States of the Council of Europe. The European Convention on Social Security was opened to signature in 1972 and accompanied by a Supplementary Agreement on the application of its provisions. The key Regulation 1408/71 comprises over 100 articles on Social Security for Migrant Workers, which have been elaborated by hundreds of decisions at the European Court of Justice and benefited millions of expatriate workers and pensioners. See E. Eichenhofer 'How to Simplify the Coordination of Social Security', *European Journal of Social Security*, 2 (2000), pp. 231–40. See also European Convention on Social Security, ETS No. 078; available at: http://conventions.coe.int/treaty/en/Treaties/Html/078.htm; Supplementary Agreement for the Application of the European Convention on Social Security, ETS No. 078A, available at: http://conventions.coe.int/treaty/en/Reports/Html/078A.htm. Since 1978, the US has established bilateral Social Security ('totalization') agreements that co-ordinate the US old age, survivors and disability (OASDI) benefits with those of other countries. See www.ssa.gov/international/totalization_agreements.html.

[86] See L. Ackers and P. Dwyer, 'Fixed laws, fluid lives: the citizenship status of post-retirement migrants in the European Union', (2004) 24 *Ageing and Society*, pp. 451–75.

[87] See G. Vonk, 'Migration, social security and the law: some European dilemmas', (2001) 3 *European Journal of Social Security*, pp. 315–32.

how the legal construction of 'residency' status affects social decisions regarding migration. Moreover, many returning retirees decide to return to reside permanently in their country of origin if they believe such a move will secure for them some advantage in public healthcare provision.[88]

Indeed, law has responded to demographic change. The ageing revolution has developed new spheres of knowledge, such as 'elder law'. On the national level, since the 1980s, the field of elder law has gained growing recognition.[89] On the international level, in recent years, there are growing calls for the establishment of specific public-international tools to handle the needs of older people around the globe.[90] The essence of these developments is to try and connect law to the changing realities and demographics.

Conclusion

Demographic realities are substantially determined by economic and social circumstances as well as sociolegal institutions. But they also influence those circumstances and institutions through a variety of potential channels.[91] Moreover, social change or demographic ageing can no longer be viewed as a 'national' problem or issue. Hence, law, in general, and 'equality', in specific, are not 'neutral' to demographic change in the European Union: they interact with each other in complex and diverse ways. Law and the concept of equality are not blind to social changes. They are both an active participant as well as a passive mirror and observant.

The literature has already revealed that older persons have been directly affected by the way international organisations have legally constructed and managed state socioeconomic policies.[92] For example, the 1994 Report of the World Bank, *Averting the Old Age Crisis*, has been highly influential in reducing state based pay-as-you-go old-age pension schemes

---

[88] P. Dwyer, 'Retired EU migrants, healthcare right and European social citizenship', (2001) 23 *Journal of Social Welfare and Family Law*, pp. 311–27.

[89] L. A. Frolik, 'The Developing Field of Elder Law: A Historical Perspective', (1993) 1 '*The Elder Law Journal*, pp. 1–18; L. A. Frolik, 'The Developing Field of Elder Law Redux: Ten Years After', *Elder Law Journal*, 10 (2002), pp. 1–14.

[90] I. Doron, 'From national to international elder law', *International Journal of Ageing, Law and Policy*, 1 (2005), pp. 45–72; D. Rodriguez-Pinzon and C. Martin, 'The international human rights status of elderly persons', *American University International Law Review*, 18 (2003), pp. 915–1007.

[91] Bloom and Canning *Global Demographic Change*.

[92] C. L. Estes, S. Biggs and C. Phillipson, *Social Theory, Social Policy and Ageing: A Critical Introduction* (Open University Press, 2003).

to a minimal role of basic pension provision, while promoting a second pension pillar around private, non-redistributive, defined contribution pension plans.[93]

Thus, it seems that in light of the demographic and social change described in this chapter, the following conclusions can be drawn:

1. Any legal discussion on equality should be contextualised within a specific social and demographic context.
2. Today's unique European Union social change, i.e. the ageing revolution, sets a contextual challenge to the legal conceptualisation and implementation of 'equality'.
3. The enlarged EU legal and policy discourse and jurisprudence on equality need to be supported with empirical social and demographic data in order to connect 'equality' to 'reality'.
4. The enlarged European Union social context is complex: on the one hand there are broad and similar 'cross-EU' demographic trends; on the other hand, however, there should be an awareness of local uniqueness and differences in each country and on each social issue.
5. The power of 'equality' and 'non-discrimination' as active social and legal tools within the enlarged EU will eventually rest upon their ability to be sensitive to the diverse and complex interactions between the law and the sociodemographic changes described above.

---

[93] R. Holtzman, *A world perspective on pension reform*, Paper prepared for the joint ILO-OECD Workshop on the Development and Reform of Pension Schemes (OECD, December 1997) World Bank *Averting the Old Age Crisis* (Oxford University Press, 1994).

PART II

5

EU sex equality law post Amsterdam

ANN NUMHAUSER-HENNING

Introduction

This chapter focuses on the development of sex equality law since the Amsterdam Treaty. The most important feature of the Amsterdam Treaty from the perspective of this book was of course the new Article 13, providing a legal basis for Community institutions to take action to combat discrimination not only on the grounds of sex but on a whole range of other grounds and within any area of Community activities. However, Article 2, as amended, Article 3(2) and Article 141 EC (see further below) are also of special interest to sex equality law, following the Amsterdam Treaty. It is also worth mentioning the new Title VIII (ex Title VIa) on employment introducing the 'open method of coordination' for employment guidelines now also extended to other areas of social cohesion. Finally, there is the inclusion of the Maastricht Social Protocol and the new rules on the Social Dialogue in Articles 137–139 EC. All of these new rules play an intrinsic role for the post-Amsterdam developments of sex equality law. To understand the development of sex equality law following the Amsterdam Treaty, its relationship with Article 13 EC and action taken on this basis it is, however, necessary to start with some remarks on the unique features of sex equality regulation in an EC law context and its roots pre-Amsterdam. After introducing these features, I will continue to describe the legal developments in the field of sex equality post Amsterdam only to end up in a discussion on the future implications of discrimination law developments in general for gender equality.

Among the issues addressed in this chapter is the convergence of discrimination concepts between different grounds. Is there a risk of erosion of the concepts of direct and indirect discrimination introducing a wider set of justifications? What are the implications for sex equality law of the new Article 13 Directives drawing upon a wider scope of *acquis communautaire* as regards the concept of indirect discrimination? Will multiple non-discrimination grounds reinforce a formal equality approach as the common denominator or, on the contrary, draw our attention to the obvious need for proactive measures? There is also the issue of non-discrimination rights for workers and its implications for discrimination law in general, working conditions being the constituent of the groups to be protected. Does the more limited coverage of the new Article 13 Directive 2004/113/EC concerning sex equality and the access to and supply of goods and services as compared especially to the Race Directive 2000/43/EC imply a new hierarchy of equalities? And, there is also the issue of enlargement and sex equality.

Something should, however, first be said on *sex as a protected ground* for discrimination, i.e. discussing the concept as such. At first sight it is clearly symmetrical. Men and women are complementary – together they make up the whole world. A ground such as disability on the other hand is clearly asymmetrical. This is a reason why the concept of 'formal equality', paradoxically,[1] is so strong within sex equality law. Favourable treatment of one sex is always to the detriment of the other.[2] Here, too, developments post Amsterdam prove to interact in a complex way with sex equality law. Already before the adoption of the first Article 13 Directives we encountered a broadened gender concept – the European Court of Justice (ECJ) had confirmed transsexuality to be a matter of sex (and sexual orientation not to be).[3] Moreover, differential treatment on the grounds of pregnancy and mothering had, ever since *Dekker*,[4] been seen as intrinsically related to the female sex and thus constituting direct discrimination. These developments contrast not only to the rights of men generally, but also of non-pregnant women as well as fathers and require a line to be drawn in relation to parental rights.[5] Here social, cultural and demographical developments within the different Member States are of

---

[1] Compare what is said below about a proactive approach as a constitutional requirement regarding precisely sex equality law.

[2] Compare, however, for instance Holtmaat, who draws our attention to the fact that the CEDAW Convention is asymmetrical so as to prohibit precisely the discrimination against women, not sex in general: R. Holtmaat, *The possible impact of other instruments to combat discrimination against women (the case of the CEDAW Convention)*, paper to the 18–19 November 2004 Hague Conference 'Progressive Implementation: New Developments in European Union Gender Equality Law'.

[3] Cases C-13/94 *P* v. *S* [1996] ECR I-2143, C-249/96 *Grant* [1998] ECR I-621 and C-117/01 *K.B.* [2004] ECR I-541.

[4] Case C-177/88 *Dekker* [1990] ECR I-3941.

[5] Compare the Council's Resolution on the balanced participation of women and men in family and working life [2000] OJ C218, pp. 0005–0007. See also, for instance, R. Nielsen,

great concern. These issues also relate to the old sameness-difference and essentialist discourses in feminist theory and to the question of multiple/ intersectional discrimination – at the heart of Article 13 EC.[6]

Unique features of sex equality regulation

One important feature is that sex equality law was part of Community Law from the very beginning

In the beginning there was only the principle of equal remuneration contained in Article 119 of the original Treaty of Rome (EEC Treaty). Gradually, as we all well know, the principle of equal treatment between men and women has gained a more general standing within Community law, as described in the introductory chapter by Helen Meenan. This background implies a double aim, still inherent in EU sex equality law, one linked to (internal) market arguments and one linked to the discourse on fundamental rights.[7]

There is a treaty based mainstreaming approach. Since 1996 the Commission's strategic approach to the question of equal opportunities between men and women is 'mainstreaming', i.e., to incorporate it into all community policies and activities,[8] a strategy now reflected in Article 3(2) EC. The mainstreaming approach has more recently spread to the new areas of non-discrimination.[9]

Gender Equality: In European Contract Law, DJF Publishing, Copenhagen (2004) and Case C-177/88 *Elisabeth Johanna Pacifica Dekker* v. *Stitching Vormingscetrum woor Jong Volwassenen (VJV Centrum) Plus*; Case C-179/88 *Handels- og Kontorsfunktionaerernas Forbund Danmark* v. *Dansk Arbejdsgiverforening, CMLR* 29 (1992) pp. 160–9.

[6] In her paper to the 18–19 November 2004 Hague Conference 'Progressive Implementation: New Developments in European Union Gender Equality Law' Dagmar Schiek argues for the use of the concept *gender* equality in the multidimensional equality strategy, see D. Schiek, *Broadening the scope and the norms of EU sex discrimination law – towards multidimensional equality law* (2004).

[7] However, the ECJ has stated that 'the economic aim is secondary to the social aim'; see Cases C-270/97 *Sievers* [2000] ECR I-933 and C-50/96 *Schröder* [2000] ECR I-774, para. 57 of both judgments. Compare also C. McCrudden, *Gender Equality in the European Constitution*, paper to the 18–19 November 2004 Hague Conference on 'Progressive Implementation: New Developments in European Union Gender Equality Law', p. 5.

[8] The European Commission's Communication incorporating equal opportunities for women and men into all Community policies and activities, COM(96) 67 final.

[9] See the 2000/750/EC Council Decision of 27 November 2000 establishing a Community action programme to combat discrimination [2000] OJ L303/23. See also the Commission's Communications regarding the EQUAL Programme, COM (2000) 853 and COM(2003) 840 final, respectively.

The 'constitutional support' for sex equality is significantly more developed than it is for other non-discrimination grounds and the crucial articles have already been referred to above.[10] However, there have been important developments at the constitutional level also since Amsterdam such as, the adoption of the EU Charter of Fundamental Rights in 2000 and its later integration into, and the adoption of a New Constitution for the European Union now supplanted by a proposed Reform Treaty (see further below). Here equality between women and men can be said to be reinforced even more. The significance of these developments for the future of EU sex equality law remains, however, as uncertain as is the future of the New Constitution itself, at the time of writing.

Moreover, the Treaty rules on equality between men and women require a proactive approach. After Amsterdam, Community law can be said to have moved from formal to substantive gender equality.[11] The new Treaty provisions proclaim equality between men and women as a 'task' and an 'aim' of the Community and impose a positive obligation to 'promote' it in all its activities.[12] Articulating the need for eliminating existing inequalities and for promoting equality between men and women, they may in fact be said to represent *a shift in the Community law gender equality approach, from a negative ban on discrimination to a positive and proactive approach to promote substantive gender equality.*[13] The wording of Article 3(2) EC in particular has been said to require a proactive approach in gender equality issues on behalf of the European Union institutions.[14] Furthermore, Article 141 EC (formerly Article 119) now provides the specific legal basis for equality of treatment between men and women not only with regard to remuneration but also in broader contexts. Article 141(4) also provides scope for positive action measures. These characteristics of sex equality law reflect the fact that it is mainly *argued in a (de facto) equality discourse*

---

[10] Article 2 and 3(2) as well as Art. 141 EC. See, for instance S. Koukoulis-Spiliotopoulos, *From Formal to Substantive Gender Equality, The Proposed Amendment of Directive 76/207, Comments and suggestions* (Athens, 2001).

[11] See, for instance, S. Koukoulis-Spiliotopoulos, ibid. See also A-G Christine Stix-Hackl, Opinion in Case C-186/01 *Dory* [2003] ECR I-2479, paras. 102–5.

[12] Articles 2 and 3(2) EC.

[13] Compare the Commission using the concept 'proactive' intervention in relation to the mainstreaming approach and 'reactive' intervention when addressing specific actions in favour of women, COM(2000) 335 final.

[14] 'In all activities the Community shall aim to eliminate inequalities and to promote equality between men and women.' However, compare R. Holtmaat (2004), who claims that there still is no clear and outright positive obligation for Member States to improve the de facto position of women.

in contrast to the other Article 13 grounds that are mainly argued within a non-discrimination framework.[15]

The importance paid to sex discrimination in working life is also reflected in the legal basis for adoption of such instruments. With regard to work-related issues, sex discrimination legislation *follows the qualified majority voting rules of Article 251* whereas Article 13 measures require unanimity. Article 13 is also argued in 'softer terms' to 'combat' discrimination. These differences may reveal precisely the double aim of sex equality law – market *and* fundamental rights interests – whereas Article 13 is more clearly within the area of human rights and social policy.

Key concepts and approaches of EC non-discrimination regulation were developed within sex equality law, such as the concepts of direct and indirect discrimination, the significant rules on the burden of proof in discrimination cases, the scope for positive action, requirements of equality plans as well as accompanying principles on direct effect, sanctions efficiency, etc.

Later action in the area of non-discrimination is – as is stated in the Green Paper on 'Equality and non-discrimination in an enlarged European Union' – built upon the EU's considerable experience of dealing with sex discrimination.[16] However, recent developments show that it also works the other way around – Article 13 developments also influence sex equality law. The current definitions of central concepts such as direct discrimination, indirect discrimination and harassment – introduced to sex equality law by Directive 2002/73 amending the Equal Treatment Directive – were articulated by the first two Article 13 Directives. The Recast Directive 2006/54/EC concerning sex equality law should also be mentioned as well as the adoption of a new Article 13 Directive 2004/113/EC (implementing the principle of equal treatment between men and women in the access to and supply of goods and services). *Due to the variable geometry*[17] *of the discrimination grounds new 'risks' now emerge as regards the application of fundamental concepts,* for instance, with regard to the justifications of direct discrimination (compare Article 6 on age discrimination in Directive 2000/78/EC), the 'test' to be met as regards indirect discrimination (compare inter alia Article 2(b)(ii)

---

[15] Compare, for instance, McCrudden, *Gender Equality,* p. 4. See, however, also S. Prechal, 'Equality of treatment, non-discrimination and social policy: Achievements in three themes', (2004) 41 *CMLR* pp. 533-51 at p. 543.

[16] The European Commission's Green Paper 'Equality and non-discrimination in an enlarged European Union', COM(2004) 379 final, p. 2.

[17] See further above on the concept of sex as a protected ground.

regarding disability in Directive 2000/78/EC), the scope for positive action and other 'fourth generation non-discrimination rights'.[18] Another aspect to be scrutinised in this context is the exemptions provided. A reason to be especially preoccupied with these general developments is the differences as regard the general aim of non-discrimination measures between the different grounds covered by Article 13 EC – to combat discrimination or to promote equality. In my opinion, there are fundamental differences here between, for instance, the regulation on sexual orientation as compared to the one concerning sex.

Post Amsterdam developments within sex equality law

In November 1997, at the Luxembourg Jobs Summit,[19] the European Employment Strategy (EES) was launched. The original guidelines revolved around four 'pillars', namely, employability, entrepreneurship, adaptability and equal opportunities. The last pillar included tackling the gender gap,[20] reconciling work and family life and facilitating the return to work after an absence, all crucial issues for *sex equality in employment*. A reform of the EES in 2003 brought the guidelines closer to the Lisbon strategy.[21] Here, gender equality is but one of ten guidelines related to the three overarching objectives: full employment, improving quality and productivity at work, and strengthening social cohesion and inclusion. Recent newly integrated guidelines are meant to achieve the Lisbon strategy in an even more efficient manner.[22] Of special interest here is Guideline 17, to promote a lifecycle approach to work, and Guideline 18, to ensure inclusive labour markets. Equal opportunities, combating discrimination

---

[18] S. Fredman, *The concept of Equality: A General Framework*, paper for a workshop in Brussels 6–7 November 2000 arranged by the Swedish Institute for Working Life.

[19] Presidency conclusions (Lisbon 23 and 24 March 2000) available at: http://europa.eu.int/ispo/docs/services/docs/2000/jan-march/doc_00_8_en.html.

[20] 'The gender gap' concept includes not only the gender *pay* gap issue but also the notorious gender gaps as regard employment as such, unemployment, the higher levels of education, family life organisation and poverty risks (including pensions).

[21] Council Decision 2003/578/EC of 22 July 2003 and the 2004 Employment guidelines [2004] OJ L326/45. The Lisbon Strategy ('to become the most competitive and dynamic knowledge-based economy in the world, capable of sustainable economic growth with more and better jobs and greater social cohesion') involves the aim to increase the overall EU employment rate to 70 per cent and that among women to more than 60 per cent by 2010.

[22] Council Decision of 12 July 2005 on guidelines for the employment policies of the Member States [2005] OJ L205/21. Here the employment rate among women is identified as currently being 56.1 per cent (for EU 27).

and gender mainstreaming, are said to be essential for progress and special attention should be paid to tackling the persistent employment gaps
between women and men (as well as the low employment rates of older
workers and young people as part of a new inter-generational approach).
Enterprises are required to respond to 'the increasing demand for job quality which is related to workers' personal preferences and family changes'.
Despite this, gender equality seems to be less visible as a priority through
these later developments of the EES.

In its Communication 'Towards a Community Framework Strategy
on Gender Equality (2001–2005)'[23] the Commission stresses the issue of
gender equality working towards an inclusive democracy and identifies
five interrelated fields of intervention: economic life, equal participation
and representation, social rights, civil life and gender roles and stereotypes. The Communication implies *a considerably broadened scope for gender equality*. The actions under 'equal participation and representation'
address women's under-representation in, among other areas, politics,
science and the Community institutions, characterised as a 'fundamental
democratic deficit'.[24] The aim of promoting equality in 'civil life' is said to
relate to 'the question of the full enjoyment of human rights and fundamental freedoms'[25] and addresses among other things the issue of violence
against and trafficking in women. In this field important policy developments have taken place both before and after Amsterdam such as the STOP
programme,[26] the DAPHNE programmes (2000–2003 and 2004–2008,
respectively)[27] and the Council Directive 2004/81/EC on the residence
permit issued to third country nationals who are victims of trafficking
in human beings or who have been the subject of action to facilitate illegal immigration, who co-operate with the competent authorities.[28] The
framework strategy has so far been monitored through the adoption of
annual work programmes and annual reports on gender equality.[29] In the
2005 equality between men and women report, the following challenges
for gender equality were identified: strengthening the position of women
in the labour market, increasing care facilities for children and other

---

[23] COM(2000) 335 final. There is a supporting programme to complement the framework
strategy, Council Decision of 20 December 2000 establishing a Programme relating to the
Community framework strategy on gender equality (2001–2005) [2001] OJ L17/22.

[24] COM(2000) 335 final, p. 7.   [25] Ibid. p. 11.

[26] Joint Action of 29 November 1996 adopted by the Council [1996] OJ L322.

[27] http://ec.europa.eu.justice_home/funding/2004_2007/Daphne/ funding_daphne_en.htm.

[28] [2004] OJ L261/19.

[29] See, for instance, the 2005 Report on equality between women and men, COM(2005) 44
final, the first to cover all twenty-five then Member States.

dependants, addressing men in achieving gender equality, integration of the gender perspective into immigration and integration policies and monitoring developments towards gender equality. There is now a Community programme for employment and social solidarity, PROGRESS 2007–2013, to replace among others, the Community action programme to combat discrimination 2001–2006 and the Council's Decision of 20 December 2000 establishing a programme relating to the Community framework strategy on gender equality 2001–2005.[30] Based on Articles 141(3) and 13(2) EC there is still an advanced proposal on the creation of an Institute for Gender Equality.[31] The objective of the Institute is to 'assist the Community institutions, in particular the Commission, and the authorities of the Member States in the fight against discrimination based on sex and the promotion of gender equality and to raise the profile of such issues among EU citizens' (Article 2).

The fact that the Amsterdam Treaty has assigned a major role to the European social dialogue, giving the social partners substantial responsibilities and powers, was mentioned earlier. The first framework agreement resulting from these provisions in their original version later resulted in the Parental Leave Directive 96/34/EC.[32] This Directive, however, predates Amsterdam and will only be dealt with here indirectly in connection with the amended Equal Treatment Directive 2002/73/EC (ETD) and in relation to case law developments.[33] The two other framework agreements which were later adopted as Directives under the Treaty, the European Council Directive 97/81/EC of 15 December 1997 concerning the Framework Agreement on Part-time Work concluded by UNICE, CEEP and the ETUC[34] and Council Directive 99/70/EC of 28 June 1999 concerning the Framework Agreement on Fixed-term Work concluded by ETUC, UNICE and CEEP,[35] however, deserve to be addressed here. Despite not constituting parts of EC sex equality law as such, they certainly have gendered implications. Then came the amended ETD, the new Article 13 Directive and the Recast Directive.

---

[30] Proposal for a European Parliament and Council Decision establishing a Community Programme for Employment and social Solidarity, PROGRESS, COM(2004) 488.

[31] Proposal for a Regulation of the European Parliament and of the Council establishing a European Institute for Gender Equality, COM(2005) 81 final.

[32] [1996] OJ L145/4.

[33] Also the Burden of Proof Directive 97/80/EC ([1998] OJ L14/6) was adopted under the Agreement on Social Policy, annexed to the Protocol (No. 14) on social policy, annexed to the Treaty establishing the European Community.

[34] [1998] OJ L14/9.   [35] [1998] OJ L14/9.

Constitutional developments post Amsterdam

Following the Cologne European Council in June 1999, the first 'Convention' was set up with the task of presenting a draft Charter of Fundamental Rights to the European Council in December 2000. The draft Charter was presented to and adopted by the Council at the Nice Summit in December 2000. Chapter III of the Charter addresses 'Equality'. Whereas Article 20 provides that 'everyone is equal before the law' and Article 21 includes a general ban on discrimination based inter alia on sex, Article 23 specifically addresses equality between men and women. According to its first paragraph, such equality 'must be ensured in all areas, including employment, work and pay'. The second paragraph makes room for positive action: 'The principle of equality shall not prevent the maintenance or adoption of measures providing for specific advantages in favour of the under-represented sex.' It is also worth mentioning Article 33 (2) here. This concerns family and work reconciliation and states that everyone shall have the right to protection from dismissal for a reason connected with maternity and the right to paid maternity leave and to parental leave following the birth or adoption of a child.

In the Commission's explanations[36] to the Charter, Article 23 is said to be based on the EC Treaty rules in Articles 2, 3(2) and 141. However, in particular, the rule on positive action has been given an apparently more narrow expression than the Treaty rule in Article 141(4). The Commission attempts to remove such doubts by referring to Article 51(2) of the Charter. Nevertheless, Article 23 can be criticised for embodying a less proactive approach even though it requires equality to be 'ensured in all areas' and the rule on 'positive measures' to reflect 'old views' of such measures as a matter of exception to non-discrimination.[37] The possible shortcomings of the Charter as regards sex equality law have been of minor importance so far, since the Charter as it stands today is not yet judicially binding but merely a 'solemnly proclaimed declaration' and the ECJ – but not so the Advocates General[38] – has displayed a considerable reluctance to refer to it.[39]

Needless to say, when and if the proposed Reform Treaty is agreed and ratified by all Member States, the exact way in which it regulates equality

---

[36] COM(2000) 559 final.
[37] For this line of argument and other critical views see further McCrudden, *Gender Equality*.
[38] See, for instance, A-G Tizzano in Case C-173/99 *BECTU* [2001]ECR I-4881.
[39] Not so the Administrative Court, see Case T-177/01 *Jégo-Quéré et Cie SA* v. *the Commission* [2002]. See also the case of the European Court of Human Rights, *Christine Goodwin* v. *The UK* (Judgment 11 July 2002).

between men and women – including the Charter of Fundamental Rights as previously integrated in Part II of the Constitution – will form the very basis for future sex equality law. This is not the place to go into the proposed Reform Treaty in detail.[40] I will discuss only the place of gender equality. Article I-2 of the unratified Constitutional Treaty that predated the Reform Treaty set out the Union's values in the following way: 'the union is founded on the values of respect for human dignity, freedom, democracy, equality, the rule of law and respect for human rights, including the rights of persons belonging to minorities. These values are common to the Member States in a society in which pluralism, non-discrimination, tolerance, justice, solidarity and equality between women and men prevail.' It is of course of particular importance that equality and specifically equality between women and men is present among the core values of the Union as expressed in the Constitution and it is now preserved by the proposed Reform Treaty. It was, however, not clear that this would always be the case. In the draft Constitutional Treaty presented to the Convention on 6 February 2003 by the Presidium equality was not included in the corresponding provision.[41]

Article I-3 of the Constitution set out the Union's objectives, and explicitly addressed promoting equality between women and men. 'When this provision is considered alongside two further provisions (Articles III-116 and III-118, sic), the mainstreaming of gender equality and non-discrimination in carrying out functions under Part III appears to become an obligation for Union institutions.'[42] The Reform Treaty, if agreed, would preserve this objective.

The Part-time Work and Fixed-term Work Directives

In general, labour-market developments have recently been perceived as forming a trend towards an increase in the peripheral and distanced workforce. This entails an increase in part-time work, fixed-term work, temporary agency work and other unstable employment relationships, i.e. flexible work as opposed to permanent, relatively secure, full-time traditional employment. These developments are of special concern to women (and thus sex equality) making up the majority of such 'flexible' workers.[43] The legitimate scope of such flexible work can be said to have been at the

---

[40] See instead further McCrudden, *Gender Equality*.
[41] CONV 528/03.   [42] McCrudden, *Gender Equality*, p. 4.
[43] In EU 25 part-time employment in 2004 represented 17.7 per cent of total employment whereas it represented 31.4 per cent of female employment. The corresponding figures as

core of labour law discourse during the last few decades. Lately, though, there have been signs indicating that all 'sides' are yielding to the trend towards more flexible working arrangements, stressing increased quality and equality of working conditions despite the mode of employment. Even so, efforts have long been made on the part of the European Commission to regulate the scope of flexible work, especially fixed-term work. We now have the European Council Directive 97/81/EC of 15 December 1997 concerning the Framework Agreement on Part-time Work concluded by UNICE, CEEP and the ETUC[44] and Council Directive 99/70/EC of 28 June 1999 concerning the Framework Agreement on Fixed-term Work concluded by ETUC, UNICE and CEEP.[45] Whereas the Part-time Work Directive was adopted on the basis of the Agreement on Social Policy contained in Protocol No 14 on social policy, annexed to the Maastricht Treaty, the Fixed-term Work Directive was adopted on the basis of Article 139(2) EC post Amsterdam. The Part-time Work Agreement's purpose is to support and facilitate part-time work more generally. Whereas the purpose of the Fixed-term Work Agreement is twofold: it sets out to improve/guarantee the working conditions of fixed-term workers. At the same time it is meant to restrict the permitted use of fixed-term work by establishing a framework to prevent abuse arising from the use of successive fixed-term employment contracts or relationships. Both Directives, however, adhere to the principle of equal treatment or non-discrimination as a central means of improving the quality of part-time and fixed-term work, respectively.

The principle of non-discrimination (Clause 4 in the respective Agreements) is that in respect of employment conditions, part-time/fixed-term workers shall not be treated in a less favourable manner than comparable full-time/permanent workers *solely* because they have a part-time/fixed-term contract or relation, unless this is justified on objective grounds.

The application of the principle of non-discrimination to part-time/fixed-term work poses special problems – as compared to other, more traditional fields of application for the equal treatment principle such as sex and nationality. One problem consists of the fact that what is forbidden by the non-discrimination provision – differential treatment as regards employment conditions – is at the same time part of what

---

regards fixed-term employment was 13.7 per cent and 14.3 per cent, respectively. Source the 'Employment in Europe 2005' report.
[44] [1998] OJ L14/9.   [45] [1998] OJ L14/9.

constitutes the groups that are to be compared. Different employment conditions pertaining to the mode of employment are a *sine qua non* even for distinguishing the protected group.[46] Moreover, Clause 4 prohibits differential treatment of part-time/fixed-term workers *solely* because of this contractual condition – that is, it forbids *direct discrimination* and not indirect discrimination. Furthermore, direct discrimination may be accepted if it is justified on objective grounds.[47] These conditions reflect in yet another way the restricted scope of the Fixed-term Work Directive/Framework Agreement; or, if we want to put it that way, the ambiguity as regards the use of fixed-term work. The existence of accepted different modes of employment where the most vital employment conditions are concerned – length of and rules on expiry of the employment contract – is a prerequisite for the regulation as such, and differential treatment is, also as regards other employment conditions, typically supposed to be objectively justified on occasion. This also reveals a somewhat limited ambition with respect to the equal treatment principle. Additionally, the principle of equal treatment is subject to the principle of *pro rata temporis*, which means that flexible employees are entitled to the same rights as permanent workers in proportion to the time for which they work.

Professor Brian Bercusson, at the VII European Regional Congress of Labour Law and Social Security held in Stockholm 4–6 September 2002, in his oral comments on the general reports, referred to these new instruments as a new right to equal treatment for workers 'turning discrimination law inside out. It is now all about the justification of differential treatment'. We will return to the implications of such a development in the last section. What is of special interest concerning the Part-time Work and the Fixed-term Work Directives in our context, however, is also the fact that there is a special relationship with sex equality law. Different working conditions for part-timers, being predominantly female, as compared to full-timers, were at the foundation of the concept of indirect discrimination as originally developed by the ECJ[48] and later case law on sex equality has concerned fixed-term work also. Both Directives include a direct statement that 'this agreement shall be without prejudice to any more specific Community provisions, and in particular

---

[46] See the judgment in Case C-313/02 *Wippel* and further below.

[47] This is usually not the case in other areas of discrimination law, with the exception of age discrimination: see further the discussion in the last section of this chapter.

[48] Compare Case 96/80 *Jenkins* [1981] ECR 911 and Case 170/84 *Bilka Kaufhaus* [1986] ECR 1607.

Community provisions concerning equal treatment of opportunities for men and women'.[49] The justification test may require a different standard within the realm of sex equality law, not least in cases of fixed-term work and pregnancy (equivalent to direct sex discrimination).[50]

The amended Equal Treatment Directive

Directive 2002/73/EC of the European Parliament and of the Council of 23 September 2002 amending Council Directive 76/207/EEC on the implementation of the principle of equal treatment for men and women as regards access to employment, vocational training and promotion, and working conditions[51] (hereafter the Amended ETD and the ETD, respectively) was due for implementation by 5 October 2005. It was adopted in light of Article 6 of the Treaty on the European Union, addressing the fundamental rights as guaranteed by the European Convention and recognised by the Union Charter of Fundamental Rights, the new provisions under Articles 2, 3(2) and 141 of the EC Treaty, the ECJ's case law on discrimination on the grounds of sex, the new Article 13 Directives and Directive 97/80/EC on the Burden of Proof in Cases of Discrimination Based on Sex.

The Amended ETD is thus an initiative to implement among other things the new EC Treaty provisions on gender equality. The Directive now includes express definitions of the central concepts of direct and indirect discrimination (Article 2(2)) consistent with the corresponding concepts in the first two Article 13 Directives. The same can be said for the concept of harassment (Article 2(3)) and also instructions to discriminate as constituting a form of discrimination (Article 2.4). Moreover, the Directive includes express definitions of two types of harassment: 'harassment related to the sex of a person' and 'sexual harassment', respectively

---

[49] Clause 6(4) of the Part-time Work Agreement and Clause 8(2) of the Fixed-term Work Agreement, respectively.

[50] The recent cases C-196/02 *Nikoloudi* and C-285/02 *Elsner-Lakeberg* concerned part-time work and indirect sex discrimination whereas Case C-313/02 *Wippel*, refers to both the Part-time Work Directive and the ETD. See also Case C-109/00 *Tele Denmark A/S* v. *Handels- og Kontorfunktionærernes Forbund in Denmark* [2001] ECR I-6993 where the ECJ stated that the dismissal of a fixed-term-employed woman on grounds of pregnancy was in conflict with the Council's Directive 76/207/EEC (Art. 5.1, direct discrimination on grounds of sex) as well as with the Pregnant Workers Directive 92/85/EEC (Art. 10). According to the ECJ there is, according to those Directives, no reason for not treating different modes of employment equally (para. 33). See also Case C-173/99 *BECTU* on the right to vacation according to the Council's Directive 93/104/EC on Working Time.

[51] [2002] OJ L269/15.

(Article 2(2)). The Amended ETD also contains improved protection for pregnant women and maternity rights, basically adjusting the Directive to the case law of the ECJ. In light of Article 141(4) the ETD's rules on positive action in the former Article 2(4) were eliminated and replaced by a reference to the Treaty rule itself (Article 2(8)). The Amended ETD also includes rules on more effective monitoring, legal protection and remedies.

The Amended ETD has thus made use of some of the innovations introduced by the first two Article 13 Directives. The definition of direct discrimination introduces the comparison of the claimant with a hypothetical worker of the other sex, in line with the ECJ's judgment in *Dekker*. The concept of indirect discrimination had developed in case law[52] and was later expressly regulated in the Burden of Proof Directive 97/80/EC. There, it was articulated so that an apparently neutral criterion could be justified 'if adequate and necessary *and due to reasons unrelated to sex*'. However, according to Article 2(2) of the Amended ETD, the concept of indirect discrimination now reads that a treatment is justified if 'objectively justified by a legitimate aim and the means of achieving that aim are appropriate and necessary'. The words 'unrelated to sex' are now missing. According to the Amended Directive national law or practice may provide in particular for indirect discrimination to be established by 'any means including on the basis of statistical evidence'.[53] The express definition here draws upon the wording of the new Article 13 Directives rather than the Burden of Proof Directive,[54] and can be said to provide a somewhat wider scope for establishing a prima facie case of indirect discrimination.[55]

The new Article 3 articulates the ban on discrimination covering both public and private sectors (including public bodies) concerning '(a) conditions for access to employment, to self-employment or to occupation, including selection criteria and recruitment conditions, whatever the branch of activity and at all levels of the professional hierarchy, including promotion; (b) access to all types and to all levels of vocational guidance, vocational training, advanced vocational training and retraining,

---

[52] See cases *Jenkins* and *Bilka Kaufhaus*.   [53] The preamble, para. 10.

[54] '*would* put . . . at a particular disadvantage' as in Art. 2(2)(b) of the Article 13 Directives compared to '*disadvantages a substantially higher proportion* of the members of one sex' in Art. 2(2) of the Burden of Proof Directive. See also, for instance, S. Koukoulis-Spiliotopoulos (2001), p. 41.

[55] Compare also the Explanatory Memorandum, Ch. 5, Art. 2 to the Commission's Proposal for the Amended ETD, COM(2000) 334 final.

including practical work experience; (c) employment and working conditions, including dismissals, as well as pay as provided for in the Equal Pay Directive 75/117/EEC; and (d) membership of, and involvement in, an organisation of workers or employees, or any organisation whose members carry on a particular profession, including the benefits provided for by such organisations'. The ban on discrimination regarding membership of, and involvement in, workers organisations, etc., apparently would put an end to such associations for only one sex. Separate women's organisations may still be accepted under Article 141(4) in the Treaty, though.[56]

Among the provisions of special importance regarding working conditions, are the new rules defining harassment since there was no EC 'hard law' on this matter.[57] There are also new provisions regarding pregnancy and maternity rights (the new Article 2(7)). Women on maternity leave will be entitled to return to the same or an equivalent job after pregnancy and maternity leave, with no less favourable working conditions, as well as to benefit from any improvement in working conditions to which they would have been entitled during their absence. While less favourable treatment of a woman related to pregnancy or maternity leave, constitutes discrimination within the meaning of the Amended ETD, these rules are without prejudice to the provisions of the Parental Leave Directive 96/34/EC and the Pregnant Workers Directive 92/85/EC,[58] respectively.

Moreover, the Amended Directive in Article 2(7) also provides an opportunity for the Member States to grant working men an individual right to paternity leave while maintaining their rights relating to employment, thus recognising distinct rights to paternity. However welcome such paternity rights may seem they can, in my opinion, also be criticised. While providing important social rights also for the fathers of small children, a different set of such paternity rights may turn out to perpetuate a distinction between maternity leave and paternity leave to the detriment of gender-neutral parental rights making their way into working life.

---

[56] Compare preamble 7 of the Amended ETD. See also R. Nielsen, 'Det nye ligebehandlingsdirektiv (2000/73/EF) – perspektiver for nordisk ret', *Arbeidsrett* 2 (2004) (Universitetsforlaget, Oslo), p. 78.

[57] Compare, however, the Commission Recommendation on the protection of the dignity of women and men at work, with an annexed Code of Practice on measures to combat sexual harassment, 92/131/EEC, [1992] OJ L49/1.

[58] [1992] OJ L348/1.

The Amended ETD contains a new rule on bona fide occupational qualifications (bfoq) defences in Article 2(6), referring to occupational activities which necessitate ('constitutes a genuine and determining occupational requirement') the employment of a person of one sex 'by reason of the nature of the particular occupational activities concerned or of the context in which they are carried out' provided that the objective sought is legitimate and subject to the principle of proportionality as laid down by the case law of the ECJ. The new writings suggest a stronger justification test than before and are a welcome elimination of the old 'derogation rule' in Article 2(2) of the 1976 ETD. This rule, too, is copied from the first two Article 13 Directives.

The remedies and enforcement rules also reflect great similarities with the Article 13 Directives – and especially the Race Directive 2000/43/EC. Thus the Amended ETD requires a special body or bodies to promote equal treatment but also with the competence to assist individual victims of discrimination pursuing their complaints of discrimination (Article 8a). It is worth mentioning the more far-reaching duty of Member States to encourage employers to promote equal treatment in the workplace 'in a planned and systematic way' (Article 8b(4)). Such equality planning has long since been a reality in Sweden, for instance, and is now spreading to other areas of non-discrimination through domestic legislation, although not required by the Article 13 Directives. The Amended ETD can be said to strengthen the general requirements as regards effective judicial protection involving effective access to court, effective judicial control and effective sanctions.[59]

Summing up, the Amended ETD means an adaptation of the concepts and the rules on remedies and enforcement to those in the Article 13 Directives. The Amended ETD extends the ban on discrimination to new situations (such as union membership) and defines harassment, instructions to discriminate and less favourable treatment related to pregnancy or maternity leave as discrimination.

A new Article 13 Directive

A significant post-Amsterdam development concerns the extension of EU sex equality law beyond the field of employment and related areas. In December 2004, the Council adopted Directive 2004/113/EC implementing the principle of equal treatment between men and women in the access to and supply of goods and services.[60] The Commission announced

---

[59] See, for instance, R. Nielsen (2004), p. 85.   [60] [2004] OJ L373/37.

its intention to put forward such a proposal in its Communication on the Social Policy Agenda,[61] as indicated above. The European Council at its meeting in Nice in December 2000 later called for such an initiative. The Directive is based on Article 13(1) EC and reference is made in the preamble, among others, to Article 6 of the TEU, Articles 21 and 23 of the Charter of Fundamental Rights and Articles 2 and 3(2) EC.[62] Discrimination based on sex and harassment in areas outside of the labour market is said to be 'equally damaging, acting as a barrier to the full and successful integration of women and men into economic and social life' and problems are said to be particularly apparent in the area of goods and services.[63] As it was based on Article 13, the Directive required unanimity within the Council for its adoption. At the first agreement on a common position within the Council (October 2004) the Directive only passed since Germany abstained from voting. Among the issues put forward by Germany were doubts concerning the compatibility of the contents of the Directive and the principle of freedom of contract as guaranteed by the German Constitution. On the 13 of December 2004, however, unanimity was reached and the Directive was finally adopted.

The Directive draws heavily upon, in particular, the Race Directive 2000/43/EC but also on the Amended ETD, now compatible with the earlier Article 13 Directives. The structure is basically the same: four Chapters dealing with general provisions, remedies and enforcement, bodies for the promotion of equal treatment and final provisions, respectively. The concepts of discrimination and harassment are the same, as are the rules on the burden of proof and the rules on remedies and procedure, there is also a requirement of a specialised body and for Member States to engage in a dialogue with NGOs, etc.

The purpose of the Directive is thus to lay down a framework for combating discrimination based on sex in access to and supply of goods and services (Article 1). The Directive, however, covers access to and supply of goods and services only when provided for remuneration and available to the public. Transactions within the private sphere, families and so on, are outside the scope of the Directive as are media, advertising and education (Article 3). The ban on discrimination does not preclude differences in treatment 'if the provision of the goods and services exclusively or primarily to members of one sex is justified by a legitimate aim and the means of achieving that aim are appropriate and necessary' (Article 4(5)). Whether

---

[61] COM(2000) 379 final.

[62] The European Parliament had examined the possibility of using Article 95 as a legal base for the Directive, see PE 337.25 final A5–0155/2004 (at 35).

[63] The preamble, recitals 8 and 9.

the Directive should apply also to insurance has been an issue of conflict. The main principle is now that Member States shall ensure that as regards contracts concluded after 21 December 2007, the use of sex as a factor in calculations shall not result in differences in individuals' premiums and benefits (Article 5(1)). However, the Directive leaves Member States a certain scope to continue to use sex as a determining factor when assessing insurance risks as long as this is based on relevant and accurate actuarial and statistical data also following December 2007. Such data must be regularly updated and made public. However, as regards insurance costs, specifically related to pregnancy and maternity they must be attributed equally to both men and women in order to provide a fairer distribution within society of such costs as of 21 December 2007 (although it is possible to extend the deadline further for two more years). The rules on insurance are to be evaluated within six years. Undoubtedly, due to societal developments such as increasing employment levels among women and the increasing use of private insurance to offset public expenditure, this is a really weak point as far as gender equality is concerned although the equality principle to a certain extent may work both ways. Whereas as regards annuities and pensions it will benefit women, as regards motor insurance it may be the other way around.

The Directive's coverage is thus limited. In the preparatory discussions it was suggested that it cover a much wider range of questions such as violence (including domestic) against women and participation in decision-making.[64] Also, early proposals by the Commission covered a number of other areas – now not covered by the Directive – such as social assistance, education, media, advertising and also taxes. Doubts regarding the legal competence of the Union in some of these areas and, possibly, extensive lobbying led to the much less extensive intervention reflected in the final Directive.[65]

The Directive is the first to bring the principle of sex equality beyond the workplace and as such, it undoubtedly represents significant progress.[66] However, drawing upon the earlier Article 13 Directives and especially the Race Directive 2000/43/EC, it is obvious that its coverage is significantly less extensive, something which has been considered as reinforcing the idea of a hierarchy of equalities where gender appears to be losing

---

[64] Compare the European Women's Lobby 'Shadow Directive on Achieving Equality of Women and Men outside the Field of Occupation and Employment' (June 2002).

[65] See, for instance, Prechal 'Equality of treatment'.

[66] Compare R. Nielsen (2004).

ground.[67] The poor scope of the Directive has also been questioned from a human rights point of view, not covering important issues such as equal treatment in the areas of media and education.[68] As regards the contents of the Directive, it is interesting to note that Article 4(5) provides for the justification of direct discrimination also. As stated by Eugenia Caracciolo di Torella, the effect of the Directive in 'real life' is likely to be a complicated mixture of gains and losses for both sexes.[69]

The Recast Directive

In 2006 the European Parliament and Council agreed a proposal for a Recast Directive bringing together some of the existing directives in a single text.[70] The Commission presented a proposal for such a Directive in 2004[71] and the Council adopted its general approach in December 2004.

The objective of the Recast Directive is to simplify, modernise and improve the Community law in the area of equal treatment between men and women by putting together in a single text provisions of Directives linked by their subject, in order to make Community legislation clearer and more effective.[72] Its legal basis is Article 141(3) EC, also the basis of the Directives amalgamated therein: the Equal Pay Directive 75/117/EEC Directive 86/378/EEC on occupational schemes as amended by Directive 96/97/EEC; the Equal Treatment Directive 76/207/EEC as amended by Directive 2002/73/EC; and the Burden of Proof Directive 97/80/EC as amended by Directive 98/52/EC.

The directive is structured in five titles. Title I, General Provisions, includes the core concept definitions taken from the Amended ETD (copying the Article 13 Directives) as well as the definition of pay from Article

---

[67] Compare E. Caracciolo di Torella at the 18–20 November 2004 Hague Conference on 'Progressive implementation; New developments in European Union Gender Equality Law' and her paper 'The Goods and Services Directive: A step forward or a missed opportunity'.

[68] Ibid. Caracciolo di Torella thus especially questions its compliance with Arts. 2, 5 and 10 in the United Nations Convention of the Elimination of all Forms of Discrimination against Women (CEDAW), already binding upon signing Member States.

[69] Ibid.

[70] Directive on the implementation of the principle of equal opportunities and equal treatment of men and women in matters of employment and occupation, 2006/54/EC, [2006] OJ L204 (to be implemented by 15 August 2008).

[71] 2004/0084/COD.

[72] Compare the Commission's Communication Updating and simplifying the Community acquis, COM(2003) 71 final.

141(2) EC and the definition of occupational social security schemes as modified by Directive 96/97/EC. Title II, Specific Provisions, comprises three chapters, concerning the principle of equal pay (Ch. 1), the principle of equal treatment in occupational social security schemes (Ch. 2) and the principle of equal treatment for men and women as regards access to employment, vocational training, promotion and working conditions (Ch. 3), recasting the respective directives as amended. Chapter 1, Article 4, on the principle of equal pay, provides:[73] 'For the same work or for work to which equal value is attributed, direct and indirect discrimination on grounds of sex with regard to all aspects and conditions of remuneration shall be eliminated.'[74] It also includes case law developments with regard to public servants' pension schemes as reflected in *Beuene* and *Niemi*.[75] Title III on horizontal provisions reflects the regulation of these matters introduced by Directive 2000/73/EC. It also relates to the contents of the Burden of Proof Directive, extending its application to the area of occupational social security schemes.

The Recast Directive can be said to signify only very moderate changes in order precisely to bring the *acquis* in line with new equality law instruments and case law developments. The ambitions to unify Community Equality Law spring clear from the Commission's explanatory memorandum: 'Legislation should . . . use the same concepts . . . in order to ensure legal and political coherence between pieces of legislation, which have similar objectives. It is therefore necessary to ensure coherence between secondary legislation on identical issues, such as the concept of indirect discrimination or the need for Member States to have bodies for the promotion of equal treatment.'[76]

Recasting a group of, often also amended, Directives into a single instrument must be regarded as an improvement. The Recast Directive will thus also provide a harmonised and coherent set of core concept definitions doing away with the current superseded definition of indirect discrimination in Article 2.2 in Directive 97/80/EC.

---

[73] An earlier version had included an interesting innovation with reference to the case. It referred to remuneration 'attributable to a single source'. Case C-320/00 *Lawrence and Others* [2002] ECR I-7325 and C-256/01 *Allonby* [2004] ECR I-873.

[74] In *Allonby*, Debra Allonby was not entitled to use as a comparator for equal pay purposes a male lecturer employed by her former employer once she herself was put to the use of her former employer through a temporary work agency.

[75] Cases C-7/93 *Beuene* [1994] ECR I-4471 and C-351/00 *Niemi* [2002] ECR I-7007.

[76] COM(2004) 279 final, p. 22.

Case law development

Community sex equality law is the basis of an impressive bulk of case law from the ECJ. It is, of course, altogether impossible to do justice to this important part of the *acquis communautaire* in such a limited space as this. On the contrary, it is my intention to discuss only the cases following Tamara Hervey's comprehensive report to the 2002 Stockholm regional European Congress on Labour Law.[77]

In her report Tamara Hervey focused on justifications of both direct and indirect discrimination on an 'uninterrupted scale'. Moreover, Hervey shows us in great detail how the strictness of the proportionality test applied by the ECJ varies according to the context. Justifications can be job-related, enterprise-related and public-interest related. The conclusion is that there are different levels of justification with regard to the concept of indirect discrimination. The Court was found to retain a relatively strong version of proportionality when assessing job-related justifications and enterprise-related justifications for indirect sex discrimination, especially when advanced by the employer. Broader public interest-related justifications advanced by a Member State are said to be subject only to a weaker, reasonableness-based proportionality test.

Hervey's line of argument fits well with Bercusson's overall comment that 'it is now all about justification', and we can expect even more diversified requirements in the future due to the impact of the new instruments on non-discrimination, ranging from the Part-time and Fixed-term Directives to the Article 13 Directives. To what extent can recent case law be said to confirm or inhibit such arguments?

First, direct discrimination has for a long time been subject to express legislative derogations in Article 2 ETD. In *Dory*, concerning compulsory military service in Germany only for men, the ECJ found Germany's choice of military organisation to be an issue outside the scope of the ETD altogether, despite the fact that the organisation of the armed forces could not be regarded *per se* to be excluded in their entirety from EC law. Community law thus does not preclude compulsory military service being reserved to men. In *Commission* v. *Austria*[78] the ECJ found, however, that Austria, by maintaining a general prohibition of the employment of

---

[77] T. Hervey, *EC law on Justifications for Sex Discrimination in Working Life*, available at the Congress website: http://www.labourlaw2002.org. Published in R. Blanpain (ed.), *Labour Law & Social Security and the European Integration, Bulletin of Comparative Labour Relations* (Kluwer Law International, 2003).

[78] Case C-203/03 *The Commission* v. *Austria* [2005] ECR I-935.

women in work in a high-pressure atmosphere and in diving work, had failed to fulfil its obligations under Articles 2 and 3 of the ETD. The ETD 'does not allow women to be excluded from a certain type of employment solely on the ground that they ought to be given greater protection than men against risks which affect women in the same way and which are distinct from women's specific needs of protection', 'nor may women be excluded from a certain type of employment solely because they are on average smaller and less strong than average men, while men with similar physical features are accepted for that employment'.[79] There is now the new rule on bfoq defences in Article 2(6) of the Amended ETD, as discussed above.

Article 2(3) of the old ETD (now Article 2(7)), despite the ban on discrimination, provides scope for provisions concerning the protection of women, particularly as regards pregnancy and maternity. However, the ECJ already ruled in *Dekker* that pregnancy and maternity are inseparable from the female sex as such and that any *inferior* treatment on these grounds amounts to direct discrimination and thus is protected by the equal treatment rule itself. This can, in fact, be regarded as the most potent protection for pregnant women and mothers. Also following important cases such as *Mahlburg*[80] and *Tele Danmark*[81] the ECJ has confirmed its fundamentalist approach in this respect. In the *Busch* case[82] the Court stated that it is an infringement of the equal treatment principle to require 'that an employee who, with the consent of her employer, wishes to return to work before the end of her parental leave must inform her employer that she is pregnant in the event that, because of certain legislative prohibitions, she will be unable to carry out all of her duties',[83] nor can the lack of such information form the basis of a decision to deny her such a re-entry. The Court reaffirmed in *Busch* that direct discrimination cannot be justified on grounds relating to the financial loss of an employer.[84] In *Merino Gómez*[85] the ECJ found that Article 5(1) of the ETD means that a worker must be able to take her annual leave – as guaranteed by Directive 93/104/EC on Working Time or the more beneficial rules in national law – during a

---

[79] Paras. 45–6 of the judgment.   [80] C-207/98 *Mahlburg* [2000] ECR I-549.

[81] See also Cases C-179/88 *Hertz* [1990] ECR I-3979, C-421/92 *Webb* [1994] ECR I-3567 and C-438/99 *Melgar* [2001] ECR I-6915.

[82] C-320/01 *Busch* [2003] ECR I-2041. Mrs Busch had required an early return from her parental leave in order to, by the time of the birth of her second child, receive (the higher) maternity allowance instead of the allowance paid during parental leave and also some supplements to the maternity allowance.

[83] Para. 47 of the judgment.   [84] Para. 44 of the judgment.

[85] C-342/01 *Merino Gómez* [2004] ECR I-2605.

period other than the period of her maternity leave and that this includes a case in which the period of maternity leave coincides with the general period of annual leave fixed by a collective agreement applicable to the entire workforce. The purpose of the entitlement to annual leave being different from that of the entitlement to maternity leave, allowing them to overlap would have entailed one of them being lost. The *Sass* case[86] regarded passage to a higher salary grade. Ursula Sass was not allowed to take into account the whole period of maternity leave (twenty weeks) taken under the legislation of the former GDR in calculating the qualifying period since the collective agreement applicable took into account only maternity leave (eight weeks) according to German federal rules. The ECJ, who found that 'a female worker is protected in her employment relationship against any unfavourable treatment on the ground that she is or has been on maternity leave', held that 'Mrs Sass is in a worse position than a male colleague who started work in the former GDR on the same day as she did because, having taken maternity leave, she will not attain the higher salary grade until 12 weeks after he does'.[87] However, it was said to be for the national court to decide whether the twenty weeks' leave actually taken by Mrs Sass was of the kind protected as maternity leave by Article 2(3) of the ETD. In *Mayer*[88] the Occupational Pension Scheme Directive 86/378/EEC as amended by Directive 96/97/EC was at stake. The Directive was found to preclude national rules under which a worker does not acquire rights to an insurance annuity during statutory maternity leave, paid in part by her employer, because the acquisition of those rights is conditional upon the worker receiving taxable pay during the maternity leave.

However, the judgment in the *McKenna* case[89] departs from this route of assuring equal rights to women on maternity leave. The employer's sick-leave scheme provided that employees were entitled to 365 days of paid sick-leave in a period of four years. Moreover, 183 days of absence in a period of twelve months were paid at full pay and any additional sick days up to the limit of 365 days over four years at half pay only. Ms McKenna was on sick leave on account of a pregnancy-related illness, at first with full pay and then afterwards for 183 days with half pay. During maternity leave she received full pay again. When that leave expired Mrs McKenna was still sick and her pay was once again reduced to half pay. The ECJ

---

[86] C-284/02 *Sass* [2004] ECR I-11143.   [87] Paras. 35 and 37 of the judgment.
[88] C-356/03 *Mayer* [2005] ECR I-295.
[89] C-191/03 *North Western Health Board* v. *Margaret McKenna* [2005] ECR I-7631.

stated that sickness-related pay was an issue under Article 141 EC and the Equal Pay Directive, not the ETD, and that despite the fact that women were protected against dismissal during pregnancy and maternity leave there was no such thing as a protection of full wages during that same time. Women making use of maternity leave deserve special protection but cannot be compared with men who are actually working. According to Article 11(b) in Directive 92/85/EC they are only guaranteed reasonable compensation. Case C-220/02[90] concerned whether not taking parental leave (following upon the expiry of maternity leave) into account for calculating a termination payment amounted to indirect discrimination of women. A comparison was made with workers performing military service (mostly men) whose leave was indeed taken into account. The Court, however, found women (and men) taking parental leave not to be in a comparable situation with workers doing national service and indirect discrimination thus not to be at stake. The Court's backward declaration that the interests of the worker and family in the case of parental leave and 'the collective interests of the nation in the case of national service ... are of a different nature'[91] is worth drawing attention to.

The question whether direct discrimination is necessarily a 'closed class' outside the presence of express legislative derogations can be said to have been addressed also in relation to the old Article 2(4) of the ETD and the scope for positive action. In *Kalanke, Marschall* and *Badeck* – despite accepting the positive action measures at stake in the latter two cases – the ECJ had argued the scope for such measures in terms of an exception to the equal treatment principle.[92] However, in the cases of *Lommers* and *Briheche* the ECJ has argued somewhat differently: 'In determining the scope of any derogation from an individual right such as the equal treatment of men and women laid down by the Directive, due regard must be had to the principle of proportionality, which requires that derogations must remain within the limits of what is appropriate and necessary in order to achieve the aim in view and that the principle of equal treatment be reconciled as far as possible with the requirements of the aim thus pursued.'[93] Sacha Prechal, at a conference on Women in Academia held

---

[90] C-220/02 *Österreichischer Gewerkschaftsbund* [2004] ECR I-5907.

[91] Para. 64 of the judgment.

[92] Cases C-450/93 [1995] ECR I-3051, C-409/95 [1997] ECR I-6363 and C-158/97 [2000] ECR I-1875.

[93] See Cases C-476/99 *Lommers* [2002] ECR I-2891, 39 and C-319/03 *Briheche* [2004] ECR I-8807, 24. In *Lommers* the test fell out positive. It was not unjustifiable to limit a number of subsidised nursery places made available by the Ministry to its staff for female officials alone whilst male officials could have access to them only in cases of emergency provided

in Lund, 2–3 December 2004,[94] claimed that now 'it's all about proportionality', a claim very much in line with the ones referred to above made by Hervey and Bercusson.

With regard to indirect sex discrimination several cases recently have concerned flexible work. *Elsner-Lakeberg*[95] deals with the question of whether national measures providing that full-time and part-time teachers were obliged to work the same number of additional hours (three) before being entitled to remuneration constituted indirect discrimination against women teachers employed part-time. With reference to *Kowalska* and *Brunnhofer*[96] the ECJ held it necessary with a separate comparison in respect of the pay for regular hours and the pay for additional hours and continued: 'Although that pay may appear to be equal inasmuch as the entitlement to remuneration for additional hours is triggered only after three additional hours have been worked by part-time and full-time teachers, three additional hours is in fact a greater burden for part-time teachers than it is for full-time teachers' and they thus 'receive different treatment compared with full-time teachers as regards pay for additional teaching hours'.[97] It is for the national court to consider the eventual justification. The *Wippel* and *Nikoloudi* cases[98] also concerned part-time employment and indirect sex discrimination. Nicole Wippel was employed part-time on the basis of a contract of employment based on the principle of 'work on demand', i.e. without specifically stated hours of work and organisation of working time. The ECJ, which found both the ETD and the Part-time Work Directive 97/81/EC in principle applicable to such a worker (in the latter case provided the Member State had not excluded them wholly or partly from the benefit of the terms of that agreement), concluded that they did not preclude a contract such as the one at stake despite all the

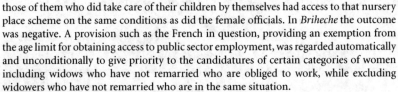

those of them who did take care of their children by themselves had access to that nursery place scheme on the same conditions as did the female officials. In *Briheche* the outcome was negative. A provision such as the French in question, providing an exemption from the age limit for obtaining access to public sector employment, was regarded automatically and unconditionally to give priority to the candidatures of certain categories of women including widows who have not remarried who are obliged to work, while excluding widowers who have not remarried who are in the same situation.

[94] The proceedings are published in R. Blanpain and A. Numhauser-Henning (eds.), *Women in Academia* (Kluwer Law International, 2006).

[95] Case C-285/02 *Elsner-Lakeberg* v. *Land Nordrhein-Westfalen* [2004] ECR I-5861.

[96] Case C-33/89 *Kowalska* [1990] ECR I-2591 and C-381/99 *Brunnhofer* [2001] ECR I-4961.

[97] Para. 17 of the judgment. Compare, however, the joined cases C-399/92, C-409/92, C-425/92, C-34/93, C-50/93 and C-78/93 *Helmig* [1994] ECR I-5727, where the ECJ held a different view.

[98] C-313/02 *Wippel* v. *Peek Cloppenburg Gmbht Co. KG* [2004] ECR 9483 and Case C-196/02 *Nikoloudi* v. *OTE* [2005] ECR I-1789.

contracts of employment of the other employees at the employer's making provision for the length and organisation of weekly working time. The principle of equality can apply only to persons in comparable situations and with reference to precisely the very conditions of the 'on demand contract'; the Court could not find any comparable worker. This case seems to confirm what was said above on the employment conditions being what constitute the very groups to be protected, as the weak point of non-discrimination of 'workers'. Ms Nikoloudi was a part-time cleaner at the public company OTE and for that reason was denied the possibility of appointment as an 'established staff member'. Established staff comprised full-time employees only. Part-time cleaners, although under contracts of indefinite duration, were regarded as 'temporary staff' and they were by definition 'female' according to the textual agreement. This amounts to direct discrimination violating the ETD. However, the Court also considered the possibility – argued by the employer – of there also being part-time employed men and conferred it upon the national court in such a case to decide whether the practice was in fact to the detriment of women and thus constituted indirect discrimination. Despite the fact that it is also for the national court to assess any eventual justification in such a case, the ECJ made some interesting remarks in that respect. Thus it ruled out the possibility that part-time work as such constitutes a sufficient reason to explain the difference in treatment. It also ruled out a public interest related justification according to which a national public utility undertaking should not bear excessive burdens, this being a mere generalisation. And, the Court continued: 'Although budgetary considerations may underlie a Member State's choice of social policy and influence the nature or scope of the social protection measures which it wishes to adopt, they do not in themselves constitute an aim pursued by that policy and cannot therefore justify discrimination against one of the sexes.'[99] In *Vergani*[100] a taxation rule providing that in order to encourage workers who had passed the age of fifty years in the case of women and fifty-five years in the case of men to take voluntary redundancy, the tax on the redundancy payment should be only half of the rate normally applied, was regarded as constituting a condition governing dismissal within the meaning of Article 5(1) ETD and amounted to discrimination. (The provision was found to be outside the scope of the exception provided for

---

[99] Para. 53 of the judgment. Compare Cases C-167/97 *Seymour-Smith and Perez* [1999] ECR I-623, C-343/92 *Roks and Others* [1994] ECR I-571 and C-77/02 *Steinicke* [2003] ECR I-9027.

[100] Case C-207/04 *Vergani* [2005] ECR I-7453.

in Article 7(1) of Directive 79/7/EEC.) The particularly interesting cases of *Lawrence* and *Allonby* have already been touched upon in connection with the Recast Directive and the provisions on equal pay.[101] In *Allonby*, however, there was also the issue of indirect discrimination enshrined in legislation: whether the requirement of being employed under a contract of employment as a precondition for membership of a legislated pension scheme for teachers could possibly amount to indirect discrimination provided it was shown that a clearly lower percentage of women than men were able to satisfy that condition and it is established that that condition is not objectively justified. This question was answered in the affirmative provided we were dealing with a worker within the meaning of Article 141(1) EC. It may be that public interest related justifications, as Hervey argues, are subject to a somewhat weaker proportionality test. However, case law developments show that the ECJ continuously scrutinises public legislation in quite disparate fields under the equal treatment regulation.[102]

Commenting on post-Amsterdam developments and pointing towards the future

As can be perceived from the foregoing, there are a number of important developments since Amsterdam in the field of sex equality law. The amended ETD and the Recast Directive may be said to signify important expressions of sex equality law developments proper. However, other important developments can be characterised, to quote Dagmar Schiek, as 'driven by the "other equalities"'.[103] This goes for the harmonisation of key concepts in the Amended ETD (and the Recast Directive) and, of course, for the new Article 13 Directive. 'The combating of discrimination is based on a hard core of rights and gives priority to synergy between all European instruments' states the Commission in its Communication on the Social Agenda 2005–2010.[104] Is this good or bad for the future of sex equality law?

---

[101] Case C-320/00 *Lawrence and Others* [2002] ECR I-7325 and C-256/01 *Allonby* [2004] ECR I-873.
[102] Compare also C-303/02 *Haackert* [2004] ECR I-2195, where the ECJ, however, accepted a pre-retirement scheme in Austria linked to unemployment and applicable to women at a lower age than men as a necessary consequence of there being a difference in normal pensionable age and thus permitted under Article 7(1)(a) of Directive 79/7/EEC.
[103] D. Schiek (2004).   [104] COM(2005) 33 final.

The wording of the Article 13 Directives explicitly takes account of the original ETD and its interpretation by the ECJ of Directive 97/80/EC and of the overall experience of fighting gender discrimination and pursuing gender equality. The Article 13 Directives, however, are also inspired by the ECJ's case law on the free movement of workers; most notably its interpretation of the concept of indirect discrimination. The Article 13 Directives can thus be said to draw from a wider scope of *acquis communautaire* than Community gender equality regulation so far. In the free movement cases the ECJ has held that 'a provision of national law must be regarded as indirectly discriminatory if it is intrinsically liable to affect migrant workers more than national workers and there is a consequent risk that it will place the former at a particular disadvantage, unless it is justified by objective considerations independent of the nationality of the workers concerned, and proportionate to the legitimate aim pursued by that law'.[105] It is thus enough to show risk. Updating gender equality regulations to this standard might actually be seen as 'building on strength' as regards gender equality, implying an instrumental and proactive approach. Sophia Koukoulis-Spiliotopoulos argues that this is precisely the approach adopted in the Amended ETD.[106] Everything would change should the ECJ accept the ban on indirect discrimination to be used instrumentally to promote substantive equality between the sexes in parallel with the use of the indirect discrimination concept in 'free movement cases'.[107] So far, however, we have seen little of this. Although the ECJ in, for instance, *Thibault* has recognised that the aim pursued by the ETD is substantive and not formal equality,[108] the 'single source argument' in *Lawrence*, confirmed in *Allonby*, seems to counteract any broader such development. This can be accredited to the 'individual complaint model' dominating EU sex equality law.[109] The test, instead of focusing on the perpetrator's guilt (a single source), could however focus on whether a rule or practice is based on the exclusion of women and is systematically detrimental to women's needs and interests – i.e. make

---

[105] Case C-237/94 *O'Flynn* [1996] ECR I-2417, para. 20.

[106] S. Koukoulis-Spiliotopoulos, *The Amended Equal Treatment Directive (2002/73) and the Constitutional Principle of Gender Equality*, paper to the 2004 Hague conference.

[107] See further A. Numhauser-Henning, 'Introduction, Equal Treatment – a Normative Challenge', in A. Numhauser-Henning (ed.), *Legal Perspectives on Equal Treatment and Non-Discrimination* (Kluwer, 2001), p. 8.

[108] Case C136/95 [1998] ECR I-2011. Compare S. Prechal (2004), p. 537.

[109] S. Fredman, *Changing the norm: positive duties in equal treatment legislation*, paper to the 18–20 November 2004 Hague Conference on 'Progressive Implementation: New Developments in European Union Gender Equality Law'.

use of 'the dominance approach'.[110] But, then again there is the argument that EU sex equality law cannot become an entirely all-embracing 'human right' due to the limited competence of EU institutions.[111] However, the need for successful integration of women as part of the Lisbon strategy for the internal market and other policies should go a long way to this end.

The Race Directive has clearly paved the way for the new Article 13 Directive 2004/113/EC broadening the scope of sex equality law beyond the area of work and employment and no doubt for significant progress. However, the fact that this Directive is considerably more limited in scope than the Race Directive has been said to create a hierarchy in discrimination to the detriment of sex equality law, despite the considerable 'heritage' of the latter as spelt out earlier in this chapter.

Another worry has been the erosion of key concepts of discrimination law as a consequence of their overall harmonisation. As regard justifications, the traditional view is that direct discrimination can never be justified. However, in her report to the Stockholm Congress already referred to above, Tamara Hervey emphasised justifications of both direct and indirect discrimination on an 'uninterrupted scale' and argued that the former Article 2 rules of the ETD will be seen as justifications within the discrimination concept.[112] Recent developments add to this picture. 'It is now all about the justification of differential treatment' said Bercusson à propos the Part-time and Fixed-term Directives banning explicitly only direct discrimination and at the same time opening up the way for its justification. There is also the very extensive rule on acceptable differential treatment in the form of direct discrimination concerning age in the Framework Directive[113] and concerning the provision of goods and services exclusively or primarily to members of one sex when justified by a legitimate aim, appropriate and necessary according to the new Article 13 Directive.[114] Future influences from the human rights approach may

---

[110] C. MacKinnon, 'Difference and Dominance, On sex-discrimination', in: K. T. Bartlett and R. Kennedy (eds.), *Feminist Legal Theory, Readings in Law and Gender* (Westview Press, 1991), pp. 81–94.

[111] S. Prechal (2004), p. 551.

[112] T. Hervey, *EC law on Justifications for Sex Discrimination in Working Life*, available at the Congress website: www.juridicum.su.se/stockholmcongress2002. In her paper to the 18–20 November 2004 Hague conference, however, she does conclude that a core general principle of justification for direct sex discrimination to date has been resisted by the ECJ, see T. Hervey, *What has EU sex equality law brought us this far: Is the glass half full or half empty?*

[113] See Art. 6 the Framework Directive 2000/78/EC.

also lead in this direction since the European Court of Human Rights permits justifications in cases of direct gender discrimination.[115] There is thus the risk of erosion of the ECJ's fundamentalist approach to direct discrimination. I have myself argued for the benefits of such an ultimate proportionality-test approach in relation to positive action measures and substantive equality.[116] Nevertheless, there are also risks attached to such a development to consider.

Then there is the concept of indirect discrimination – of special interest when it comes to substantive equality and equally adequate working conditions. Whereas the ban on direct discrimination concentrates on what is to be regarded as alike[117] and not on the treatment as such – what I will call the reference norm – the concept of indirect discrimination has a special potential. An apparently neutral reference norm with detrimental effects for a protected group must be objectively justified by a legitimate aim, represent a necessary means and be proportionate to its purpose.[118] The new and harmonised definition of this concept now present in the Amended ETD (and the Recast Directive) has already been discussed from the angle of providing new options as regards how to prove discrimination. This is a good thing. However, there is also here *the risk of erosion of the concept of indirect discrimination*. The variable geometry of different grounds for discrimination bans may turn out to erode the concept. We can already discern a tendency to stress differences in recent case law not finding the situations at hand comparable.[119] As regard the disabled, the concept of reasonable accommodation makes room for economic arguments on behalf of the employers as justifications, something which may turn out to undermine other grounds of discrimination in the long run, also.

The potential of the concept of indirect discrimination has thus so far been hampered in the process of application. However, there are also some more positive lines of argument. Bercusson, at the Stockholm conference, recalled how the issue of justifications is related to managerial prerogatives at the heart of labour law. Discrimination law and the requirements

---

[114] See Art. 4(5) of the Directive 2004/113/EC.   [115] C. McCrudden (2004).

[116] See A. Numhauser-Henning, 'On Equal Treatment, Positive Action and the Significance of a Person's Sex', in A. Numhauser-Henning (ed.), *Legal Perspectives on Equal Treatment and Non-Discrimination* (Kluwer, 2001).

[117] I.e. what are to be regarded as similar cases.

[118] On this line of argument, see A. Christensen 'Structural Aspects of Anti-Discriminatory Legislation' and 'Processes of Normative Change', both in A. Numhauser-Henning (ed.), *Legal Perspectives on Equal Treatment and Non-Discrimination* (Kluwer, 2001).

[119] Compare S. Prechal (2004).

of justifications for differential treatment may well develop into a general duty for employers objectively to justify their managerial decisions.[120] Equal treatment law may also aim at formulating positive/substantial requirements on managerial decisions/working conditions. Marie-Ange Moreau, also at the Stockholm conference, presented the very interesting idea of a widened scope for the requirement on adjustment measures now applying to disabled people to all under-represented groups.[121] Such ideas relate in an interesting way to the Amended ETD's new rules on preventive measures, equality plans and special bodies to promote equality between men and women.[122] However, the special rights already in place for pregnant and breastfeeding women – and to some extent for fathers and parents in general – are perhaps the best examples of such accommodation outside the area of disability, so far.

Article 13 and the widened scope for the non-discrimination principle to cover a number of new groups, further expanded by the Union Charter on Fundamental Rights[123] and a number of Community law instruments as regards atypical employment, threaten, however, to weaken the ban on discriminatory treatment, reducing it to the notion of formal equality already at the heart of the ECJ's case law. There is, in my opinion, a considerable risk that an ever-growing number of groups to be protected against discrimination will incline the notion of discrimination even closer to the Aristotelian concept of formal equal treatment as the least common denominator than hitherto. The Article 13 Directives here build on weaker ground than gender equality due to the new provisions after the Amsterdam Treaty, which in the area of gender equality thus demand a positive and proactive approach. Such fears can, to some extent, be said to have been confirmed by the Commission's Green Paper on 'Equality and Non-discrimination in an Enlarged Union' which clearly focuses on Article 13 and the two Directives then adopted on this basis and articulated in

---

[120] See further, for instance, M. Rönnmar, 'The Right to Direct and Allocate Work – From Employer Prerogatives to Objective Grounds', in A. Numhauser-Henning (ed.), *Legal Perspectives on Equal Treatment and Non-Discrimination* (Kluwer, 2001).

[121] M.-A. Moreau, 'Justifications of Discrimination', available at the Congress website: http://www.juridicum.su.se/stockholmcongress2002 published in R. Blanpain (ed.), *Labour Law & Social Security and the European Integration, Bulletin of Comparative Labour Relations* (Kluwer Law International, 2002).

[122] As regards this line of argument, see also A. Neal, 'Disability Discrimination at Work' in A. Numhauser-Henning (ed.), *Legal Perspectives on Equal Treatment and Non-Discrimination* (Kluwer, 2001).

[123] Article 21(1) of the Charter.

terms of non-discrimination to the detriment of the duty of the Union to promote equality in general and sex equality in particular.[124]

The situation in many of the new Member States – the post-communist countries – adds to this picture. To quote Csilla Kollonay Lehoczky: 'while conservatives favour "restoring classic family values" and this necessarily is a threat to already won labour market positions and social equality, liberals – in the name of private autonomy – feel reluctant to interfere with market freedom, and with the freedom of the owner (employer) in using their property.'[125] However, as formal equal treatment has proven ineffective or at least insufficient to come to terms with substantive differential treatment in the real world there is also the possibility that such a general development will open up for a more proactive approach to tackle the real problems of labour-market and society.[126] In a report on equal opportunities for women and men in the new Member States and accession countries from the Open Society Institute[127] it was clearly indicated that whereas the EU integration process had been a catalyst for improvements in the legislative framework on gender equality this legal change had not really made an impact on substantive equality in the daily lives of men and women. To this end the report recommends 'the European Commission should strengthen its role in monitoring the transposition and implementation of legislation', gender mainstreaming strategies should really be applied and relevant authorities should acquire a real commitment to equality between men and women.[128] As can be seen from a number of Community policy documents, the question of social inclusion – not least into the labour market – whether of women and the elderly, or of the citizens of new Member States or the disabled, must be considered a major concern for the future. The fundamental rights approach requires the scope of equality to be broadened further beyond the traditional area

---

[124] Compare E. Caracciolo di Torella at the 2004 Hague conference.

[125] C. Kollonay Lehoczky, *The significance of existing EC sex equality law for women in the new Member States. The case of Hungary*, paper to the 18–19 November 2004 Hague Conference.

[126] Compare the Commission's proposal on an Institute for Gender Equality, where the possibility to integrate sex equality matters in one Fundamental Rights Agency was rejected since it could imply that 'gender equality would remain a peripheral matter and would not receive the necessary attention and priority and as a result the impact would be very limited' (p. 5).

[127] Equal Opportunities for Women and Men, Monitoring law and practice in new member states and accession countries of the European Union, Network Women's Program, Open Society Institute 2005, see www.soros.org/initiatives/women/articles_publications/publications/equal_20050502.

[128] Ibid, at p. 53.

of the economically active not only with regard to women but also with regard to the other marginalised groups outside the Race Directive. The issue of political representation has not yet been addressed, nor has the monumental issue of domestic violence. To further such developments the Aristotelian concept of equality is clearly not enough but must be complemented by a plurality of different equality concepts and positive measures in the broadest definition.

6

EU anti-racism policy: the leader of the pack?

MARK BELL*

Introduction

In November 2004, the former Directorate-General for Employment and Social Affairs became the Directorate-General for Employment, Social Affairs and Equal Opportunities. This change in nomenclature was accompanied by a refreshing of the Commission's Internet pages on anti-discrimination. In the transition to the new pages, the dedicated website on 'anti-racism policy' disappeared and was consigned to the archives section.[1] This could be dismissed as a small matter of information presentation, but could it also be viewed as symptomatic of the current state of the Union's anti-racism policy?

The conventional view amongst many academic commentators is that race and ethnicity find themselves at the pinnacle of the so-called 'hierarchy of equality'.[2] The main reason for this perception is the relative strength of the Race Equality Directive[3] when compared to other areas of EU anti-discrimination law. Notably, the prohibition of discrimination on grounds of racial or ethnic origin applies to a wider range of areas than equivalent legislation on discrimination on grounds of sex, religion or belief, disability, age and sexual orientation. Given such disparities within EU anti-discrimination legislation, there are good reasons to argue that a higher level of protection exists in respect of discrimination on grounds of

---

* I wish to acknowledge the helpful comments and suggestions from Helen Meenan, Erik Bleich and the participants at the 'Equality and Diversity' Conference held at the University of Leicester on 13 May 2005.

[1] http://europa.eu.int/comm/employment_social/fundamental_rights/ public/arcr_en.htm.

[2] For example, C. Brown, 'The Race Directive: towards equality for *all* the peoples of Europe?' (2002) 21 *Yearbook of European Law* pp. 195–227, at p. 222; H. Meenan, 'Age equality after the Employment Directive', (2003) 10 *Maastricht Journal of European and Comparative Law*, pp. 9–38, at p. 10.

[3] Directive 2000/43/EC implementing the principle of equal treatment between persons irrespective of racial or ethnic origin, [2000] OJ L180/22.

racial or ethnic origin. Nevertheless, does this fully reflect the strength of the Union's commitment to combating racism? This chapter asks whether the picture painted by an exclusive focus on anti-discrimination *legislation* may be misleading. Whilst the Directives are central elements in the Union's efforts to combat discrimination, they are not isolated legal initiatives. Instead, they form part of a wider policy framework on equality. Alongside the legal instruments there are a range of other measures that need to be considered. For example, the specialised action programmes on equality[4] and initiatives taken in other policy fields where equality objectives have been integrated through the process of mainstreaming.[5] By stepping back from the Directives and broadening the horizon, this chapters suggests that the assumed equality hierarchy becomes more debatable. To this end, the chapter begins with an overview of the principal poles around which EU anti-racism policy has been organised. It identifies three main fields: legislative instruments, mainstreaming and an institutional commitment. Each of these is then examined in turn before concluding with an overall assessment of the state of anti-racism policy.

The construction of a policy against racism

The adoption of a Directive devoted to racial discrimination reflected the growing dynamism of EU anti-racism policy during the 1990s. Various factors combined to propel race up the political agenda. High profile incidents of racist violence occurred alongside a significant improvement in the electoral fortunes of parties from the extreme right-wing. These movements often placed anti-immigrant rhetoric at the centre of their policy platforms. During the same period, the role for the European Union in immigration and asylum grew considerably. Critics argued that the emerging policies were unduly restrictive, frequently captured in the notion of 'Fortress Europe'.[6] Anti-racism policy became a means for the EU to counter such criticisms by presenting evidence that it was taking initiatives to assist those migrants already residing within the Union. Against this backdrop, issues of racism assumed a greater political salience than other discrimination grounds. Combating racism came to feature

---

[4] E.g. Council Decision 95/593/EC concerning a medium-term Community action programme on equal opportunities for women and men (1996–2000), [1995] OJ L335/37.

[5] S. Mazey, 'Gender mainstreaming strategies in the E.U.: delivering on an agenda?' (2002) 10 *Feminist Legal Studies* pp. 227–40.

[6] L. Fekete and F. Webber, *Inside Racist Europe* (Institute of Race Relations, 1994), p. 28.

regularly on the agenda of European Council meetings[7] and the antecedents of Article 13 EC lie, in part, in the decision of the European Council in 1994 to create a Consultative Commission on Racism and Xenophobia.[8] This group, mainly composed of representatives of Member State governments, made a wide range of recommendations for constructing a comprehensive EU policy against racism.[9] Whilst the group's support for an amendment of the Treaty helped lead towards Article 13 EC, this was just one element of a much broader strategy. For example, the Council subsequently agreed to designate 1997 as European Year Against Racism, an initiative that served to spotlight the increasingly prominent role of the EU in this area.

Drawing together the various developments during and since this period, three principal policy strands can be identified. The first strand is *legislative initiatives*. As already discussed, the Race Equality Directive is obviously the shining example of legal measures taken by the European Union to combat racism. Less frequently noted is the fact that the Directive was preceded in 1996 by the adoption of the Joint Action concerning action to combat racism and xenophobia.[10] This instrument aimed to promote cross-border judicial cooperation in relation to racist criminal offences. As such, it reveals a twin-track legislative strategy; on the one hand, anti-discrimination legislation and, on the other, measures to combat racism as a crime. This was also reflected in the changes introduced by the 1999 Treaty of Amsterdam. Anti-racism was inserted as a core objective of the newly proclaimed Area of Freedom, Security and Justice:

> the Union's objective shall be to provide citizens with a high level of safety within an area of freedom, security and justice by developing common action among Member States in the fields of police and judicial cooperation in criminal matters and by preventing and combating racism and xenophobia.[11]

The legislative initiatives against racism were not intended to be self-standing and in 1998 the Commission published its 'Action Plan Against Racism'.[12] One of the hallmarks of the Action Plan was a new commitment to *mainstreaming* anti-racism. This evidently borrowed from the language

---

[7] It was mentioned six times in European Council conclusions between 1990 and 1994: see M. Bell, *Anti-discrimination law and the European Union* (Oxford University Press, 2002), p. 69.

[8] *Bulletin-EU*, Issue 6-1994, point I.29.

[9] Consultative Commission on Racism and Xenophobia, 'Final Report', 6906/1/95 Rev 1, RAXEN 24 (General Secretariat of the Council of the European Union, 1995).

[10] [1996] OJ L185/5.   [11] Article 29 EU.

[12] Commission, 'Action Plan Against Racism' COM (1998) 183.

and tools of EU gender equality policy, where mainstreaming became a central strategy during the 1990s.[13] The Commission promised to 'actively develop a mainstreaming approach to combating racism',[14] listing a range of policy fields, such as employment, education, youth and research, where anti-racism objectives would be integrated.

The final element to EU anti-racism policy was an *institutional commitment* in the form of the European Union Monitoring Centre on Racism and Xenophobia (EUMC). This arose from a recommendation of the European Council's Consultative Committee and its establishment was approved in 1997.[15] At the time, this represented a strategic commitment by the Union to provide an entrenched focus on racism. The EUMC seemed to promise an institutional source of expertise, supporting analysis and the future development of anti-racism policy. These three policy pillars – legislation, mainstreaming and an institutional commitment – constructed a relatively elaborate framework. The rest of this chapter considers each of these pillars in order to review their evolution and current status.

Legislative initiatives

The Race Equality Directive

Although the Race Equality Directive sits amidst a range of EU anti-discrimination legislation, it possesses three features that have underscored its relative strength. First and foremost, the Directive's material scope is broad: it applies to employment, vocational training, education, social protection, social advantages and access to goods and services, including housing.[16] Immediately, this distinguished the Directive from the pre-existing legislation on sex equality, which was limited to employment and social security. Moreover, the accompanying Framework Employment Directive provided protection against discrimination on grounds of religion or belief, disability, age and sexual orientation, but only in respect of employment and vocational training.[17] This situation has altered slightly following Directive 2004/113/EC implementing the

---

[13] Commission, 'Incorporating equal opportunities for women and men into all Community policies and activities' COM (1996) 67.

[14] Commission, Action Plan, p. 3.

[15] Regulation 1035/97/EC establishing a European Monitoring Centre for Racism and Xenophobia, [1997] OJ L151/1.

[16] Article 3(1), Directive 2000/43.

[17] Directive 2000/78/EC establishing a general framework for equal treatment in employment and occupation, [2000] OJ L303/16.

principle of equal treatment between men and women in the access to and supply of goods and services.[18] This instrument goes some way to levelling-up protection against sex discrimination. Nevertheless, there remain important areas where the scope of the Race Equality Directive is not mirrored elsewhere; most notably, sex discrimination in the field of education is still not prohibited by EU law.[19]

The second noteworthy dimension to the Race Equality Directive is its combination of a wide material scope of application with relatively few exceptions to the principle of equal treatment. Here, the contrast with Directive 2004/113/EC is stark. Although protection against sex discrimination has been extended beyond labour market matters, this is counterbalanced by a number of significant exceptions. Whilst there is no possibility to justify taking racial or ethnic origin into account in the provision of financial services, it remains open to Member States to permit sex to be taken into account in calculating risk assessments (e.g. in setting insurance premiums).[20] Finally, the Race Equality Directive was the first instrument to require Member States to create a body for the promotion of equal treatment with functions such as assisting individual victims of discrimination.[21] This obligation now also exists in respect of sex discrimination,[22] but not for any other ground.

Although the Race Equality Directive contains its own weaknesses and limitations (in particular the broad exception for difference of treatment based on nationality[23]), it remains strong in comparison to other EU anti-discrimination legislation. It is fair to conclude that the Directive was a relatively bold step that transformed a policy history of hesitancy into a concrete legal commitment on the part of the Union. The roots of this turnaround lie in the political consensus built during the 1990s on the need for an EU dimension to anti-racism policy. The high-level commitment to taking action against racism was not equally evident on issues such as age or sexual orientation and this factor encouraged the Commission to propose separate and more ambitious legislation on racial

---

[18] OJ 2004 L373/37.

[19] This is excluded from the scope of Directive 2004/113 (Art. 3(3)).

[20] Ibid., Art. 5(2). See further, E. Caracciolo di Torella, 'The goods and services Directive: limitations and opportunities' *Feminist Legal Studies*, 13 (2005), pp. 337–47.

[21] Article 13, Directive 2000/43.

[22] Article 8a, Directive 2002/73/EC amending Directive 76/207/EEC on the implementation of the principle of equal treatment for men and women as regards access to employment, vocational training and promotion, and working conditions, [2002] OJ L269/15; Article 12, Directive 2004/113.

[23] Article 3(2), Directive 2000/43.

discrimination.[24] The final proposal was informed by evidence that many Member States already possessed laws against racial discrimination, but that these were rarely used in practice.[25] The requirement to create an equal treatment body aimed at constructing an institutional dimension that would embed anti-racism policies at the national level, echoing the Union's own decision to create the EUMC.

The longer term construction of support for anti-racism laws combined in 2000 with short-term political circumstances. The entry into the Austrian government of Jorg Haider's Freedom Party (from the extreme right) galvanised the desire of the other Member States to send a signal of their rejection of this political drift. This resulted in the 'fast-track' adoption of the Race Equality Directive within the space of six months.[26] Although the short-term impetus is not a sufficient explanation of the Directive's origins, it did contribute to ensuring the swift adoption of comparatively far-reaching legislation. In contrast, Directive 2004/113/EC was scarred by protracted bargaining, first within the Commission and then subsequently within the Council of Ministers.[27] This resulted in a gradual reduction in the material scope of the original proposal and a significant increase in the range of exceptions necessary to accommodate Member States' objections.

An enduring question concerns the choice to isolate race in a separate Directive. The principal explanation, as discussed above, lies in the greater political consensus that prevailed on this form of discrimination. Whilst this pragmatism paid dividends in the form of a stronger and broader Directive, its legacy is the legal stratification of race and ethnicity as separate from the other discrimination grounds. This fails to engage with evidence that manifestations of discrimination are not neatly compartmentalised according to the categories constructed through law. First, there are grey areas around the boundaries of what is meant by 'racial or ethnic origin'. The intersection between race and religion is a good example of the problems encountered in distinguishing discrimination grounds

---

[24] Commission, 'Communication on certain Community measures to combat discrimination' COM (1999) 564, p. 8.

[25] Commission, 'Legal Instruments to Combat Racism and Xenophobia' (Office for the Official Publications of the European Communities, 1992).

[26] A. Geddes, 'Integrating immigrants and minorities in a wider and deeper Europe', in W. Spohn and A. Triandafyllidou (eds.), *Europeanisation, national identities and migration – changes in boundary constructions between Western and Eastern Europe* (Routledge, 2003), pp. 83–98, at p. 94.

[27] A. Masselot, 'Gender equality outside the labour market' in M. Mateo Diaz and S. Millns (eds.), *The future of gender equality in the European Union* (Palgrave, forthcoming).

in the manner imagined by the Directives. The post-9/11 context has highlighted the interlocking nature of race and religion with respect to Muslim communities of migrant origin. Secondly, although other grounds, such as age or disability, are easier to distinguish from race and ethnicity, they can combine to produce specific forms of inequality. In his contribution to this book, Israel Doron draws attention to the impact of earlier periods of migration on the contemporary ethnic profile of older people in Europe. Health and social care services will require re-examination in order to respond to cultural, religious and linguistic diversity. Alternatively, labour market data indicate that some groups of third country national women have markedly lower employment rates than those of either women in general or third country national men.[28] Given the very limited experience to date of litigation under any of the Article 13 Directives, it is difficult to reach firm conclusions on how cases raising more than one ground of discrimination will be handled. Nonetheless, the variations in the legal framework do not facilitate an integrated legal analysis of cumulative discrimination.

Combating racism through EU criminal law

One of the issues that originally located racism within the EU's political agenda was evidence that individuals and organisations were exploiting differences in national criminal law relating to racist offences. For example, racist publications were being produced in a Member State where this was not illegal and then being distributed in other states where this activity was prohibited.[29] Restraining such action was more difficult in the context of the EU internal market (with its emphasis on reducing border controls), as well as the opportunities presented by the rapid diffusion of the Internet.[30] As already mentioned, the Union adopted a Joint Action in 1996 in order to 'ensure effective judicial cooperation' with respect to incitement to discrimination, Holocaust denial, dissemination of racist material and the activities of racist organisations.[31] Although Joint Actions were legally binding instruments adopted under the aegis of

---

[28] Commission, 'Employment in Europe 2003' (Luxembourg, Office for the Official Publications of the European Communities), p. 198.

[29] P. Rodrigues, 'Cross-border discrimination: private international law, the denial of the Holocaust and the Internet' in T. Loenen and P. Rodrigues (eds.), *Non-discrimination law: comparative perspectives* (Kluwer, 1999), pp. 397–410.

[30] Commission, 'Communication on illegal and harmful content on the Internet' COM (1996) 487.

[31] Title 1, Article A, Joint Action, [1996] OJ L185/5.

the EU Treaty, no possibility was provided for enforcement by the Commission or the Court of Justice. Unsurprisingly, the impact of the Joint Action seemed to be limited. A Council report in 1998 identified only two Member States which had taken specific measures to implement the Joint Action, although the report also concluded that national law in most Member States was already largely in conformity.[32]

The Treaty of Amsterdam introduced significant reforms to the functioning of the EU Treaty 'third pillar' on police and judicial co-operation. Notably, the amendments replaced the Joint Action instrument with a new legal tool, the Framework Decision. Unlike its predecessor, the contents of a Framework Decision can be interpreted by the Court of Justice.[33] Whilst the EU Treaty expressly excludes a Framework Decision from having direct effect,[34] the Court of Justice has held that national courts are under a duty to interpret national law in conformity with the provisions of a Framework Decision.[35] Taking advantage of the new possibilities this offered, in 2001 the Commission proposed a Framework Decision on combating racism and xenophobia.[36]

The Commission proposal identified six conducts that would be punishable as a criminal offence in all Member States:

- public incitement to violence or hatred for a racist purpose;
- public insults or threats for a racist purpose;
- public condoning for a racist purpose of crimes of genocide, crimes against humanity and war crimes;
- public denial or trivialisation of the Holocaust in a manner liable to disturb the public peace;
- public dissemination or distribution of tracts, pictures or other material containing expressions of racism;
- directing, supporting or participating in the activities of a racist group.[37]

Additionally, the Commission proposed that racist or xenophobic motivation in any other criminal offence should be deemed an aggravating circumstance and a factor to be taken into account in determining the penalty.[38]

---

[32] UE Conseil, 'Note de Comité K.4 au Coreper', 7808/1/98 REV 1, Brussels, 29 April 1998. Austria and Luxembourg had taken specific implementing measures.
[33] Article 35 EU.   [34] Article 34(2)(b) EU.
[35] Case C-105/03 *Pupino*, [2005] ECR 5285.
[36] COM (2001) 664. For a more detailed discussion, see R. Nickel, A. Coomber, M. Bell, T. Hutchinson and K. Zahi, *European strategies to combat racism and xenophobia as a crime* (European Network Against Racism, 2003).
[37] Article 4.   [38] Article 8.

Unlike the Race Equality Directive, reaching agreement on this legislative proposal has proven extremely difficult. Consensus was almost achieved at the Justice and Home Affairs Council on 27–28 February 2003.[39] Nonetheless, the Italian government (then holding the Presidency) submitted an alternative text in March 2003 which was rejected by all other delegations. At this stage, the Council decided to suspend negotiations and these were not recommenced until almost two years later in February 2005.[40] During these negotiations, numerous changes have been made to the draft Framework Decision. For example, the list of offences has been reduced and the description of each of the remaining offences has been altered.[41] It is, though, possible to underline certain key themes in the debate.

The definition of 'racism and xenophobia'

The Commission proposed to define 'racism and xenophobia' as 'the belief in race, colour, descent, religion or belief, national or ethnic origin as a factor determining aversion to individuals or groups'.[42] Perhaps the most significant aspect of this definition is how it contrasts with the concept of racism implicit in the Race Equality Directive. The latter contains no specific definition of 'racism' and the list of prohibited grounds is simply left at 'racial or ethnic origin'. As mentioned earlier, the separate treatment of discrimination on grounds of 'religion or belief' under the Framework Employment Directive indicates that religious discrimination is viewed as conceptually distinct.

A number of states, including the UK, Austria and the Netherlands, raised questions over the inclusion of religion in the draft Framework Decision.[43] These discussions resulted in the addition of the following derogating clause:

> A Member State may exclude from criminal liability conduct . . . where the conduct is directed against a group of persons or a member of such a

---

[39] Council, 'Proposal for a Framework Decision on combating racism and xenophobia', 6229/05 DROIPEN 10, 10 February 2005, p. 2.

[40] Ibid. Political agreement was reached in April 2007.

[41] Directing, supporting or participating in the activities of a racist group is no longer included in the list of offences under discussion. At the time of writing, the latest draft available was Council, 'Proposal for a Council Framework Decision on combating racism and xenophobia', 8994/1/05 DROIPEN 24, 27 May 2005.

[42] Article 3(a), COM (2001) 664.

[43] Council, 'Proposal for a Council Framework Decision on combating racism and xenophobia', 14665/02 DROIPEN 86, 25 November 2002, p. 3.

group defined by reference to religion and this is not a pretext for directing acts against a group of persons or a member of such a group defined by reference to race, colour, descent, or national or ethnic origin.[44]

This provision bifurcates offences linked to religion, distinguishing between those that are a pretext for racism and those which are entirely severable. The mischief that this is designed to address is a situation where conduct of a racist nature is constructed in terms of hostility to a particular religion, such as Islam, in order to evade the scope of racist criminal offences. Nevertheless, it may produce some unusual lacunae. For instance, incitement to hatred directed against religious converts (e.g. white Europeans converting to Islam) might not be regarded as a 'pretext' for acts against ethnic minority groups. More generally, this debate reveals a lack of consensus amongst the Member States as to what is meant by 'racism'. The rapid adoption of the Race Equality Directive side-stepped a more profound interrogation on the relationship between race and religion. In contrast, the Framework Decision negotiations have illustrated the problematic nature of drawing strict boundaries.

Balancing freedom of expression with combating racism

Another thread running through the negotiations is how to strike the correct balance between respecting freedom of expression and using the criminal law to combat racism. Notably, a broad exception protecting constitutional principles of free expression has been inserted.[45] In addition, various derogations would permit Member States to restrict the circumstances under which an offence would be committed. For example, Article 8(1)(d) allows Member States to exclude from criminal liability conduct which 'is not threatening, abusive or insulting'.[46] These extra exceptions are bound up with an underlying debate around the application of the principle of double criminality in relation to racist criminal offences. This general principle requires conduct to be contrary to the legislation of both the requesting and the receiving state in order to permit judicial

---

[44] Article 8(1), Council, 8994/1/05 DROIPEN 24, 27 May 2005.
[45] Article 7(2): 'This Framework Decision shall not have the effect of requiring Member States to take measures in contradiction to their constitutional rules and fundamental principles relating to freedom of association, freedom of the press and the freedom of expression in other media or rules governing the rights and responsibilities of, and the procedural safeguards for, the press or other media where these rules relate to the determination or limitation of liability', ibid.
[46] Ibid.

co-operation, such as the seizure and confiscation of materials in one state at the request of prosecutors elsewhere. The basic rationale of the Framework Decision was to create a common corpus of racist criminal offences across all Member States, thus avoiding gaps in legislation that give rise to judicial co-operation problems where there is a lack of double criminality. Yet, the derogations now found within the Framework Decision risk undermining the anticipated convergence in the substantive content of national criminal law. The current text aims to guarantee cross-border judicial co-operation even where national laws differ as a result of Member States choosing to take advantage of the permissible derogations,[47] however, this has proven controversial.

Combating racism with legal instruments

Reviewing the Union's legislative strategy against racism, evidence of progress is highly unbalanced. There is a great disparity between the steps taken through discrimination legislation and the 'difficulties' encountered in the criminal law field. In part, this may reflect wider issues of institutional resonance.[48] Although the Race Equality Directive departed from the traditional labour market focus of earlier discrimination legislation, it built on an established model. In contrast, the Union's role in criminal law is more recent, albeit an area of significant change in recent years. The lack of agreement on criminal law instruments suggests that the Union's policy frame on anti-racism is becoming more defined. Bleich highlights the contrast between the dominant policy frames on racism found within the UK and France. Whereas the UK has focused on tackling 'access racism', such as discrimination in access to employment, France has historically concentrated on 'expressive racism', such as racist speech within the media.[49] The evolution of the Union's legislative strategy on racism indicates a greater consensus on using law to combat 'access racism' than in respect of 'expressive racism'.

Mainstreaming

A clear commitment to mainstreaming anti-racism was first espoused in the Commission's 1998 Action Plan Against Racism. Since then, adherence

---

[47] Article 8(3), ibid.
[48] M. Pollack and E. Hafner-Burton, 'Mainstreaming gender in the European Union' (2000) 7 *Journal of European Public Policy* pp. 432–456, at p. 436.
[49] E. Bleich, *Race politics in Britain and France – ideas and policymaking since the 1960s* (Cambridge University Press, 2003), p. 170.

to this strategy has been reiterated in various policy documents. In 2000, the Commission presented an initial report on the implementation of the Action Plan, which confirmed the priority attached to the mainstreaming approach.[50] In its contribution to the 2001 UN World Conference Against Racism, the Commission highlighted its own efforts at mainstreaming and recommended that all states should follow this approach.[51] Indeed, in 2005 the DG Justice, Freedom and Security website declared: 'the Commission has endeavoured to pursue a coherent strategy of integrating anti-racism into EU policies, known as mainstreaming. This has proved successful across a number of Community policies.'[52] Although the 'success' of mainstreaming may be proclaimed on the Commission's Internet pages, this proposition demands further scrutiny. In particular, it is necessary to consider evidence relating to both the process and product of mainstreaming.

The process of mainstreaming

Mainstreaming is a broad concept that encapsulates a rich array of different methods and strategies for promoting equality.[53] Various typologies for categorising mainstreaming models can be identified. For example, a distinction can be drawn between those which are 'elite-bureaucractic' as opposed to 'democratic-participatory'.[54] In the former, the existing circle of decision-makers is retained, but an attempt is made to adjust the factors influencing policy decisions. In the latter, the very style of decision-making is challenged, with the introduction of new actors from affected communities. Alternatively, mainstreaming models may be distinguished by their choice of instruments. In some cases, there has been a preference for non-binding guidance coupled with procedural requirements for decision-makers, such as undertaking impact assessment analysis. Other

---

[50] Commission, 'Report on the implementation of the action plan against racism – mainstreaming the fight against racism', January 2000. Available at: http://europa.eu.int/comm/employment_social/ fundamental_rights/public/arcr_en.htm.

[51] Commission, 'Contribution to the World Conference Against Racism, Racial Discrimination, Xenophobia and Related Intolerance' COM (2001) 291, p. 13.

[52] See: http://europa.eu.int/comm/justice_home/fsj/rights/discrimination/fsj_rights_discrim_en.htm (visited 24 April 2005).

[53] Group of Specialists on Mainstreaming, *Gender Mainstreaming – conceptual framework, methodology and presentation of good practice. Final report of activities of the Group of Specialists on Mainstreaming (EG-S-MS)* (Council of Europe, 1998).

[54] F. Beveridge and S. Nott, 'Mainstreaming: a case for optimism and cynicism' (2002) 10 *Feminist Legal Studies* pp. 299–311, at p. 301.

approaches have sought to underpin mainstreaming duties by making them legally binding and ultimately open to judicial enforcement.[55]

The first weakness that seems evident in the Commission's approach is the failure to articulate the process through which mainstreaming would be accomplished. Both the 1998 Action Plan and its 2000 review refer to the creation of an inter-service group to promote mainstreaming.[56] Yet, there was little detail on how this group would accomplish the systematic integration of anti-racism objectives across all areas of EU law and policy. This vagueness in the original plan was criticised by the Parliament's Civil Liberties Committee, which emphasised the need for 'clear objectives and set timetables'.[57] Indeed, Shaw reports that whilst the inter-service group was active in the run-up to the 2001 World Conference Against Racism, it has not met since then.[58]

A more structured approach to mainstreaming may be emerging through Commission impact assessment techniques. In 2005, the Commission announced its intention to include fundamental rights within existing impact assessment requirements for all legislative proposals.[59] Oversight will be exercised by the Group of Commissioners on Fundamental Rights, Anti-Discrimination and Equal Opportunities.[60] This could be a vehicle for mainstreaming race issues into new initiatives, however, there is no apparent mechanism for reviewing the effects of pre-existing law and policy.

The product of mainstreaming anti-racism

In assessing the Commission's mainstreaming activities, two aspects can be highlighted: financial support for projects on racism and the integration of anti-racism into policy objectives.

[55] This has been a distinctive characteristic of the statutory duty to promote equality of opportunity in Northern Ireland: see C. McCrudden, 'Equality' in C. Harvey (ed.), *Human rights, equality and democratic renewal in Northern Ireland* (Hart Publishing, 2001), pp. 75–112.

[56] COM (1998) 183, 16; Commission, Implementation of the action plan against racism, p. 19.

[57] European Parliament, 'Report on the Communication from the Commission, An Action Plan Against Racism' [Oostlander], A4-478/98, 3 December 1998, p. 13.

[58] J. Shaw, 'Mainstreaming equality in European Union law and policymaking' (European Network Against Racism, 2004), p. 23.

[59] Commission, 'Compliance with the Charter of Fundamental Rights in Commission legislative proposals – methodology for systematic and rigorous monitoring' COM (2005) 172.

[60] Ibid. p. 6.

One possible indicator of mainstreaming is the growth in the number of EU-funded projects on issues relating to racism. These stretch beyond the anti-discrimination and employment programmes overseen by DG Employment, Social Affairs and Equal Opportunities and consequently illustrate some permeation of anti-racism objectives. This is especially evident in the fields of education and youth, where a considerable range of projects on anti-racism have been funded.[61] Furthermore, combating racism has been entrenched as a horizontal objective of the Union's Youth Action Programme.[62] Naturally, these projects hold the potential to advance knowledge and understanding of racism, which can in turn stimulate future policy development. Nevertheless, the rather disparate nature of anti-racism projects makes it difficult to evaluate their long-term impact or direction. For instance, the 2004 report 'Minority elderly health and social care in Europe' was funded under the Fifth Framework Research Programme.[63] It highlights the situation of older people from minority communities when accessing healthcare, such as their greater need for language interpretation, differences in disease prevalence rates and religious requirements that vary between communities. The capacity for the Union to respond to these research findings is far from evident. Such matters would fall within the ambit of policy co-operation on social protection, but this remains rather loose and confined to broad macro-policy objectives.[64] The questions raised around the coherence and effectiveness of these funding programmes can be traced back to the fragile institutional resources for overseeing anti-racism mainstreaming. It is difficult to see how systematic co-ordination of anti-racism policy is ensured without clear structures for interdepartmental communication and planning.

Whilst the ad hoc funding of specific projects provides evidence of mainstreaming, in the long-term it is more crucial to ensure that anti-racism is embedded within the underpinning policy objectives. An example of mainstreaming at the level of policy aims can be found in the European Employment Strategy. The core goal of the Strategy is to raise

---

[61] See: http://europa.eu.int/comm/education/archive/raci/e1_en.html.

[62] Article 2(1)(a), Council Decision 1031/2000/EC establishing the 'Youth' Community action programme [2000] OJ L117/1.

[63] PRIAE Research Briefing, 'Minority elderly health and social care in Europe' (2004), available at: http://www.priae.org/docs/MEC%20European%20Summary%20Findings2.pdf.

[64] See further, Commission, 'Modernising social protection for the development of high-quality, accessible and sustainable healthcare and long-term care: support for national strategies using the open method of coordination' COM (2004) 304.

employment participation rates, with the flagship target of achieving a 70 per cent employment rate by 2010.[65] Whilst race issues were not mentioned in the original Employment Guidelines, by 2000 the Commission was able to cite concrete evidence of mainstreaming in practice because the second set of guidelines specifically called on Member States to 'give special attention to the needs of the disabled, ethnic minorities and other groups and individuals who may be disadvantaged, and develop appropriate forms of preventive and active policies to promote their integration into the labour market'.[66] The objective of promoting labour market inclusion of ethnic minorities and immigrants has featured in all subsequent versions of the guidelines. Nevertheless, the case of the Employment Strategy serves to illustrate the complexity involved in implementing mainstreaming. Although race made the transition from invisibility to being expressly on the agenda, this has not guaranteed genuine and thorough policy integration. On the one hand, the specific race guideline remained marginal, receiving limited attention in either the annual National Action Plans or the Council's Recommendations directed at individual Member States.[67] On the other hand, it is difficult to find evidence of race mainstreaming within the Employment Strategy. Aside from the dedicated guideline, there was no parallel attempt to weave race into other limbs of the Strategy, such as policies on entrepreneurship or on equal opportunities for women and men. Indeed, there is a contrast here with gender, where originally the specific equal opportunities pillar was combined with a horizontal objective of gender mainstreaming throughout all other parts of the Strategy.[68]

Rhetoric or reality?

Although the Commission continues to express its commitment to mainstreaming anti-racism, the first seven years of this approach have revealed a rather slow gestation. Pointing to lists of funded projects on race-related

---

[65] Council Decision on guidelines for the employment policies of the Member States, [2003] OJ L197/13.
[66] Guideline 9, Council Resolution on the 1999 Employment Guidelines, [1999] OJ C69/2.
[67] For more detailed analysis, see M. Bell, 'Racial discrimination and the European Employment Strategy', in J. Bell and C. Kilpatrick (eds.), *The Cambridge Yearbook of European Legal Studies. Volume 6. 2003–2004* (Hart Publishing, 2005) pp. 55–71, at p. 59.
[68] For an assessment, see J. Rubery, 'Gender mainstreaming and gender equality in the EU: the impact of the EU employment strategy' (2002) 33 *Industrial Relations Journal*, pp. 500–22.

issues provides evidence of policy activity, but this is not a sufficient indicator of a coherent and comprehensive mainstreaming strategy. The picture emerging is one of sporadic initiatives that lack a linking narrative.

The European Union Monitoring Centre on Racism and Xenophobia

The creation of the Monitoring Centre (EUMC) represented a distinctive strand to anti-racism policy and one which set it apart from other areas of equality law and policy. Its establishment was a key recommendation of the 1995 Council Consultative Commission on Racism and Xenophobia[69] and it formed an integral element in building the anti-racism policy infrastructure. What was the purpose of the EUMC? Article 2(1) of its constituting Regulation states:

> the prime objective of the Centre shall be to provide the Community and its Member States . . . with objective, reliable and comparable data at European level on the phenomena of racism, xenophobia and anti-Semitism in order to help them when they take measures or formulate courses of action within their respective spheres of competence.[70]

This imagines the Centre as a source of expertise in an evolving policy field; an institutional commitment that would bring focus and an ongoing source of knowledge. In practice, the EUMC has experienced considerable difficulties. These might be summarised under two headings: finding an institutional identity and fulfilling its mandate.

Finding an institutional identity

Although Regulation 1035/97 provided the legal foundation for the EUMC, breathing life into the agency proved challenging. On the one hand, there were administrative problems, such as finding appropriate premises,[71] which retarded its practical functioning and indeed the Centre was unable to spend a significant proportion of its budget in 1998 and 1999.[72] Concerns were also expressed surrounding the political

---

[69] Consultative Commission on Racism and Xenophobia, 'Final Report', 6906/1/95 Rev 1, RAXEN 24 (General Secretariat of the Council of the European Union, 1995).

[70] Regulation 1035/97/EC.

[71] Commission, 'Report on the activities of the European Monitoring Centre on Racism and Xenophobia' COM (2000) 625, p. 4.

[72] There was a 73 per cent underspend in 1998 and a 26 per cent underspend in 1999: Commission, ibid., p. 9.

independence of the Management Board and the attitude of certain national governments.[73] Alongside these organisational matters, the EUMC initially struggled to locate a distinctive role for itself. On the one hand, the task of monitoring national compliance with EU legislation, most notably the Race Equality Directive, lies primarily with the Commission. In fact, the Commission created its own group of legal experts on discrimination on grounds of racial or ethnic origin which it tasked with preparing national reports on the transposition process.[74] Furthermore, all aspects of national law and policy on racism were already kept under periodic review by the European Commission for Racism and Intolerance of the Council of Europe. Looking in a different direction, the EUMC was not originally equipped to become 'a major centre of original research'.[75] Nevertheless, its early activities oscillated between 'monitoring' activities (such as the review of national legal developments in its annual reports) and pursuing an independent research agenda.

Fulfilling the mandate

In 2002, an external evaluation reached the conclusion that 'the EUMC cannot be said to have demonstrated value for money for the €13 million it has committed'.[76] One of the principal criticisms of the Centre's work was a failure to concentrate on the primary objective of providing 'objective, reliable and comparable data'. This finding was echoed by the Commission in 2003: 'the objective of comparability has not yet been achieved to any substantial degree'.[77] Both reviews raised questions as to whether the original mandate could effectively be completed.

The distinctive focus of the EUMC mandate was the compilation of *comparable* data on racism in the Member States. This reflected a visible gap in the information resources available within Europe. Data collection practices in relation to race and ethnicity vary greatly across the

---

[73] European Parliament Resolution on the European Monitoring Centre on Racism and Xenophobia, [2001] OJ C121/409.

[74] http://europa.eu.int/comm/employment_social/fundamental_rights/public/pubsg_en.htm#Race.

[75] Commission, 'Communication on the activities of the European Monitoring Centre on Racism and Xenophobia, together with proposals to recast Council Regulation (EC) 1035/97' COM (2003) 483, p. 6.

[76] Centre for Strategy and Evaluation Services, 'Evaluation of the European Monitoring Centre on Racism and Xenophobia', May 2002, p. 79: http://europa.eu.int/comm/employment_social/fundamental_rights/pdf/ arcg/eumc_eval2002_en.pdf.

[77] Commission, Activities of the European Monitoring Centre, p. 4.

Member States. In some states, such as the UK and the Netherlands, data disaggregated by reference to ethnic origins is available and has been encouraged through legislation. Yet, in other states, the collection of such data has been officially opposed or even rendered unlawful. Various objections have been raised, such as protection of individual privacy, potential misuse of ethnic data and the implicit reinforcement of ethnic categorisations within society.[78] In retrospect the EUMC was placed in the invidious position of being charged with producing comparable data, but lacking the institutional resources to bring this about. It has no powers to impose common standards on national statistical collection systems. Indeed, the Commission's 2003 review concluded that 'ultimately the Monitoring Centre's remit is unachievable unless national authorities adopt compatible if not common classification systems'.[79]

Certainly, there is no immediate prospect of the Member States agreeing to collect ethnic data, for example, through national census surveys. Nonetheless, the objective of 'comparable' data might be achievable even in the absence of identical data sets. In some instances, the data subject to comparison will not be exclusively quantitative in nature, such as comparative analysis of legal instruments. Elsewhere, it may be possible to draw upon surrogate or associated data in the absence of direct information according to ethnic origin. For instance, data on the employment and unemployment rates of third country nationals has been utilised within the Employment Strategy. Although nationality is not a satisfactory substitute for ethnic data, it can provide a useful indicator in the absence of other options. More recently, there is evidence that the EUMC has refocused its work towards the collection of comparable data. Specifically, it is producing a series of comparative baseline studies covering topics such as employment, education and racist violence.[80]

From EUMC to Fundamental Rights Agency

Given the EUMC's growing pains, it is not surprising that questions were raised surrounding its viability. During the 2003 review, the Commission identified various options: retaining and revising its existing mandate; extending its remit to cover a wider range of equality grounds or human

---

[78] For a critical analysis of these arguments, see J. Goldston, 'Race and ethnic data: a missing resource in the fight against discrimination', in A. Krizsán (ed.), *Ethnic monitoring and data protection – the European context* (Central European University Press, 2001).

[79] Commission, Activities of the European Monitoring Centre, p. 5.

[80] See www.eumc.at/eumc/index.php?fuseaction = content.dsp_ cat_content&catid = 1.

rights in general; abolition. As with the 2002 external evaluation, the Commission concluded that expanding its remit 'would be an unwelcome distraction within the limit of the resources likely to be available to the Centre and [. . .] it would lead to a weakening of the emphasis on racism'.[81] Despite this finding, four months later the European Council peremptorily announced that it had 'agreed to build upon the existing European Monitoring Centre on Racism and Xenophobia and to extend its mandate to become a Human Rights Agency'.[82] A subsequent Parliament report noted that 'this decision came as a complete surprise – even to insiders. It has been criticised as a bad example of political horse-trading.'[83] Although the Commission's proposal for the Fundamental Rights Agency includes a commitment to continue dedicated work on racism and xenophobia,[84] concerns remain. At an organisational level, there are clearly great risks involved in this process of restructuring. Will it be possible to ensure that equivalent resources are devoted to issues of racism within the new agency? Might the reorganisation undermine the experience and specialisation of the EUMC? Setting these important practical issues to one side, this chapter will focus on the implications for anti-racism policy. These can be analysed by reference to two issues: race and other equality grounds; and race and human rights.

Race and other equality grounds

When considering the origins of the EUMC, it is necessary to bear in mind that its conception preceded Article 13 EC and arose from the 1994/5 Consultative Commission. Indeed, its approval was presented as one of the concrete outputs of the 1997 European Year Against Racism. Consequently, there was relatively little debate at that time about whether its remit should extend to other forms of discrimination. In the period since its creation, however, the salience of other equality issues has risen considerably. There are three potential benefits from moving towards a broader equality mandate.

---

[81] Commission, Activities of the European Monitoring Centre, p. 9.

[82] Council, 'Brussels European Council: 12 and 13 December 2003. Presidency Conclusions' POLGEN 2, 5 February 2004, p. 27. See further, C. McCrudden and H. Kountouros in this volume.

[83] European Parliament, 'Working document on the proposal for a Council Regulation on the European Monitoring Centre on Racism and Xenophobia (Recast version)', PE 339.635, 25 March 2004, p. 2.

[84] Article 5(1)(b), Commission, 'Proposal for a Council Regulation establishing a European Union Agency for Fundamental Rights' COM (2005) 280.

First, the existing work of the EUMC has already engaged with the boundaries between racism and other forms of discrimination. It has conducted several studies on discrimination against Islamic communities,[85] as well as a research project on Roma women and access to healthcare.[86] In fact, the Commission's aborted proposal in 2003 to revise the constituting Regulation of the EUMC sought to broaden its mandate to cover racism, xenophobia, anti-Semitism and 'related intolerance'.[87] That proposal also uncovers a second reason favouring a wider horizon. In order to strengthen the independence and expertise of the Management Board, the Commission suggested that the national representatives should be drawn from the persons responsible for running the national equal treatment bodies established pursuant to the Race Equality Directive.[88] When considering the identity of these organisations, it becomes clear that in many cases the EUMC's interlocutors would not be race-specific bodies, but rather agencies with a mandate for a range of equality grounds. Admittedly, the picture varies considerably across the Member States. In a few cases, national authorities have chosen to create or retain organisations with a mandate dedicated to combating racism.[89] Nevertheless, there is a discernible trend towards single equality bodies.[90]

Finally, the challenges faced in constructing comparable European data are arguably not unique to issues around race and ethnicity. Problems relating to data protection and individual privacy will be applicable to the collection of data on personal characteristics such as religion, disability or sexual orientation. Debates surrounding the appropriate classifications are also present. The meaning of 'disability' is contested and gaps emerge between self-perception and external categorisations. The definition of disability for the purposes of discrimination law may not correspond to an individual's assessment of whether they have a disability. Alternatively, concerns have been expressed that classifications of sexual orientation may reify the notion that sexual identities are stable and unambiguous.[91] This debate is not dissimilar to that surrounding the potential for ethnic data to solidify perceptions of ethnic divisions in society.

[85] Commission, Activities of the European Monitoring Centre, p. 4.
[86] 'Romani women and access to health care' *Equal Voices*, Issue 11, (2003).
[87] Commission, Activities of the European Monitoring Centre, p. 20.   [88] Ibid., p. 24.
[89] For example, the Ombudsman on Ethnic Discrimination in Sweden or the National Office Against Racial Discrimination in Italy.
[90] Commission, 'Equality and non-discrimination in an enlarged European Union' COM (2004) 379, p. 12.
[91] H. Oliver, 'Sexual orientation discrimination: perceptions, definitions and genuine occupational requirements', *Industrial Law Journal* 33 (2004), pp. 1–21, at p. 20.

The fact that there are overlapping and shared features in the process of equality data collection does not by itself require the creation of a single organisation. It does suggest that there is at least space for mutual learning and synergies through a co-ordinated approach. This is especially true when seeking to construct data relating to multiple discrimination; for example, the situation of older people from minority ethnic communities. The shift, therefore, to the Fundamental Rights Agency might be viewed as an opportunity to develop a more integrated equality perspective. This logic is contradicted, however, by the Commission's subsequent proposal to create a separate Institute for Gender Equality.[92] The mandate of the Institute will be remarkably similar to that of the EUMC: 'to collect, record, analyse and disseminate relevant objective, reliable and comparable information as regards gender equality'.[93] In its explanatory statement, the Commission argues that 'the advanced state of development and the specificity of gender equality policy, which goes beyond the fight against discrimination and the respect of a fundamental right, are such that justify a separate agency'.[94] In addition, the Commission suggests that 'gender equality would remain a peripheral matter' if located in an agency with a wider remit.[95] The difficulty with this reasoning is that it raises profound questions over the earlier decision to extend the EUMC's mandate. The risk that racism becomes marginalised within a broader organisation seems equally serious. With regard to the specificity of gender equality as a fundamental right, the Commission points to the dedicated agencies and instruments found at the international level.[96] Yet, the same argument would be valid in respect of racism where specialised international human rights protection exists under the Convention on the Elimination of All Forms of Racial Discrimination.

Race and human rights

The arguments in favour of a broader equality mandate are substantial and they echo the widespread national debates on the appropriate structure of equality bodies. Yet, the choice of the European Council was to make a more radical shift towards a human rights agency. There are some examples at the national level where this approach has been followed. In Latvia, the National Human Rights Office performs functions

---

[92] Commission, 'Proposal for a Regulation of the European Parliament and Council establishing a European Institute for Gender Equality' COM (2005) 81.
[93] Ibid. Art. 3(1)(a).   [94] Ibid. p. 4.   [95] Ibid. p. 5.   [96] Ibid. p. 4.

similar to those required by the Race Equality Directive[97] and in Britain recent legislation will replace the existing equality bodies with a Commission for Equality and Human Rights.[98] There is not, though, an evident trend at national level to wrap together equality and human rights.

It is not difficult to identify examples of issues that link race and human rights. State measures to fight terrorism frequently create tensions with the protection of human rights, such as the right to a fair trial or freedom from arbitrary detention. Where such measures are more likely to be used against persons from minority ethnic communities, then a race equality dimension combines with broader human rights analysis. Similarly, there is a close relationship between human rights and race equality in any assessment of immigration law and policy. The handling of asylum applications presents human rights questions, such as the right to a fair hearing or respect for family life. Simultaneously, it is difficult to dissociate asylum policies from wider debates on ethnic diversity within society.

In this light, the Fundamental Rights Agency has an opportunity to contextualise anti-racism policy by situating it within the human rights agenda. This could be particularly valuable in addressing issues related to ethnic diversity, but which do not fit neatly within an 'anti-discrimination' paradigm. Most notably, the 2004 enlargement of the European Union has drawn greater attention to the situation of historic national minorities. Kymlicka defines national minorities as 'groups that formed complete and functioning societies on their historic homeland prior to being incorporated into a larger state'.[99] This is not an entirely new issue for the European Union; national minorities also exist within many western European states, such as German-speakers in northern Italy. Nevertheless, the treatment of national minorities has received greater prominence in relation to the countries of the '2004/2007' enlargement. The wars in the former Yugoslavia graphically illustrated the ultimate risks posed by post-communist conflicts linked to the treatment of national minorities. Moreover, in some acceding states national minorities form very significant proportions of their population. In Slovakia, for example,

---

[97] G. Feldhune, 'Report on measures to combat discrimination in the 13 candidate countries: Latvia' (2003), p. 20.

[98] See further, Equality Act 2006.

[99] W. Kymlicka, 'Western political theory and ethnic relations in Eastern Europe' in W. Kymlicka and M. Opalski (eds.), *Can liberal pluralism be exported? Western political theory and ethnic relations in Eastern Europe* (Oxford University Press, 2001), pp. 13–105, at p. 23.

the Hungarian minority forms around 10 per cent of the population.[100] Non-discrimination is undoubtedly a central element of the minority rights agenda and here there is a crossover with combating discrimination against communities of migrant origin.[101] Yet, certain aspects of minority rights can be distinguished from anti-discrimination. One example could be claims for national minority languages to be granted a 'recognised' status, either within the territory as a whole or in respect of a particular region.[102] Indeed, the protection of national minority languages may even come into conflict with measures to promote race equality. Such tensions are exposed in recent debates in Ireland on whether to remove Irish language entry requirements for police officers in order to promote recruitment from communities of migrant origin.[103]

Alongside the question of national minorities, the '2004/2007' enlargement placed a spotlight on the situation of Roma communities in Europe. The entrenched inequality and exclusion of the Roma poses challenges for the limits of anti-discrimination legislation. In particular, a strategy based on individual litigation is unlikely to prove sufficient to break the cumulative disadvantage experienced in education, housing, healthcare and the labour market.[104] A human rights perspective does not necessarily provide any simple answers to such issues. Nonetheless, the broader mandate of the Fundamental Rights Agency could facilitate a more comprehensive overview of the interaction between anti-discrimination, minority rights and human rights.

Conclusion

The changed context following the 2004/2007 enlargement underlines the need for a reflective approach to diversity. Diversity exists both between discrimination grounds, but also within the concepts of race and ethnicity. The situation of Afro-Caribbeans in the UK, Roma in the Czech Republic or Russians in Latvia is different, although the Race Equality Directive

---

[100] Commission, 'Equality, diversity and enlargement' (Office for the Official Publications of the European Communities, 2003), p. 104.

[101] G. Toggenberg, 'Who is managing ethnic and cultural diversity in the European condominium? The moments of entry, integration and preservation' (2005) 43 *Journal of Common Market Studies*, pp. 717–37, at p. 729.

[102] The Council of Europe's Framework Convention on National Minorities contains a range of provisions relating to the use of minority languages (e.g. Arts. 9–11).

[103] 'Údarás member criticizes plan to waive Irish rule for Garda entry', *Irish Times*, 24 August 2005.

[104] B Hepple, 'Race and Law in Fortress Europe', (2004) 67 *Modern Law Review*, pp. 1–15, at p. 8.

may be relevant to all. The sources of discrimination and manifestations of disadvantage vary and consequently the appropriate response needs to be tailored. For example, the aim for Roma children might be to encourage their integration into mainstream education following practices of forced segregation. In contrast, national and religious minorities might view separate educational provision as a valuable means of preserving distinctive cultural and religious traditions.

The response of the Union to race and ethnic discrimination appears to be characterised by uneven evolution. The rapid progress made through anti-discrimination legislation is not matched elsewhere. In some places, such as criminal law instruments, policy stagnated. In other areas, such as mainstreaming, there is a sense of policy drift; the underlying plan or direction is difficult to detect. Looking back to the policy's origins in the 1990s, at that time there was a vision for a comprehensive, multi-faceted anti-racism policy. Initiatives, such as the EUMC, were race-centred and did not engage extensively with other equality grounds. This approach has altered considerably in recent years. Bleich and Feldmann suggest 'it is possible that antiracism will never crystallize as a coherent, well-developed European policy domain. More general domains of "antidiscrimination" and "human rights" may subsume antiracism as an issue area.'[105] Certainly, the debate surrounding the future of the EUMC is illustrative of the tensions between pursuing an integrated approach to equality and human rights and the desire to retain focus and specialisation. On the one hand, experience has demonstrated that issues of racism are difficult to disentangle from some other equality grounds, most especially religion. On the other, certain aspects of combating racism differ from other forms of discrimination. Most notably, promoting equality for minority ethnic communities is clearly related to the status and treatment of third country nationals. Therefore, migrant integration, as well as immigration and asylum policies, have a particular resonance.

The discussion in this essay calls into question the impression given by the equality legislation hierarchy. By shifting to a broader focus, the pre-eminence of race becomes more questionable and the waters are muddied. The purpose is not to suggest a revised hierarchy, where sex moves back up the ladder. Rather, the intention is to highlight the relevance of measures beyond the EU Equality Directives. By stepping back, a richer impression can be gleaned of the broader directions in equality law and policy.

---

[105] E. Bleich and M. C. Feldmann, 'The rise of race? Europeanization and antiracist policy-making in the EU'. Paper presented at the conference 'The impact of Europeanization on Politics and Policy in Europe: Trends and Trajectories' (University of Toronto, 7–9 May 2004).

7

Religion or belief: aiming at the right target?

GWYNETH PITT[1]

History and context

The modern continent of Europe has been fashioned by religious conflict. The fifteenth to eighteenth centuries in Europe were characterised by wars of religion, primarily between Catholics and Protestants, although neither sect omitted to persecute the Jews, heretics within their own ranks and anyone else of a different persuasion. At the same time, Western Christendom engaged in an outward-facing war against the Islamic Ottoman Empire and some of what are seen as key moments in European history relate to this struggle. The re-conquest of Granada by the Spanish in 1492 ensured that the lands north of the Mediterranean remained part of the Holy Roman Empire, but in 1453 the Ottoman Turks conquered Constantinople and as late as 1653 they launched a massive operation to take Vienna, an attack ultimately repelled by the Habsburg army. Thus western Europe remained decisively Christian and mainly Roman Catholic.[2] The Balkans remained a maelstrom in the nineteenth century and the collapse of Communism in Yugoslavia in the 1990s brought unspeakable atrocities committed by ethnic groups on each other, their ethnicity generally coextensive with their religious culture.

The European countries who drafted the European Convention on Human Rights and the smaller subset who formed the EEC in the 1950s had largely buried the differences between Catholics and Protestants and saw themselves as an essentially homogeneous community. In his speech to the Consultative Assembly on the Convention on Human Rights the British representative, Sir David Maxwell-Fyfe, referred to those present

---

[1] I am grateful to the editor, co-authors and Peter Edge for comments on this chapter. The usual disclaimers apply.

[2] A. Wheatcroft, *Infidels* (Viking, 2003).

as 'those nations who belong to and revere the great family of Western Europe and Christian civilization'.[3]

Not much has changed in the present European Union, even after enlargement. Today the European Union consists of mainly Christian Member States. Fourteen are predominantly Catholic (Austria, Belgium, France, Hungary, Ireland, Italy, Lithuania, Luxembourg, Malta, Poland, Portugal, Slovakia, Slovenia and Spain), five are predominantly Protestant (Denmark, Estonia, Finland, Sweden and the UK) and three are mainly Christian with no denomination predominating (Germany and the Netherlands have approximately equal numbers of Catholics and Protestants; the population of Latvia is a mixture of Catholic, Protestant and Russian Orthodox). Of the remaining Member States, the populations of Cyprus and Greece mainly adhere to the Greek Orthodox Church and the population of the Czech Republic consists of 40 per cent who describe themselves as atheists as well as 47 per cent who are Christian (mainly Catholic). With the important exception of Northern Ireland, differences between Catholics and Protestants no longer give rise to significant tensions and discrimination in the employment field. If the discussions opened between the EU and Turkey in autumn 2005 were to result in that country joining the EU there would be some rebalancing since its 69.5 million population is virtually all Muslim.[4]

The Member States cleave to different philosophies as to the relationship of religion and the state. The UK has an established church, as did Italy until 1984, while France and Germany insist on the separation of church and state as part of their constitutions, although in Germany the church is a major employer in the public sector, running schools and hospitals with the aid of the public sector. Other Member States can be located along an axis between these two extremes. The Greek constitution guarantees freedom of religion, but states that Eastern Orthodoxy is the prevailing religion. Portugal, Spain and Sweden give special privileges to the dominant church, even though it is not established. The Irish Constitution of 1937 expressly provides that blasphemy is a ground for

---

[3] *Travaux préparatoires* for the ECHR, quoted in C. Evans, *Freedom of Religion under the European Convention on Human Rights* (Oxford University Press, 2001), p. 39.

[4] Country reports on the implementation of anti-discrimination legislation 2004–2005, from the Network of Independent Legal Experts, available at: http://europa.eu.int/comm/ employment_social/fundamental_rights/index_en.htm, under 'Publications' (accessed October 2005). For the enlargement countries and Turkey, see www.religioustolerance. org/rel_coun.htm (accessed January 2006).

limiting freedom of expression, and in the UK also, blasphemy is a crime, but only where the Christian religion is insulted.[5]

While formal levels of religious observance vary considerably across Europe and are generally in decline, it is nonetheless the case that many aspects of social and cultural life are rooted in Christianity. This applies to some fundamental conceptions of marriage and the family as well as the rhythm of working life. Thus, Sunday is a non-working day for the majority of workers in all the Member States and most public holidays coincide with major mainstream Christian festivals. To turn that statement around, a Christian worker is unlikely, most of the time, to find that the demands of normal work schedules conflict with the requirements of religious observance in any European Union country. The same is not true for other religions, whose holy day may fall on Friday or Saturday and whose major religious festivals are not recognised in national calendars.

A number of Member States report that Muslims now represent a significant religious grouping in the state, usually as a result of immigration over recent decades, although the percentage of the population is only between 3 per cent and 7 per cent. The exception is Cyprus, where 18 per cent of the population are Muslim (reflecting the Turkish heritage of many Cypriots). There is no doubt that there are tensions between Muslim and Christian communities in many of the Member States, especially since the 11 September 2001 terrorist attacks in the US, the murder of Theo van Gogh in the Netherlands in 2004, and the 7 July 2005 terrorist incidents in London which were found to have been perpetrated by British Muslims of Asian origin. These have prompted anti-Muslim reactions, especially in some sections of the media, compounded by perceptions of the war in Iraq as, in some sense, imperialist and oppressive of Muslim communities. The tensions are manifest in debates in France (and Austria and Germany) over Muslim girls being able to wear headscarves in schools, in Denmark over the representation of the prophet Mohammed in cartoons and in arguments in the UK as to whether incitement to religious hatred should be a crime. They are also behind much opposition in Europe to the inclusion of Turkey as a member of the European Union, although ironically Turkey is a more determinedly secularist state than many of the existing members.[6]

---

[5] Held not to breach Article 9 of the ECHR in this respect in *Choudhury* v. *UK*, App. No. 17439/90, 12 HRLJ 172 (1991).

[6] See the discussion in the ECtHR in *Refah Partisi* v. *Turkey* (2003) 37 EHRR 1 and P. M. Taylor, *Freedom of Religion: UN and European Human Rights Law and Practice* (Cambridge University Press, 2005), pp. 314–18.

Many different strands can be detected in the current debates: concern over national identity, an atavistic fear of the 'other', the perception that Islam discriminates against women, the association of race and religion in the case of Muslims and some other ethnic groups, and the collision between the demands of freedom of expression and freedom of religion. It is beyond the scope of this chapter to deal with these issues in sufficient depth, but some of them will be touched upon in what follows. One of the main questions which will be explored is whether the classification of religion alongside belief in the scheme of EU equality law is appropriate or whether the problem of exclusion would be better addressed through an expanded notion of race and ethnicity: whether, in fact, Article 13 and the Framework Employment Directive[7] are aiming at the right target in relation to this protected ground.

Scope of the protected ground

Inclusion of 'belief'

When amendment to the EC Treaty to extend anti-discrimination protection was first seriously mooted in the early 1990s, religion was one of the grounds included, but other beliefs were not. Thus, the Commission's 1994 White Paper[8] included 'religion' among the grounds to be covered, but made no mention of 'belief'. The European Parliament's resolution on the Inter-Governmental Conference in 1995 called for the Treaty to be amended to include a reference to equal treatment 'irrespective of race, sex, age, handicap or religion' – again, with no mention of belief.[9] The conclusions of the Italian Presidency, indicating some of the tasks for its successor, raised the issue, 'whether non-discrimination . . . should also apply to other factors: religion, beliefs and opinions, disability, sexual orientation, age'.[10] This suggests that at this stage, beliefs other than religious beliefs were seen as a separate ground, perhaps having more in common with political and other opinions. Yet the final version of Article 13 of the EC Treaty and the Framework Employment Directive refer to prohibition of discrimination on grounds of 'religion or belief'. It seems likely, not least from the absence of recorded discussion, that

---

[7] Directive 2000/78/EC establishing a general framework for equal treatment in employment and occupation, 2000 OJ L303/16.

[8] *European Social Policy – a way forward for the Union*, White Paper, COM (1994) 333 final.

[9] [1995] OJ C151, 156 (17.9.95).   [10] EU Bulletin 6–1996, 43/108.

the inclusion of belief was in order to make it clear that non-religious beliefs, such as atheism, were covered as well as religious beliefs[11] rather than to widen the protection to all kinds of beliefs or opinions, which would have been a substantial change from what had been agreed hitherto. This formulation also has the advantage of making European Union equality law congruent with European and international human rights law.

The fundamental human rights treaties dealing with freedom of religion are the Universal Declaration of Human Rights 1948 (UDHR),[12] the International Covenant on Civil and Political Rights 1966 (ICCPR),[13] the Declaration on the Elimination of all Forms of Intolerance and Discrimination Based on Religion or Belief 1981[14] and the European Convention on Human Rights (ECHR),[15] all of which include belief as well as religion. The UDHR Article 18 states:

> Everyone has the right to freedom of thought, conscience and religion; this right includes freedom to change his religion or belief, and freedom, either alone or in community with others and in public or private, to manifest his religion or belief in teaching, practice, worship and observance.

The main areas for debate around the drafting of Article 18 were not whether 'belief' should be included as well as 'religion', but whether or not freedom to change religion should be explicitly guaranteed.[16] It was intended from an early stage that some non-religious beliefs, such as atheism, should be equally protected and there was little debate as to the meaning of the terms 'religion' and 'belief'. The right to change religion (opposed by some Middle Eastern countries on the basis that the Koran forbids Muslims to change their religion) remained highly contentious during the drafting of ICCPR Article 18, with the result that it refers only to 'freedom to have or to adopt a religion or belief of his choice'. This is thought by most commentators to amount to the same thing, but without express mention of the right to change.[17] There was similar disagreement when the 1981 Declaration was drafted, with the same result.

---

[11] While some would argue that atheism is a religious belief, this is not universally accepted.
[12] UN Doc A/3/810 (1949).   [13] 999 UNTS 171 (1966).   [14] UN Doc A/36/51 (1982).
[15] European Convention for the Protection of Human Rights and Fundamental Freedoms, 213 UNTS 221 (1950).
[16] Evans, *Freedom of Religion under the European Convention*, Ch. 3; Taylor, *Freedom of Religion*, Ch. 2.
[17] Reinforced by the UN Human Rights Committee General Comment No. 22, UN Doc CCPR/C/21/Rev. 1/Add. 4 (1993).

ECHR Article 9 provides:

(1) Everyone has the right to freedom of thought, conscience and religion; this right includes freedom to change his religion or belief and freedom, either alone or in community with others and in public or private, to manifest his religion or belief, in worship, teaching, practice and observance.

(2) Freedom to manifest one's religion or beliefs shall be subject only to such limitations as are prescribed by law and are necessary in a democratic society in the interests of public safety, for the protection of public order, health or morals, or for the protection of the rights and freedoms of others.

Like the UDHR Article 18, this expressly includes freedom to change religion, not a particularly controversial issue in mainly Christian Europe. Like the ICCPR, ECHR Article 9 distinguishes between an absolute right to freedom of thought, conscience and religion in the first paragraph and a more restricted right to manifest one's religion in the second paragraph, subject to limitation where this is necessary for the reasons specified.

The ECHR formulation in relation to religion or belief was followed when the EU Charter of Fundamental Rights was adopted at Nice in 2000. Thus, Article 10(1) of the Charter provides:

Everyone has the right to freedom of thought, conscience and religion. This right includes freedom to change religion or belief and freedom, either alone or in community with others and in public or in private, to manifest religion or belief, in worship, teaching, practice and observance.

Article 21 prohibits discrimination on grounds, inter alia, of religion or belief and Article 22 enjoins the EU to 'respect cultural, religious and linguistic diversity'.[18] While the Charter of Fundamental Rights has no direct legal effect at present, it is an important statement of values and is already being used in interpreting other EU provisions.[19]

If religious belief is recognised as worthy of protection then it seems logical that comparable philosophical belief systems which do not involve a deity should be covered as well. It may be felt that earlier EU communications on the subject referred to 'religion' only as a sort of shorthand, and that it would always have been intended that non-religious beliefs would receive similar protection. However, it is submitted that the focus on

---

[18] These would have become Art. II-10, Art. II-21 and Art. II-22 under the proposed EU Constitution.

[19] See further C. McCrudden and H. Kountouros, in Chapter 3 of this volume.

religion (only) in the discussion leading up to Article 13 is actually indicative of the fact that it was the problem of discrimination against members of particular religious groups in many areas of social life, including
employment, which was seen by the EU as the major issue to be addressed,
rather than the problem which could be conceptualised as one of employers discriminating against people on grounds of their personal belief systems. While the inclusion of non-religious beliefs may seem logical in one
sense, the question as to whether there should be any limitation on the
kinds of belief attracting protection has not been seriously addressed and
may yet give rise to problems of interpretation, to be considered below.

Relationship of the ECHR and the Framework Employment Directive

Religion or belief is unique compared with the other grounds protected
by Article 13 in that it is the only one which also appears as a positive
freedom in the ECHR. While all the grounds covered by Article 13 of the
EC Treaty also appear in ECHR Article 14 (along with others such as political opinion and social origin), Article 14 only prohibits discrimination
in relation to the enjoyment of the other rights and freedoms under the
Convention and thus will only come into play if another Convention right
is engaged.[20] While Protocol 12 would create a free-standing prohibition
on discrimination, it has been ratified by only three Member States.[21]
However, the positive guarantee of freedom of religion in Article 9 means
that there is quite a lot of jurisprudence of the European Court of Human
Rights (and the European Commission of Human Rights until 1998[22])
dealing with aspects of religion or belief, much of which may be relevant
in interpreting the requirements of the Framework Employment Directive in relation to religion or belief. While Article 13 and the Framework
Employment Directive do not purport to introduce a positive right to freedom of religion in their sphere of operation, discrimination on grounds
of religion or belief in employment could amount to an infringement of

---

[20] Although it is possible to find a breach of Art. 14 even if the substantive right is not
infringed: see the discussion in O. de Schutter, *The Prohibition of Discrimination under
European Human Rights Law* (European Commission, 2005), available at: http://europa.
eu.int/comm/employment_social/fundamental_rights/legisln/prohib_en.pdf   (accessed
March 2006).

[21] See further C. McCrudden and H. Kountouros, above, Chapter 3.

[22] Until 1998 cases could only be taken to the European Court of Human Rights by nations or
by the European Commission of Human Rights. Thus claims by individuals were effectively
screened by the Commission, whose decisions up to that date are therefore important on
the interpretation of the Convention.

the right to have or to manifest a religion or belief contrary to Article 9 and the ECHR jurisprudence will clearly be relevant.

One of the crucial questions which will arise in relation to the religion or belief ground is how far the jurisprudence of the European Court of Human Rights will be seen as determinative of the issues which will arise under the Directive. According to Article 6(2) of the Treaty on European Union,[23] the EU should 'respect fundamental rights as guaranteed by the ECHR and as they result from the constitutional traditions common to the Member States, as general principles of Community law'. This is reinforced by Article 52(3) of the Charter of Fundamental Rights, which provides that rights in the Charter which correspond to rights in the ECHR shall have the same scope and meaning as the ECHR rights. However, while there is a clear steer towards consistency of approach, it is submitted that this does not necessarily commit the ECJ to accepting the European Court of Human Rights' interpretation of those principles in all cases, especially since Article 52(3) of the Charter also adds that, 'This provision shall not prevent Union law providing more extensive protection.'

As many commentators regard the European Court of Human Rights as having taken an unduly narrow view of the protection offered by Article 9 in relation to claims by employees,[24] if a similar approach is taken to the legal interpretation of the Directive, the Directive may be found to have a disappointingly limited impact. This is discussed further below.

Definition of 'religion or belief'

There is no attempt to define the terms 'religion or belief' in the Framework Employment Directive. In this the Directive follows the international human rights treaties and the ECHR. Member States have adopted a similar policy.[25] However, leaving definitional issues to national courts with, eventually, guidance from the ECJ could lead to difficulties. A number of important questions are left open by the Directive: first, whether the definitional tests used in other legal contexts should be applicable here;

---

[23] [2002] OJ C325/5 (24.12.2002).
[24] Evans, *Freedom of Religion under the European Convention*, pp. 127–132; G. Moon and R. Allen, 'Substantive rights and equal treatment in respect of religion and belief' [2000] EHRLR 581, 590. See also the discussion of *Ahmad* v. *UK* and *Stedman* v. *UK infra* p. 215.
[25] 'No Member State has attempted to provide a comprehensive definition of "religion or belief" within anti-discrimination legislation.' J. Cormack and M. Bell, *Developing Anti-Discrimination Law in Europe: the 25 EU Member States Compared* (European Commission, 2005), available at: http://europa.eu.int/comm/employment_social/fundamental_rights/public/pubst_en.htm

secondly, what are the characteristics of a qualifying religion or belief; thirdly, whether political beliefs will come within the protection; and finally, whether the requirements of any religion or belief will be judged objectively by the court (perhaps with the assistance of expert evidence) or subjectively according to the conscience of the individual worker.

In a wide-ranging review of UK anti-discrimination legislation, Hepple *et al* found that the main reservation expressed by those consulted on prohibition of religious discrimination in the UK 'was the difficulty in defining religion or belief, and the problem of distinguishing a "genuine" religion from a cult with harmful beliefs or practices'.[26] This is an issue which has already faced municipal and international courts in a variety of contexts. Courts have already had to decide these questions in relation to immigration and asylum (whether an individual belonging to a harmful religion should be admitted to a country; whether an asylum seeker is in danger of religious persecution if she or he is returned home); in relation to charity and tax law (whether a particular religious organisation should be recognised as such for fiscal benefits); in relation to conscientious objection (e.g. to military service, or to belonging to an organisation such as a trade union), as well as in interpreting instruments guaranteeing a positive right to freedom of religion or belief and a negative right not to be discriminated against on grounds of religion or belief.

It is important to recognise that these different contexts may quite properly entail different factors being given different weight. For example, when what is at issue is whether or not an organisation should receive financial privileges or whether members of a sect alleged to engage in harmful practices should be allowed to enter a country, it may be appropriate to focus on the formal structure, authoritative statements of doctrine and official publications of the organisation. In the case of someone seeking exemption from military service, the person's sincerity, as measured in part by the coherence of his beliefs and the consistency of his behaviour can properly be regarded as the most important factors. It is also at least arguable that different considerations apply to a positive freedom compared with a negative protection from adverse treatment. These caveats should be borne in mind in defining religion or belief for the purposes of the Framework Employment Directive.

The most important and difficult question is deciding what are the boundaries of protected belief. Where this has arisen in relation to the

---

[26] B. Hepple, M. Coussey and T. Choudhury, *Equality: A New Framework* (Hart Publishing, 2000), p. 47.

ECHR a fairly liberal approach has been taken. There is, of course, no problem in including well-known, longstanding religions within the protection of Article 9. In relation to newer, smaller or even unknown religions, Convention jurisprudence seems to have placed some burden on the claimant to show its existence (e.g. in X v. UK^{27} the Commission rejected the claim of a prisoner allegedly denied the right to practise the Wicca religion on grounds, inter alia, that he had not mentioned any facts making it possible to establish the religion's existence). Taylor suggests that the European Court of Human Rights has become more generous in this regard,[28] accepting as religions almost without question the Church of Scientology,[29] the Moon Sect,[30] the Divine Light Zentrum[31] and Druidism.[32] However, as Evans points out, this is in part because of the practice of the Commission and the Court to move straight to a consideration of whether or not the respondent country has a defence under Article 9(2) without first examining closely whether the religion or belief qualifies as such.[33] It appears that under the terms of the Directive this approach would not be possible and it will be necessary for courts to decide as a prior issue whether or not a particular belief qualifies as a protected 'religion or belief'.

Some Member States have attempted to establish boundaries through guidance to the legislation. In relation to 'religion' the explanatory notes to the Austrian Equal Treatment Act state that, 'for a religion there are minimum requirements concerning a statement of belief, some rules for the way of life and a cult'.[34] In the UK, the Explanatory Notes to the Employment Equality (Religion or Belief) Regulations 2003 refer to beliefs having 'a certain level of cogency, seriousness, cohesion and importance, provided that the beliefs are worthy of respect in a democratic society and are not incompatible with human dignity'.[35] Curiously, the guidance given to the UK legislation by the Advisory, Conciliation and Advisory Service (Acas) is different from this, stating that courts are likely to take account of factors such as collective worship, a clear belief system and a profound

---

[27] App. No. 7291/75, 11 D&R 55 (1977).   [28] Taylor, note 6 above, p. 208.
[29] X and Church of Scientology v. Sweden App. No. 7805/77, 16 D&R 68 (1978).
[30] X v. Austria App. No. 8652/79, 26 D&R 89 (1981).
[31] Omkarananda and the Divine Light Zentrum v. UK App. No. 8188/77, 25 D&R 105 (1981).
[32] Chappell v. UK App. No. 12587/86, 53 D&R 241 (1987).
[33] Evans, note 3 above, p. 56.
[34] Cormack and Bell, note 25 above, p. 21.
[35] Department for Trade and Industry (DTI) Explanatory Notes on the Employment Equality (Religion or Belief) Regulations 2003, para. 12, referring to the ECtHR's judgment in Campbell and Cosans v. UK (1982) 4 EHRR 293, 304. These notes have no legal force but are an indication of prevailing government opinion.

belief affecting the way of life or view of the world.[36] However, this may be unduly restrictive, reflecting a Western, Christian, ethnocentricity and discriminating against newer religions.[37]

In relation to 'belief' the UK Employment Equality (Religion or Belief) Regulations 2003 originally contained a definition in the following terms: 'religion, religious belief, or similar philosophical belief'.[38] This suggested a restrictive approach which many considered to be unwarranted – a criticism finally accepted by the UK government, which introduced a new definition of religion or belief in the Equality Act 2006, removing the word 'similar' and making it absolutely unambiguous that lack of belief was included.[39] It is submitted that the reference to 'religion' separately from 'religious belief' is apt to extend protection to people who practise a religion at some level, whether or not they actually believe in it. However, it seems highly likely that a worker seeking protection under the Directive for non-religious beliefs will have to demonstrate some sort of belief system, rather than just a strong belief on one or two issues. Again, the Convention jurisprudence supports the idea that there should be 'a coherent view on fundamental problems';[40] in *Pretty* v. *UK*[41] the applicant's sincere and profound belief that assisted suicide should be allowed was held to be outside Article 9 for this reason.

An important boundary issue to be resolved in relation to the Directive will be the extent to which political beliefs can come within the protection. It is worth noting that the majority of Member States have expressly included protection for political beliefs in their anti-discrimination provisions.[42] However, others appear anxious to ensure that political opinion should not be covered. The Explanatory Notes to the Employment

---

[36] Acas, *Religion or Belief and the Workplace: a guide for employers and employees* (2004), para.1.1.

[37] See, e.g., J. Gunn, 'The complexity of religion and the definition of "religion" in international law', (2003) 16 *Harvard Human Rights Journal* 189.

[38] Employment Equality (Religion or Belief) Regulations 2003, reg. 2(1).

[39] UK Equality Act 2006, s. 44: 'In this part –

    (a) "religion" means any religion,
    (b) "belief" means any religious or philosophical belief,
    (c) a reference to religion includes a reference to lack of religion, and
    (d) a reference to belief includes a reference to lack of belief.'

[40] *X* v. *Germany* App. No. 8741/79, 24 D&R 137 (1981).   [41] (2002) 35 EHRR 1.

[42] These are: Cyprus, the Czech Republic, Denmark, Estonia, Finland, France, Hungary, Italy, Latvia, Luxembourg, Malta, the Netherlands, Poland, Portugal, Slovenia and Spain. Political opinion is also a protected ground in Northern Ireland, but not in the rest of the UK. See Cormack and Bell, above, n. 25.

Equality (Religion or Belief) Regulations 2003,[43] implementing the Directive in Great Britain, categorically state that political beliefs will not be included unless they are similar to a philosophical belief.[44] However, it seems likely that some political beliefs, even party political beliefs, will qualify as protected beliefs. Convention case law has recognised pacifism,[45] Nazism,[46] fascism,[47] Communism[48] and even principled opposition to corporal punishment[49] and anti-abortion beliefs[50] as prima facie falling within the protected range. Again, some of these cases involved the European Court (or Commission) for Human Rights moving directly to a consideration of the respondent state's power to restrict manifestations of the belief rather than being fully considered conclusions, and so they need not be highly persuasive when the Directive is being interpreted. But they illustrate the important point that there is apparently no scope for any evaluation of the worth or potential harmfulness of the belief in question.

This highlights a difference between the religion or belief ground compared with other protected grounds. Anti-discrimination provisions for the other protected grounds express a consensus about particular values of equality and the irrelevance of certain characteristics which are relatively straightforward to understand and uncontroversial (the protection extended to sexual orientation is probably the most controversial, but even then not to the extent of there being any real opposition to its inclusion on the part of any Member State). However, a blanket protection for religion or belief potentially provides protection for the holders of completely abhorrent, or irrational, or bigoted beliefs, including those which would certainly not accord equal rights to others if they were to prevail. This may seem to be inevitable, given the pluralist conception of religion or belief underpinning the Directive and the obvious difficulties in ruling on such matters. But if it is accepted that a belief system can be evil as well as good, a premise which, it is submitted, is self-evident, then this criticism is valid – and fundamental. While Article 2(5) of the Framework

---

[43] SI 2003/1660.
[44] DTI Explanatory Notes on the Employment Equality (Religion or Belief) Regulations 2003, para. 13: this probably still stands despite the revised definition of religion or belief above, note 35.
[45] *Arrowsmith* v. *UK* App. No. 7050/75, 19 D&R 5 (1980).
[46] *X* v. *Austria* App. No. 1747/62, 13 CD 42 (1963).
[47] *X* v. *Italy* App. No. 6741/74, 5 D&R 83 (1976).
[48] *Hazar, Hazar and Açik* v. *Turkey* App. No. 16311,16312 16313/90, 72 D&R 200 (1991).
[49] *Campbell and Cossans* v. *UK* (1982) 4 EHRR 293.
[50] *Plattform 'Ärzte für das Leben'* v. *Austria* App. No. 10126/82, 44 D&R 65 (1985).

Employment Directive does state that it is 'without prejudice to measures laid down by national law which, in a democratic society, are for public security, for the maintenance of public order and the prevention of criminal offences, for the protection of health and for the protection of the rights and freedoms of others',[51] this would not appear apt to cover an employer's less favourable treatment of, say, someone professing Nazi sympathies on grounds that the employer fears that this would be unpopular with other workers.[52]

This raises the final definitional issue, which concerns what evidence a worker will have to adduce in order to show that she or he has a particular religion or belief so as to come within the Directive's protection. Sincerity of practice or belief is bound to be a necessary condition and to this extent, the prior behaviour of the worker and how far it is consistent with the religion or belief claimed is clearly relevant. Rationality of the belief, as mentioned already, is equally clearly not relevant. A particular difficulty here is where discrimination occurs because of the claimant's personal interpretation of his religion, although the 'official doctrine' of the religion (assuming that (a) this exists, and (b) that there is general agreement on what it means, both of which assumptions may be contentious in practice) is different. Should the belief be judged subjectively, according to the individual's interpretation, or objectively, according to the religion's 'authorised version'?

As this is not addressed directly in the Directive or the implementing legislation of Member States, an authoritative answer will have to await decision by the ECJ. Evans[53] notes that the European Court of Human Rights has usually taken an objective view of what a particular religious belief requires, citing *Valsamis* v. *Greece*[54] and *Efstratiou* v. *Greece*,[55] both cases where Jehovah's Witnesses argued a breach of their rights under Article 9 when their children were suspended from school for refusing to take part in a parade on Greek National Day. They regarded the parade as militaristic and thus contrary to their pacifist beliefs. In both cases the

---

[51] Compare ECHR Art. 9(2), which is in similar, but not exactly the same, terms.

[52] According to H. Meenan, 'Age Equality after the Employment Directive', (2003) 10 *MJ* 1, this clause was inserted during negotiations in the Council of Ministers in response to concerns expressed by some Member States that the prohibition of discrimination on the grounds of sexual orientation should not interfere with the need to control criminal sexual behaviour such as paedophilia.

[53] C. Evans, above n. 3, at p. 120. Moon and Allen, n. 24 above, go so far as to say, 'It cannot be a wholly subjective test, since rights are in issue.' *Sed quaere?*

[54] (Series A) No. 2312 (1996-VI) 2 ECtHR.

[55] (Series A) No. 2347 (1996-VI) 27 ECtHR.

Court held that there was nothing in the parade to offend their beliefs. Thus the judges of the European Court of Human Rights in effect substituted their subjective judgment of what the applicants' religion required for the judgment of the applicants themselves.[56] In contrast, in the US, where a similar issue arose in relation to Jehovah's Witness schoolchildren saluting the flag, the Supreme Court upheld their exemption, stating: '[N]o official, high or petty, can prescribe what shall be orthodox in politics, nationalism, religion or other matters of opinion.'[57] The subjective approach was also taken when this issue arose in English law at the time when religious objection to trade union membership was the only legally protected reason for not joining where a closed shop was in operation.[58] It is submitted that the subjective test is to be preferred. The focus should be on the individual and his or her actual belief – not the belief which others may think that he or she ought to have.

Hepple and Choudhury[59] argue that there should be a liberal approach to the definition of religion or belief on the grounds that anti-discrimination legislation is aimed at protecting individuals from arbitrary treatment on the basis of beliefs which they are believed to hold (whether rightly or wrongly) – thus the validity of the belief itself should not be a major issue. This argument is valid up to a point, as we will see when we consider the meaning of discrimination, below. However, if this approach is correct, it has the result that an employer could be liable for discrimination if he or she rejects a job applicant because that person professes belief in a theory of racial superiority but not if the rejection is because the job applicant is a supporter of a particular political party. Is this a satisfactory state of affairs?

The concept of discrimination

The Framework Employment Directive deals with discrimination only 'as regards employment and occupation'.[60] This includes access to employment, self-employment or occupation, selection and recruitment,

---

[56] See P. W. Edge, 'The European Court of Human Rights and Religious Rights', (1998) 47 *ICLQ*, p. 680, 685.

[57] *West Virginia State Board of Education* v. *Barnette*, 319 US 624, 642 (1943), cited in Evans, note 3 above, p. 121.

[58] Between 1976 and 1980, in accordance with the Trade Union and Labour Relations Act 1974, Sch. 1, para. 5 (as amended). See *Goodbody* v. *BRB* [1977] IRLR 84.

[59] B. Hepple and T. Choudhury, *Tackling Religious Discrimination: practical implications for policy-makers and legislators* (Home Office Research Study 221, 2001), p. 31.

[60] Article 1.

promotion, access to vocational guidance and training, employment and working conditions, terms of employment and dismissal as well as membership of relevant organisations such as trade unions, employers' associations or professional bodies.[61] It makes four kinds of discrimination unlawful on grounds of religion or belief: direct discrimination, indirect discrimination, harassment and instructions to someone else to discriminate.[62] In addition, employees must be protected from victimisation resulting from any complaint or proceedings relating to equal treatment.[63] There is no defence to direct discrimination, although there may be exceptional circumstances where having a particular religion or belief is a genuine and determining occupational requirement, discussed further below.

Unlike ECHR Article 9, the Directive makes no overt reference to *manifestation* of religion or belief. It could be argued that 'on the grounds of religion or belief' must include manifesting that belief at least to some extent, but given that ECHR Article 9 specifically differentiates between having a belief and manifesting it, there may doubt as to whether such an argument would be successful. This is something which will have to await decision by the ECJ. It is of some importance, because if manifestation is not included in the concept, then discrimination on grounds of the worker's manifestation of his or her religion or belief would be actionable only if it constituted indirect discrimination or harassment. This point can be illustrated by an example from one of the two areas where the issue is likely to arise in practice in employment: these are dress codes and time off for religious observance. In relation to dress codes, the problem is either that the employer has a uniform requirement which conflicts with the employee's religious beliefs or the employee wishes to wear a symbol of her religion contrary to the wishes of the employer. In relation to religious observance, the issue could be about time off during the working day, for example, to pray, or it could be about accommodating working patterns so that the employee need not work on his or her holy day.

If a male Sikh was refused employment because he wanted to wear a turban, which would contravene the employer's uniform requirements, it might be possible to argue that this was less favourable treatment of him on grounds of his religion. This would mean that the ground of religion would be taken to include not only the worker's inner religious belief but also the outward manifestation of it, in his appearance. If so, this would be

---

[61] Article 3.   [62] Article 2.   [63] Article 11.

direct discrimination. However, if this situation is read as the imposition of a rule as to uniform which puts male Sikhs at a particular disadvantage, it will be indirect discrimination and the issue of objective justification will arise. One reason for preferring the indirect discrimination approach is that it gives greater discretion to the adjudicator to weigh the competing interests of the employer and the worker.[64]

Indirect discrimination is defined by Article 2(b) as occurring where 'an apparently neutral provision, criterion or practice would put persons having a particular religion or belief . . . at a particular disadvantage compared with other persons' unless the provision, criterion or practice can be objectively justified by the employer as being an 'appropriate and necessary means' of achieving a legitimate aim. Whereas indirect discrimination is normally thought of as something which bears more heavily on one group than another, Hepple and Choudhury point out that this formulation could be applied provided that at least more than one person would be put at a disadvantage by the provision, criterion or practice.[65]

The stipulation that the employer should have to show that the practice having an adverse effect is objectively justified as an appropriate and necessary means of achieving a legitimate aim suggests that a fairly high standard of objective justification will be required. This further implies that national courts and the ECJ should not follow Convention case law in this particular context. In cases such as *Ahmad* v. *UK*[66] and *Stedman* v. *UK*,[67] the first involving a Muslim schoolteacher seeking time off to attend Friday prayers and the second a Christian travel agent who did not want to work a Sunday shift, it was held that by accepting a contract of employment with terms inconsistent with their religious observance the applicants had forfeited any right to claim a breach of Article 9. The fact that they could give up their jobs was seen as an adequate safeguard of their right to freedom of religion. This line of cases was recently followed by the English Court of Appeal considering the impact of the Human Rights Act 1998 on the law of unfair dismissal, rejecting the application of an employee who claimed that he was unfairly dismissed when he refused

---

[64] Cases on dress codes in the UK have usually been treated as raising an issue of indirect discrimination: see, e.g., *Panesar* v. *Nestlé* [1980] ICR 64; *Singh* v. *BRB Engineering* [1986] ICR 22 *Azmi* v. *Kirklees MBC* [2007] IRLR 484.

[65] B. Hepple and T. Choudhury, *Tackling Religious Discrimination: practical implications for policy-makers and legislators* (Home Office Research Study 221, 2001), Ch. 6.

[66] (1982) 4 EHRR 126. See *Ahmad* v. *ILEA* [1978] QB 36 for the proceedings in the Court of Appeal.

[67] App. No. 29107/95, 89-A D&R 104 (1997).

to work on Sundays.[68] It is inconceivable that the same approach could be taken under the Directive.

In relation to dress codes, the European Court of Human Rights has been similarly restrictive. In *Karaduman* v. *Turkey*[69] the European Commission of Human Rights held that there was no violation of Article 9 in requiring the claimant to be bare-headed in a photograph attached to a degree certificate instead of wearing a Muslim headscarf as she wished. The Commission accepted the argument that the principle of secularity was seen by Turkey as essential to maintaining a democratic and pluralist society, but also referred to the fact that the claimant had chosen to enrol at the university, knowing its rules. Exactly similar reasoning was applied more recently by the European Court of Human Rights in *Leyla Sahin* v. *Turkey*,[70] upholding a student's exclusion from examinations and suspension from the university for wearing an Islamic headscarf. But in reality, if all higher education institutions in the country impose this rule, the 'choice' of complying, forgoing higher education or going abroad to study is not really meaningful, any more than it is meaningful for an employee to choose between a job on the employer's terms and unemployment.

The decisions in *Karaduman* and *Leyla Sahin* could be seen as justified under the margin of appreciation because of the particular importance of the secularity principle for Turkey, but in *Dahlab* v. *Switzerland*[71] the European Court of Human Rights upheld a ban on a woman teacher wearing a Muslim headscarf in order to protect the rights and freedoms of others – namely, the pupils, who might be affected (in some rather unclear way) by this display of religious symbolism. Again, it would seem that this line of cases would need to be reconsidered when the issue arises under the Framework Employment Directive.

The limitations of the protection against indirect discrimination should not be overlooked. Where an employer, for example, imposes a dress code or uniform requirement which conflicts with a Muslim woman's desire to wear a headscarf or to keep her legs covered, there will no doubt be a prima facie case of indirect discrimination, and in practice, it is hard imagine situations where this could be justified by an employer today. Similarly, if an employer refuses all leave because of a rush order to be completed, thus preventing Muslim employees taking holiday for Eid,[72] again it would be

---

[68] *Copsey* v. *WWB Devon Clays Ltd* [2005] IRLR 811.
[69] App. No. 16278/90 74 D&R 93 (1993), discussed in Taylor, n. 6 above, pp. 253–6.
[70] App. No. 44774/98 (2004)
[71] App. No. 42393/98 (2001), discussed in Taylor, n. 6 above, pp. 254–5.
[72] *Cf J H Walker* v. *Hussain* [1996] IRLR 11.

prima facie indirect discrimination and the issue would be whether or not this was necessary and proportionate. But what if an employer is asked by a single employee for time off for a day of religious obligation and refuses, simply because the employee's absence would cause a mild inconvenience to the business? It could be argued that the employer's decision is a 'provision' or could be extrapolated as a 'practice' of not allowing leave where this would cause mild inconvenience and would thus constitute prima facie indirect discrimination (which would be unlikely to be justified in these circumstances).[73] However, the alternative and, it is submitted, better view is that it would be stretching the meaning of 'provision, criterion or practice' too far to include in it a one-off decision of this kind. Furthermore, it would effectively obliterate any distinction between indirect discrimination and the duty to make reasonable accommodation, whereas the concepts are clearly differentiated in the Framework Employment Directive, which shows a definite intention to restrict the duty of reasonable accommodation to disability only. If this view is correct, it does demonstrate an unfortunate gap in protection for workers, contrasting unfavourably with the position in the US[74] and some Canadian provinces[75] where employers are under a duty reasonably to accommodate the religious needs of their employees.

De Schutter[76] argues that this is one area where Convention case law could be of assistance to workers. *Thlimmenos* v. *Greece*[77] concerned a Jehovah's Witness who had been convicted of a felony because of his refusal, based on his religious beliefs, to wear military uniform during compulsory military service. He was later refused entry to the Greek Institute of Chartered Accountants because of his criminal conviction. His claim under Article 9 was not based on the fact that he had received different treatment because of his religious belief, but rather that he had been treated the same as any other criminal, with no allowance having been made for the fact that his conviction had arisen directly because of his adherence to his religious belief. The European Court of Human Rights dealt with this under Article 14 in conjunction with Article 9 and held that

---

[73] The view taken by the EAT in *British Airways plc* v. *Starmer* [2005] IRLR 862.

[74] Title VII of the Civil Rights Act 1964, s. 701(j) (as amended) states: 'The term religion includes all aspects of religious observance and practice, as well as belief, unless an employer demonstrates that he is unable to reasonably accommodate to an employee's or prospective employee's religious observance or practice without undue hardship on the conduct of the employer's business.'

[75] E.g. Ontario Human Rights Code 1990.   [76] See n. 20 above.

[77] (2001) 31 EHRR 411.

a breach of his rights had occurred. The judgment explicitly recognises that discrimination occurs not only when different treatment is meted out, but also 'when States without an objective and reasonable justification fail to treat differently persons whose situations are significantly different'.[78] De Schutter argues that this could be used as a springboard to expand the concept of indirect discrimination to include an obligation of reasonable accommodation. This is an interesting possibility which again must await authoritative decision. Against this view, as noted already, it may be argued that the express inclusion of reasonable accommodation for disability implies that it was not intended to be covered by the general concept of indirect discrimination in the Directive.

Article 2(3) of the Framework Employment Directive defines harassment as occurring 'when unwanted conduct related to any of the grounds referred to in Article 1 takes place with the purpose or effect of violating the dignity of a person and of creating an intimidating, hostile, degrading, humiliating or offensive environment' – although it follows this definition with a stipulation that the concept may be defined by Member States. One of the key issues to be decided, therefore, is whether the effect on an individual should be judged purely subjectively or whether some level of objectivity should be introduced through the concept of a reasonable person holding the religion or belief of the person harassed. In English law of sex and race discrimination, influenced by the US, harassment has traditionally been held to occur *either* when the conduct has the purpose or effect of violating the recipient's dignity *or* where a hostile environment is created, and it is to be hoped that a similar test will be applied in relation to harassment on grounds of religion or belief.

The concept of harassment raises interesting possibilities for the collision of rights. In considering the right to manifest one's religion under ECHR Article 9(2) the European Court of Human Rights has been called on to decide whether or not proselytism is part of the right to manifest religion (within the rubric of 'teaching, practice, worship and observance') – or whether it can in fact be seen as an interference with other people's freedom of religion. In *Kokkinakis* v. *Greece*[79] (concerning a Jehovah's Witness convicted of an offence under a Greek law forbidding proselytism) the European Court of Human Rights held that proselytism was part of the freedom to manifest religion, but that if it became 'improper' it could be regarded as infringing other people's rights to freedom of religion. Unfortunately, the Court gave no real guidance on the limits of

[78] Ibid., para. 44.   [79] (Series A) No. 260-A (1993) ECtHR.

proper and improper behaviour. In *Larissis* v. *Greece*,[80] where Pentecostal air force officers had been convicted of a similar offence for attempting to convert some of their subordinates, the Court commented, 'what would in the civilian world be seen as an innocuous exchange of ideas which the recipient is free to accept or reject, may, within the confines of military life, be viewed as a form of harassment or the application of undue pressure in abuse of power'.[81] While ordinary employment relations are less confining than military life, it may well be the case that attempts by a manager to influence the religion or belief of his or her subordinates could be regarded as harassment on grounds of religion or belief through interfering with the employees' own beliefs, and it is also possible to imagine situations where one employee attempts to convert others to his or her own religious or similar beliefs and deeply offends his or her colleagues in the process. An employer might end up in the unenviable position of either trying to justify a ban on discussing certain kinds of 'sensitive' subjects in the workplace, which could potentially be indirect discrimination on grounds of religion or belief, or else facing claims of harassment from harangued employees on grounds of a hostile environment. That this situation also engages the ECHR Article 10 right to freedom of expression adds another layer of complexity.[82] It has been held in the UK that where an employer allows employees to chat while working, to forbid an employee to try and persuade others of the benefits of trade union membership was an unwarranted interference with his or her right to take part in trade union activities and similar reasoning could apply here.[83]

Exceptions

Three exceptional situations are allowed for by the Directive: where religion or belief is a genuine and determining occupational requirement for the job; organisations with a religious ethos; and certain public services in Northern Ireland. An exception is also made for positive action for all the grounds.

---

[80] (Series A) No. 65 (1998-V) ECtHR 263.   [81] Ibid., para. 51.

[82] The England football manager, Glenn Hoddle, was sacked for expressing his belief that disability was some kind of divine punishment: see P. Elias and J. Coppel, 'Freedom of Expression and Freedom of Religion: some thoughts on the *Glenn Hoddle* case', in J. Beatson and Y. Cripps (eds.), *Freedom of Expression and Freedom of Information*, Oxford University Press (2000). See also *Otto-Preminger-Institut* v. *Austria* (1994) 19 EHRR 1; *Wingrove* v. *UK* (1997) 24 EHRR 1; Edge, above note 56.

[83] *Zucker* v. *Astrid Jewels* [1978] ICR 1088.

Requirements of the post

Article 4(1) provides a general exception for all grounds protected under the Framework Employment Directive which, in the case of religion or belief, allows this to be required where, 'by reason of the nature of the particular occupational activities concerned or of the context in which they are carried out' being of a particular religion or belief constitutes a 'genuine and determining occupational requirement', provided also that the objective of the requirement is legitimate and the requirement itself is proportionate. This would obviously cover ministers of religion and could perhaps also cover teachers of a religion or belief or people providing services to a particular religious denomination. The latter two examples are jobs which could be carried out by a non-adherent, but it would probably be legitimate for an employer to conclude that the job would be better performed by someone with a personal commitment to the same religion or belief and that adherence to it is therefore a genuine and determining requirement.

Organisations with a religious ethos

However, in relation to religion or belief only, Article 4(2) provides a further exception for churches and other organisations 'the ethos of which is based on religion or belief'. This permits differences of treatment where a person's religion or beliefs 'constitute a genuine, legitimate and justified occupational requirement, having regard to the organisation's ethos'. Furthermore, such bodies may require people working for them 'to act in good faith and with loyalty to the organisation's ethos'. It seems that this exception was in part included to allow continuance of practices to this effect in some Member States, such as Germany, where both the Protestant and Catholic churches are major employers, in health and education as well as direct church activities.[84] In part it seems also to be motivated by a desire to allow communities based on a particular belief system to maintain their identity through demanding that anyone belonging to them should subscribe to the same belief system. Many commentators suggest that this exemption will be and should be narrowly interpreted, since it is an exception. But where communities exist based on a particular faith or belief which is accepted as a blueprint for every aspect of members' lives, it is difficult to see why they should not be able to require that everyone within the community should share the same faith. This must be relevant

[84] See Recital 24 of the Preamble to the Framework Employment Directive.

to the strength and sustainability of the community in that form and seems unremarkable. The issue really is more one of scale. Faith communities of such a kind are actually rare and are almost bound to be small. What is more difficult is the situation where (as in Germany) the church is a major employer and its right to require employees to show loyalty to the ethos has justified quite major incursions into people's private lives. It is submitted, therefore, that the basic idea behind this special exception for religion or belief is well-founded, but that its expression in the Directive is not.

Northern Ireland

Recital 34 of the Preamble to the Framework Employment Directive recognises that 'the need to promote peace and reconciliation between the major communities in Northern Ireland necessitates the incorporation of particular provisions into this Directive'. Those provisions are found in Article 15 and allow discrimination on grounds of religion first, in relation to recruitment to the police service (including support staff), to address the historic under-representation of Roman Catholics in the police force, and secondly, in relation to recruitment of teachers (given that most schools in Northern Ireland are denominational).

Positive action

As with the other grounds in the Framework Employment Directive, Article 7(1) allows Member States to establish an asymmetrical model, giving advantages to adherents of particular religions or beliefs in order to prevent disadvantage or to compensate for past disadvantage. However, no Member State has indicated any intention to legislate along these lines in relation to religion or belief.[85]

Evaluation: aiming at the right target?

The protected grounds under Article 13 can be categorised in a number of different ways. It has become commonplace to talk of a hierarchy of

---

[85] Country reports on the implementation of anti-discrimination legislation 2004–2005, from the Network of Independent Legal Experts, available at: http://europa.eu.int/comm/employment_social/fundamental_rights/index_en.htm, under 'Publications' (accessed October 2005).

protected grounds in European equality law,[86] with race equality now at the top, having overtaken sex equality law with the passage of the Race Directive.[87] Race equality law now extends to social protection, education, housing and the supply of goods and services, while sex equality law is limited (in the short term) to the fields of employment and social security.[88] Discrimination on grounds of religion or belief thus comes further down the hierarchy, along with sexual orientation, age and disability, because it is only prohibited in the field of employment. In this categorisation, it is ahead only of discrimination on grounds of nationality, which is unevenly protected because of the exclusion of third country nationals from some aspects of the coverage of anti-discrimination measures.

The 'hierarchy of protected grounds' approach provides a useful descriptive classification of the factual matrix of European equality law, but is limited as a tool for evaluating the differences between the grounds and the level of protection afforded to them. It is often used to argue for an extension of the level of protection to the 'lesser' grounds and it could be used as a device to explain the evolution of anti-discrimination or equality law, on the basis of an underlying assumption that eventually the levels of protection for all grounds will be levelled up to the standard now established for race equality law. This in turn presupposes that all the Article 13 grounds are worthy of similar treatment and protection, which may be contested, as we will see.

Dagmar Schiek proposes a different taxonomy based on whether the grounds relate to ascribed differences, actual and unalterable biological differences or differences which are the product of choice.[89] She would place race discrimination, gender discrimination and some aspects of disability discrimination in the top category of ascribed difference – i.e., she contends that these are not based on any kind of factual difference between those placed in different groups, but merely on socially constructed differences arising from the reactions and opinions of others. 'Gender' is used

---

[86] E.g., S. Fredman, 'Equality: a New Generation?', *ILJ*, 30 (2001) p. 145; M. Bell, *Anti-Discrimination Law and the European Union* (Oxford University Press, 2002); C. McCrudden, 'Theorising European Equality Law', in C. Costello and E. Barry (eds.), *Equality in Diversity: the New Equality Directives* (Irish Centre for European Law, 2003).

[87] Council Directive 2000/78/EC, [2000] OJ L303/16, (27.11.00).

[88] This will change following implementation of Directive 2004/113/EC on equal treatment between men and women in the access to and supply of goods and services, which is due by 21 December 2007. However, the material scope of this Directive is narrower than that of the Race Directive.

[89] D. Schiek, 'A new framework on equal treatment of persons in EC law?', (2002) 8 *European Law Journal*, pp. 290, 309–312.

in this context with precision to refer to socially constructed differences between men and women as opposed to 'sex' which refers to biological differences. In the second category – those which at least in part reflect genuine biological differences – she would put sex discrimination (properly so-called), disability and age. The final category, those which depend on choice, would include religion and belief and sexual orientation.

The strength of this taxonomy is that it is based on a set of reasons which provide a rationale for possible differences in treatment of the different protected grounds. However, the allocation of grounds to the different categories is far from uncontroversial. Most people – gay, lesbian and heterosexual – would deny that their sexual orientation is a lifestyle choice and the same is frequently true of religious adherence. The House of Lords in the UK famously rejected the argument that a Sikh boy could comply with a school requirement to have his hair cut short and that it was simply his choice not to do so.[90] Discussing whether or not the boy 'could comply' with a requirement to wear his hair cut short the House of Lords said that in this context, 'can comply' must mean, not 'can physically comply' but 'can in practice comply'. In practice, the boy could not comply with the rule because it conflicted with an important religious and/or cultural requirement.

This highlights an important feature about the religion or belief ground which is probably unique to it: namely, that it covers both situations where adherence to a religion – or being thought by others to adhere to a particular religion – is a mark of group identity and situations where it is a matter or personal belief or conscience. Gunn[91] helpfully identifies three overlapping meanings of religion which clarify this point. The first is religion as belief, which focuses on the individual's own feelings and understanding about the religion. The second is religion as identity, which emphasises group affiliation and is based as much on cultural tradition and ethnicity as religious doctrine. Religion by this meaning is an important component in the glue which binds the community together and also which makes it identifiable as a social grouping. The third is religion as a way of life, where adherence to the religion is not something which is only manifested quietly and privately but which requires certain kinds of outward expression, either in dress or prayers or pervasively in expected standards of behaviour. The first and third meanings could also be applied sensibly

---

90 *Mandla* v. *Dowell Lee* [1983] ICR 385.
91 J. Gunn, 'The complexity of religion and the definition of "religion" in international law' (2003) 16 *Harvard Human Rights Journal* 189.

to other belief systems as well as religion, but it is difficult to see the second as anything but an affinity into which a person is born.

The Directive draws no distinction between these different meanings of religion and thus implies that they are equally deserving of protection. The inclusion of 'religion or belief' indeed implies that personal belief or conscience is as worthy of protection as religion as identity, although it is fairly clear that the latter has much more in common with race discrimination. Indeed, as Gunn points out, it is frequently impossible to distinguish between discrimination on grounds of race, ethnicity and religion.[92]

Returning to Schiek's taxonomy, religion or belief can thus be seen as a ground which cuts across her categories. At least in some respects, discrimination on grounds of religion or belief ought to be treated as a matter of ascribed characteristics, because there is no doubt that people who are, or who are perceived to be, members of some religious groups, notably Muslims in Europe at the present time, are likely to be discriminated against because of their group identity. Interestingly, this can occur regardless of their personal belief systems and thus they are liable to discrimination not so much on grounds of their religion or belief but because of their group membership, the associated socially constructed differences and the perception of them as 'other' to the majority of European society.

At the other end of the spectrum, the religion or belief ground is perhaps the only ground within the expanded protectorate of Article 13 which really can depend on choice – ranging from the sometimes ephemeral adoption of the latest fad to a rigorously thought-through belief system which informs a way of life and which may or may not admit of supernatural powers. Insofar as choices may change, the protection for religion or belief has something in common with protection from age discrimination, where the characteristics of those protected obviously change over time, and disability discrimination, where not only characteristics of individuals may change, but also the kinds of characteristic which are comprised in the category are hugely various and where individuals who appear to have the same disability may be differently affected by it. However, in the case of age and disability, the change in the individual's characteristics does not happen by choice.[93]

---

[92] Ibid., p. 212.

[93] Although it is accepted that disability can result from lifestyle choices, e.g. emphysema from smoking. Lifestyle choices can also affect someone's apparent age.

The question to be asked is whether or not these different meanings of religion or belief in fact require the same levels of protection. It is submitted that they do not and that what would be desirable would be to expand the notion of race and ethnicity to include what has been described above as religion as an ascribed characteristic while leaving at its current place in the hierarchy religion or belief which is the product of free choice, regardless of its merits or demerits.[94] The concept of religion as an ascribed element of identity is recognised in the Council of Europe's Framework Convention for the Protection of National Minorities 1995,[95] which implicitly defines national minorities in terms of 'the essential elements of their identity, namely their religion, language, traditions and cultural heritage'.[96] The Convention aims not only to protect national minorities from discrimination but also to enable them to maintain and develop their own culture and to promote a climate within which cultural diversity is recognised as a source of enrichment for society rather than being seen as potentially divisive. This approach accurately identifies the central problem of religious discrimination and its precepts would provide a better framework for dealing with it.

This recognition of a hierarchy based on reason might also provide a rationale for deciding the 'collision of rights' situations which are bound to occur. As with other grounds, discrimination on grounds of religion or belief may well intersect with other grounds protected under Article 13. The overlap with race has been discussed already. There is also a clear intersection with sex discrimination, since religious requirements may bear more heavily on women than on men within religious communities and it is not uncommon for religious doctrines to hold that women occupy a different (and lesser) place compared with men. Thus, religions may require men and women to worship separately, or to be divided from each other during the act of worship, or may reserve positions of authority and power (such as the priesthood) to men only. The religious ethos exception allows most such practices to continue.

The possibility of conflict between grounds is also to be considered. It is likely that there could be internal conflict in this ground itself – because intolerance of other belief systems may explicitly or implicitly be part of the fundamental doctrine of a religious belief. There is also likely to be a clash with the provisions protecting against discrimination on grounds

---

[94] See P. W. Edge, 'Religious rights and choice under the European Convention on Human Rights' [2000] 3 Web *JCLI*.
[95] 157 ETS.   [96] Article 5(1).

of sexual orientation, since some religions regard homosexual behaviour as 'unnatural' and incompatible with the doctrine of the religion. While Article 4(2) allows 'churches and other public or private organisations the ethos of which is based on religion or belief' to stipulate religion or belief as a 'genuine, legitimate and justified occupational requirement, having regard to the organisation's ethos', it specifically states that this 'should not justify discrimination on another ground'. Maybe it should not, but almost certainly at some point there will be a need to decide whether or not this can stand. In the UK the Employment Equality (Sexual Orientation) Regulations 2003, implementing the Framework Employment Directive, were challenged by some trade unions on grounds of incompatibility with the protection from sexual orientation discrimination in the Directive because they allow an employer to discriminate on grounds of sexual orientation where the employment is for the purposes of an organised religion and the discrimination is either to comply with the doctrines of the religion or to avoid conflicting with the strongly held beliefs of a significant number of the followers of that religion.[97] The case was rejected by High Court on the basis that the exception was bound to be narrowly construed and represented an appropriate balance between the competing interests. This is despite the fact that the exception allows sexual orientation discrimination purely to pander to the prejudices of the religion's followers, unfounded in doctrine, provided that their views are held with sufficient strength! However, in this respect, it also follows the exception allowed in English law for sex discrimination in relation to ministers of religion.[98]

Conclusion

The desire for consistency between EU equality law and European and international human rights law has led to an articulation of the protected ground of religion which conflates the human right to freedom of religion with the duty to prevent discrimination on unjustified grounds. This articulation treats religion as an aspect of personal identity and conviction and, having done so, must protect beliefs which are the product of reflection and conscience (whether rational or irrational) as well as religious beliefs which share similar characteristics. It would be irrational and wrong to privilege religious belief over comparable holistic belief systems.

[97] *Amicus and others* v. *Secretary of State for Trade and Industry* [2004] IRLR 485.
[98] See the Sex Discrimination Act 1975, s. 19.

However, it may be doubted whether it is appropriate, in a measure preventing irrelevant discrimination in employment, to include protection against discrimination on grounds of 'religion or belief'. There is a sense in which religion needs to be included in the prohibition on discrimination in order to ensure that racial discrimination is dealt with adequately. In British law, for example, the prohibition in the Race Relations Act 1976 on discrimination on grounds of 'colour, race, nationality and ethnic or national origin' has been held to cover discrimination against Jews[99] and Sikhs[100] but not Rastafarians[101] and probably not Muslims.[102] Since discrimination against members of the latter two groups would be most likely to occur because of their group membership and its near-identity with minority racial groups in the UK, it is clear that if they were not covered by the Race Relations Act then there was a definite gap in legislative protection. It is much less clear that protection of say, Satanists, Druids and animal rights activists serves an equally important purpose. An expanded definition of race and ethnicity, along the lines of the Framework Convention for the Protection of National Minorities, would serve this purpose better.

If, however, it is argued that there should indeed be protection from discrimination on grounds of religion or belief in the wider senses identified above, then the important question of the basis for selecting the grounds to be protected by Article 13 is raised. Bell[103] notes a move in EC law from a market integration model of social policy (the model which certainly underpinned the original Article 119 of the Treaty of Rome) to one of social citizenship, involving dual concepts of individuals identifying themselves with membership of the European Union and the EU recognising and valuing the diverse groups and individuals comprising the citizens of the Union. The latter could be regarded as a rationale for the inclusion of a wide conceptualisation of religion and belief within the anti-discrimination regime. If so, however, it is illogical to confine protection to the employment field (not including the provision of goods and services, housing, transport, education, etc.) and it is also not obvious why the protection should be confined to the grounds mentioned in Article 13 of the EC Treaty rather than the grounds identified in Article 14 of the European Convention on Human Rights. If that formula were adopted, there would be explicit protection from discrimination on grounds such

---

[99] *Seide* v. *Gillette Industries* [1980] IRLR 427.   [100] *Panesar* v. *Nestlé* [1980] ICR 64.
[101] *Dawkins* v. *Dept of the Environment* [1993] IRLR 284.
[102] *J. H. Walker* v. *Hussain* [1996] IRLR 11.
[103] M. Bell, *Anti-Discrimination Law and the European Union* (Oxford University Press, 2002).

as language, political opinion, social origin, birth or other status and indeed it would be possible to argue for wider protection, since the categories protected by Article 14 are not closed. The question remains – in its prohibition of discrimination on grounds of religion or belief, is the Framework Employment Directive aiming at the right target?

8

Disability discrimination law in the European Union*

GERARD QUINN

Member States are generally taking a civil rights approach to disability: from seeing people with disabilities as the passive recipients of benefits, they acknowledge the legitimate demands of people with disabilities for equal rights. Accordingly, they are making efforts to develop policies that aim at the full participation of people with disabilities into the economy and society. It implies equal opportunities, empowerment and active citizenship in mainstream society.[1]

1. Introduction – the emergence of the rights-based approach to disability in the EU

The main purpose of this chapter is to assess the significance and future potential of the Framework Employment Directive in the specific context of disability.[2]

A recent report by the European Foundation for the Improvement of Living and Working Conditions on the status of persons with disabilities in Europe makes for sober reading.[3] It recalls that disability (which it combines with chronic illness) affects 17 per cent of Europe's general population and about 15 per cent of the working population.[4] Disabled people are reported to have twice the rate for non-participation in the labour market as compared to persons without disabilities. The

---

* Dedicated to Niamh and Anne, an inspiring duo of solidarity and love.
[1] *Joint Report on Social Inclusion* (2004), p. 91. Text available at: http://www.europa.eu.int/ comm/employment_social/social_inclusion/ docs/final_joint_inclusion_report_2003_en.pdf.
[2] Council Directive 2000/78/EC establishing a general framework for equal treatment in employment and occupation [2000,] OJ L303/16.
[3] *Illness, Disability and Social Inclusion*, Dublin, European Foundation for the Improvement of Living and Working Conditions (2003): text available at: http://www.eurofound.ie/ publications/htmlfiles/ef0335.htm.
[4] It should be emphasised there is, of course, no obvious or necessary link between disability and illness since the vast majority of persons with disabilities do not have any illness.

unemployment rate for persons with a severe disability is about three times the level for non-disabled persons. Workers with disabilities typically receive a lower wage than others and segregation is reported to begin at an early age 'with children often pushed into parallel education networks or otherwise excluded from mainstream society'.[5]

The drafting of a United Nations (UN) convention on the rights of persons with disabilities is but the latest expression of a global law reform trend in the disability context.[6] The text of the treaty was agreed in August 2006 and formally adopted by the United Nations General Assembly in December of that year. It was opened for signature and ratification on 30 March 2007. Nearly one hundred states have already signed the treaty since then. It should have particular potency in stimulating law reform in developing countries where at least 500 million of the estimated 650 million persons with disabilities in the world live.[7] As will be seen, key parts of the draft treaty dealing particularly with non-discrimination on the ground of disability are clearly inspired by EU law.[8]

Disability discrimination is bad enough on its own. Its effects are magnified many times over when combined with overlapping grounds of discrimination including age, race, sexual orientation and religion. With respect to age, improved medical care combined with profound demographic change is leading to an absolute growth in the number of persons with disabilities in the EU and is also creating a much larger cohort of elderly persons with disabilities. As a report published by the European Commission in 2001 states:

> The clearest and most consistent relationship across countries is between age and disability. Higher age groups have a higher share of disability. Or, in other words, the disabled population is old in comparison to the

---

[5] *Information sheet on Illness, Disability and Social Inclusion*, Dublin, European Foundation for the Improvement of Living and Working Conditions (2003), available at: www.eurofound.ie/publications/htmlfiles/ef0332.htm.

[6] The drafting process for this convention commenced in 2002 and is ongoing. For the background on the draft United Nations convention see: www.un.org/esa/socdev/enable/rights/adhoccom.htm.

[7] The World Health Organization has recently lent its authority to the authenticity of this estimate. See statement on *Access to Rehabilitation for the 600 million people living with disabilities* (World Health Organization, 2003); text available at: www.who.int/mediacentre/news/notes/2003/np24/en/.

[8] The European Commission participates actively in the deliberations alongside the Council. For its position on the UN draft treaty see, 'Towards a United Nations Legally Binding Instrument to promote and protect the rights and dignity of persons with disabilities', COM(2003) 16 final, 24 January 2003.

population in general . . . This is mainly explained by the fact that the health conditions of individuals generally deteriorates with age . . . There is also a generation factor. Younger age groups meet with better health and working conditions in their early working life and better health care and rehabilitation provisions, than persons from older generations.[9]

In as much as the prevalence of disability increases with age, it is obvious that age and disability interact as operative grounds of discrimination.[10] A recent 2005 NGO report in the UK charts the various disadvantages suffered by older people generally as well as older people with disabilities.[11] It makes for similarly depressing reading. It asserts that those:

> who become disabled once they are already over pensionable age are likely to be disadvantaged as compared to their younger (disabled) peers due to age discrimination in the benefit, health and care systems . . . Symptoms that develop into impairment may be seen as a 'normal' part of ageing, and appropriate disability-related help may not be offered or sought. By contrast, those who have been disabled in earlier life may have very different expectations about their entitlement to the kind of support they require.[12]

Strikingly, the Report continues:

> The disability benefit system is overtly discriminatory on the grounds of age: people who become disabled before the age of 65 are eligible for Disability Living Allowance which includes a 'mobility component' . . . and access to an adapted vehicle scheme: this entitlement is retained after their 65th birthday provided they have already qualified for it. However, those who become disabled after the age of 65 are eligible only to apply for Attendance Allowance, which is less generous, takes longer to qualify for, and has no comparable mobility scheme.[13]

The disadvantages that accrue through the interaction of disability and age as grounds of discrimination are felt in a diverse range of fields

---

[9] *The Employment Situation of Persons with Disabilities in the European Union: Study Prepared by EIM Business and Policy Research* (European Commission, 2001), p. 36. Report available at, www.europa.eu.int/comm/employment_social/ news/2001/dec/2666complete_en.pdf.

[10] Indeed, this interaction between age and disability was the subject of a Finnish Presidency Ministerial Conference in 1999: *Conference on the Independent Living of Older Persons and Persons with Disabilities* (Helsinki, 1999) The papers for this conference are available at: http://pre20031103.stm.fi/english/presidency/independ/independ.htm.

[11] *Discussion Paper, Age, Multiple Discrimination and Older People* (Age Reference Group on Equality and Human Rights, London, 2005), The paper is available from 'Help the Aged' group at: http://policy.helptheaged.org.uk/_policy/AgeEquality/_default.htm.

[12] Ibid, p. 21.   [13] Ibid, p. 23.

such as social care, healthcare and poverty and benefits. It is submitted that these disadvantages are not just confined to the UK but are in fact widespread throughout Europe. Although not all these disadvantages relate to employment – and thus fall outside the scope of the Framework Employment Directive – they do give a sense of just how pervasive discrimination is on the overlapping grounds of disability and age.

With respect to gender and disability, an excellent 2003 publication of the Council of Europe dealing with women and disabilities highlights the disadvantages suffered by women because of discrimination based on the overlapping grounds of disability and gender.[14] It states:

> There is still insufficient awareness of the existence of this twofold source of discrimination: its effects have been largely unresearched. It remains masked behind each of its constituent parts and any measures taken seem to be based on the idea that the two aspects of the discrimination should be dealt with separately. Such an approach, however, common in all European countries, does a disservice to women with disabilities and to society as a whole, which has much to lose as a result.[15]

On the question of discrimination in the specific sphere of employment on the overlapping grounds of gender and disability the Council of Europe report went on to say:

> [here too] . . . the needs of women with disabilities and those of men with disabilities are perceived differently. It is accepted that men must have access to work, but there is no such consensus about women with disabilities, who tend to be steered towards a passive existence. All too often, the prevailing idea is that employment fulfils a different role for women with disabilities than for men. For women, work would appear to represent a means of filling time rather than offering a guarantee of independence. Occasionally, women with disabilities will develop this negative idea. Women with disabilities are more likely to be employed in low-status, lower-paid jobs with poorer working conditions. Lack of self-esteem and education further complicates the matter.[16]

Perhaps the greatest testament to the prevalence of discrimination on the ground of gender and disability is evidenced by the fact that the framers of the United Nations Treaty on the Rights of Persons with Disabilities

---

[14] *Discrimination Against Women with Disabilities* (Strasbourg, Council of Europe, 2003). Report available at: www.coe.int/T/E/Social_Cohesion/soc-sp/Discrimination%20Women._E%20in%20color.pdf.
[15] Ibid., p. 10.   [16] Ibid., p. 35.

felt it necessary to include a specific Article dealing with disability and gender. Article 6 states:

> 1. States Parties recognise that women and girls with disabilities are subject to multiple discrimination, and in this regard shall take measures to ensure the full and equal enjoyment by them of all their human rights and fundamental freedoms.

An analysis of discrimination on the overlapping grounds of race can be found in the United Nations 2002 Study on the *Current Use and Future Potential of United Nations Human Rights Instruments in the Context of Disability*.[17] With respect to disability within the *International Convention against All Forms of Racial Discrimination (ICERD)* the Study states:

> The Convention is of obvious relevance and use to persons who experience discrimination on account of a combination of their racial status and disability. Racial discrimination can itself cause disability. In health services, for example, it may result in failure to treat conditions that can deteriorate into a disability.

> Many State party reports already contain references to disability. This demonstrates that a wide array of States parties already consider disability to be an issue worth reporting on under the [race] Convention. While they may not view disability as a separate ground for reporting (i.e. separate from race), the fact that they report on disability at all provides a basis for useful dialogue between the Committee and States parties.[18]

Religion has proved interesting in jurisdictions like the US where, because of the First Amendment separation of church and state, non-discrimination law tends not to reach religious denominations. That explains why, for example, there is an express provision in the Americans with Disabilities Act (ADA) excluding religious denominations from its coverage (section 307). This exclusion covers the entirety of the ADA which extends far beyond the employment context. This means, for example, that places of worship need not be accessible – although in fact most are through voluntary compliance. Similarly, the ADA contains a provision equivalent to that contained in Article 4.2 of the Framework Directive according to which a person's religion or belief may constitute a *bone fide occupational requirement* for a job (see the analysis that follows in section 4(f) below).

---

[17] The UN Study is available at: www.unhchr.ch/html/menu6/2/disability.doc.
[18] Ibid., p. 240.

For a long time in Europe, and indeed throughout the world, persons with disabilities were seen as the 'deserving poor'. That is, while they were deemed more deserving of states largesse than others they were also considered to be both perpetually and 'naturally' poor. They were frequently regarded as objects of pity, charity and care rather than as subjects in their own right and incapable of directing their own personal destiny. Of course, their status as the 'deserving poor' placed them not so much on a pedestal as in a gilded cage from which it was nearly impossible to emerge and participate as an equal in civil society.

A worldwide law reform movement is now well and truly underway in the disability field – one that tackles the legacy of the past and helps create a more equal society and economy.[19] It is animated by basic human values such as dignity, autonomy, equality and social solidarity and by human rights law. It is also animated by a commitment to reduce economic inefficiency since the exclusion of so much human talent from the labour market is damaging to employers, creates needless dependence on the welfare rolls, diminishes the overall tax take of governments and leads to reduced levels of overall economic activity to the detriment of all. These twin impulses – enhancing economic rationality and honouring human rights – converge to provide a strong forward drive for disability law reform in the EU and elsewhere throughout the world.

The European Union is part of that worldwide trend away from paternalism and towards basic rights for all in the disability context. The groundwork for this shift was laid in the early 1990s at European level. In its 1994 Green Paper on European Social Policy the European Commission famously asserted that 'social segregation *even with adequate income maintenance and special provision* is contrary to human dignity' in the context of disability (emphasis added).[20] This simple statement was a genuine breakthrough. In other words, money alone is not a sufficient answer unless linked to a rights-based reform agenda. The 'poor law' approach of largesse and pity would no longer do – even if lavishly funded.

The United Nations had previously adopted the UN Standard Rules for the Equalisation of Opportunities of persons with Disabilities in 1993.[21]

---

[19] For an overview of this trend, see generally, M. Breslin and S. Yee (eds.), *Disability Rights Law and Policy: International and National Perspectives* (Transnational, 2000). See also, P. Blanck (ed.), *Disability Rights: International Library of Essays on Rights* (Ashgate, 2005).

[20] Green Paper on European Social Policy – Options for the Union, COM(93), November 1993, 551 at p. 48.

[21] *United Nations Standard Rules for the Equalization of Opportunities for Persons with Disabilities*, New York, United Nations, General Assembly Resolution 48/96, 1993. Full text is

Even before the process for drafting the Treaty of Amsterdam had begun in earnest in 1997 a momentous decision was taken within the European Commission to find some way of giving expression to the principles contained in the UN Standard Rules in EU law and policy (effectively the latter since treaty reforms had to wait for the Treaty of Amsterdam which came one year later). The vehicle for doing so was a landmark Communication of 1996 in which the European Commission set out a clear vision of the equal opportunities model in the disability field and asserted that there was a need to move toward it in European policy.[22] This shift in thinking was obvious even from the title of that Communication: *Equality of Opportunities for People with Disabilities – A New Community Disability Strategy.*

The 1996 strategy entailed three basic thrusts. Firstly, political dialogue on the issue was intensified and focused. A High Level Group of Member States representatives was set up to exchange information and best practice. Surprising as it may now seem, such political dialogue was wholly new in 1996. It continues to function. Secondly, and not without some resistance especially from elements within the Council, the Commission proposed to mainstream disability into its own internal processes – which, crucially, included the legislative process. An inter-service working group was set up to carry mainstreaming forward. It too continues to function. The Commission is, however, commendably alive to the need to maintain a disability-specific focus notwithstanding its commitment to mainstreaming. In a 2005 speech Commissioner Spidla stated, for example:

> We do however recognise that it may be sometimes necessary to have a disability-specific approach. This can be an essential first step in overcoming the disadvantages linked to disability and to putting disabled people on an equal footing with non-disabled people.[23]

Thirdly, dialogue with civil society was further consolidated by the 1996 Communication in a spirit of partnership. Indeed, in the aforementioned speech, Commissioner Spidla explicitly endorsed the universal rallying call of the disability NGO movement of '*nothing about us*

---

available at: www.un.org/esa/socdev/enable/dissre00.htm. See generally, 'Human Rights and Disabled Persons: Essays and Relevant Human Rights Instruments', in T. Degener and Y. Koster Dreese (eds.), (Kluwer, 1994).

[22] *Communication of the Commission on Equality of Opportunity for People with Disabilities – a New European Community Disability Strategy*, COM(96) 406 final, 30 July 1996.

[23] See speech of Commissioner Spidla to the Deaf and Hearing Impaired Conference, London on 13 May 2005. The text is available at: www.europa.eu.int/comm/ employment_social/speeches/2005/ vs_130505_en.pdf.

without us. This relationship with civil society has produced a fruitful and informed dialogue and has helped ensure responsiveness on the part of the Commission to the rights and felt needs of Europeans with disabilities. It is, in its way, a model for the rest of the world.

Even as it approaches its tenth anniversary, the basic strategy of the 1996 Communication remains vital and continues to be built on. The year 2003 was denominated the European Year of Persons with Disabilities (EYPD) which had some notable successes in raising the profile of disability as a civil rights issue throughout the Union.[24] Wisely, the EYPD focused on awareness raising at national and regional levels. This served to ensure that the core message of the EYPD – linking rights with the pursuit of justice for persons with disabilities – truly belongs (and was seen to belong) to the people in their own local communities.[25]

In order to capitalise on the success of the 2003 Year the Commission issued a new action plan to maintain momentum: *Equal Opportunities for People with Disabilities: a European Action Plan*.[26] The plan proposes to intensify efforts at co-ordinating the rights-based approach to disability across an impressively broad range of competencies. It will begin with employment since economic independence is so foundational in pro- viding the means for self-determination in so many spheres of life. The Commission will henceforth issue a biennial report on the overall situ- ation of people with disabilities in the enlarged EU. This report will be used as the basis for identified new or emerging priorities in the years up to 2010. This coincides nicely with a parallel commitment by the Council of Europe (whose membership ranges far beyond the borders of the EU) to produce a similar ten year action plan on disability (see the analysis in section (2) below).[27]

Although the focus of this chapter is on legislation – and specifically the Framework Employment Directive – it is important to keep in mind the other policy tools that can and are being brought to bear on the issue of disability discrimination by the Commission. Apart from the

---

[24] Council Decision of 3 December 2001, on the European Year of People with Disabilities 2003, [2001] OJ L335/15.

[25] For a review of the generally positive effects of the EYPD see *Special Eurobarometer Report on the European Year of People with Disabilities* (Brussels, 2004). The text is available at: www.europa.eu.int/comm/employment_social/index/eurobar_ report_en.pdf.

[26] COM(2003) 650 30 October 2003.

[27] The commitment to do so is contained in the *Political Declaration* adopted by the Second Council of Europe Ministerial Conference in Disability (Malaga, 2003), at para. 49. The text of the Declaration is available at: www.coe.int/T/E/Social_Cohesion/soc-sp/Integration/.

European Social Fund, which in obvious ways complements the thrust of the legislation, there are other policy tools available to the Commission.

The Lisbon Strategy (adopted at the Lisbon Council Summit of 2000) aims at making Europe the most competitive and knowledge-based economy in the world by 2010. This requires the co-ordination of efforts in fields such as employment and social inclusion where the EU does not have clear legislative competence. The so-called Open Method of Co-ordination (OMC) is used to identify common policy goals toward which the Member States pledge to co-ordinate their efforts and according to which their performance is peer reviewed.[28]

Interestingly, and apparently at the early insistence of Spain, disability has figured from the outset on the European Employment Strategy (EES – which dates back to the Luxembourg Jobs Summit of 1997) which uses the OMC. A recent review by the Commission of the accomplishments of the EES on the disability ground noted some limited success and outlined future potential.[29] Likewise, disability has figured prominently in the Social Inclusion Strategy which also uses the OMC approach of co-ordinating the policy efforts of the Member States. The Commission recently announced that it will apply the OMC method to health and long-term care with obvious beneficial applications in the context of disability at least to the extent that there is any overlap with disability.[30]

Important new initiatives in the disability field include a new 2005 EU strategy on eAccessibility whose main objective is 'to promote a consistent approach to eAccessibility initiatives in the Member States on a voluntary basis, as well as to foster industry self-regulation'.[31] A draft Regulation has been proposed by the Commission in 2005 dealing with accessibility in air transport which would prohibit a refusal to carry a person with a disability on account of their disability and also provide for a right to assistance.[32] To be sure, this latter initiative – like so many others in the

---

[28] See generally, S. Smismans, 'How to be Fundamental with Soft Procedures? The Open Method of Coordination and Fundamental Social Rights', in G. De Búrca and B. De Witte (eds.), *Social Rights in Europe* (Oxford University Press, 2005).

[29] For an assessment see, *Disability mainstreaming in the European Employment Strategy*, Brussels, European Commission, EMCO/11/290605 (2005).

[30] COM(2005) 33 final, on the Social Agenda, at p. 9.

[31] COM(2005) 425 final, on eAccessibility, 13.09.2005.

[32] COM(2005) 47 final, 16.2.2005, Proposal for a Regulation of the European Parliament and of the Council concerning the rights of persons with reduced mobility when travelling by air. The text of the draft Regulation is available at: www.europa.eu.int/comm/transport/air/rights/doc/com_2005_047_en.pdf.

disability field – comes nearly twenty years after the enactment of the Air Carrier Access Act in the US.[33] Yet it is nonetheless a vital step in the right direction.

The prevalence of discrimination against disabled air travellers was recently underscored by a case brought against Ryanair in the British courts. The airline charged a wheelchair levy for all disabled passengers using wheelchairs. The British courts ruled that this constituted discrimination contrary to the UK Disability Discrimination Act 1994.[34] The court held that the airline was under a duty to provide 'reasonable adjustment' in the form of providing the use of a free wheelchair to enable the complainant to get to the plane. The draft Regulation on air accessibility would add much needed specificity to the broad duty to accommodate such travellers.

The Commission also provided support for a recent and highly important study on community-based alternatives to institutionalisation for persons with disabilities.[35] It is perhaps fair to say that the need for de-institutionalisation and the related need for greater community-based care has yet to be faced throughout Europe. Indeed, a group of European NGOs have come together to 'promote the provision of comprehensive, quality and community-based services as an alternative to institutionalisation' (European Coalition for Community Living).[36]

There is therefore a very rich backdrop of ideas and policy in the EU dealing with disability. The thrust of this policy is positive and rests squarely on an appreciation of the equal rights of European citizens with

---

[33] For a comprehensive overview of US disability law see P. Blanck *et al. Disability Civil Rights Law and Policy*, (Thompson & West, 2003). In 2004 the US National Council on Disability (an advisory body to the President and Congress) recommended further amendments to the Federal Air Carrier Access Act to clarify the right of individuals to institute private suits; see www.ncd.gov/newsroom/publications/2004/aircarrier.htm. The draft EU Regulation requires the designation of a domestic body to handle complaints (Art. 11) and also requires penalties that would be 'effective, proportionate and dissuasive' (Art. 12).

[34] *Ross* v. *Ryanair*, decision of the Central London County Court, 30 January 2004. Reference and discussion of the decision is to be found on the website of the Disability Rights Commission (DRC) of the UK: www.drc-gb.org/newsroom/newsdetails.asp?id = 618&section = 1.

[35] Included in Society: Results and Recommendations of the European Research Initiative on Community-Based Alternatives for Disabled People, Brussels, European Commission, 2004. The text is available at: www.europa.eu.int/comm/employment_social/index/socinc_en.pdf.

[36] The website of the European Coalition for Community Living is available at: www.community-living.info/documents/AboutECCL.pdf.

disabilities. The Framework Employment Directive is part of that mosaic. It should be viewed – and ultimately judged – by how it fits with this overall thrust and how it helps to advance it.

2. Anchoring the rights-based approach in EU law

It was perhaps inevitable that the paradigm shift at the level of ideas set out by the 1996 Communication would eventually be reflected in EU legislation. The competencies added to the Treaties by Article 13 of the Treaty of Amsterdam of 1997 transformed the capacity of Europe to tackle discrimination on a number of new grounds including disability.

Less well known is the fact that European level disability NGOs had played an active part in making the case for these new competencies. Indeed a famous Report of the 'European Day of People with Disabilities' issued in 1995 detailed the case for treaty changes in the disability context and provided an essential backdrop to the negotiations with respect to disability.[37] A subsequent 'European Day Report' in 1996 set out what a Directive should be like in the disability context.[38]

On foot of Article 13, a Directive combating racial discrimination was adopted by Council in June 2000.[39] On the basis of a proposal from the European Commission the Council unanimously adopted the Framework Employment Directive on Employment in November 2000.[40] It is this latter Directive that now explicitly covers disability in its relevant non-discrimination provisions. There is now a considerable body of literature on the two new anti-discrimination Directives adopted under Article 13.[41]

---

[37] *Invisible Citizens: Disabled Persons' Status in the European Treaties*, Brussels, Report of the European Day of Disabled Persons, 1995.

[38] *Mainstreaming of Equal Opportunities: The Campaign for Article 13 Continues*, Brussels, Report of the European Day of Disabled Persons, Brussels, 1997.

[39] Council Directive 2000/43/EC on Equal Treatment between persons irrespective of racial or ethnic origin [2000] OJ L180, p. 22 (Race Directive).

[40] Council Directive 2000/78/EC/

[41] For a useful summary of this literature see, *Critical Review of Academic Literature Relating to the EU Directives to Combat Discrimination*, Brussels, European Commission, 2004. For a review of the situation leading up to the inclusion of Article 13 into the TEU see G. Quinn, 'The Human Rights of People with Disabilities under EU Law', in P. Alston, M. Bustello and M. Keenan (eds.), *The EU and Human Rights* (Oxford University Press, 1999), p. 281. For an overview of the Framework Employment Directive in the Disability context see R. Whittle, 'The Framework Employment Directive for Equal Treatment in Employment and Occupation: an Analysis from A Disability Rights Perspective', (2002) 27 *ELRev* p. 303.

The values of the Framework Employment Directive are further reflected in and reinforced by the Charter of Fundamental Rights for the European Union adopted in 2000 which expressly mentions disability in two substantive Articles. Article 21(1) of the Charter sets out a general prohibition against discrimination on several grounds which explicitly includes disability (as well as providing for a separate ground on 'genetic features'). The addition of 'disability' to the protected grounds was perhaps unthinkable in 1990 – a mere ten years before the adoption of the Charter. And it is certainly arguable that 'genetic features' is already implicit in the ground 'disability' under the Framework Employment Directive (see section 4(b) below).

Article 26 of the EU Charter of Fundamental Rights deals with the more disability-specific right to integration. It purports to recognise and respect the 'right of persons with disabilities to benefit from measures designed to ensure their independence, social and occupational integration and participation in the life of the community'. This language is ambiguous to say the least. It could be argued that there is a further substantive right to these measures – not just a right to benefit from them whenever they happen to be provided for. That is, of course, where cross reliance on the provisions of the Revised European Social Charter comes in useful.[42]

Absent the adoption of the Constitutional Treaty which would confer legal status on the Charter, it is perhaps best to think of the above provisions as mirroring and encapsulating the values and principles already animating EU disability policy. They may, however, provide useful interpretive tools which could be used to reinforce an interpretation of the Framework Employment Directive as a human rights measure.

As a result of the adoption of the Framework Employment Directive the European Union is now an acknowledged world leader in developing appropriate anti-discrimination law on the ground of disability in the employment context.[43] Symbolically – and for the first time in EU law – the Directive situates disability where it should be; namely, within a high

---

[42] Revised European Social Charter, ETS no 163 (1996). See generally the website of the European Social Charter at: www.coe.int/T/E/Human_Rights/Esc/.

[43] In its recently adopted Framework Strategy on Non-Discrimination the Commission asserted, with a large amount of justification,

> These efforts [since the Treaty of Amsterdam] have produced results including the development of some of the most comprehensive and far reaching anti-discrimination legislation to be found anywhere in the world.

COM(2005) 244 final, non-discrimination and equal opportunities for all – a framework strategy, p. 1.

profile civil rights instrument and alongside other prohibited grounds of discrimination.

3. The value added of the non-discrimination tool

Why is the anti-discrimination idea of relevance and of use in the disability context? What value does it add to the traditional policy response of social provision? What kind of job do we expect the Framework Employment Directive to do in the disability context and by what criteria is its success (or failure) to be judged in the future?

For the purposes of this chapter one may leave to one side the academic debate about the 'social construct' of difference.[44] There is much to the view that persons are often 'marked apart' or labelled by their supposed group affiliations in order to be 'kept apart'. That is to say, human difference (including the difference of disability) is imagined or created in order to set the terms of entry and participation into the lifeworld (e.g., the world of work and social interaction, etc.) which have the unintended (and sometimes intended) effect of excluding those who are deemed different. However, my primary focus is not so much on the origin of the 'difference' in question but on how those who are different – or who are labelled as different – are in fact treated.

It proves important to distinguish between the various ways in which people may be discriminated against – or the motives of the would-be discriminator – to grasp the import of the non-discrimination model in the disability context. Individuals who belong to – or are assumed to identify with – a particular group or clustering of persons may be treated negatively in part because of the historically low status of that group in society. This can result from (or give rise) to feelings of superiority on the part of one group as against another. In this context one of the main functions of anti-discrimination law is to valorise the group and group identity.[45] The paradigm case is race. The vast majority of commentators on disability law assume that the main challenge is the prevalence of inaccurate proxies about disability. And yet increasingly, persons with disabilities, like racial minorities, are beginning to express group pride in their affiliation and are seeking to have this pride valorised by the law. For

---

[44] A recent interesting work on the social construct of disability is C. Barnes and G. Mercer (eds.), *Implementing the Social Model of Disability: Theory and Research*, (Disability Press, 2004).

[45] See, e.g., L. Alexander, 'What makes Wrongful Discrimination Wrong; Biases, Preferences, Stereotypes and Proxies', *U Pa L Rev* 1(1992), p. 149.

example, some disability NGOs argued that there should be a right to be disabled inscribed into the draft UN Convention on the Rights of Persons with Disabilities.

Alternatively, discrimination may be motivated less by feelings of moral superiority by one group over another and more by the use of proxies or stereotypes concerning the assumed characteristics of group members. These proxies are usually highly inaccurate and diminish the individuality of the individual. Disability is a classic case in point. Here the reduction of personal 'use value' is even implicit in the very word 'dis-ability'. Disability is commonly – and mistakenly – taken as a proxy for inability to perform the routine tasks of life. So the resulting exclusion (which is extremely pronounced in the employment sphere) appears all the more 'natural'. Any countervailing ethic of integration is put automatically on the defensive as cost-ineffective since it is simply presumed that persons with disabilities are less productive.

It is sometimes said that the doctrine of 'separate but equal' – long and rightly rejected in the area of race – still lives on (and thrives) in the field of disability.[46] From this perspective, not only is the exclusion 'natural' but its recipients are sometimes expected to be thankful for state support and largesse. Arguably at play here is the conflation of biological fact (impairment) with social role. The end result can be a crude and pernicious form of social determinism that arbitrarily telescopes the life chances of persons with disabilities. Such social determinism suggests that persons with disabilities have no place in the mainstream and no productive role to play in the labour market. Indeed, according as the labour market does not adjust to allow such persons to express their abilities then, through time, this proxy becomes a self-fulfilling prophesy – a vicious circle of exclusion.

An important point of principle needs to be stressed in this context. Even where the relevant proxies may have some basis in fact (e.g. some categories of persons with disabilities have a lower productivity rate compared to others) it is still impermissible to use them to cloud rational judgments about individual ability since it is always possible that individuals will not conform to the stereotype. It is fundamentally unfair not to afford everyone an equal chance of proving themselves.

[46] The seminal case rejecting the doctrine of 'separate but equal' on the ground of race is *Brown v. Board of Education*, 347 US 483, 495 (1953). For a discussion of its relevance in the cognate field of Disability see G. Quinn, 'Disability Discrimination Law in the United States', in G. Quinn, M. McDonagh and K. Kimber (eds.), *Disability Discrimination Law in the United States, Australia and Canada*, (Oak Tree Press, 1993), pp. 26–7.

However, the main problem in the field of disability is not so much that the proxies are accurate but should not be used. Rather, it is that the proxies are highly inaccurate and rest on encrusted layers of unexamined presuppositions that have piled up over the centuries. So one of the main tasks of non-discrimination law in the context of disability is to separate fact from fiction – to place a spotlight on the person behind the disability and, in the employment context, to get employers to focus much more rationally on what the individual has to offer as distinct from what the proxies suggest he has to offer. To a large extent the non-discrimination principle (both direct and indirect) helps to reverse the presumptions of inability accreted through the centuries about persons with disabilities. It therefore adds to market rationality.[47]

Furthermore, and crucially, to fully respect the difference of disability will sometimes (though not always) entail positively accommodating that difference. This much is plain as a matter of principle from the rulings of the European Court of Human Rights.[48]

Hence, the significance of the concept of 'reasonable accommodation' as a way of moving beyond respecting difference to accommodating it. The obligation of 'reasonable accommodation' is distinct from 'positive action measures' and is intimately tied to the non-discrimination idea. For one thing, positive action measures are general and not tailored to the individual. The notion of 'reasonable accommodation' is, on the other hand, quintessentially individualised. It involves the person in an inter-active dialogue with the employer to search for the right kind of accommodation needed in the overall circumstances of the case. Importantly, positive action measures do not generally create subjective rights. That is to say, persons with disabilities are not generally given any legal standing to challenge how (or whether) the relevant positive action measures are implemented. To the contrary, and precisely because of the intimate link with non-discrimination, the concept of 'reasonable accommodation' creates clear legal standing for the person to challenge the manner by which they are being accommodated.

[47] See generally, *The Business Case for Diversity – Good Practices in the Workplace*, Brussels, European Commission, 2005. Text available at: www.europa.eu.int/comm/employment_social/fundamental_rights/pdf/events/busicase_en.pdf.

[48] On positive obligations generally under the ECHR see A. Mowbray, *The Development of Positive Obligations under the European Convention on Human Rights by the European Court of Human Rights* (Hart, 2004). On positive obligations as they apply to disability under the ECHR see O. De Schutter, 'Reasonable Accommodations and Positive Obligations in the European Convention on Human Rights', in A. Lawson and C. Gooding (eds.), *Disability Rights in Europe: From Theory to Practice* (Hart, 2005), pp. 35–65.

Since one of the drawbacks of positive action measures has been this lack of direct accountability to the person there does not tend to be a close correlation between the measure provided and individual needs. This is redressed by the notion of 'reasonable accommodation'. All of which is not to say that positive action measures are not required. They obviously are. But the notion of 'reasonable accommodation' ensures a more direct link between the accommodation to be provided and the circumstances of the person and it also affords the person the opportunity to challenge accommodations and truly adjust them to his or her realities.

The text of the Framework Employment Directive is alive to the need for positive action measures. Naturally such positive action measures are needed in the disability context. A chief distinguishing feature of the European social model has been its commitment to provide the material 'underpinning to freedom' through social support. The inter-linkage drawn between positive action measures and non-discrimination in the Framework Employment Directive may well provide an opportunity to reflect on how social support might be better directed to achieve the main goal of both non-discrimination and social provision – namely to honour persons and create the conditions for their personal fulfilment and success. Useful pointers are to be found in the recent Conclusions and case law of the European Committee of Social Rights of the Council of Europe. This case law shows how the non-discrimination ideal can refresh social rights.[49]

How then, does the Framework Employment Directive do the job that one would ideally expect of the non-discrimination ideal in the disability context?

4. Anatomy of the Framework Employment Directive on the disability ground

This section reviews the manner by which the Framework Employment Directive extends and tailors the protection of the non-discrimination idea on the ground of disability.

Much of the analysis in this section is based on and develops Part II of the Baseline Study on Disability Discrimination Law in the EU Member States (hereafter, Disability Baseline Study) which the author prepared within

---

[49] On the disability case law under the European Social Charter see G. Quinn, 'The European Social Charter and EU Anti-Discrimination Law in the Field of Disability: Two Gravitational Fields with one Common Purpose', in G. De Búrca and B. De Witte (eds.), *Social Rights in Europe* (Oxford University Press, 2005), 279–304.

the EU Network of Independent Experts on Disability Discrimination for the European Commission in 2004.[50]

(a) The Recitals as windows on to the values of the Directive in the disability context

Of some significance in setting the context for the Directive are Recitals 1 and 6 that refer, essentially, to the fact that the Union is primarily a community of shared values with a commitment to the achievement of human rights for all. This backdrop is important since it situates the equal treatment ideal of the Directive squarely in a human rights context.

Recital 8 refers to the Employment Guidelines (of the European Employment Strategy agreed for 2000) which stress the need to foster a labour market favourable to social integration 'by formulating a coherent set of policies aimed at combating discrimination against groups such as persons with disability'. From this may be inferred a broad goal of social integration to be advanced through non-discrimination law and policy.

Discrimination based, inter alia, on disability, is stated by Recital 11 as undermining the achievement of the objectives of the EC Treaty, in particular the attainment of a high level of employment. Because of this, Recital 12 states that any direct or indirect discrimination based, inter alia, on disability, in the employment field covered by the Directive should be prohibited throughout the Community. Recital 16 states that the provision of measures to accommodate the needs of disabled people in the workplace plays an important role in combating discrimination on the grounds of disability.

In sum, the achievement of equal treatment on all grounds including disability is both a productive factor in the marketplace as well as a civilising factor in democratic society. These two rationales should be seen as mutually supportive and in this they reflect the dynamic interaction between the Inter State Commerce Clause (Article 1(8)(3)) and Section 5 of the 14th Amendment to the US Constitution.[51]

---

[50] The *Disability Baseline Study* is available on the website of the European Commission at: www.europa.eu.int/comm/employment_social/fundamental_rights/public/pubsg_en.htm.

[51] Both of these provisions are asserted on the face of the Americans with Disabilities Act as providing twin constitutional authority for its enactment. The Inter State Commerce clause provides authority to Congress to regulate economic transactions even within states provided there is some link to Inter State Commerce. Section 5 of the 14th Amendment provides added authority to Congress to enact civil rights legislation advancing the 14th

The recent decision of the European Court of Justice (ECJ) in *Mangold* lends credence to the view that the human rights rationale of the Framework Employment Directive is its dominant rationale.[52] In that case the Court asserted that the Framework Employment Directive 'does not itself lay down the principle of equal treatment in the context of employment'.[53] Instead the sole purpose of the Directive is to 'lay down a framework for combating discrimination (on the various enumerated grounds)'.[54] Importantly, the Court identifies the source of the principle is to be found in various international instruments (i.e. human rights treaties) and in the constitutional traditions common to the Member States. This could be a mixed blessing given the recent *D.H.* judgment of the European Court of Human Rights.[55]

(b) The crucial absence of a definition of disability

The Framework Employment Directive does not define disability.[56] Naturally this affords Member States considerable latitude in how, or whether, they define disability for the purposes of transposing the Framework Employment Directive. The question that immediately arises is whether this discretion is unlimited.

In this regard, it is important to note that Article 1 states that the general purpose of the Directive is to lay down a general framework for combating discrimination on the 'grounds of' disability with a view to putting into effect the principle of equal treatment. What is prohibited is *discrimination* or negative treatment '*on the ground*' of disability. It could be strongly argued that this formulation would appear to place the focus of attention on the phenomenon of discrimination as such and not so much

---

Amendments' general protection of equal protection under the law. For a discussion as to these two bases of Congressional authority see S. L. Milochik, 'The Constitution and the Americans with Disabilities Act: Some First Impressions', (1991) 64 *Temple L. Rev.* 619. With respect to recent difficulties with the constitutionality of certain aspects of the ADA see J. Lav, 'Conceptualizations of Disability and the Constitutionality of Remedial Schemes under the Americans with Disabilities Act', (2002–03) 34 *Colum Hum Rts L Rev.* 197.

[52] Case C-144/04, decision of the ECJ, 22 November, 2005.
[53] Ibid. at para. 74.   [54] Ibid.
[55] *D. H. and Ors* v. *Czech Republic*, App. No. 57325/00, Judgment of the Court, 7 February, 2006.
[56] See T. Degener, *Definition of Disability*, Research Paper for the EU Network of Legal Experts on Disability Discrimination Law (2004): the text of the paper is available at: www.europa.eu.int/comm/employment_social/fundamental_rights/pdf/aneval/disabdef.pdf.

on the peculiarities or the person. After all, a woman does not generally have to prove that she is a woman before invoking anti-discrimination law.

To the latter point, it may be retorted that it is obvious who is a woman. That is probably true in the vast majority of instances although gender identity is 'not without its complexities' at least with respect to transsexuals ('gender dysporia'). Even if it is obvious who is a man and a woman, the same, however, could not be said with respect to race and ethnic origin. Indeed, it is interesting to note in passing that a failure to reach a consensus on the definition of 'national minority' did not stop the Council of Europe from adopting the landmark Framework Convention for the Protection of National Minorities.[57] To limit the benefits of anti-discrimination law to certain kinds of disability or to disabilities reaching a certain degree would not appear to be consistent with the underlying goals of the Directive.[58]

Interestingly, the draft UN treaty on the rights of persons with disabilities also prohibits discrimination on the 'basis' of disability and similarly lacked a definition of disability until the last drafting session in August 2006. The absence of a definition in the draft UN treaty was strongly favoured by the EU during the negotiations (at least until the last session in August 2006).

As to the potential scope of the protectorate, several possibilities present themselves. It will be seen that the European Court of Justice has not gotten off to a good start in this vital field.

First of all, it is certainly arguable that people may be discriminated against 'on the *basis of disability*' who may not themselves have a disability but who are nevertheless treated negatively because of the assumption that they have a disability. An example is someone with a facial disfigurement who is not thereby disabled but who might be treated negatively by others *as if* he were disabled. This is certainly the view clearly held by the Canadian Supreme Court. In a major decision in 2000, *Quebec* v. *Montreal et al.*, known as the *Mercier* case, that Court specifically endorsed the tendency of Canadian lower courts to include subjective perceptions of disability within the definition of disability.[59] It stated:

---

[57] European Treaty Series (ETS) No. 157 (1995) (entered into force in 1998).

[58] A useful background survey of the variety of definitions extant in comparative European law was carried out for the European Commission by Brunel University and published in 2002: *Definitions of Disability in Europe – a Comparative Analysis*, Brussels, European Commission, 2002.

[59] *Quebec (Commission de droits de la personne et des droits de la juenesse)* v. *Montreal; Quebec (etc.,)* v. *Boisbriand (City)* [2000] 1 SCR

Whatever the wording used in human rights legislation [essentially provincial non-discrimination codes], Canadian courts tend to consider not only the objective basis for certain exclusionary practices (i.e., the actual existence of functional limitations). But also the subjective and erroneous perceptions regarding the existence of such limitations. Thus, tribunals and courts have recognized that even though they do not result in functional limitations, various ailments such as congenital physical malformation, asthma, speech impediments, acne and, more recently, being HIV positive, may constitute grounds for discrimination.[60]

The Canadian Supreme Court continued:

Thus, a 'handicap' may be the result of a physical limitation, an ailment, a social construct, a perceived imitation or a combination of all these factors. Indeed, it is the combined effect of all these circumstances that determines whether the individual has a 'handicap' [for the purposes of Quebec law] . . .

Courts will therefore have to consider not only an individual's biomedical condition, but also the circumstances in which a distinction is made. In examining the context in which the impugned act occurred, courts must determine, *inter alia*, whether an actual or perceived ailment causes the individual to 'experience the loss or limitation of opportunities to take part in the life of the community on an equal level with others'.

The fact remains that handicap also includes persons who have overcome all functional limitations and who are limited in their everyday activities only by the prejudice or stereotypes that are associated with this ground.[61]

The Court concluded:

That is not to say that the biomedical basis of 'handicap' should be ignored, but rather to point out that, for the purposes of the Charter, we must go beyond this single criterion. Instead, a multi-dimensional approach that includes a socio-political dimension is particularly appropriate. By placing the emphasis on human dignity, respect, and the right to equality rather than on a simple biomedical condition, this approach recognizes that the attitudes of society and its members often contribute to the idea of perception of 'handicap'. *In fact, a person may have no limitations in everyday activities other than those created by prejudice and stereotypes.*[62]

Secondly, those who may be susceptible to disability (revealed for example, through genetic testing) may also be treated negatively 'on the ground of

---

[60] Ibid., para. 48.   [61] Ibid., paras. 79–81.   [62] Ibid., para. 77 (emphasis added).

disability' even though they do not themselves currently have a disability. Again, if a consistent focus is maintained on the phenomenon of discrimination on the ground of disability then it makes sense to bring this category within the protective coverage of the relevant anti-discrimination law. It bears recalling that Article 21(1) of the EU Charter of Fundamental Rights includes 'genetic features' as one of the prohibited grounds. Indeed, Article 10 of the Council of Europe Convention on Biomedicine specifically bans any form of discrimination on the basis of a persons' 'genetic heritage'.[63] Article 12 of the same Convention also controls (limits) the use of genetic tests. This Convention has been ratified by nineteen Council of Europe Member States. It is submitted that the fact that disability is listed separately from 'genetic features' in the EU Charter of Fundamental Rights should not automatically mean that it is excluded from coverage under the Framework Employment Directive since the two grounds concatenate.[64]

Thirdly, there are others who may not have a disability but who work with or associate with those who have a disability. They would include a mother with a disabled child seeking to re-enter the labour market or a volunteer in a hospice for those with AIDS. Such people are likely to be treated negatively 'on the ground of disability' even though they do not themselves have a disability. Logically, if a consistent focus is maintained on the phenomenon of discrimination 'on the ground of disability' then it also makes sense to bring this category within the coverage of the relevant anti-discrimination law. Indeed, a reference on this very point from the UK is currently pending before the European Court of Justice as of October 2006 (*Coleman* v. *Law & Law*).[65] In that case a mother claims she was dismissed because she cares for a disabled son. The net point posed to the Court is whether 'associative discrimination' is covered by the Directive.

Irish discrimination law is particularly illuminating on the question of definition. Section 2 of the Employment Equality Act 1998 specifies a mainly medical definition of disability for the purposes of that Act. In fact many disability NGOs took exception to the inclusion of a medical

---

[63] Convention for the Protection of Human Rights and Dignity of the Human Being with regard to the Application of Biology and Medicine: Convention on Human Rights and Biomedicine, Council of Europe Treaty System (CETS) No. 164 (1997).

[64] Perhaps the best and most recent analysis of the non-discrimination principle in the context of genetic testing is M. Stein and A. Silvers, 'An Equality Paradigm for Preventing Genetic Discrimination', (2002) 55 *Vand. L. Rev.*, 1341.

[65] *Coleman* v. *Law and Law*, Case No. 2303745/2005, decision of the Employment Tribunal, 17 February 2006.

definition when the Bill was being debated.[66] Essentially, section 2 lists several (fairly exhaustive) medical conditions and deems them to be a 'disability' for the purposes of the Act. Interestingly, it then proceeds to declare these medical conditions to amount to a disability if they:

> exist at present, or which previously existed but no longer exists, or which may exist in the future or which is imputed to a person.[67]

It is clear, therefore, that the Irish definition includes a record of a disability, a perceived disability and a future disability. Subsequent practice before the Irish courts has shown that the medical definition (as expanded above to sweep in putative as well as future disabilities) has not placed insurmountable obstacles in the way of litigation. If litigants fail they generally fail for other reasons and on the merits. So, even though not ideologically pure, the Irish statutory definition has 'worked'.

By way of contrast, the definition of disability in the UK Disability Discrimination Act (DDA) of 1994 followed the 'social model' approach which was based loosely on the definition under the Americans with Disabilities Act (ADA). Section 1 of the DDA states that a persons with a disability is:

> a person who has a physical or mental impairment which has a substantial and long term adverse effect on their ability to carry out normal day-to-day activities.

In this sense, the British definition is ideologically pure. And yet it has led to many obstacles in the way of litigation. As indicated in the aforementioned Disability Baseline Study:

> Normal day-to-day activities include mobility, manual dexterity, physical coordination the ability to lift, carry or otherwise move everyday objects, hearing or eyesight, memory or the ability to concentrate, learn or understand, the perception of the risk of danger. The adverse effect must also be long-term, that is, having lasted for at least 12 months, or the period that it can be reasonably expected to last is at least 12 months or the rest of the persons life (whichever is the shorter).

> Thus the focus is on what the individual cannot do as opposed to what they can do. So far, cases involving acute vertigo, chronic pain in the legs and feet induced by fallen arches, transient epileptic fits, a sight loss in

---

[66] The Irish approach was in fact modelled on Australian disability law. See s. 4 of the Disability Discrimination Act (Australia) 1992, available at: http://scaleplus.law.gov.au/html/pasteact/0/311/top.htm.

[67] Employment Equality Act 1998, s. 2(e): available at: www.irishstatutebook.ie/front.html.

one eye, back strain with a continuing ability to carry out light duties and rheumatoid arthritis in the absence of independent medical evidence have all failed the test of having a 'substantial adverse impact' upon normal day-to-day activities. Increasingly it is the practice for tribunals to hear medical evidence as to whether an impairment objectively exists. The determination of whether the impairment is 'substantial' remains a question of fact for the tribunal alone to determine.[68]

The fact the definition on the DDA had proved a hindrance rather than a help drew criticism from the Disability Rights Commission (DRC) as well as many other groups. The definition was broadened somewhat by the Disability Discrimination Act 2005.[69] Section 18 of that Act adds that a person who 'has cancer, HIV infection or multiple sclerosis is to be deemed to have a disability'. In anticipation of a Single Equality Act (merging all existing equality legislation), and as of January 2006, the British government has requested the DRC to carry out a further consultation exercise on what any future definition of disability should look like.[70]

That the British definition proved problematic was not perhaps a surprise given the fate of the definition under the ADA in the US Courts.[71] Section 3(2) of the ADA defined disability with respect to an individual as:

(A) a physical or mental impairment that substantially limits one or more of the major life activities of such individual;

(B) a record of such an impairment; or

(C) being regarded as having such an impairment.

A series of US Supreme Court decisions has considerably narrowed this section. By so doing the courts have effectively raised the hurdles through which litigants must jump before their case can be dealt with on the merits.[72] The effects of these and lower court decisions in the US have been summarised by Peter Blanck (and others) as follows:

---

[68] At p. 81.

[69] The Act is available at: www.opsi.gov.uk/ACTS/acts2005/20050013.htm.

[70] The Disability Rights Commission Consultation Paper is available at: www.drc-gb.org/ uploaded_files/documents/20_916_Consultation %20on%20definition%20of%20 disability.doc.

[71] The Civil Rights Division of the US Department of Justice maintains a comprehensive website on ADA related legal materials. It is available at: http://www.ada.gov.

[72] See, e.g., *Sutton* v. *United Air Lines, Inc.*, 527 US 471 (1999), *Albertsons Inc.* v. *Kirkingburg*, 527 US 555 (1999), *Murphy* v. *United Parcel Service Inc.*, 527 US, 555 (1999). See generally, *Righting the ADA: National Council on Disability Policy Paper no 7 (2003) The Impact of the US Supreme Court's ADA Decisions on the Rights of Persons with Disabilities*, available at: www.ncd.gov/newsroom/publications/2003/decisionsimpact.htm. See also, L. Krieger (ed.), *Backlash against the ADA: Reinterpreting Disability Rights* (Michigan, 2003).

1. Persons who use mitigating measures are not protected by the ADA.
2. Persons whose impairments could be mitigated by medication are not protected by the ADA.
3. It is difficult for individuals to establish that they are substantially limited in the major life activity of working.
4. Individuals must prove not only that they are substantially limited in major life activities, but that they are substantially limited in 'activities central to daily life'.
5. It is almost impossible for individuals to establish that they fall within the 'regarded as' prong of the ADA's definition of disability.[73]

French law also follows the trend toward a more social definition of disability. Article 2 of Law 2005–102 inserts the following definition of disability into Article L114 of the Code of Social Welfare:

> A person has a disability for the purposes of this Code if he has, a complete limitation of activity or restriction of the ability to participate in society encountered by a person in his or her environment by reason of a substantial, lasting or definitive alteration of one of the many physical, sensory, mental, cognitive or psychological faculties, of multiple disabilities or of a disabling illness.

Austria has recently legislated to include family members (including relatives with caring responsibilities) within the scope of protection of its equality legislation.[74]

Fittingly, given the importance of the issue of definition, the first case on the ground of disability under the Framework Employment Directive to reach the European Court of Justice was decided in July 2006 on the definition (*Chacon Navas* referral).[75] A Spanish judge (Judge Pablo Aramendi of Social Court no. 33 in Madrid) referred two issues for a preliminary ruling in May 2005. The issues were:

1. Does the protection of Directive 2000/78, insofar as Article 1 lays down a general framework for combating discrimination on the grounds of disability, cover a worker who has been dismissed from his or her company solely because he or she was ill?
2. In the alternative, in case it is deemed that illness does not fall within the protective framework provided by Directive 2000/78 for combating discrimination on the grounds of disability, and the answer to the first

---

[73] P. Blanck (*et al.*), *Disability Civil Rights Law and Policy* 3–17/3–18.
[74] See the Austrian Equal Status Act for People with Disabilities 2005.
[75] Case C-13/05 [2005] OJ C69, 19.03.2005, p. 8.

question is no, may illness be regarded as an identifying attribute in addition to the ones in relation to which Directive 2000/78 prohibits discrimination.

The net questions posed were whether sickness, as such, counts as a disability and, if not, could sickness (or health status) be considered covered by analogy. This would amount to an extension – although arguably not an unwarranted extension – of the received understanding of the term disability. It would appear that at least some countries (France, Belgium) include 'health status' as a ground of discrimination in their legislation. The judge appeared to be asking whether the ground of disability could encompass health status at least to some degree.

On 16 March 2006 the Advocate General (M. L. A. Geelhoed) handed down an opinion on the *Chacon Navas* referral.[76] The Opinion of Advocate General Geelhoed in the *Chacon Navas* case was very regrettable.[77] Both net questions were answered in the negative.[78]

Somewhat disturbingly, the Advocate General's Opinion gives the impression that financial costs play a major, if not a predominant role in determining the outer boundaries of the definition of disability.[79] The motive seems to have been to cabin the potentially 'far reaching' obligations of the relevant actors. Financial costs are, of course, an important consideration. But it is respectfully submitted that an approach which deliberately sculpts the definition of disability in order to control costs is not consistent with the underlying goal of the Directive which is to provide a 'level playing field as regards equality in employment' (Recital 37). The Opinion of the Advocate General uses a highly consequentialist approach to the question of definition (need to avoid costs) rather than one that seeks to give precedence to the civil rights of the individual and explore other and more sophisticated ways of balancing the achievement of these rights with other reckonable interests.

Further, in the course of his Opinion, the Advocate General held that current medical conditions that might presage future disabilities do not bring the individual within the protective scope of the Directive.[80] This is doubly to be regretted since genetic testing is likely to become ever more prominent in Europe in the years ahead thus leaving many (if not the majority) vulnerable to discrimination based on putative disabilities.

---

[76] Case C-13/05, Opinion of the Advocate General, 16 March, 2006: available in French at: //http://curia.eu.int/jurisp/cgi-bin/form.pl?lang = EN&Submit = Rechercher$docrequ.
[77] Case C-13/05 [2005] OJ C69/8, 19.3.2005. [78] 16 March 2006.
[79] See para. 52 of the Advocate General's Opinion. [80] Ibid. at para. 62.

The European Court of Justice handed down its ruling in the *Chacon Navas* case in July 2006.[81] The Court reasoned that the concept of 'disability' as used in the Directive 'must be understood as referring to a limitation which results in particular from physical, mental or psychological impairments and which hinders the participation of the person in professional life'. No specific reasons were advanced by the Court as to why this must be so.

The Court continued that the use of the term 'disability' in Article 1 of the Directive meant that the legislature intended to distinguish it sharply from sickness. The Court pointed to Recital 16 which is to the effect that the 'provision of measures to accommodate the needs of disabled people at the workplace plays an important role in combating discrimination on the grounds of disability' and concluded that the need for such measures adapting the workplace meant that the disability had to be long term or carried a probability that it would last over a long time.[82] This is a curious use of a positive norm in the Directive to restrict the scope of the potential protectorate. It was then a rush to the conclusion that 'a person who has been dismissed by his employer solely on account of sickness does not fall within the general framework laid down for combating discrimination on grounds of disability by Directive 2000/78'.[83]

As to the second question the Court strictly construed the Directive to exclude the possibility of extending an existing ground by analogy. It refused to consider that the general principle of non-discrimination in EU law – a principle that encompassed and transcends the Directive – could or should have this effect.[84]

The *Chacon Navos* ruling has one dramatic effect on the drafting of the UN treaty on disability. As previously mentioned, the EU Presidency has insisted throughout the drafting of the UN Convention on the Rights of Persons with Disabilities that there was no need for a definition of disability under the Convention. It pointed to the absence of a definition under the Directive and argued that a definition was out of place in a human rights instrument. However, the EU appears to have relented on the point in part because of the *Chacon Navos* ruling. The treaty as finally agreed in August 2006 does in fact contain a definition of a person with a disability which reads (Article 1):

> Persons with disabilities include those who have long-term physical, mental, intellectual, or sensory impairments which in interaction with various

---

[81] Judgment of the Court (Grand Chamber), 11 July 2006.   [82] Ibid., para. 45.
[83] Ibid., para. 47.   [84] Ibid., para. 56.

barriers may hinder their full and effective participation in society on an equal basis with others.[85]

It can at least be said of the definition in the UN Convention that it makes an effort to understand and express the basic point that it is the interaction of disability with social processes (i.e. the absence of sensitivity in such processes to disability) that causes the main problem. Regrettably, the formula used by the ECJ (an impairment that *itself* hinders the participation) does not demonstrate any similar depth of understanding.

However, since the Directive provides a floor there is nothing to stop Member States from going beyond its minimum requirements. Arguably, according as EU Member States ratify the UN treaty, the UN definition should become the norm while the ECJ's ruling could represent a very low floor. In short, the *Chacon Navos* ruling was a missed opportunity on the part of the ECJ and compares extremely poorly with the reasoning of the Canadian Supreme Court in *Mercer*. The *Coleman* referral on 'associative discrimination' poses the next challenge to the Court and it is hoped it will use the opportunity to reflect much deeper on the ripple effects of disability-based discrimination.

(c) The prohibition on direct and indirect discrimination on the ground of disability (Article 2)

The drafting history of Article 2 is quite important to a proper appreciation of the non-discrimination principle in the disability context and especially with respect to the interaction with Article 5 which particularises the obligation of 'reasonable accommodation'.

In explaining its original proposal for a Directive and with respect to the disability ground the Commission stated:

> Various official estimates suggest that people with disabilities are at least two to three times more likely to be unemployed and to remain unemployed for longer periods than the rest of the working population. A contributory factor to this situation is the prevalence of discrimination based on disability. *Such discrimination* would include *inter alia* the existence of inadequately adapted workplaces, workstations and work organisation design.[86]

The language used above is important for it shows that the Commission clearly saw that inadequately adapted workplaces, etc., was a form of discrimination in the employment context. It is worth emphasising that the

[85] Article 1.   [86] COM(1999) 656 final, at 3 (emphasis added).

original text of Article 2 (general prohibition on non-discrimination) as proposed by the Commission contained four subparagraphs – the fourth of which contained the original reference to 'reasonable accommodation' as a way of tackling such inadequately adapted workplaces.[87] As originally proposed, Article 2(4) read:

> In order to guarantee compliance with the principle of equal treatment for persons with disabilities, reasonable accommodation shall be provided, where needed, to enable such persons to have access to, participate in, or advance in employment, unless this requirement creates an undue hardship.

In the ensuing negotiations within Council no delegation objected to the linkage drawn in the above formulation between non-discrimination and 'reasonable accommodation'. However, a purely technical drafting decision was taken to move subparagraph 4 to a new Article (now Article 5). This was done because it was felt out of place to overburden the general or headline prohibition against discrimination with overly detailed or prescriptive rules dealing with only one ground among the many. It was felt that if any detailed prescriptive rules on particular grounds were needed they should be provided for elsewhere in body of the Directive.

For example, Article 6 on the age ground elaborates certain justifications for discrimination on that ground. And Article 5 now particularises the obligation of 'reasonable accommodation'. However, and in order to maintain the organic link with the general prohibition against non-discrimination contained in Article 2, the opening line of the original subparagraph 4 (above) proposed by the Commission was retained in the opening words to the new Article 5:

> In order to guarantee compliance with the principle of equal treatment in relation to persons with disabilities, reasonable accommodation shall be provided

Suffice it to say that the original Article 2 contained an explicit reference to the obligation of 'reasonable accommodation' and its displacement for purely technical drafting reasons from Article 2 to the new Article 5 should not be seen as breaking the link between the general prohibition against non-discrimination of Article 2 and the obligation to provide 'reasonable accommodation'.

As a historical aside, the fact that the two provisions were separated out in the Directive was invoked by the EU Presidency during the negotiations

---

[87] COM (1999) 565 final. Proposal for a Council Directive Establishing a General Framework for Equal Treatment in Employment and Occupation.

that took place in a United Nations Working Group in 2004. This Working Group was tasked with the job of elaborating a working text for the UN disability treaty. The EU presidency argued that is was necessary to separate out the prohibition against non-discrimination from the obligation to provide 'reasonable accommodation' in order to maintain parity with the Framework Employment Directive. Unfortunately this separation was allowed to stand in the treaty from 2004 until the seventh Ad Hoc Committee (drafting body) met in January 2006 and restored the link. Discrimination, for the purposes of that draft treaty, is now defined as:

> any distinction, exclusion or restriction on the basis of disability which has the purpose or effect of impairing or nullifying the recognition, enjoyment or exercise, on an equal basis with others, of all human rights and fundamental freedoms in the political, economic, social, cultural, civil or any other field. It includes all forms of discrimination, *including denial of reasonable accommodation* [and direct and indirect discrimination].[88]
>
> (emphasis added)

The principle of equal treatment is stated in Article 2(1) of the Directive to mean that there shall be no direct or indirect discrimination on the ground, inter alia, of disability.

Direct discrimination is defined under Article 2(2)(a) to occur where 'one person is treated less favourably than another is, has been or would be' on the ground, inter alia, of disability 'in a comparable situation'. This encompasses straightforward cases of direct and intentional discrimination against persons with disabilities motivated primarily by prejudice. It is noteworthy that no defence whatsoever is allowable for direct discrimination. If 'reasonable accommodation' can place the individual in a 'comparable situation' then the individual is, by definition, in a comparable situation for the purposes of the Framework Employment Directive.

A recent 2005 and very clear example of direct discrimination on the ground of disability – albeit outside the employment context – arose recently in Latvia.[89] The plaintiff, who was a wheelchair user, was denied access to a nightclub. He was told there were no more spaces even though a non-disabled friend of his got in later. On a different occasion he was similarly denied entry and was told that there was a 'private party' taking place. Again, another (non-disabled) person sought entry without any

---

[88] For the latest draft of the treaty see: www.un.org/esa/socdev/enable/rights/ahc7ann2rep. htm.

[89] Riga Regional Court, Case No. 04386004, C 20203 (12 July 2005).

difficulty later. The club tried to defend its actions by saying that it required several days notice for the presence of a disabled patron. The court found against the club under defamation proceedings (offence to honour and reputation). But it seems a clear and blatant form of direct discrimination on the ground of disability.

The notion of direct discrimination under Article 2(2)(a) may also reach the issue of 'reasonable accommodation' in an indirect manner. For example, direct or intentional discrimination might arise because the would-be discriminator may fear having to provide 'reasonable accommodation'. In other words, the prospect of having to provide 'reasonable accommodation' may motivate an employer to discriminate directly on the ground of disability.

The added value of indirect discrimination is that it is capable of reaching systemic issues of discrimination not normally covered by the prohibition against direct discrimination. It is defined in Article 2(2)(b):

> where an apparently neutral provision, criterion or practice would put persons . . . [with a disability] . . . at a particular disadvantage compared with other persons.

This prohibition is of inestimable value in the disability context. This is so because much discrimination on the ground of disability arises through thoughtlessness or the unquestioning acceptance of long established practices. And it is this form of discrimination that impacts most in the context of disability and that has left a legacy of practices that effectively exclude. In other words, indirect discrimination will not generally be motivated by malice or forethought. But it is devastating in its effects and the reach of the indirect discrimination provisions of the Framework Employment Directive to disability is crucial.

Indirect discrimination may on occasion be motivated by prejudice. That is to say, in order deliberately to screen persons with disabilities out of the workplace employers might adjust the qualification standards to have that effect. It is fairly clear that this concept of 'indirect discrimination' in the Framework Employment Directive reaches both disparate impact (unmotivated indirect impact) as well as intentional discrimination through the guise of apparently neutral provisions. That is, it would not appear to be necessary to prove a discriminatory intent. This can also be inferred from existing European case law dealing with indirect discrimination on the ground of sex.[90]

---

[90] See, e.g., Case 170/84 *Bilka-Kaufhaus GmbH* v. *Weber von Harzt* [1986] ECR 1607.

Unlike the situation pertaining to direct discrimination, two defences are allowed to a charge of indirect discrimination under the Framework Employment Directive.

The first defence is of general application to all the grounds (including disability) and it allows for an objective justification with a legitimate aim and pursued by necessary and appropriate means: Article 2(2)(b)(i).

The second defence deals more specifically with the concept of indirect discrimination as applied to disability. At the time of the drafting of the Framework Employment Directive the most advanced legislation in Europe on this ground was the British *Disability Discrimination Act* (DDA) of 1995. At that time the DDA did not contain any express prohibition on 'indirect discrimination'. The DDA did, however, provide for an obligation of 'reasonable accommodation' (called 'reasonable adjustments') and deemed a failure to provide such accommodations to amount to discrimination.

During negotiations on the Directive within Council it was apparently felt that the provision of 'reasonable accommodation' was a sufficient answer to a charge of 'indirect discrimination' since many if not all of the obstacles that arise through indirect discrimination can be removed by invoking such an obligation. For this reason a specific reference was retained to 'reasonable accommodation' under Article 2(2)(b)(ii) notwithstanding the removal of the substance of the obligation to Article 5. The end result is that the disability-specific defence to 'indirect discrimination' under Article 2(2)(b)(ii) now reads:

> As regards a person with a particular disability, the employer or any other person or organisation to whom this Directive applies, is obliged, under national legislation, to take appropriate measures in line with the principles contained in Article 5 in order to eliminate disadvantages entailed by such provision, criterion or practice.

A few points may be noted with respect to Article 2(2)(b)(ii). First of all, it assumes that national legislation actually provides for the obligation to engage in 'reasonable accommodation' and that such legislation accords with the requirements of the Framework Employment Directive. Secondly, it assumes that such legislation has actually been complied with. Thirdly, it implicitly assumes that 'indirect discrimination' will arise unless effectively responded to with 'reasonable accommodation'. Fourthly, it assumes that the only available response or cure to 'indirect discrimination' where it is proven to occur on the ground of disability is the provision of 'reasonable accommodation'. Certainly the provision of 'reasonable accommodation' will answer a charge of indirect discrimination in many instances. This leaves open the theoretical possibility of indirect discrimination arising on the ground of disability for which the provision of 'reasonable accommodation' is no answer or solution. In such cases the general defence to indirect discrimination (objective justification with a legitimate aim pursued proportionately) would need to be relied upon to defend an allegation of discrimination on the ground of disability.

When 'reasonable accommodation' is an answer to indirect discrimination and where it is not possible due to the defence of 'disproportionate burden' provided for by Article 5 then presumably the charge of indirect discrimination has been fully answered. So the notion of 'reasonable accommodation' can operate as the 'cure' to indirect discrimination and also as a defence against a charge of indirect discrimination when it is shown not to be possible to achieve in practice.

An interesting point with respect to the material scope of the Directive (Article 3) is posed in the disability context. Are sheltered workshops covered and, if so, what implications will this have for 'employment and working conditions, including . . . pay'. The question of the status of sheltered workshops has rumbled for years. The main argument against extending the protective coverage of legislation such as the Directive has generally been that the activity in question is primarily non-economic and any remuneration given does not necessarily convert the 'work' into 'real' economic work. The issue surfaces from time to time and most recently in a 2005 decision of the Danish High Court. The High Court reasoned that the money received was not a salary (entitling the individual in question to an employment contract) but was more in the nature of a 'work award'.[91] Although the ECJ has looked at the issue in a different context it will no doubt be required to look at it afresh in the context of the Framework Directive.

(d) From formal rights to effective rights: the key obligation of 'reasonable accommodation' (Articles 2 and 5)

At least one eminent commentator has sought to link strands of the concept of 'reasonable accommodation' to the case law of the European Court of Human Rights.[92]

---

[91] Eastern High Court of Denmark, UfR, 2005, p. 1492. See also *Sheltered employment in five member states of the Council of Europe*, Strasbourg, Council of Europe, 1997.

[92] See O. De Schutter, 'Reasonable Accommodations and Positive Obligations in the European Convention on Human Rights', in A. Lawson and C. Gooding, *Disability Rights in Europe* (2005). ch. 4.

As previously mentioned, the substance of subparagraph 4 of Article 2 contained in the original Commission proposal which dealt with 'reasonable accommodation' was removed to the new Article 5 even though Article 2(2)(b)(ii) retains a reference to the notion as a specific justification for indirect discrimination on the ground of disability.

Article 5 is in many respects the linchpin of the Framework Employment Directive on the ground of disability.[93] It reads as follows:

> In order to guarantee compliance with the principle of equal treatment in relation to persons with disabilities, reasonable accommodation shall be provided. This means that employers shall take appropriate measures, where needed in a particular case, to enable a person with a disability to have access to, participate in, or advance in employment, or to undergo training, unless such measures would impose a disproportionate burden on the employer. This burden shall not be disproportionate when it is sufficiently remedied by measures existing within the framework of the disability policy of the Member State.

The conceptual linkage between non-discrimination and 'reasonable accommodation' was clearly explained by the Commission in its original proposal. The Commission explained:

> The principle of equal treatment under Article 2 as applied in the context of disability entails an identification and removal of barriers in the way of people with disabilities who, with reasonable accommodation, are able to perform the essential functions of a job. *The concept has become central in the construction of modern legislation combating disability-based discrimination* [citing the British DDA which specifically deems a failure to provide 'reasonable accommodation' or its equivalent as discrimination] and is also recognised at an international level.[94]

The Commission continued:

> Essentially the concept stems from a realization that the achievement of equal treatment can only become a reality where some reasonable allowance

---

[93] See generally, L. Waddington, *Implementing and Interpreting the Reasonable Accommodation Provision of the Framework Employment Directive – Learning from Experience and Achieving Best Practice* (EU Network of Disability Discrimination, 2004), available at: www.europa.eu.int/comm/employment_social/fundamental_rights/pdf/aneval/reasonaccom.pdf. See also L. Waddington and A. Hendricks, 'The Expanding Concept of Employment Discrimination in Europe: From Direct and Indirect Discrimination to Reasonable Accommodation Discrimination', *International Journal of Comparative Labour Law and Industrial Relations* 18 (2002) p. 403.

[94] COM (1999) 565 final at 8, 9 (emphasis added).

is made for disability in order to enable the abilities of the individual concerned to be put to work. It does not create an obligation with respect to
individuals who, even with reasonable accommodation, cannot perform
the essential functions of any given job.[95]

The link between failure to provide 'reasonable accommodation' and the
proscription against discrimination was more recently underlined by the
Commission in its aforementioned working paper on disability and the
European Employment Strategy. It stated:

> Reasonable accommodation is not a positive action left to the discretion of
> public or private operators, but an obligation whose failure can constitute
> unfair discrimination.[96]

Under Article 5, 'reasonable accommodation' in the form of 'appropriate
measures' shall be taken 'where needed in a particular case'. This rightly
assumes that such accommodation will not be required in all cases. Of
importance is Recital 17 which asserts that the Directive only covers those
who can perform the 'essential functions' of a job with or without 'reasonable accommodation'.

The reference to 'essential functions' in Recital 17 is important on a
number of levels. First of all, it serves to underscore the point that the quest
for a particular 'reasonable accommodation' should be an interactive one
between the employer and individual. The employer will need to identify
carefully the truly 'essential functions' of a given job and to distinguish
them from marginal functions. Obviously, if an employer over-conflates
the 'essential functions' of a job in order deliberately to screen a person with a disability out or if such over-conflation has that result, then
the employer is guilty of at least indirect discrimination. Adjudicatory
bodies including courts must obviously retain jurisdiction to review how
the 'essential functions' of any particular job are defined and should not
automatically defer to the employer's own judgments. Otherwise the prohibition on discrimination will have little effect.

Secondly, the reference to 'essential functions' is also relevant to the
kind of 'reasonable accommodation' that an employer might be required
to engage in. For example, if the marginal or non-essential functions of
a job could be transferred to another employee in order to enable an
employee with a disability to perform the 'essential functions' of the job
then such 'reasonable accommodation' might be required.

---

[95] Ibid., at 9.
[96] See, *Disability Mainstreaming in the European Employment Strategy*, Brussels, European
Commission, EMCO/11/290605 (2005), at p. 3.

A good example of a case turning on the 'essential functions' notion arose in 2005 in Cyprus.[97] The Cypriot Ombudsman entertained a complaint dealing with entry requirements for obtaining placement in a nursing school. Among the requirements was one that stated that the candidate should be 'in good health'. The applicant in question had reduced hearing and was on that count refused entry. The refusal was defended on the basis that a nurse would have to be capable of hearing. The Ombudsman concluded that this amounted to direct discrimination on the ground of disability. Interestingly, the Ombudsman pointed to many examples of deaf persons being admitted to educational and training establishments worldwide. And revealingly the Ombudsman stated that many new opportunities were opening up for graduates of the nursing school and may include positions that do not require excellent hearing or vision. Therefore, it might be conjectured (although this did not form part of the ratio of the decision) that being able to hear or see fully was not necessarily an 'essential function' of the range of jobs to which the applicant might be able to apply for in the future. In essence, to deny the applicant entry into nursing school might be said to deny a right to work in jobs whose 'essential functions' did not require excellent hearing or sight. Bearing in mind that the material scope of the Framework Directive reaches to 'all types and to all levels of vocational guidance, vocational training, advanced vocational training retraining' (Article 3(1)(b)) and that this enables the Directive to reach into many types of education (if not general education) this precedent could prove extremely important.

Article 5 does not itself provide an exhaustive or even an indicative list of 'appropriate measures' of accommodation. But the object of such accommodation is stated to be to 'enable a person to have access to, participate in, or advance in employment or to undergo training'. Recital 20 does, however, refer to some illustrative examples including:

> adapting premises, and equipment, patterns of working time, the distribution of tasks or the provision of training or integration resources.

Given the potential range of accommodations (e.g. reassignment of non-essential or marginal functions to other employees) and the amount of variables at play, it follows that the process of identifying any particular 'reasonable accommodation' must, perforce, be interactive and individualised to the needs of the person in question.

---

[97] The Ombudsman Office: Decision of the Equality Authority, No. 16/2005 regarding the Nursing School's entry requirements and the exclusion, on that basis, or persons with disabilities.

The concept of 'reasonable accommodation' ('reasonable adjustment' under UK law) has been most developed under British and Irish disability discrimination law. With respect to British law and practice, and as pointed out in the aforementioned Disability Baseline Study:

> Typical 'reasonable adjustments' under the DDA include making physical adjustments to premises, re-assigning 'non-essential' duties of the job to other employees, flexible working hours, acquiring or modifying equipment, modifying procedures or reference manuals, modifying procedures for testing and assessment, providing a reader or interpreter and providing supervision.[98]

The recent 2004 House of Lords decision in *Archibald* v. *Fife Council* is illustrative of the kinds of issues that arise and how they can be creatively handled by the courts.[99] This case involved a roadsweeper for a local council who became unable to walk and therefore unable to continue working as a roadsweeper. Section 6(2)(b) of the DDA states that 'reasonable adjustments' to work arrangements can include:

> Any term, condition or arrangement on which employment, promotion, a transfer training or any other benefit is offered or afforded.

Archibald was temporarily reassigned to a sedentary job at the council which did not require walking but which the council considered to be a promotion since it carried a higher pay scale. The redeployment procedure then in force required each candidate for such a 'promotion' to undergo an examination without any exceptions. Archibald took the examination but failed and was therefore dismissed. The House of Lords held that the duty to make 'reasonable adjustments' effectively obliges an employer to treat a disabled person 'more favourably' than others. By this it did not mean to suggest that persons with disabilities should be afforded 'special rights'. What it meant, instead, is that the regulations that apply to promotions (i.e. requiring satisfactory performance of the test) should themselves be adjusted to take account of the rights of workers with disabilities. The ruling affects the operation of ancillary legislation which mandates that appointment to public posts should be strictly on merit. That is to say, the latter legislation should be interpreted in light of the DDA and not the other way around – thus erecting a sort of lexical hierarchy in favour of the DDA.

---

[98] See *Disability Baseline Study*, at p. 80.
[99] [2004] UKHL 32. Available at: www.publications.parliament.uk/pa/ld200304/ldjudgmt/jd040701/arch-1.htm.

A series of Irish cases reveals that the process for identifying a 'reasonable accommodation' must be an individualised and participatory one. In the 2003 Irish case of *A Computer Component Company* v. *A Worker* an employer was found liable because it had not conducted an assessment of the potential range of abilities of the worker in question.[100] In another Irish case of 2003 evidence that a railway crossing attendant suffered from depression – and so might pose a danger to the public – was held to be insufficient ground for letting him go. The Equality Officer (part of the Equality Tribunal in Ireland) held that such assumptions in the absence of an individualised assessment was not enough to ground a negative decision against the worker in question.[101]

A defence of 'disproportionate burden' is provided for by Article 5. Any assessment of when an otherwise 'reasonable accommodation' reaches the threshold of 'disproportionate burden' involves a complex balancing of the circumstances of the employer with the rights and interests of the employee or prospective employee. Recital 21 asserts that within this calculus account should be taken of:

> financial and other costs involved, the scale and financial resources of the organisation or undertaking and the possibility of obtaining public funding or any other assistance.

This defence is a key element to Article 5. A wide variety of factors will no doubt be relevant in the determination of whether the threshold of a 'disproportionate burden' has been exceeded. Among other things, it brings the intersection between general social provision and non-discrimination law into sharp focus in the disability context. Many employers are in fact directly or indirectly assisted in several Member States to employ persons with disabilities.[102] This assistance takes many forms including capital grants, technical advice and assistance, tax credits and other tax breaks. If such aid is taken into account then there will be a reduced opportunity to plead 'disproportionate burden' in many instances.

A recent example of innovative legislation in this field is the new Estonian Law on Employment Services and Allowances which entered into force on 1 January 2006.[103] According to this law, the Estonian state will

---

[100] ED/00/8 Determination No. 013 (July 2001).
[101] *C* v. *Iarnrod Eireann* DEC E/2003/054.
[102] These positive action measures are usefully summarised in a Council of Europe publication, *Legislation on the rehabilitation of people with disabilities: Policy and legislation*, Strasbourg, Council of Europe, 2002 (6th edn).
[103] RT I 2005, 54, 430.

compensate employers for up to 50 per cent of expenses necessary for job accommodations up to a specified maximum amount.

However, if this state assistance were not to be factored into the equation then there would have been many more opportunities for employers to avail of the defence. The drafters of the Directive were keenly aware of the problem and Article 5 now specifically provides that the burden shall not be considered disproportionate when it:

> is sufficiently remedied by measures existing within the framework of the disability policy of the Member State concerned.

So the availability of state aid and assistance to employers is relevant to the identification of the thresholds. Interestingly, the Irish Equality Tribunal has held in *An Employee* v. *A Local Authority* that an employer may be denied recourse to the defence of 'disproportionate burden' if it had in fact access to state resources and technical assistance to help offset the costs of 'reasonable accommodation'.[104]

Indeed, the fact that the state itself may be the employer is highly relevant on the assumption that it can bear a higher threshold. In the above case the Irish Equality Tribunal held that the extent of the obligation to engage in 'reasonable accommodation' might vary according to whether the entity in question was in the public or the private sector – the latter could be presumed to be able to bear a higher burden.[105]

Other relevant factors will include the financial capacity of the enterprise (which brings the link between parent and subsidiary companies into focus) and its overall capacity to concede the accommodation required. All of which must be balanced against the overall objective of the Framework Employment Directive which is to lay down a 'level playing field' for all in the employment context (Recital 37).

It is worthy of note that the European Committee of Social Rights – the treaty monitoring body that interprets the European Social Charter – now interprets the Charter to require anti-discrimination law on the ground of disability in the employment sphere and that such law should expressly require an obligation of 'reasonable accommodation'.[106]

It is not an exaggeration to say that the way in which the obligation of 'reasonable accommodation' is handled will probably determine whether

---

[104] DEC E/2002/4, at para. 6.13.   [105] Ibid., para. 51.

[106] See, *Conclusions XVI-2*, Vol 1 and 2, European Committee of Social Rights (covering Article 15 of the Charter). All conclusions of the Committee are available at: www.coe.int/T/E/Human_Rights/Esc/3_Reporting_procedure/.

national legislation will be effective in combating discrimination on the ground of disability.

(e) The space provided for 'positive action' (Article 7)

Positive action measures have traditionally proliferated in the field of disability. Article 7 of the Framework Employment Directive is drafted with care in order to carve out a protected space for such measures on all grounds including disability. It is to the effect that the Framework Employment Directive shall not prevent Member States from 'maintaining or adopting specific measures to prevent or compensate for disadvantages' linked to the grounds of prohibited discrimination (including disability). Nor, of course, can the Directive be used to require such positive action measures where they do not already exist.

An important point of principle arises. Does Article 7(1) immunise all forms of positive action from scrutiny under the prohibition against discrimination under the Framework Employment Directive? After all, Article 7(1) is geared to ensure 'full equality of treatment in practice'. It might plausibly be argued that a positive action measure that makes it less likely that the public (and employers) will be sensitised to the need for a rational appraisal of the abilities of persons with disabilities is open to question.[107] This would appear to arise in the context of legislative measures or practices that reserve certain categories of low status jobs for certain categories of workers with disabilities (e.g. to persons with certain impairments of a certain degree). It is too early to say how the European Court of Justice might react to this issue if squarely put.

Since quotas were widely used throughout Europe at the time of the negotiations leading up to the adoption of the Framework Employment Directive it is unlikely that Article 7(1) (whether taken alone or when read in conjunction with Article 2) was meant to subvert them. This issue would not therefore appear to arise with respect to quota systems.

Portugal recently enacted *Law 38/2004* which concerns rehabilitation and participation of persons with disabilities. Interestingly, while the UK repealed its quota system for the hiring of persons with disabilities upon the enactment of its DDA in 1995, Portugal has used the opportunity of transposing the Directive to establish a quota system on a legislative

---

[107] An interesting example is the Cypriot legislation, Law on the Engagement of Trained Blind Telephone Operators (1988), which gives priority in the public service for blind telephone operators over others.

footing. It creates a 2 per cent quota for private enterprise and a 5 per cent quota for the public administration.

An interesting case is presently pending in Greece concerning its quota system. A person with a disability applied for a job with a Greek bank only to be turned away on the basis that the relevant quota (2 per cent) was full. It raises the interesting question whether the prohibition against discrimination (with an associated obligation of 'reasonable accommodation') continues to function after a quota is full. Since the Directive does not indicate that the filling of a quota (as a form of 'positive action measure') places a 'stop' on the application of the non-discrimination principle, it would be reasonable to surmise that 'positive action' measures simply rounds out – and does not displace the prohibition. The case was remitted from the Equal Treatment Committee to the Labour Inspectorate in January 2006 on jurisdictional grounds. A decision is pending before the latter body.

A disturbing decision was handed down by the Supreme Court of Cyprus in 2005 which held that legal measures giving priority in employment in the public sector to persons with disabilities violates the guarantee of equality under the Cypriot Constitution (Article 28). Effectively, the Court held that the priority in question amounted to reverse discrimination against other equally qualified candidates.

A striking and positive example of developments in this field is the recently enacted duty to eliminate unlawful discrimination and to promote equality of opportunity for disabled persons contained in the DDA of 2005.[108] Section 3 of the 2005 Act inserts a new provision into the 1995 DDA to the effect that every public authority shall in carrying out its functions have due regard to:

(a) the need to eliminate discrimination that is unlawful under this Act;
(b) the need to eliminate harassment of disabled persons that is related to their disabilities;
(c) the need to promote equality of opportunity between disabled persons and other persons;
(d) the need to take steps to take account of disabled persons' disabilities, even where that involves treating disabled persons more favourably than other persons;
(e) the need to promote positive attitudes towards disabled persons; and
(f) the need to encourage participation by disabled persons in public life.

---

[108] See generally C. O'Cinneide, 'A New Generation of Equality Legislation? Positive Duties and Disability Rights', in A. Lawson and C. Gooding, *Disability Rights in Europe* (2005), chapter 12.

The British Disability Rights Commission drafted a Code of Practice outlining what is entailed by the above duty which has been approved by the UK Secretary of State for Work and Pensions.[109] This is an exceptionally clear and helpful Code and indeed sets a model for what can, and ought to be done, in the other Member States. The Directive, in itself, does not require this extra step to be taken but it is clear (from a moral if not a legal perspective) that such an approach to 'positive action' measurably enhances the success of the underlying anti-discrimination legislation.

Recently the Administrative Court of the City of Braga (Portugal) took into account the positive duties of the state towards persons with disabilities outlined in the Constitution (presumably Articles 13(2) and 71) in order to reinforce a decision against a local inaccessible bank.[110]

Article 7(2) of the Directive is even more specific (providing a *lex specialis*) with respect to 'positive action measures' in the specific context of disability. In this specific context it goes on to carve out an exception for the protection of health and safety at work. It reads:

> With regard to disabled persons, the principle of equal treatment shall be without prejudice to the right of Member States to maintain or adopt provisions on the protection of health and safety at work or to measures aimed at creating or maintaining provisions or facilities for safeguarding or promoting their integration into the working environment.

The drafting history of this provision reveals that the intention behind it was positive and not negative.

Clearly, the European Commission saw health and safety measures as an added way of creating space in the workplace for persons with disabilities and not as a drag on the achievement of the same. It is noteworthy that in its original proposal the Commission justified the notion of 'reasonable accommodation' in part on the basis that:

> it would supplement and reinforce the employer's obligation to adapt the workplace to disabled workers, as provided by Framework Employment Directive 89/391/EEC [Health & Safety Directive].[111]

The Commission's original proposal did not contain an equivalent to Article 7(2). Apparently it was added during negotiations in Council and

---

[109] See www.drc-gb.org/documents/DED_Code_Dec05_pdf.pdf.
[110] *Caixa Geral de Depositos* v. *Camara Municipal de Barcelos*, Case No. 712/04 OBEBRG, 23 June 2005.
[111] Council Directive 89/391 of 12 June 1989 on the introduction of measures to encourage Improvements in the safety and health of workers at work, [1989] OJ L183, 29.06.1989, p. 1.

in a positive spirit. It is noteworthy that it was put into the Article dealing with 'positive action' and not in any Article dealing with (or entitled) 'exemptions'.

It is therefore plain that the Framework Employment Directive does not contemplate health and safety law and policy as an obstacle to the achievement of a non-discriminatory and integrated work environment. Rather, it sees the non-discrimination principle as being complemented by health and safety law and especially by the latter's focus on adapting the workplace to suit the employee. On occasions, however, employers might plead health and safety concerns in order either to exclude persons with disabilities from the workplace or to segregate them from the main workforce. Given the drafting history of the Directive and in particular the emphasis placed on the potential synergy between both sets of laws (anti-discrimination laws on the one hand and health and safety laws on the other), it follows that such a negative invocation of health and safety issues should be strictly scrutinised and placed firmly on the defensive.

An excellent approach – indeed a model – is the one set out by a 2002 publication of the Northern Irish Equality Commission – *Balancing Disability Rights with Health and Safety Requirements – new guide for employers.*[112] In the relevant part the publication states:

> In certain circumstances some actions may be 'justified', even if there is a negative impact on the disabled person so long as the decision to take the action was reached after a careful balancing of obligations under the 'reasonable adjustment' duty and the duty to ensure, as far as is reasonably practicable, the health and safety of employees and others.[113]

It is submitted that the approach set out by the Northern Irish Equality Commission best fits the underlying purposes of the Framework Directive. An interesting case arose in the UK concerning a directive from a local council against manual handling of persons with disabilities (*R (on the application of A & B) v. East Sussex CC).*[114] The Directive was motivated out of concerns for the health and safety of staff. This had disastrous effects for two disabled sisters who, as a result could not go shopping, swimming or horseriding (activities that were central to their lives). In a lengthy and careful judgment the High Court judge in question (Munby J) declared that an absolute ban on lifting was unlawful. It did not amount to a fair

---

[112] Available at: www.equalityni.org/uploads/word/DR&HS.pdf.   [113] Ibid., p. 12.
[114] High Court (Admin) CO/4843/2001.

balancing between the rights of the sisters and the legitimate concerns for health and safety.

Undoubtedly, cases will come before the ECJ seeking to scope out the interface between non-discrimination and health and safety law.

(f) Exemptions: 'genuine and determining occupational requirement'

If the defences available under Article 2 are not proven then discrimination will ordinarily be deemed to arise in a suitable case. Other parts of the Framework Employment Directive carve out exemptions to the operation of the non-discrimination principle.

Article 4(1) of the Framework Employment Directive is careful to carve our space for employers to make distinctions which are 'based on a characteristic related to any of the [prohibited] grounds' where:

> by reason of the nature of the particular occupational activities concerned or of the context in which they are carried out, such a characteristic constitutes a genuine and determining occupational requirement.

The original proposal of the Commission dealing with this exemption stated that the 'justification in these cases relate to the nature of the job concerned and the context in which it is carried out'.[115] Great care will be needed to police the invocation of this defence successfully in the disability context. Otherwise a segregationist ethic could too easily masquerade as a genuine and determining occupational requirement.

With respect to the 'nature of the job' a key concern on the disability ground will again be the accurate identification of the 'essential functions' of any given job. Is it, for example, really essential that a delivery van driver should be able-bodied when vehicles can easily be adjusted to enable a person with a disability to drive?

With respect to the 'context' in which the job is to be carried out it is surely of relevance whether or not 'reasonable accommodation' is provided. The 'context' of the job will include many things. One thing it should not include would be the potential reaction (or predictions about these reactions on the part of employers) of customers, consumers or indeed fellow-workers to the presence of a person with a disability on the job. Even if these negative reactions occur (and even where predictions of their occurrence are accurate) it would undermine the purpose of the

[115] COM(1999) 565, at p.10.

Framework Employment Directive if employers were permitted to use it in order exempt their behaviour from examination.

(g) Permission for armed forces exemption: Article 3(4)

Recital 18 of the Framework Employment Directive is to the effect that the armed forces and police are not required to maintain in employment:

> persons who do not have the required capacity to carry out the range of functions that they may be called upon to perform with regard to the legitimate objective of preserving the operational capacity of those services.

The reference to 'required capacity' is probably meant to embrace the actual capacity (occupational and otherwise) of an individual to perform a job. Logically this concept relates to the 'essential functions' of the job. And presumably, the phrase 'required capacity' includes the possibility of 'reasonable accommodation'.

Article 3(4) of the Directive proceeds to grant states a discretion not to apply the provisions of the Framework Employment Directive to all or part of their armed forces on the grounds of age and disability. Recital 19 rationalises this discretion on the basis of the need to safeguard the combat effectiveness of the armed forces of the Member States. It probably follows that any derogations that go beyond what is objectively needed to safeguard the combat readiness of the armed forces go beyond the scope of the permission created under Article 3(4). Recital 19 also requires that the scope of any derogation on this ground must be defined.

5. Conclusions

It is too early yet to say whether the Framework Employment Directive will make a substantial difference to the lives of millions of Europeans with disabilities. The first few test cases will probably prove crucial in influencing the mindset of the Court and in framing the issues. In a hopeful sign some countries are using the transposition process to reflect more broadly on disability law reform.[116] However, the decision of the Court in the *Chacon Navas* referral is disappointing to say the least.

---

[116] In Austria, for example, a new Act has been enacted in December 2005 which repeals many provisions on the statute book deemed to be at odds with the rights of persons with disabilities: Supplementary Act to the Disability Equality Act (*Bundes-Nehindertengeichstellungs-Begleitgesetz*).

It is fascinating to observe that the rationale for much that is proposed or planned by the Commission in its new Social Agenda is not confined to economics and the need to inject greater rationality into market mechanisms. In its recently adopted Framework Strategy for non-discrimination the Commission asserted that discrimination:

> blights individual lives. It is also bad for the economy and society as a whole. Moreover it undermines confidence in and support for the fundamental European values of equality and the rule of law.[117]

It is submitted that this dual approach – human rights together with market rationality – should inform the interpretation and application of the Framework Employment Directive on the disability ground. Yet, when they diverge – as they sometimes will, the human rights provenance of the Framework Employment Directive should be dispositive. The previously discussed *Mangold* decision of the European Court of Justice would appear to be a step in the right direction.

In the aforementioned Framework Strategy the Commission also signalled the need to go beyond traditional non-discrimination policies in order to prevent discrimination – tough on discrimination and tough on the causes of discrimination. It clearly stated:

> the implementation and enforcement of anti-discrimination legislation on an individual level is not enough to tackle the multifaceted and deep-rooted patterns of inequality experienced by some groups. There is a need to go beyond anti-discrimination policies designed to prevent unequal treatment of individuals.[118]

It continued:

> it is difficult for legislation alone to tackle the complex and deep-rooted patterns of inequality experienced by some groups. Positive measures may be necessary to compensate for long-standing inequalities suffered by groups of people who, historically, have not had access to equal opportunities.[119]

Such an approach is particularly relevant in the context of disability since it is obvious that profound structural change will be required to puncture the cycles of exclusion that lead to discrimination. The move by the British government to create positive duties on public bodies to advance the rights of persons with disabilities is to be greatly welcomed and hopefully widely emulated. Indeed, it will become more and more necessary

---

[117] COM(2005) 244 final, Non-Discrimination and equal opportunities for all – A Framework Strategy.
[118] Ibid., p. 2.   [119] Ibid., p. 6.

to link up substantive social rights with non-discrimination if the ultimate goals of discrimination law are to be achieved in the context of
disability.[120]

In its new Social Agenda (2005–2010) the European Commission has
correctly identified three main drivers of change in contemporary Europe
as: (1) increased competition in a global market; (2) rapid technological
change; and (3) population ageing.[121] It is suggested that all of these
drivers point to a need to intensify the equal opportunities agenda in the
disability context. Increased competition should logically lead to more
inclusive markets in which all talent is put to productive use without
prejudgment. Rapid technological change provides new opportunities to
enable the true talents of persons with disabilities to be put to productive
work. And any rational response to Europe's ageing population must
entail providing more economic and social opportunities for our elderly
population which includes a substantial and growing number of persons
with disabilities.

The Commission reported in 2006 on the implementation of the Race
Directive and initially was not committed to introducing fresh legislative proposals that would apply the prohibition against disability discrimination into fields such as goods and services. Its main focus was
to ensure the effective transposition of the existing Directives. Toward
that end it commissioned a study on the impact assessment of non-
discrimination law – a science with a long pedigree in the US and
only beginning in Europe. It also, however, commissioned a study on
national law that goes beyond the minima set by the Framework Employment Directive. This was awaited with keen interest as it could and now
has laid the ground for plans by the Commission as to fresh legislative
proposals.

The year 2007 was designated the European Year of Equal Opportunities
for all. There is already some substantive case law from the European Court
of Justice on the Framework Employment Directive. We should have a
clearer indication soon whether the Framework Employment Directive is
working and what kinds of further flanking measures are needed to make
European citizenship a reality for persons with disabilities.

This is not simply right because Europeans with disabilities say it is
right. As the Eurobarometer study of 2001 on Attitudes of Europeans

---

[120] See, e.g., S. Fredman, 'Disability Equality: a Challenge to the Existing Anti-Discrimination
Paradigm', in A. Lawson and C. Gooding (eds.), *Disability Rights in Europe* (2005), at
pp. 199–219.
[121] COM(2005) 33 final, on the Social Agenda (Social Agenda 2005–2010).

towards Disability showed, 97 per cent of Europeans think that something more should be done to integrate people with disabilities into society.[122] Europe is ready. The next moves must come from the European Court of Justice. It is hoped that the *Chacon Navas* decision represents an aberration.

[122] *Attitudes of Europeans to Disability*, Brussels, Eurobarometer Study 54.2 (2001). Text is available at: www.europa.eu.int/comm/ employment_social/disability/eu_bar_en.pdf.

9

Age discrimination – Of Cinderella and
The Golden Bough[1]

HELEN MEENAN[*]

One of the powerful themes in this chapter is the role physical appearance plays in age discrimination. This is vaguely reminiscent of ancient kings being executed at the first sign of physical defect.[2] The purpose of regicide was to avert decay in the country and was best carried out when the king was still healthy. While these customs have disappeared, many otherwise erudite thinkers see age as different from other grounds and age discrimination as more acceptable than other forms. This acceptance is sometimes based on stereotypes of people of a certain age or on the traditional use of age as a rational management and organisational tool. Confusion has even surrounded what age discrimination actually is. This chapter has two deceptively simple aims: first, to explore age as a human characteristic and how it can impact on work and life; and second, to examine the age strand within the Employment Equality Directive (Employment Directive) and wider contexts.[3] It will emerge that although age differs in some respects from the other Article 13 EC Treaty grounds, just as they all differ from each other, age discrimination is not necessarily different and may particularly hurt those at the intersection of age and other grounds. The inclusion of age in the Employment Directive has already achieved two important results. Firstly, age discrimination is prohibited in each Member State, nominally providing a uniform minimum level of protection, and secondly, there now exists a definition of age discrimination in European law.[4]

[*] I am indebted to Mark Bell, Ruth O'Connell-Doyle, Frances Meenan, Barrister, and my colleague Graeme Broadbent for their valuable comments on an earlier draft.
[1] Sir J. G. Frazer, *The Golden Bough* (Macmillan, 1922), Ch 24, ss. 2 and 3.   [2] Ibid.
[3] Council Directive 2000/78/EC establishing a general framework for equal treatment in employment and occupation [2000] OJ L303 at p. 16.
[4] With very few exceptions, the Member States have followed the definitions in the Race and Employment Equality Directives across all grounds, J. McCormack and M. Bell for

Age as a unique characteristic

Age is unique among the family of Article 13 grounds. It has the greatest potential to overlap with all other grounds of discrimination and to unify all people as everyone has an age and everyone will hopefully grow older. Multiple discrimination involving age can occur when those who already experience discrimination grow older and age discrimination can compound other forms or it may result from a particular combination of identities.[5] Age is also fluid yet at any point in time chronological age is static and can ascribe legal powers or prohibitions to individuals. A person's age cannot be changed, unlike names or even gender. Thus age goes to our core identity in ways that are inescapable. A person's state of being at a given age is intimately bound up with the ageing process in ways that cannot be generalised.

Meanings of age

Sociologists assign three principal meanings to age.[6] The first is chronological age, which refers to years and changes to one's place in society.[7] This meaning is most at play in law, employment law and practice and pensions. It also underpins many age limits justified by health and safety regulations. The second meaning is social age, relating to transitions in the life course. Arber and Ginn maintain that social age is gendered due to the impact of women's reproductive roles on the pattern of their working lives.[8] The third meaning is physiological age, referring to functional ability and the gradual decline in physical strength and form that occurs with ageing.[9] This meaning helps to mark out the highly individualised nature of age as it is affected by factors that play out differently in each individual; gender and class are said to play a role in the speed and timing of physiological ageing, so are occupation and lifestyle.[10] This chapter will argue that it is the chronological meaning of age that is intended by the Employment Equality Directive.

---

the European Network of Legal Experts in the non-discrimination Field 'Developing Anti-Discrimination Law in Europe The 25 EU Member States Compared' (European Commission, 2005).

[5] Age Reference Group on Equality and Human Rights, UK 'Age and multiple discrimination in older people – A Discussion Paper', (October 2005) at p. 3, available at: http://policy.helptheaged.org.uk.

[6] See, for instance, S. Arber and J. Ginn (eds.), *Connecting Gender and Ageing: A Sociological Approach* (Open University Press, 1995), pp. 5–11.

[7] Ibid.   [8] Ibid.   [9] Ibid. at p. 10.   [10] Ibid.

Demographic change and caring

The twentieth century witnessed a dramatic increase in life expectancy – twenty years have been added to the average life span since 1950, with a further ten years predicted by 2050.[11] The United Nations (UN) describes population ageing as a universal force with the same power to shape the future as globalisation.[12] Demographic change in the European Union (EU) echoes global trends, with an older, shrinking working-age population and growth in the number of workers over 60 that is due to continue until 2030.[13] Some estimates predict a new threshold of old age (when the population starts to suffer real incapacities) as 82 years by 2040.[14] This leads to the question: when does a worker become old today? The answer depends on factors such as the sector worked in, the job and the educational status and personal qualities of the worker.[15] However, the workplace is crucial for coping with longer lives. Most people will need to work for longer to help finance their extra years. This means reversing the trend of early retirement in the European Union, which some regard as a 'new right', and working at least beyond 60.[16] Working for longer will also be important to enhance access to rights of social citizenship and to public life.[17]

Socio-demographic changes are also increasing the amount of time spent on caring.[18] The ageing population will have a particular impact on working carers, especially those combining eldercare with childcare. Part-time work is recommended to help those who need to work and also provide some form of family care.[19] Israel Doron describes eldercare as taking many forms, including caring from a distance.[20] Supportive measures may be required to enable those who wish to or who need to, work longer than today.[21] A broadening of Article 13 and the Employment

[11] Report of the Second World Assembly on Ageing, Madrid, 8–12 April 2002, UN Doc. A/CONF.197/9 (2002), at p. 5.

[12] Ibid. at p. 6.

[13] European Commission's 'Green Paper Confronting demographic change: a new solidarity between the generations', COM(2005) 94 final, at p. 3.

[14] G. Reday-Mulvey, *Working Beyond 60 Key Policies and Practices in Europe*, (Palgrave Macmillan, 2005), at p. 31 referring to P. Bordelais.

[15] Ibid. at p. 64.   [16] Reday-Mulvey *Working Beyond 60*, at p. 96.

[17] Arber and Ginn, *Connecting Gender and Ageing*, at p. 175 go further, saying that the rights of social citizenship are bound up with being a worker.

[18] A. Walker and T. Maltby, *Age in Europe* (Open University Press, 1997), p. 37.

[19] Ibid. at p. 91.   [20] In this volume.

[21] Note Ireland's Carer's Leave Act 2001 provides for temporary unpaid leave on a full-time basis for up to 65 weeks. In the UK the Work and Families Act 2006 provides a new right for carers to request flexible work.

Directive to include carer status may be prudent; caring could interact with a worker's late working life and trigger discrimination for a combination of age and caring. Against this background, two new concepts are emerging – lifelong work and the lifelong worker.[22] These require a life-course approach to working that demands a re-examination of working life. For Stein *et al.*, this may mean a more dynamic workplace for older workers, comprising periods of active employment, disengagement from the workplace and re-entry into the same or a new career.[23] For others a reduction in the working time of the older worker is essential to this process.[24] However, not all jobs are suited to part-time work.[25] Another approach would involve a horizontal rather than a vertical approach to the life cycle – a continual blending of life's major activities rather than a hitherto largely segmented approach.[26] However, attempting to mix most of life's significant activities throughout the life course may be a strain for some.

Ageing: a highly individualised process

Sometimes age discrimination is treated as though it is less wrong than other forms.[27] There is evidence of a contrary attitude to age discrimination altogether, with one commentator asking 'Is age discrimination (sometimes) wrong? If so, why and in what circumstances?'[28] It is not clear what forms the basis of this approach. One danger of downgrading age as a ground of discrimination is that it facilitates stereotypes and classifies the individual *solely* according to their actual or perceived chronological age. The ageing process is in fact highly individualised, and any stereotyping of people of the same age is therefore misplaced. The idea that older people are not a homogenous group can be documented at least as far back as 1948, at that time this was based on the ability to lead an active

---

[22] Reday-Mulvey *Working Beyond 60*, at p. 89. M. Bury describes 'the concept of the life course is . . . fast becoming the predominant focus of sociological work on ageing' in Arber and Ginn, *Connecting Gender and Ageing*, at p. 24.

[23] D. Stein, T. S. Rocco and K. A. Goldenetz, 'Age and the University Workplace: A Case Study of Remaining, Retiring or Returning Older Workers', *Human Resource Development Quarterly*, 11: 1 (spring 2000) at p. 61 and pp. 76–7.

[24] Reday-Mulvey *Working Beyond 60*, at p. 89.   [25] Ibid. at p. 86.   [26] Ibid. at p. 22.

[27] In the US, C. Ventrell-Monsees and L. McCann have spoken inter alia of the lack of punitive damages for age discrimination as implying that age discrimination is somehow less wrong, in 'Ageism: the Segregation of a Civil Right', Annual Meeting of the Gerontological Society of America, 24 November 1991.

[28] E. Holmes poses these questions in her review of S. Fredman and S. Spencer (eds.), *Age as an Equality Issue* (Sweet and Maxwell, 2003) in *Public Law* (2004), 913–15.

life.[29] More recently, Walker and Maltby see the perception of older people as a homogenous group as itself condoned by ageism.[30] Many different attributes contribute to the heterogeneity of people of all ages. They can also interact to contribute to different forms of discrimination. A large body of research now exists on 'gendered ageism' in the workplace and the intersection of race and age is gradually receiving more focused attention.[31] Age and disability also overlap in at least two ways. Some people develop a disability after state pension age and other people with a disability grow older.[32] Despite the negative beliefs held by some employers about older workers[33] there is a considerable body of industrial gerontological research showing that age is a poor proxy for performance.[34] In general, age and job performance are found to be unrelated[35] and age-related changes 'have little effect on workers' output except in the most physically demanding tasks'.[36]

However, two phenomena exist for age in particular. One is intra-group discrimination whereby older managers discriminate against older workers.[37] The other concerns far greater functional variations between workers of the same age than between workers of different ages.[38] But there may be some likelihood of individual functional disability after the age of 45.[39] Finnish studies have found that individual differences vary greatly with age within an occupational group and even among people of the same age within that group; these differences are particularly striking after the age of 55.[40] These studies indicate a need for individual solutions to work

[29] J. H. Sheldon, *The Social Medicine of Old Age Report of an Inquiry in Wolverhampton* (Oxford University Press, 1948), at p. 2.

[30] Ibid. at p. 9.

[31] A. Walker's paper 'Age and Employment' (1997), *World Congress of Gerontology Ageing Beyond 2000: One World One Future*, available at: http://cas.flinders.au/iag/proceedings/proc0033.htm. Note also TUC labour market report 'Double discrimination: older black workers & the need for a new deal', (ESAD, July 1998), pp. 1–13.

[32] Age Reference Group on Equality and Human Rights, at p. 21.

[33] W. Loretto, C. Duncan and P. J. White, 'Ageism and employment: controversies, ambiguities and younger people's perceptions', (2000) 20 *Ageing and Society*, pp. 279–302 at p. 283.

[34] Ibid.

[35] N. B. Kurland, 'The Impact of Legal Age Discrimination on Women in Professional Occupations', (2001) 11 *Business Ethics Quarterly*, pp. 331–348 at p. 340.

[36] G. F. Shea, *Managing Older Employees* (Jossey-Bass, 1991) at p. 153 discussed in Stein *et al.* 'Age and the University Workplace' p. 73.

[37] C. Oswick and P. Rosenthal in M. Noon and E. Ogbonna, *Equality, Diversity and Disadvantage in Employment* (Palgrave, 2001), at p. 9.

[38] Ibid. and Stein *et al.*, 'Age and the University workplace', p. 73.

[39] Stein *et al.*, Age and the University Workplace', p. 79.

[40] J. Ilmarinen, 'Ageing Workers in Finland and in the European Union: Their situation and the Promotion of Their Working Ability, Employability and Employment', (2001) Vol. 2, No. 4 *Geneva Papers on Risk and Insurance*, pp. 623–41.

and age.[41] The European Commission too has recently recommended personalised approaches to help older people return to employment.[42] In light of older people's vulnerability to early exit this recommendation should be broadened to cover retention.

Accommodating the effects of ageing

There is a good deal of confidence in the idea that physiological changes associated with ageing can generally be offset by ergonomic arrangements, reorganised working time and redesigned jobs.[43] The idea that the traditional model of anti-discrimination law does not work sufficiently well for age and disability, and that the reasonable accommodation approach of disability law could be applied to physiological changes associated with ageing, is not new.[44] However, with very few exceptions, reasonable accommodation has not been applied beyond disability during the implementation process in the enlarged EU, to date.[45]

While all older workers do not suffer the same functional deterioration at the same rate, stress does appear to increase with age.[46] This too can be accommodated and is another reason why part-time work is important for older workers.[47] The Employment Directive encourages the EU Member States to treat all persons in the same way by virtue of their chronological age alone.[48] Lawful (and unlawful) discrimination on the basis of chronological age ignores the great individual physiological differences there may be even among persons of the same age in the same branch of work. They also mask the fact that there can be other differences between younger and older workers such as, different training approaches needed for each group. Recognising and catering for these differences constructively contributes to a life-course approach to working. The European Work Organisation Network has called for 'age suitable' workplaces where working conditions are adapted to the health and safety

---

[41] Ibid.
[42] European Commission 'Communication Increasing the employment of older workers and delaying the exit from the labour market', COM(2004) 146 final.
[43] See Reday-Mulvey, *Working Beyond 60*, p. 80 and Stein *et al.* 'Age and the University Workplace', p. 62, discussing Shepherd and Rix.
[44] Gerard Quinn's paper 'Non-discrimination in the context of age and disability sometimes requires reasonable accommodation to the difference', *European Conference on Independent Living of Older Persons and Persons with Disabilities*, Helsinki, 6–7 October 1999.
[45] 'Developing Anti-Discrimination Law in Europe' (2005), at p. 35.
[46] Reday-Mulvey, *Working Beyond 60*, pp. 84 and 91.   [47] Ibid.
[48] Referring in particular to Art. 6.

needs of older employees and in which experience-based knowledge plays an important role.[49]

Defining age discrimination

For some, age discrimination is particularly difficult to define compared with longer-standing forms of discrimination.[50] The Employment Directive now facilitates a core definition of age discrimination that conforms with other grounds and across the EU.[51] Given initial opposition by some Member States to the inclusion of age in Article 13 and the Employment Directive, this is an advance that should not be taken for granted. For Oswick and Rosenthal, age discrimination can potentially affect everyone; people move in and out of ageism throughout their lives and the type of ageism will change at different stages.[52] This view acknowledges the experiences of younger as well as older people. The Employment Directive facilitates protection from discrimination at any age during working or occupational life. However, it is possible that in the hands of individual Member States, Article 6 will erode this promise held out by the Directive.

Different age cohorts: shared and distinct experiences

Age discrimination can potentially occur when working life begins – for example, does the minimum wage discriminate against young workers? While the minimum wage can be justified, a generalised minimum wage

[49] Thematic Paper No. 3, M. Krenn and P. Oehle (eds.), *Integration of the Ageing Workforce* (November, 2001) at p. 10 available at: www.europa.eu.int/comm/employment_social/pub_integr.pdf.

[50] See, John Cridland, deputy Director General, Confederation of British Industry in European Foundation for the Improvement of Living and Working Conditions, eironline, 'Overview of the implementation of the framework equal treatment Directive', at p. 14 available at: www.eiro.eurofound.eu.int/2004/02/study/tn0402102s.html. Where he opines 'much more than any previous discrimination law, age discrimination is particularly difficult to define'.

[51] Article 2.2 (a) direct discrimination is taken to occur where one person is treated less favourably than another, is, has been or would be treated on any of the grounds, referred to in Art. 1. Article 2.2 (b) indirect discrimination shall be taken to occur where an apparently neutral provision, criterion or practice would put persons having a particular religion or belief, a particular disability, a particular age, or a particular sexual orientation at a particular disadvantage compared with other persons. This provision is subject to objective justification by a legitimate aim or reasonable accommodation for disabled persons, see Art. 2.2. (b)(i) and (ii).

[52] Noon and Ogbonna, *Equality, Diversity and Disadvantage in Employment*, at pp. 8–9.

does not always make sense, particularly when a young worker is performing simple 'like work' with an older co-worker.[53] In an interesting
contrast, older workers in the Netherlands lose the right to a minimum
wage, among other rights, if they work beyond the state pension age of
65.[54] Research on discrimination in the EU prior to the 2004 enlargement,
found that young people aged 15–24 were five times more likely than those
aged 65+ and twice as likely as any other age group to report age discrimination.[55] Age was the most frequently cited ground of discrimination
overall. However, the idea of 'prime age' labour has emerged in the literature to refer to those between the ages of 25 and 35 who seem to be
favoured over both older and younger workers, especially in hiring.[56] This
concept now makes the American Age Discrimination in Employment Act
1967 (ADEA) look somewhat outdated as it only protects employees from
the age of forty.

Trends can be discerned whereby different age cohorts are vulnerable
to both overlapping and differing forms of age discrimination. For workers in their 40s, age discrimination relates particularly to promotion and
recruitment and from 40, to training.[57] Training has a special role to play
for all workers and is crucial as both a preventive and remedial measure.[58]
It becomes more important with age and needs to continue until retirement and be adapted to the experienced worker.[59] Age discrimination in
training is widespread in the US, where chronological rather than functional age is said to decide training opportunities.[60] The Employment
Directive by contrast includes training within its scope.

---

[53] Note, in the Netherlands workers under 23 qualify for a lower minimum wage than those
above 23, on the basis that they are professionally immature and have lesser needs, see Lan-
delijk Bureau Leeftijds-discriminatie's (LBL) summary 'Age limits in the labour market',
available at: www.leeftijd.nl/p0165.html.

[54] E. Smolenaars, *65 Jaar als uiterste houdbaarheidsdatum* (LBL, Utrecht, 2005) at pp. 164–5,
who argues that using 65 as a limit on benefits and entitlements in a number of acts is not
justifiable.

[55] A. Marsh and M. Sahin-Dikmen, *Discrimination in Europe (Report B)* (Policy Studies
Institute, 2002) at pp. 2 and 15.

[56] Loretto *et al.*, 'Ageism and Employment', at p. 285. See also, L. Bennington, 'Prime age
recruitment: The Challenges for Age Discrimination Legislation', (2004) 3 *Elder Law
Review*.

[57] Walker and Maltby, *Age in Europe*, at p. 75 and E. Drury, 'Older Workers in the European
Community: Pervasive Discrimination, Little Awareness', (1993) 20 *Ageing International*
pp. 12–16 at p. 12.

[58] A. Walker and Reday-Mulvey at p. 108, cite ETUC.

[59] Reday-Mulvey, *Working Beyond 60*, at p. 202.

[60] Stein *et al.*, *Age and the University Workplace*, at p. 76.

Vulnerability of older workers

Lyon and Pollard describe mid-to-late working life as a period of considerable vulnerability for many.[61] Older workers, particularly those in their 50s, are susceptible to early exit from the workforce that often becomes permanent.[62] Periods of low income for older workers can also lead to enduring poverty in old age.[63] Those over 45 in the UK who are lucky enough to find a new job following a gap will usually have to accept a 26 per cent drop in pay from their previous job.[64]

In the post-2004 enlargement Member States (new Member States), the employment rate for older workers averages 30.5 per cent.[65] Prior to enlargement, age discrimination was a rather unfamiliar concept in the new Member States.[66] However, a radical change in the concept of ageing workers has occurred in Hungary. Many Hungarian firms now consider workers to be *elderly* at 40–45 rather than 70–75 under the socialist model when it was common for firms to re-hire their workers on pension, giving them a supplemental income.[67] A central factor in this change has been the entry of the baby-boomers of the 1970s into the workforce in the 1990s, which apparently pushed more 40- to 54- year-olds into unemployment.[68] This appears illogical when viewed against overall gains in human longevity.

Older workers' wages may also contribute to their situation. The Lazear model revealed that younger workers are traditionally paid less than their relative productivity whereas older workers are paid more than their relative productivity in efficient long-term incentive contracts.[69] The working world accepted this *contract* between younger and older workers. Reday-Mulvey highlights the problematic nature of such practices when

---

[61] P. Lyon and D. Pollard, 'Perceptions of the Older Employee: is anything really changing?' (1997) 26 *Personal Review* 4, pp. 245–55.

[62] Loretto *et al.*, 'Ageism and Employment', at p. 281.

[63] Walker and Maltby, *Age in Europe*, at p. 77 and F. Lackzo and C. Phillipson, 'Defending the right to work age discrimination in employment', in E. McEwen (ed.), *Age the Unrecognised Discrimination Views to Provoke a Debate* (Age Concern, 1990), at p. 95.

[64] TAEN, 'Experience of Age Discrimination', at p. 1.

[65] European Commission Green Paper, 'Equality and non-discrimination in an enlarged European Union', COM(2004) 379 final, 28.05.2004 at p. 13.

[66] Ibid.

[67] Z. Szeman, 'Ageing and the Labour Market in Hungary', in T. Maltby, B. De Vroom, M. L. Mirabile and E. Øverbye, *Ageing and the Transition to Retirement: a Comparative Analysis of European Welfare States* (Ashgate, 2004).

[68] Ibid. at p. 205.

[69] E. P. Lazear, 'Why Is There Mandatory Retirement?' (1979) 87 *Journal of Political Economy*, pp. 1261–84. Note the analysis of the Lazear model in D. Neumark and W. A. Stock, 'Age Discrimination Laws', (1999) 107 JPE 5, pp. 1081–125.

the average age of the workforce increases and workers nearing the end of working life are more likely to be made redundant first.[70] Removing expensive older workers during redundancy on the basis of their higher cost may well be objectively justifiable under Article 6.1 of the Employment Directive, which will be discussed below.[71] The European Commission among others suggests that the seniority element of pay be reconsidered to bring pay closer to productivity as an incentive for employers to hire and retain older workers.[72] Part-time work can additionally help to reduce the cost of older workers. The European Commission also suggests envisaging work across the whole life cycle, allowing scope for flexible, part-time working and career breaks.[73] For this to work, a massive co-ordinated effort is required across the working world. All workers, especially older workers, may need to agree a different tacit contract in which wages reflect productivity and performance more than seniority. However, performance-related pay systems may contain hazards of their own. Two recent surveys in the UK found that male academics in higher education are 1.5 times more likely to be awarded discretionary pay, a form of performance-related pay than their female colleagues.[74] While white academics in higher education, are 1.6 times more likely to be awarded discretionary pay than their black and ethnic minority (BME) colleagues.[75]

Vulnerability of women

Older women outnumber older men, especially at very old ages, at global and European levels although population ageing will narrow the gap.[76] The UN refers to the *feminisation of poverty* and calls for special measures to address this issue especially among older women.[77] Within the EU prior to enlargement, the problem was particularly bad in the UK, with one

---

[70] Reday-Mulvey, *Working Beyond* 60, at 179.

[71] C. O'Cinneide for the European Network of Legal Experts in the Non-discrimination Field, 'Age Discrimination and European Law' (European Commission, 2005), at p. 26.

[72] 'Increasing the Employment of Older Workers'.   [73] Ibid. at p. 14.

[74] Association of University Teachers, Performance related pay in UK higher education: gender and the use of discretionary pay points 2002–3 (January 2005) available at: www.aut.org.uk/media/pdf/b/5/dps_gender_2002-3.pdf.

[75] Association of University, Teachers Ethnicity and the use of discretionary pay in UK HE (AUT Research, October 2005) available at: www.aut.org.uk/media/pdf/n/h/eth_discpay_oct05.pdf.

[76] According to the UN the average of 71 men per 100 women is expected to increase to 78, Report of the Second World Assembly on Ageing, Madrid, 8–12 April 2000.

[77] World Conference, above at p. 18.

in four single British female pensioners living in poverty.[78] Women's life course also means they are more likely than men to experience poverty for the first time in old age.[79] A number of factors contribute to women's life and career patterns: child-rearing, interrupted careers, shorter working lives, caring, lower salaries, lower status work, predominance in atypical work, education, lower pensions and discrimination. The pay gap between men and women also increases with age.[80] Thus women (especially widows and divorced women), frequently have a particular need to improve their retirement income, which they must rely on for longer and so are likely to favour working beyond pension age.[81]

However, sex discrimination and the inter-sectionality of sex and age also play a role in women's situations. Theories such as the 'double jeopardy' or 'double whammy' of age and sex discrimination abound in relation to women.[82] Bernard *et al.* point to increasing evidence that age combines with gender to disadvantage women in organisations at all ages,[83] while Itzin and Newman have conceptualised 'gendered ageism' as a significant aspect of organisational culture.[84] A critical factor in older women's problems is that they experience the same problems as older workers but to a greater extent and earlier in the life course.[85] A key reason is that women are viewed, as being older sooner than men are, usually by men, leading to the idea of a glass ceiling of age for women.[86] This appears to be in addition to any discrimination experienced by younger women, by virtue of being of childbearing age which is now regarded as up to

---

[78] Age Concern England *One in Four – A quarter of single women pensioners live in poverty: this scandal must end* (2003) available at: www.ageconcern.org.uk.

[79] J. McMullin, 'Theorizing age and gender relations', in Arber and Ginn, *Connecting Gender and Ageing*, at p. 34.

[80] Age Reference Group on Equality and Human Rights, at p. 14. This is also true in the US see D. Rodeheaver 'Labor Market Progeria', at p. 105.

[81] Reday-Mulvey, *Working Beyond* 60, at 98. Davis *et al.* 'Alone and Poor: the Plight of Elderly Women', in L. Glasse and J. Hendricks, *Gender & Aging* (Baywood Publishing Company Inc., 1992), at pp. 81–4 report that poverty will practically disappear among elderly couples and older men living alone; by 2020 elder poverty will be almost exclusively a problem for elderly women in the US.

[82] As discussed by McMullin 'Theorizing age and gender relations', at p. 36 and Loretto *et al.* 'Ageism and Employment', at p. 296.

[83] M. Bernard, C. Itzin, C. Phillipson and J. Skucha, 'Gendered Work, Gendered Retirement', in S. Arber and J. Cuinn at p. 59.

[84] C. Itzin and C. Phillipson, 'Gendered Ageism' (below) at p. 88.

[85] D. Rodeheaver 'Labor Market Progeria: On the Life Expectancy of Presentability among Working Women,' in Glasse and Hendricks, *Gender & Aging*, at p. 104.

[86] C. Itzin and C. Phillipson, 'Gendered Ageism A double jeopardy for women in organizations,' in C. Itzin and Newman (eds.), *Gender, Culture and Organizational Change* (Routledge, 1995), at p. 82 and Bernard *et al.*, 'Gendered Work, Gendered Retirement', at p. 61.

the age of 40.[87] British research finds that an older worker is a woman over 35 but a man over 42.[88] Social standards of appearance are found to be partly responsible for the combination of age and sex discrimination experienced by older women in the US.[89] Rodeheaver describes a shorter life expectancy of presentability for working women than men as *labour market progeria*.[90] Unemployed older women may also face discrimination in getting jobs involving traditional feminine qualities due to social standards that regard ageing women as less attractive and less feminine.[91] Thus some women grow into discrimination as they grow older for reasons of a changing appearance and some jobs will be more prone to produce these effects than others will.

This leads us back to a social meaning of age and a perception of physiological age. Yet appearances can be deceptive. Direct discrimination under the UK Employment Equality (Age) Regulations 2006, includes discrimination based on the perception of a person's age, whether it is correct or not.[92] In Ireland the definition of discrimination was expanded in 2004 to include discrimination based on a ground that is imputed to the person concerned and discrimination by association with another person.[93] The foregoing would tend to suggest that these meanings of discrimination would be particularly helpful to those women who look older than they are and also those young people who are frequently perceived as too young.[94] It also suggests another reason to reduce the lower age limit of 40 for protection from age discrimination in the US, for example. The phrase 'the pale, stale, male' has been coined to describe the typical beneficiary of age discrimination laws, the white middle-aged male executive.[95] Apart from

---

[87] Equal Opportunities Commission, 'Greater expectations Final report of the EOC's investigation into discrimination against new and expectant mothers in the workplace' (2005) at pp. 45–7, which reveals evidence of considerable bias by British HR professionals against employing women of child-bearing age, available at www.eoc.org.uk/PDF/pregnancy_gfi_final_report.pdf.

[88] Employers Forum on Age Fact Sheet, *Age – the Issues fort today's workplace* (undated) and Itzin and Phillipson 'Gendered Ageism' at p. 85, respectively.

[89] Rodeheaver in Glasse and Hendricks, *Gender & Aging*, at p. 101.

[90] Ibid.   [91] Ibid. at 105.

[92] *Employment Equality (Age) Regulations 2006, Notes on Regulations* at note 10, July 2005, available at: www.dti.gov.uk/files/file27136.pdf.

[93] Employment Equality Act 1998 s.6 as amended by Equality Act 2004 s.4.

[94] This is particularly true for young people trying to access services, Marsh and Sahin-Dikmen, *Discrimination in Europe (Report B)*, at p. 16.

[95] More men than women have traditionally filed age discrimination claims in the US. However, the number of claims filed by women doubled from 16 per cent in the first eighteen years of the ADEA to 32 per cent in 1996, Prof. Eglit 'The Age Discrimination in Employment Act at Thirty: Where its Been, Where it is Today, Where its Going', *University of Rich.L.Rev.* 31 (1997), p. 579.

being offensive, this term encourages the perception that age discrimination is less important than other forms and can obscure discrimination arising from the multiple and intersecting identities of people of all ages. The Preamble to the Employment Directive acknowledges that women are frequently the victims of multiple discrimination.[96] Moreover, the idea of age triggering sex discrimination has been with us for some time in European law.[97]

The situation of young people

The European Commission has begun to see young people as a rare yet undervalued resource, stating that society needs to devise new ways of liberating the potential of both the young and the old.[98] It encourages better integration of young people in economic life against a background of youth unemployment in the EU especially among the under 25s. The European Commission warns that young people are at risk of poverty, which is at a higher rate of 19 per cent for those aged 16–24 compared to 12 per cent for those aged 25–64 and 17 per cent for 65+. It reports that young people can encounter discrimination based on their age and lack of occupational experience, which together with other factors such as gender, social origin or race, make it difficult for them to integrate into economic life and society. Importantly, the Commission for one is quite clear that demographic ageing does not mean an automatic solution to the problems of unemployment and the integration of young people.[99]

Key contexts and factors

European policy initiatives

The European Commission believes it is necessary for all age groups to achieve activity rates that are as high as possible in order to avoid the problems of a smaller workforce, pressures on pensions, public finances, old age care and healthcare, and risks of social exclusion for older people.[100] It suggests that if the male retirement age could be increased to between 64 and 65 years and present growth in female activity rates could

---

[96] Recital 3.
[97] Most notably in Case 152/84 Marshall v. Southampton and South West Hampshire Area Authority [1986] ECR 723.
[98] 'Confronting demographic change', COM (2005) 94 final, pp. 6–7.
[99] Ibid., p. 7.   [100] Ibid., p. 9.

be maintained, it would be possible to make up for most of the expected increase in the old age dependency burden.[101] The gender issue located at national and international levels is also reflected in the EU, with women making up almost two-thirds of those over 65.[102] However, the challenge of an ageing society is only one aspect of a broader agenda.

The Lisbon European Council in 2000 set the goal for the EU to become, by 2010, 'the most competitive and dynamic knowledge-based economy in the world, capable of sustainable economic growth with more and better jobs and greater social cohesion'.[103] Actions to achieve these aims include raising the overall employment rate to 70 per cent and raising the employment rate of women to more than 60 per cent by 2010. Full employment lies at the heart of the Lisbon Strategy, but the elderly initially featured only in the context of social inclusion. The Stockholm European Council 2001 referred more overtly to population ageing, seeing the goal of full employment as an important way of dealing with this challenge.[104] It set a target of 50 per cent of older women and men in employment by 2010.

The Barcelona European Council 2002 advocated the reduction of early retirement and a progressive increase of five years in effective average age of retirement by 2010.[105] In 2004, the High Level Group on the future of social policy in an enlarged European Union (HLG) identified enlargement, population ageing and globalisation as the three great challenges for the European social agenda.[106] It also highlighted a policy of extending working life by increasing the employment rate of senior workers, women and the young. This could be achieved through a flexible life pattern and mobility over the life cycle.[107] The HLG describes the period from 2006 to 2010 as the last window before the working age population begins to shrink and 2010 as a pivotal year during which Europe will take a major demographic turn.[108] It suggests that after this date, employment can only grow if immigration increases, the employment rate carries on rising or both happen together. However, the mid-term review of the Lisbon strategy in 2004 revealed declining economic growth and mixed

---

[101] European Commission 'Communication Towards a Europe for All Ages – Promoting Prosperity and Intergenerational Solidarity', COM(1999) 221 final at p. 14.

[102] Ibid. at 5.

[103] 23 and 24 March 2000, Conclusion 5 available at: http://ue.eu.int/cms3_applications/Applications/newsRoom/loadbook. ASP?MAX=1&BID=76&LANG=1&cmsId=347.

[104] 23 and 24 March 2001.   [105] 15–16 March 2002.

[106] DG Employment and Social Affairs 'Report of the High Level Group on the Future of Social Policy in an Enlarged European Union' (2004) at p. 7.

[107] Ibid. at pp. 7–8.   [108] Ibid. at pp. 20 and 38.

progress.[109] The Lisbon Strategy has been re-launched and the European Commission now recommends exceeding the Lisbon target of 70 per cent employment and continually raising the retirement age to compensate for the reduction in size of the working age population.[110] Its emphasis on flexible working lives and extending working life at both ends shows it is generally in sync with key commentators noted above. However, these policies appear to be motivated primarily by releasing reserves of labour to pursue productivity goals.

Enlargement

At present the post 2004 EU Member States (EU+10) are experiencing a surge in the number of young people.[111] This makes them an obvious source of immigration to EU 15. However, two factors mitigate against this – the prospect of an influx of immigrants is said to be exaggerated, and the rejuvenating effects of enlargement are predicted to be small and temporary.[112] The median age in Central and Eastern Europe (CEE) is predicted to outstrip that of Western Europe by 2035 but life expectancy is currently lower than in EU 15.[113] Many older people in CEE have been bereft of family, home and means of support as a result of conflict and have experienced the breakdown of a social and political system that offered them some measure of security in old age.[114] In some of these countries, older people feel that their situation is worse than it was after the Second World War.[115] HelpAge International reports that older people have not had access to the new opportunities that political change has given to young people, which affects their ability to develop new forms of work. However, the unemployment rate for young people aged 15–24 is on

---

[109] Report from the High Level Group chaired by Wim Kok, *Facing the Challenge The Lisbon strategy for growth and employment* (European Communities, Luxembourg, 2004).

[110] European Commission 'Communication to the Spring European Council Working together for growth and jobs A new start for the Lisbon Strategy', COM(2005) 24 at pp. 3–7 and 'Confronting demographic change', COM(2005) 94 final, p. 4.

[111] In 2003 children under 15 made up 19 per cent of the population in the new Member States, European Commission 'The social situation in the European Union 2003 – In brief', at p. 7. The HLG also reports a 'baby boom' in the 1970s and 1980s in the new Member States which has since noticeably declined, pp. 7 and 18.

[112] Ibid. and HLG on the Future of Social Policy at pp. 11–12.

[113] 65–72 for men compared to 73–78 in EU 15 and 75–78 for women compared to 79–83 in EU 15, HLG on the Future of Social Policy at pp. 12 and 17.

[114] HelpAge International 'A generation in transition: Older people's situation and civil society's response in East and Central Europe', (HelpAge International, 2002) pp. 2–3.

[115] Ibid. at 4.

average double that of adults throughout the EU as a whole, with hotspots in both EU 15 and EU+10.[116] At the time of enlargement, unemployment rates in the new Member States were almost double the EU 15 average with a growing number of long-term unemployed.[117]

'Street elderly' who engaged in begging or marginal work, became a new phenomenon in CEE prior to enlargement.[118] At the other end of the age spectrum, large numbers of street children are an ongoing phenomenon in CEE.[119] These groups, possibly among others, may well benefit from a variety of EU programmes, but it is unknown to what extent the Equality package adopted in 2000 can assist them. Further targeted research into the causes of the problems faced by younger and older people in CEE seems wise in order to assess this. In particular whether there may be appropriate positive action by Member States, in line with Article 6.1(a) or the more substantive equality provision, Article 7.1 of the Employment Directive.

The role of quality in work

The quality of work appears to have a distinct and important effect on the life experience[120] and is recognised by the European Commission as a multidimensional concept that embraces diversity and non-discrimination.[121] Improving quality and productivity in work are also part of the Lisbon strategy. Positive links are found between employment growth, good job quality and productivity.[122] Conversely, there are negative links between low quality work and social exclusion and poverty. In general, almost a third of workers who move from unemployment to

---

[116] HLG on the Future of Social Policy at p. 43, hotspots in EU 15 are Greece, Italy, Spain, Finland, France and Belgium and in EU+10 they are Poland and Slovakia.

[117] Ibid. at 50.   [118] Ibid. at 9.

[119] European Foundation for Street Children World-wide (EFSCW) *Summary Report on the Symposium on Street children and youth as a priority of the EU's social inclusion policy for the New Member States in Central and Eastern Europe*, 9–10 December 2004, Brussels available at: www.enscw.org/documents/Summary%20Report% 2017-03-2005%20Logo.pdf.

[120] 'The Social Situation in the European Union 2003', at p. 16. A negative correlation has also been found between health and leaving work and a positive correlation has been found between health and returning to work for those who prefer to work, J. E. Mutchler *et al.*, 'Work Transitions and Health in Later Life' (1999) 54 *Journal of Gerontology Series B: Social Sciences* 5 (1999), S252–S261.

[121] European Commission Communication 'Employment and social policies: a framework for investing in quality', COM(2001) 313 final, identifies ten dimensions of quality.

[122] European Commission Communication 'Improving quality in work: a review of recent progress', COM(2003) 728 final at pp. 3 and 6.

low-quality jobs are at a high risk of becoming unemployed again within a year.[123] Quality also plays a role in retaining older workers in work for longer and is important for attracting older people and those with caring responsibilities back to work.[124] Whereas lower quality jobs can act as a bridge to better employment for young or high skilled people, older and unskilled workers can stay in cycles of unemployment, inactivity and low skilled employment.[125] This may explain why the withdrawal of older workers in low quality jobs from the labour market is said to be four times higher than that of older workers in jobs of high quality.[126]

Age and the Employment Directive

Among the Article 13 grounds, age has struggled for recognition as an equality issue rather than a social policy or labour market issue.[127] Article 6.1 of the Directive arguably preserves the inherent tension between these two positions and the preamble hints at a labour market impetus for the inclusion of age.[128] It permits cut-offs and limits based on a chronological age approach that apply to all persons of the same age or age group but this denies recognition of the great diversity in characteristics, competencies and abilities among people of the same age or age group. Despite any potentially diminishing effects of Article 6.1, the inclusion of age in the Employment Directive is a cause for celebration. Its incorporation arguably owes a good deal to the pragmatism of the Community lawmakers and the Member States in seizing an opportunity. Article 6.1 reflects the role of unanimity and the various pre-existing age-based measures throughout the enlarged EU. Colm O'Cinneide speaks of issues that arise for age that distinguish it from other grounds, such as the fact that there are no fixed characteristics that define particular age groups and the fact that individuals do not remain fixed within particular age groups.[129] While these points are acknowledged, a person's chronological age is a fixed characteristic at that moment for legal, social and employment purposes.

---

[123] Ibid. at pp. 6–7.   [124] Ibid. at pp. 6 and 10.

[125] 'The Social Situation in Europe 2003', at p. 9.

[126] 'Improving quality in work: a review of recent progress', at p. 6.

[127] Quinn, Helsinki conference, at p. 7 and C. O'Cinneide, 'Comparative European Perspectives on Age Discrimination Legislation', in Fredman and Spencer (eds.) (2003), pp. 195–217 at pp. 196 and 200.

[128] Recital 8 emphasises 'the need to pay particular attention to supporting older workers, in order to increase their participation in the labour force'.

[129] O'Cinneide, 'Age Discrimination and European Law', at p. 5.

Moreover, the arguments that age lacks a fixed characteristic or that it is fluid may also apply to other grounds. A person's sexual orientation can change; adherence and non-adherence to a religion can vary throughout life; and some medical, psychiatric and psychological conditions give rise to periods of disability, remission or abatement. It must not be forgotten that women change their status through pregnancy. But the fixed nature of chronological age can have a *snakes and ladders* effect on employment and life activities due to age barriers imposed by law, employers and service providers. The wide range of age-based rules across different employment fields and conditions throughout the EU[130] arguably constitutes a barrier to equality, especially as Article 6.1 provides a mechanism to accept, retain and legitimise them. O'Cinneide also speaks of a differentiation for age, between unfair assumptions and stereotypes that are undesirable and legitimate age-based distinctions.[131] For him the Directive achieves this differentiation with its particular framework. By contrast, Clare McGlynn sees Article 6.1 as entrenching certain forms of discrimination.[132]

It is true that the Employment Directive 'singles out' age discrimination.[133] Firstly, the Directive, and Article 6.1 in particular, give the Member States the possibility to shrink the material scope for different age groups substantially. Secondly, the Directive excludes certain areas from its ambit altogether. This can make the Directive's overall minimum aims somewhat porous for the age ground in the hands of the individual Member States. The preamble foretells a patchwork of protection throughout the EU, stating: 'However, differences in treatment in connection with age may be justified under certain circumstances and therefore require specific provisions which may vary in accordance with the situation in Member States.'[134] Three categories of non-application and potential non-application (by choice or through justification) can be identified.

---

[130] For the UK see, Department for Education and Skills, 'Occupational Age restrictions: Summary QPID Study Report No. 96' (December 2001).

[131] Ibid., the latter being rooted in rational considerations that 'are not incompatible with the recognition of individual dignity, serve valuable social and economic objectives, and often are designed to protect particular age groups'.

[132] 'EC Legislation Prohibiting Age Discrimination: "Towards a Europe for All Ages?"' (2000) 3 *Cambridge Yearbook of European Legal Studies* (2000), pp. 279–299 at p. 290.

[133] Note 'Opinion of the Economic and Social Committee on certain Community measures to combat discrimination', CES 596/2000, E/o SOC/029 of 5 June 2000 at para. 6.6, p. 13 where it states that the action programme should have a strong focus on age discrimination for this reason.

[134] Recital 25.

In the first category, the Directive does not affect two areas that would ordinarily concern age as follows:

- Recital 14 states that the Directive is without prejudice to national provisions laying down retirement ages;
- Article 3.3 excludes payments made by state schemes, including social security or social protection schemes payments.

Arguably, social security laws would have been unworkable without these, so age may have remained isolated outside the Directive without such political compromises. Recital 14 was not included in the proposal for the Directive but was included later largely at the request of the British government.

The second category gives Member States a choice whether effectively to exempt two fields from the age strand. It comprises:

- Article 3.4 permitting Member States not to apply the age and disability provisions of the Directive to their armed forces;
- Article 6.2 allowing Member States to provide that fixing ages of admission or entitlement to retirement or invalidity benefits for occupational social security schemes will not be age discrimination provided this does not result in sex discrimination.

Article 6.2 again goes to the workability of the law and national social security systems. Article 3.4 was required by the British government.[135] A number of Member States have made special provision for the application of age and disability to the armed forces during the implementation process.[136]

The third category contains just one provision – Article 6.1, which is unique within the anti-discrimination package adopted in 2000, in that it permits the Member States to justify direct discrimination solely on the ground of age.

- Article 6.1 allows Member States to provide that differences of treatment based on age will not be discrimination 'if, within the context of

---

[135] A. Evans-Pritchard 'Business criticises EU ban on jobs bias', *Daily Telegraph*, 18 October 2000.

[136] In Denmark the armed forces may ask the Ministry for permission to exclude applicants of a particular age or with disabilities from specific positions by virtue of genuine occupational qualifications. By contrast Maltese regulations do not apply to the armed forces in respect of discriminatory treatment on grounds of age and disability, see European Network of Legal Experts in the non-discrimination field, *European anti-Discrimination Law Review*, Issue 1, April 2005, at pp. 44 and 61 respectively.

national law, they are objectively and reasonably justified by a legitimate aim, including legitimate employment policy, labour market and vocational training objectives, and if the means of achieving that aim are appropriate and necessary'.

This is neither a case of exclusion from the Directive's ambit or a case of choosing not to apply a provision. It is also vague and potentially infinitely elastic.[137]

Article 6.1 and 'legitimate' age discrimination?

Article 6.1 lists three examples of differences in treatment on grounds of age that may be justified and refers to them as not constituting discrimination rather than permitted forms of discrimination.[138] The first difference in treatment is the setting of special conditions on access to employment and vocational training (including dismissal and pay) for young people, older workers and persons with caring responsibilities to promote their vocational integration or ensure their protection. Some commentators refer to this provision in purely positive action terms.[139] While the potential for positive action is an obvious merit of this provision, others believe that the special conditions are likely to include not only more favourable but also less favourable conditions.[140] This view is consistent with the wording of Article 6.1. For Clare McGlynn, this first possibility could be used to justify the kind of differential treatment associated with the labour market 'which it might be hoped that age discrimination legislation would prohibit' such as, the minimum wage for young workers.[141]

The second example of justifiable differential treatment is the fixing of minimum conditions of age, professional experience or seniority for access to employment or to certain advantages linked to employment. This seems designed to facilitate the maintenance of the status quo within national employment practices and also to prevent a flood of litigation by generally younger workers challenging long service pay awards and

---

[137] John Cridland, CBI is quoted in the *Daily Telegraph* article by A. Evans-Pritehord, as saying that the age clause 'leaves too many unanswered questions'.

[138] L. Waddington, 'Article 13 EC: Setting Priorities in the Proposal for a Horizontal Employment Directive', (2000) 29 *ILJ* 2, p. 176 at p. 178.

[139] S. Fredman, 'The Age of Equality', at p. 57 and B. Hepple at pp. 86 and 88 in Fredman and Spencer *Age as an Equality Issue*.

[140] P. Skidmore, 'The European Employment Strategy and Labour Law: A German Case Study' (2004) *ELRev* 29(1), pp. 52–73 at p. 61 and C. McGlynn pp. 279–99 at p. 290.

[141] C. McGlynn, pp. 279-99 at p. 290.

benefits. Bob Hepple warns that such advantages linked to employment in this way can amount to indirect discrimination if they are not justified.[142] However, one-off benefits for long service should become less plentiful over time with more non-linear careers and greater reliance on career breaks.[143] But if age or long service were a (sole) determining factors for higher salaries, it would be hard to see how such a practice might be defensible.

The third example concerns the fixing of a maximum age for recruitment, which is based on the training requirements of the job or the need for a reasonable period of employment before retirement. This is particularly troubling for Sandra Fredman as training and retirement ages are both in the hands of the employer.[144] Others see it as denying the transferability of prior experience and that specifying it in the Directive will entrench its use.[145] There is no doubt that retirement ages exert downward pressure on training and maximum recruitment ages. Yet they are left in the hands of the Member States or employers following the Directive. Three further aspects of this example give cause for concern. The first is the vagueness of the term training. The second is the vague notion of employer payback for training or recruitment costs, there is no indication how these should be measured; approaches based on years of service may exclude others based on productivity, for example. The third is the inherent scope for misusing the requirement of a reasonable period of employment before retirement.

Both the Directive and Article 6.1 have drawn much comment for their treatment of age. Article 6.1 has been described as an open-ended possibility to justify age discrimination, a 'catch-all' justification for discrimination on grounds of age (as long as the provisions are objectively and reasonably justified) and is generally regarded as highly permissive.[146] The proposal for the Directive was also described as seeking to 'legalise age discrimination'.[147] Is this fair? Article 6 is indeed 'qualitatively different'[148] both from the provisions applicable to all the grounds in the Article 13 Directives and importantly even from tailormade provisions

---

[142] Hepple at pp. 86 and 88 in Fredman and Spencer, *Age as an Equality Issue.* p. 87.

[143] 'Green Paper Confronting demographic change', at p. 3.

[144] S. Fredman, 'The Age of Equality', p. 57.

[145] C. McGlynn above at pp. 290 and 291.

[146] See L. Waddington, 'The New Directives: Mixed Blessings', in Costello and Barry (eds.), *Equality in Diversity The New Equality Directives* (Ashfield, 2003), at p. 48 and C. McGlynn above at p. 292 and O'Cinneide, 2003, fn. 127, p. 200.

[147] Eurolink Age cited in Waddington 'Article 13 EC: Setting priorities', p. 179.

[148] So described by Waddington in 'The New Directives: Mixed Blessings'.

for three other grounds in the Employment Directive: Article 5, Article 2.2(ii), Article 4.2 and Article 15. Article 5 obliges employers to provide reasonable accommodation for those with disabilities. Article 4.2 permits Member States to provide or maintain religious ethos as an occupational requirement of churches or other organisations whose ethos is based on religion or belief. Gwyneth Pitt explores the rationale and scope of this exception in her contribution to this volume. Article 15.1 (police services) is devoted to mending equality of opportunity damaged by religious and political historical divisions in Northern Ireland.

Therefore a degree of specificity exists elsewhere in the Directive relating to grounds other than age and some of these provisions also refer to a difference in treatment as not constituting discrimination, as in Article 6.1. However, it is arguable that the reasonable accommodation and Northern Ireland (police services) provisions have almost exclusively positive connotations for target groups and aim at making equality of opportunity a reality. All of these provisions compare favourably with Article 6.1 in that they are finite, clearer and more specific. Perhaps the only one that can be said to excuse discrimination is the religious occupational requirement. It is arguably a provision that contributes to the workability of the Directive and implementing law.

Adapting to the peculiarities of age

Perhaps the examples of different treatment for age can be explained by the school of thought represented by Gerard Quinn: 'It is best to try to be honest about the objective differences and attempt to adjust common rules where needed to meet the peculiarities of each group.'[149] While Waddington asks whether the special attention for age, disability, religion and belief reflect a further prioritising of these grounds, 'or whether they seek merely to ensure that all groups, in spite of their different needs, are able to benefit equally from the eventual Directive, or are excluded when their "differentness" requires this'.[150] For Eilis Barry the 'hierarchy of grounds' is very much a product of political pragmatism leaving the opportunity for a more robust model of equality to emerge through their judicial and legislative implementation.[151] All three stances are discernible within the Employment Directive.

[149] Quinn, Helsinki paper, at p. 13.
[150] Waddington 'Article 13 EC: Setting priorities', at p. 176.
[151] 'Different Hierarchies – Enforcing Equality Law', in Costello and Barry (eds.), *Equality in Diversity*, pp. 411–434 at p. 414.

Perception, acceptance or exclusion of 'differentness' has particular resonance for age, as intra-group 'differentness' may be more likely to be at play than for other grounds. If the Directive sought to ensure that all grounds benefit equally, then reasonable accommodation might have been extended to age and some of the examples of different permitted treatment might no longer be required. Despite the scope for positive or protective measures, Article 6.1 also has the potential to preserve pre-existing discrimination and employment practices and to deny employment, occupational and training opportunities to younger and older people. By contrast, Article 5 only facilitates access to these areas for disabled persons.

A good deal of Article 6.1 is unlikely to adapt to the peculiarities of particular age groups and seems aimed at balancing the interests of employers with employees in ways that would be unacceptable for other grounds. It arguably perpetuates the use of age as a convenient criterion for workforce management. However, it is difficult to think of an alternative organisational tool that is as easy, cheap and effective to apply. O'Cinneide refers to the necessity of age limits where individual assessment of each person's competencies and qualities is not possible and states 'the text of Article 6(1)(a) makes it clear that such measures are regarded as potentially objectively justifiable'.[152] Thus for him general age limits will be problematic where individual assessment is possible.[153]

This is not to disagree with those who believe that different equality responses may be required for different grounds (and in different contexts).[154] Article 6.1 in its present form may not be what they had in mind but perhaps it reflects the idea that different motives may have underpinned the inclusion of different grounds[155] and the political agreement needed to get all Member States to accept the inclusion of age. It is tempting to think of Article 6.1 as possessing a carte blanche quality that sets age apart from the other grounds in the Employment Directive. Article 6.1 at first seems to reserve considerable power and control to employers over the working lives and choices of employees at a time when they are being asked to extend their working lives, thus potentially pulling against current thinking emerging from the European Commission, the UN and NGOs concerned with ageing and older people. However, the ECJ's judgment in *Mangold* v. *Helm*, below demonstrates the

---

[152] O'Cinneide, 2005 at 39.   [153] Ibid. at 6.

[154] For example, C. McCrudden, 'Theorising European Law', in Costello and Barry (eds.) *Equality in Diversity*, at pp. 1–38.

[155] Ibid. at 11.

effectiveness in particular of the 'appropriate and necessary' means limb of the justification test in Article 6.1 despite any apparent *boundlessness* in the permitted differences in treatment. Notwithstanding this workable test, some workers will suffer in the meantime, while waiting for an individual to emerge and instigate litigation and for the judicial outcome, even where this is ultimately in their favour.

The 'kernel' effect

Quinn refers also to there being some kernel of truth in the common perception that age impacts on capacity.[156] No one can vehemently disagree as disability and long-term conditions do increase with age in general.[157] But he also argues that this 'truth' masks the large degree of individual variations and fails to take account of healthier lifestyles and preventive medicine.[158] This kernel of truth is evident in the Directive. It has influenced the age ground inter alia by permitting Member States to treat all persons of a given age in identical fashion on the basis of their chronological age alone, through the use of minimum and maximum ages. Another truth is that many workers in the EU cease working long before retirement age.[159] Thus maximum recruitment ages and mandatory retirement do not respond to a large-scale need for workforce management. They also go against efforts to delay exit and swell the numbers of workers in the population as a whole in the face of demographic ageing.

A similar kernel effect would be judged very harshly if applied to pregnant women or working mothers. However, age is seen as a rational criterion for employment decisions in some circumstances while race and sex (generally) should not come into the decision-making process.[160] Bell and Waddington argue that age and disability can sometimes result in an individual being unable to perform work or restrict availability for work

---

[156] G. Quinn, 'Walking the talk-Equal Rights in an Enlarged European Union Or The Importance of Talking While walking: A Reflection Paper', European Commission Conference, Prague, 5–6 July 2004 at p. 12.

[157] Age Reference Group on Equality and Human Rights, at p. 10.   [158] Ibid.

[159] The age of early exit also varies throughout EU 25 with the average exit age at 56.9 years in Poland, for example, see 'Increasing the employment of older workers', at p. 7. In the UK some older workers have recently started to work for longer.

[160] For age, see B. Hepple 'Age Discrimination in Employment: Implementing the Framework Directive 2000/78/EC', in Fredman and Spencer (eds.) above at p. 95. For grounds that are always irrelevant and those that are sometimes relevant to decisions on employment/access to goods and services see, Bell and Waddington 'Reflecting on inequalities in European equality law', (2003) 28 *ELRev*, pp. 349–69 at p. 361.

but the Directive's lack of reasonable accommodation provisions for age is inconsistent when compared with disability. They point to the contrast represented by Article 6 'which will place older workers at a disadvantage if acted upon by the Member States'.[161] Article 6 may also make it more difficult for those experiencing multiple discrimination on age and another ground to seek redress.

The chronological age approach

It is strongly arguable that the chronological age approach is embedded in Article 6.1. But this approach leaves no room for positive individual variations. Moreover, maximum recruitment ages are also bound up with retirement ages and the lifespan has grown by twenty years since 1950[162] and by longer still since British male and female pension ages were fixed at 65 and 60 respectively in 1925.[163] On this basis a retirement age of 65 or below is founded on obsolete information about life expectancy. O'Cinneide has asserted that measures to eliminate discrimination against older workers 'reflect the fact that the primary concern of policy makers is to deal with the more troubling economic and social consequences of age discrimination, while minimising alterations to existing business and public sector policies'.[164] The broad range of get-outs for age in the Directive may hint at an ongoing reluctance on the part of some Member States to treat age as an equality issue. An Irish court, in *Equality Authority* v. *Ryanair*, has already considered chronological age and has clarified that the term 'young', in a job advertisement, referred to chronological age and not those who were 'young at heart', and regarded this as age discrimination.[165]

Examples of direct age discrimination

Age limits and mandatory retirement are two of the clearest examples of direct age discrimination, and both impact on other areas, such as hiring and training. Arguably, employers will need to use maximum recruitment ages for jobs requiring lengthy and expensive training for as long as they are allowed to set mandatory retirement ages by national law. Recital 14 of the Directive states that it shall be without prejudice to national provisions

---

[161] Ibid.   [162] Report of the Second World Assembly on Aging.
[163] Widows', Orphans' and Old-Age Contributory Pensions Act 1925.
[164] O'Cinneide, 2003 above at 196.
[165] DEC-E/2000/14 available at: http://www.equalitytribunal.ie.

laying down retirement ages. The full meaning and effect of this clause is difficult to gauge. Prior to agreement on a national default retirement age of 65, Hepple wrote that as the UK had no national retirement age, mandatory retirement ages would have to be justified under Article 6.1.[166] Others view Recital 14 as meaning variously that Member States retain the right to fix national mandatory retirement ages, that state-imposed retirement ages related to pensions are exempt from the Directive or are more like an exclusion from the Directive.[167] Notwithstanding Recital 14, Article 6.1 appears to allow Member States to permit age limits and mandatory retirement ages (if they are objectively justifiable within its terms).

It is important to read Article 6.1 in light of Article 8.2, which requires that implementation of the Directive does not reduce the level of protection from discrimination already existing in the Member states. Protection must stay at the same level at the time of implementation but may possibly be reduced later.[168] Article 6.1 allows Member States to retain and entrench a number of age-based employment practices. However, it also appears to allow Member States to set various age limits and special conditions for different ages for the first time. There is no indication in the Directive that any of the age exemptions or justifications is constrained by Article 8.2. Therefore Article 6.1 enables Member States to disapply some anti-discrimination cover for age and may possibly disapply Article 8.2 from some aspects of the age ground. For O'Cinneide however, Article 8.2 means that if the introduction of a national default retirement age deprives employees of employment rights, it may not be permissible.[169] Ultimately, the European Court of Justice (ECJ) will resolve any tension between these two provisions.

In the meantime, a Dutch case concerning the retirement age of 56 for airline pilots helps to shed some light on issues raised by retirement ages. *Martinair* has successfully defended this retirement age in the Dutch Supreme Court, by justifying it as necessary for ensuring promotion

---

[166] Hepple in Fredman and Spencer, *Age as an Equality Issue*, p. 89.

[167] See respectively, P. Skidmore, 'EC Framework Directive on Equal Treatment in Employment: Towards a Comprehensive Community Anti-Discrimination Policy?' (2001) 30 *Industrial Law Journal*, pp. 126–32 at p. 130, O'Cinneide, 2003 above at 15 and Clare McGlynn above at 290.

[168] H. Meenan, 'Age Equality after the Employment Directive', *MJ* 1 (2003), pp. 9–38 at p. 14.

[169] O'Cinneide, 2005 above at 43.

opportunities for all pilots before retirement.[170] This is an unusual justification for the airline industry, which normally relies on health and safety justifications. It also puts the Netherlands out of step with the US and European countries such as France, which have a mandatory retirement age of 60 for pilots. Pilots from Member States with a later retirement age find that they cannot fly into or over these countries and are therefore restricted in their routes. This situation also highlights a very important issue that has not been covered by the Directive – the cross-border effects of different age limits for particular sectors among Member States. This hampers employers' ability to roster pilots and other transport workers for cross-border or international work and potentially makes them more vulnerable when downsizing takes place. In *Martinair*, neither the Dutch Age Discrimination Act nor the Employment Directive could be relied on at the relevant time;[171] these retirement provisions may yet be revisited for compatibility with Article 6.1.

Interpreting Article 6 – issues

For some the greatest flexibility has been given to the Member States in respect of age discrimination.[172] This appears deserved as the legitimate aims are examples, but they span the whole scope of the Directive, sending the signal that age is less equal than other grounds. It is impossible to say where the legitimate aims begin and end or to see how vast the range of permissible differences of treatment will be. Article 6.1 also blurs the lines between direct and indirect discrimination as the latter is frequently spoken of as discrimination affecting a group rather than the individual.[173] Yet a Member State can allow employers to treat all persons of a given age or age group in the same way by virtue of their age under Article 6.1.

In effect therefore, the only types of age discrimination totally untouched by Article 6.1 and the Directive are instructions to discriminate and harassment, which would encompass ageist language adduced with some success in age discrimination cases in Ireland and the US.[174] The

---

[170] *Martinair Holland NV* v. *Vereniging van Nederlandse Verkeervliegers* Nr. C03/077HR, Dutch Supreme Court, 9 October 2004, available at: www.rechtspraak.nl.
[171] O'Cinneide, 2005, ibid, footnote 94 at p. 38.   [172] Paul Skidmore, 2001, at 130.
[173] Meenan, 'Age Equality after the Employment Directive', at pp. 20–21.
[174] For Ireland see, *Equality Authority* v. *Ryanair* DEC-E/2000/14 which involved a job advertisement for 'a young and dynamic professional' and *A Named Female* v. *A Named Company* DEC-E/2002/013 which involved profane language, berating a young female for her inexperience and youth. By contrast for the US, see H. Meenan, 'Age Discrimination: Law-Making Possibilities Explored', (2000) *IJDL* pp. 247–92 at pp. 265 –8.

wide drafting of Article 6.1 gives an initial impression that Member States will easily sustain justifications for direct age discrimination. A number of approaches foresee a generous interpretation in favour of the Member States. One is represented by Paul Skidmore and is based on a comparison with the ECJ's treatment of sex discrimination.[175] Another is represented by McGlynn who finds clues in the Preamble to suggest the 'Member States' concern to ensure that the prohibition on discrimination does not encroach too far on domestic traditions or impact on controversial policy questions'.[176] Recital 25 contains such a clue alluding to differences in treatment for age that may be justified and which may vary in accordance with the situation in Member States.[177] It suggests to her a wide margin of appreciation for Member States, 'which may encourage the Court to provide considerable leeway to Member States'. There are now some indications from the national courts and tribunals and indeed from the ECJ that justification could be tested more vigorously than Skidmore and McGlynn suggest.

Interpreting Article 6 – case law

The ECJ's first preliminary reference ruling on Article 6, in *Mangold* v. *Rudiger Helm*,[178] concerned the unlimited use of fixed-term contracts (FTCs) for workers over the age of 52.[179] The ECJ has ruled that this practice infringed Article 6.1. This ruling is of major significance for a number of reasons. The aim of the German rule was to promote the vocational integration of unemployed older workers, insofar as they have difficulties in finding work.[180] The age above which FTCs were justified for older workers in Germany had been successively reduced from 60 to 58 and then 52. The ECJ found that these reductions were not contrary to the non-regression clause of the Framework Agreement on fixed term contracts (FTC Agreement) as they were justified by the need to encourage the employment of older persons. However, the German law did constitute a difference in treatment directly on grounds of age and the Court tested it against Article 6.1. The Court found that the aim of the legislation to promote the vocational integration of unemployed older workers 'objectively and reasonably' could justify the difference in treatment.

---

[175] Ibid.   [176] McGlynn above at 292.   [177] Ibid.
[178] Case C-144/04, Judgment 22 November 2005.
[179] Paul Skidmore has already critically discussed this type of measure, 2004 at pp. 64–71.
[180] Case C-144/104, Judgment 22 November 2005, Paragraph 59.

However, in testing whether the means used to achieve the objective were 'appropriate and necessary' the Court took issue with the application of this law to all workers who have reached the age of 52, without differentiating between their employment status before the FTC.[181] The Court noted that this large number of workers could lawfully be employed on successive FTCs until retirement age and thereby denied stable employment and objected to the use of age as the sole criterion. It had not been shown that the fixing of an age threshold 'regardless of any other consideration linked to the structure of the labour market in question or the personal circumstances of the person concerned', was appropriate and necessary to attain the integration of older workers.[182] The German law had breached the principle of proportionality and could not therefore be justified.

The Court relying on the various international treaties and constitutional traditions of the Member States, mentioned in the preamble to the Directive, declared that the principle of non-discrimination on grounds of age must be regarded as a general principle of European law. This was enormously helpful, as the date for transposition of the Employment Directive had not expired. According to the Court, previous case law and Article 18 of the Employment Directive prevented a Member State from adopting measures that were incompatible with the Directive.[183] This ruling is also significant for the other grounds as the Court was referring to the sources of the principle of non-discrimination for all of the grounds contained in the Employment Directive when it declared the general principle of non-discrimination on grounds of age. Finally, the Court confirmed that the Employment Directive does not itself lay down the principle of equal treatment in employment and occupation.[184] Thus *Mangold* demonstrates the effectiveness of Article 6.1. However, despite a number of positive and significant features in its ruling, the Court regrettably missed a golden opportunity additionally to make a contextual argument based on demographic ageing and increases in human longevity, to defeat a blanket sole criterion of the low age of 52.

One question left unanswered by *Mangold* is whether the use of fixed-term contracts for older workers can collide with Article 8.2 (non-regression of legal protection) of the Employment Directive or whether a measure that is *successfully* justified under Article 6.1 is automatically unaffected by Article 8.2? The answer to this question may bear a good deal on the factual and legal circumstances of the case in hand.

---

[181] Ibid., paragraph 64.   [182] Ibid., paragraphs 64 and 65.   [183] Ibid., paragraph 67–72.
[184] Ibid., paragraph 74–76.

Interestingly, Irish law now provides that it is not discrimination to offer a FTC to a person over the compulsory retirement age for that employment.[185] There is now no upper age limit on claims for unfair dismissal in Irish law.[186] This may well be a disincentive for Irish employers to offer a permanent contract to either an internal or external employee above the relevant retirement age.

FTCs for older workers also prompt reflection on the issue of quality in work, a point not lost on the ECJ in *Mangold*. For some older workers, a FTC may be preferable to no work and may be conducive to working in later life, especially after retirement or for those who wish to re-enter the labour market. But for those with the greatest financial need, FTCs may represent a measure of insecurity and continued inability (especially in the case of women) to build up savings and pensions. It may also be asked whether FTCs and other measures targeted at older workers, will help produce and sustain the long-term growth needed to counter the effects of population ageing and globalisation on the labour market. It is uncertain whether the dilution of employment rights for those over retirement age may yet be seen as an age-based difference in treatment that infringes the Directive or requires justification.[187]

National case law: the Netherlands

Mangold contrasts with a Dutch case decided by the Dutch Equal Treatment Commission (ETC) in 2004, concerning the compatibility of three practices with the Dutch Act on Equal Treatment on the Grounds of Age.[188] These practices, referred by an employer, were a gradual reduction of working hours to employees aged 57.5 years or older, a requirement that employees be employed continuously for ten years by the employer to qualify for this reduction and granting extra holidays to older workers. The ETC viewed the first practice based on seniority as failing the objective justification test, it did not consider that a person needed 7.5 years to prepare for full retirement. Moreover, the length of service requirement was unlawful '*indirect* age distinction' because older workers could

---

[185] EEA 1998, s. 6 as amended by Equality Act 2004, s. 4 (c).

[186] Unfair Dismissals Act 1977, s. 2 (1)(b) as amended by Equality Act 2004, s. 4.

[187] On 6 December 2006, an age organisation, Heyday, backed by the National Council on Ageing and Age Concern, succeeded in having its challenge on retirement ages in the UK Government's Employment Equality (Age) Regulations 2006 referred to the European Court of Justice. These Regulations involve a national default retirement age of 65.

[188] Case no. 2004/150 of 15 November 2004 also as discussed in the *European Anti-Discrimination Law Review*, 1 (2005) at pp. 62–63. The identity of the parties remains confidential in ETC case law.

comply more easily than younger workers could. Granting extra holidays for workers over 50 was a distinction on grounds of age that was not justified by a legitimate aim. The employer's reason was that extra holidays would help prevent absence due to illness but failed to adduce evidence that absence was a real problem.

This case demonstrates how difficult it may be to justify differences in treatment that would otherwise amount to indirect age discrimination against younger workers. It is even more interesting for showing how the justification process may deny older workers some of the strategies and flexibility they need to stay in the workplace until 65 and beyond. Allowing none of these may have a heavier impact on those with a real need to work for more years. However, this case may not be the last word in the Netherlands as a different sector or job may have a significant bearing in another case, so might more measured provisions for older workers.

Human rights, equality and justice

In the context of the European Convention on Human Rights (ECHR) and the European Social Charter (ESC), Olivier De Schutter refers optimistically to 'age and disability, the next candidates for being treated as suspect grounds . . . rapidly rising in the hierarchy of prohibited grounds'.[189] However, Article 13 EC and the Employment Directive arguably provide the strongest foothold yet for age within the broader European human rights matrix. They give age some parity of esteem with the other grounds, notwithstanding any permitted exclusions or justifications. The EU Charter of Fundamental Rights (EUCFR) also represents a symbolic peak for age and elder rights in the EU. Article 21.1, the non-discrimination provision incorporates all of the Article 13 grounds. Additionally the EUCFR contains rights of the child in Article 24 and rights of the elderly in Article 25. Christopher McCrudden has argued that equality law in the EU is in the process of being subsumed within a broader human rights discourse encompassing 'a more inclusive ideal of equality'.[190] This process is welcome and reflects *inter alia* a growing rights-based approach to equality embedded in the Article 13 Directives.[191]

---

[189] Prof. O. De Schutter for the European Commission, *The Prohibition of Discrimination under European Human Rights Law* (European Commission, Belgium, 2005), at p. 15.

[190] In Costello and Barry (eds.) *Equality in Diversity*, p. 9.

[191] O'Cinneide highlights this approach, 2005 at p. 11 and Fredman above at p. 145.

Access to justice and promoting age equality

The Employment and Race Directives rely principally on the long-standing individual litigation model of EC law, reflecting in part at least the individual justice model of equality. They also contain quite a number of 'new' features that move away from this model and seek to achieve equality by other means.[192] While the shortcomings of the individual litigation model in fighting discrimination have been well documented, it still represents a major advance for age, as the Employment Directive has ensured that age discrimination has been outlawed in most EU Member States for the first time. But age differs from other Article 13 grounds, in that a Member State can objectively justify both direct and indirect age discrimination.[193] However, a number of problems have been identified with actively enforcing the prohibitions on direct and indirect age discrimination per the Directive. There are perceived difficulties in locating a suitable comparator for direct age discrimination but the use of a hypothetical comparator can help to overcome them.[194]

This is demonstrated by the Irish case *Perry* v. *Garda Commissioner* where, relying on a hypothetical comparator, established that a gap of two days was significant.[195] This was in the context of a voluntary early retirement scheme that paid a much higher gratuity to a 59-year-old colleague of the 64-year-old complainant. The Equality Officer applied the scheme to two hypothetical workers aged 60 less one day and 60 plus one day with the same service record, revealing that the younger worker, by two days, received more money and concluded that the difference was based on age. Other problems have been identified for indirect age discrimination – the fact that almost any employment provision, criterion or practice will probably put some age group at a disadvantage[196] but it is important not to exaggerate them. Furthermore, it may not be possible in every situation to achieve age equality, or combat age discrimination, in employment in the absence of equivalent legislation in goods and services. This is especially needed for older people in pursuit of services that could equally enable them to obtain a job, such as in motor insurance, exemplified by the Irish case *Jim Ross* v. *Royal & Sun Alliance plc.*[197] The Equality Officer found on the facts, that a blanket refusal to give quotations for insurance to drivers over 70 infringed the Equal Status Act 2000.

---

[192] Eilis Barry above at pp. 411, 412 and 418.
[193] The possibility to justify direct discrimination for any other ground is limited to genuine occupational requirements which is generally quite narrowly construed.
[194] O'Cinneide, 2005 above at 22.   [195] DEC-E2001-029.
[196] Ibid at 26 to 27.   [197] DEC-S2003-116.

Positive action

Examining the intersection of age with gender has shown that women have unique problems with this combination. This strongly suggests the need for comprehensive research at European and national levels into the combined effects of gender and age. There is also a need to disaggregate older and younger workers to scrutinise diverse groups within them and seek appropriate equality responses for different subgroups where required. Positive action is permitted by Article 6 of the Directive for age and Article 7 for all grounds. However, Article 6 permits the setting of special conditions on access to employment and training 'for young people, older workers and persons with caring responsibilities to promote their vocational integration or ensure their protection'. While Article 7 states in substantive equality terms: 'With a view to ensuring full equality in practice, the principle of equal treatment shall not prevent any Member State from maintaining or adopting specific measures to prevent or compensate for disadvantages linked to any of the grounds.'[198] While both are merely permissive, Article 6 arguably nods at a lower level of attainment.

In the past, Hepple has written that age does not have underrepresented groups in the same way as gender, racial equality and disability, or in Northern Ireland community affiliation. He has argued that: 'in the case of age it would be difficult and arbitrary to treat people in particular age bands as "groups" who must be fairly represented. Older workers, unlike women and ethnic minorities, are not segregated into particular job categories.'[199] He recommended that the removal of barriers for older and younger people and the promotion of their special needs should be encouraged as voluntary positive action.[200] This chapter suggests that dismantling age groups by gender (and indeed other grounds) may reveal clearer pockets of under-representation that call for more targeted and reliable approaches (than voluntary positive action). Some research indicates that the majority of women are segregated into low status, low-paid jobs, with stagnation in career paths and clear inequity in pay.[201] Also apparent are problems experienced by many older workers in a particular age group that exist now but may change with time. For example, some older workers still have poorer basic skills such as literacy

---

[198] For a discussion of substantive equality see among others, M. Bell 'Equality and the European Union', (2004) 33 *ILJ* pp. 242–60 at p. 247.

[199] In Fredman and Spencer (eds.), ibid at pp. 84–5.   [200] Ibid.

[201] Miriam Bernard *et al.* in Arber and Ginn (eds.) above at pp. 57 and 62–3 and European Commission Staff Working Paper, 'Gender pay gaps in European labour markets-Measurement, analysis and policy implications', SEC (2003) 937, 4.9.2003.

and numeracy not to mention computer skills, and in general have fewer formal qualifications than younger workers.[202]

Conclusion

The inclusion of age in Article 13 and the Employment Directive was indeed a cause for celebration but the time for celebration has passed. Our focus must now change. This chapter has revealed several compelling reasons why Member States should rely on Article 6.1 with caution and the European Commission ought to revisit this provision following a survey of its implementation throughout the enlarged European Union. The first concerns the contexts against which Article 6.1 was adopted, most notably demographic ageing. All stakeholders have a vested interest in a working environment that welcomes workers of all ages. The second concerns the broad categorisation of age as an anti-discrimination ground: younger and older workers have some overlapping but also many different experiences and needs. The third concerns intersectionality among the grounds, the combination of age and gender produces significant (negative) effects for women. This demands serious research at both national and European levels so that further action can be considered to produce effective equality responses. This signals above all a need for a general awareness-raising of the potential for intersectionality among all grounds and how this impacts on discrimination and equality. The fourth reason identifies an enduring tension between age's struggle to be treated as an equality issue and Article 6.1's ability to entrench and legitimise differences of treatment based on the chronological meaning of age alone. The fifth highlights the effect of this entrenchment as perpetuating outdated maximum age limits partially driven by (obsolete) mandatory retirement ages.

The overarching message of this chapter is that condoning any lesser treatment for age risks hurting those who find themselves at the intersection of age and at least one other ground. Furthermore, from an equality perspective, the homogenous treatment of any age group is unlikely to achieve anymore than formal equality. As regards age, it seems that the law has not yet caught up with some realities driven by the contexts within which the Directive was adopted such as population ageing. Certain other realities cannot be ignored such as the kernel of truth that age affects

---

[202] For the UK see G. Ford and J. Soulsby, 'Mature Workforce Development: East Midlands 2000 Research and Report' (Leicester, NIACE (National Organisation for Adult Learning), 2001), at pp. 22–7.

capacity. But this is so highly individualised that age limits, mandatory retirement and the application of *legitimate* differences in treatment on age grounds are blunt tools with which to manage younger and older workers. The traditional use of age as a means of ensuring *fair* treatment of the whole workforce on retirement, risks foreclosing badly needed employment opportunities for women, possibly among other groups. Age limits may also be a lazy way of organising the workforce especially as the problem until now in Europe has been voluntary and involuntary early exit rather than the majority of workers wanting to stay in work up to and beyond retirement. The UK's right to request work after retirement age is an interesting partial solution as some employees have the chance, no matter how uncertain, to work beyond retirement age.[203] But the employer arguably retains ultimate power in this process. Employers should be encouraged to use voluntary reasonable accommodation in the short term in the EU to cater for any deterioration associated with ageing where feasible, pending any potential change in legislation. Part-time work and flexible work are highly important for older workers and may be seen as a form of reasonable accommodation. They enable workers with caring responsibilities, those in stressful jobs and those who would work for longer if they were allowed, to rebalance their lives.

Everyone must now reflect on a design for their own life, against the background of increased longevity, all their identities and responsibilities. This approach should engender a sense of excitement and greater control about the possibilities presented by a longer life. However, the quality of each person's experience will also depend on factors that will vary to an extent throughout the EU. The life course must also be re-thought by all other stakeholders. In time, ordinary European citizens, such as Werner Mangold will emerge through the national and European Courts, who will help to clarify the unanswered questions concerning the Employment Directive and age. While it would be wrong to place too great a burden on many such shoulders, their contribution is essential and promises to unite pre- and post-Article 13 eras to exciting effect.

---

[203] Schedule 6 and 7 to the Employment Equality (Age) Regulations 2006.

10

The 'mainstreaming' of sexual orientation into European equality law[1]

BARRY FITZPATRICK

Introduction

This chapter will examine the development of European equality law in the context of the emergence of sexual orientation as an equality law ground. Its focus will be an examination of the provisions of the Framework Directive[2] as they particularly apply to sexual orientation discrimination and the rights of lesbians, gays and bisexuals (LGBs). It is considered necessary, when approaching new equality grounds, to take an integrated but differentiated approach integrated in the sense that many of the legal definitions (and practical implications) of new grounds are common to those of pre-existing grounds,[3] but also differentiated in that each new ground presents issues and controversies which are particular to that ground. The latter perspective is not to endorse a hierarchy of inequality[4] but rather to acknowledge the differences between them.

In this sense, at the level of European equality law, sex equality has been the 'mainstream' focus of attention for over 30 years. The main challenge

---

[1] I am particularly grateful to the Editor and to Mark Bell for comments on an earlier draft of this paper.

[2] Directive 2000/78 establishing a general framework for equal treatment in employment and occupation, referred to in the text as 'the Framework Directive', and, by way of abbreviation, as 'FEED'.

[3] See C. McCrudden, 'Theorising European Equality Law', in C. Costello and E. Barry (eds.), *Equality in Diversity The New Equality Directives* (Irish Centre for European Law, 2003) p. 16, where he says: 'It might be thought, indeed, to be in the nature of courts such as the ECJ, to see such individual pieces of legislation as arising from a common principle of equality, leading to a presumption that the same concept should be interpreted equivalently in different Directives. Is this a desirable development? Should we view emerging European equality law as espousing a common conception of equality?'

[4] See, McCrudden, 'Theorising European Equality Law', p. 17.

of the Race[5] and Framework Directives is partly to integrate the new equality grounds into established practices on recruitment, harassment, etc. But the second challenge is to appreciate that women, racial and religious minorities, the disabled, younger and older people and LGBs all face differing issues and that what has been a sensible approach to established grounds may need rethought and modification to deal with new grounds. However, from a legal perspective, the Race and Framework Directives are based on well-established EC provisions of sex equality law, supported by a rich case law from the European Court of Justice (ECJ) which has significantly strengthened the principle of equal treatment irrespective of sex as a fundamental principle of EC law. This has now been augmented by the ECJ's judgment in *Mangold*,[6] in which the principle of equal treatment irrespective of age has been acknowledged as a fundamental principle of Community law. It is therefore clear that all the equal treatment principles manifested in the two Directives are equally fundamental. Although the Race and Framework Directives reflect broadly a 'common template' for European equality law, subject to some significant 'variations' from ground to ground, there are aspects of sexual orientation which differentiate it, at least to some extent, as an equality ground from other grounds. First, it might be anticipated that most of the attention will be on the 'anti-discrimination' aspects of sexual orientation discrimination, that is issues of combating prejudice through use of direct discrimination and harassment principles, rather than 'equality of opportunity' aspects, that is issues of alleviating disadvantage through use of indirect discrimination and positive action principles. To the extent that there is a 'lifestyle' aspect to sexual orientation discrimination, it is not that sexual orientation is a 'lifestyle choice' but rather that different LGBs express their sexual orientation to differing degrees. Hence, on one end of the 'outness' spectrum, issues will arise over same-sex relationships.[7] For those who are less 'out', there will be issues of privacy. It may also be the case that those LGBs who are more 'out' about their sexuality may be more liable to discrimination than those who are not. On the other hand, many LGBs

---

[5] Directive 2000/43 implementing the principle of equal treatment between persons irrespective of racial or ethnic origin, referred to in the text as 'the Race Directive', and, by way of abbreviation, as 'REOD'.

[6] Case 144/04 *Werner Mangold* v. *Rüdiger Helm*, Judgment 22 November 2005.

[7] It is not possible in this chapter to chart the significant development of same-sex partnership rights in the EU (see M. Bell, *Anti-Discrimination Law and the European Union*, ch. 4, 'Sexual Orientation Discrimination' (Oxford University Press, 2002).

may wish to conceal their sexual orientation or curtail their 'outness' to certain categories, e.g. close personal friends.[8]

An interesting analysis on sexual orientation discrimination is provided by Yoshino,[9] in which he argues that various categories of LGBs try to avoid discrimination by way of three strategies, 'conversion', where LGBs adopt a straight life, including heterosexual relationships, 'passing', where LGBs pass themselves off as straight and 'covering', where LGBs are relatively 'out' about their sexual orientation but in ways which involve assimilation into a predominant straight society. As he states, 'Covering means the underlying identity is neither altered nor hidden, but is downplayed. Covering occurs when a lesbian both is, and says she is, a lesbian, but otherwise makes it easy for others to disattend her orientation.'[10] His basic hypothesis, which he applies also to issues of race and sex (and to a lesser extent, religion) is that 'assimilation can be an *effect* of discrimination as well as an *evasion* of it'. In this sense, Yoshino is demonstrating the tension between social inclusion and respect for diversity. But he is also indicating aspects of discrimination against LGBs, initially on the basis of a failure to 'convert', then on a failure to 'pass' (both still powerful motivations for homophobic discrimination and harassment) and more recently a failure to 'cover', for example from an LGB perspective, asserting sexual orientation through openness and activism or, from a homophobic perspective, 'flaunting' sexual orientation. Therefore, he states: 'As time progresses, I posit that more and more discrimination against gays will take the form of covering demands, rather than taking the historical forms of categorical exclusion or "don't ask, don't tell".'[11] Hence a significant factor in sexual orientation discrimination, which is applicable to other grounds, is that discrimination is rarely on the 'prohibited factor' alone but on a 'prohibited factor plus' basis. It may well be that certain LGBs, in particular those less willing to 'cover', are more prone to discrimination than others.

The emergence of a broad framework of European equality law, starting with the inclusion of Article 13 in the Treaty of Rome, through the Treaty of Amsterdam 1997, is a product of the past ten years. By 1997, Article

---

[8] As the Commission states in its Communication on the original Framework Directive proposal: 'However, such cases are hard to prove and examples of discriminatory practices do not always come to the fore. This seems to be because employment is an area in which people may hide their sexual orientation for fear of discrimination and harassment.' (COM(1999) 566, s. 2).

[9] K. Yoshino, 'Covering', (2001) 111 *Yale L.J.* 769. [10] Ibid., p. 772. [11] Ibid., p. 776.

13 EC provided the platform for the inclusion of race, religion or belief, sexual orientation, disability and age on the agenda. However, various attempts were being made at that time to develop sexual orientation as an equality ground,[12] particularly by way of sex equality litigation in the UK. In a 'twin-track' approach, cases were brought both to the European Court of Justice and the European Court of Human Rights (ECtHR) from the British courts. The case before the ECJ, *Grant* v. *South West Trains Ltd*,[13] focused on the argument that 'equal treatment irrespective of sex', in both Article 141e EC (ex Article 119) and in the sex equality directives, included 'equal treatment irrespective of sexual orientation'. The latter duo of cases, *Lustig-Prean and Beckett* v. *UK*[14] and *Smith and Grady* v. *UK*,[15] sought to exploit rights to privacy and non-discrimination in the European Convention. The ECJ-focused litigation strategy failed while the ECtHR-focused strategy enjoyed considerable success.

Ms Grant made two main arguments, first, that if her partner had been a man, he would have enjoyed free travel and therefore that it was sex discrimination to deprive her partner of the same benefit and, secondly, that 'sex' includes 'sexual orientation'. The Court rejected both arguments. First, it concluded that, since the partner of an employee in a same-sex male couple would also have been deprived of the free travel, there was no discrimination on grounds of sex in Ms Grant's case and, secondly, stated that 'sex' could not be equated with 'sexual orientation'. The latter conclusion was barely consistent with the Court's earlier ruling in the gender reassignment case *P* v. *S and Cornwall County Council*.[16] Here the Court concluded P's dismissal in consequence of her gender reassignment affected her fundamental human rights and that such a dismissal was clearly 'on grounds of her sex', despite the respondents' argument that a female-to-male transsexual would have been treated in the same fashion.

P v. *S* can be seen as an unusually progressive decision for the Court in the mid 1990s when much of the rest of its jurisprudence was consolidating the dramatic advances in sex equality law from the mid-to-late 1980s. In this sense, *Grant* can be seen a cautious judgment, more in keeping with the judicial mood of the times. The Court was also aware that sexual orientation was included as a potential equality ground in Article 13 EC and that negotiations were underway on both the Race and the Framework Directives.[17]

---

[12] For a full discussion of sexual orientation as an EU equality ground, see Bell, *Anti-Discrimination Law*, ch. 4.

[13] Case C-249/96, [1998] ECR I-621.   [14] (2000) 29 EHRR 548.

[15] (2000) 29 EHRR 493.   [16] Case C-13/94, [1996] ECR I-2143.

[17] Para. 48 of the judgment.

On the other hand, the exploitation of the ECHR has had a positive contribution to the 'mainstreaming' of sexual orientation discrimination in EC equality law, first, in establishing significant human rights in relation to sexual orientation discrimination and, secondly, by providing a significant underpinning to the provisions of the Framework Directive, particularly in light of the inclusion of 'sexual orientation' in the non-discrimination provision of the European Charter of Fundamental Rights. *Dudgeon* v. *UK*[18] had established that gay men enjoyed rights to privacy under Article 8 ECHR and, in the landmark judgments in *Lustig-Prean and Beckett* v. *UK*[19] and *Smith and Grady* v. *UK*,[20] the Court concluded that LGBs in the UK military had suffered serious breaches to their rights to privacy both through intrusive investigations into their private lives and through their subsequent dismissal from the armed services. In the slightly later decision in *Salguerio da Silva Mouta* v. *Portugal*,[21] the Court finally accepted the argument put by Dudgeon nearly twenty years before, namely that sexual orientation was an 'other status' ground under Article 14 ECHR (non-discrimination).

'Sexual orientation' as a ground in the Framework Directive

The recognition of 'sexual orientation' as an 'other status' ground in Article 14 ECHR and the application of 'the right to privacy' in Article 8 reflect a significant 'human rights' dimension to sexual orientation discrimination law. It is tempting to take a largely human rights approach to discrimination and equality law generally, particularly in relation to the issue of inclusion of a particular ground in the equality law framework. This is an easier process if the focus of equality law is non-discrimination. For example, the ECJ in *P* v. *S* relied heavily on the abuse of the applicant's human dignity in concluding that the sex equality regime should be extended to transgendered people. In essence, an equality ground is identified as a 'prohibited factor', a ground upon which reliance may not be placed. Decisions in the labour market, in the provision of goods and services and by public authorities should not take the 'prohibited factor' into account. Whether we are considering a black woman being evicted from a bus in 1950s Alabama,[22] an air stewardess arguing for equal

---

[18] (1981) Series A No 45.   [19] (2000) 29 EHRR 548.
[20] (2000) 29 EHRR 493.   [21] (2001) 31 EHRR 47.
[22] The arrest of Rosa Parks on 1 December 1995 in Montgomery, Alabama for refusing to give up her seat to a white man (see her obituary at http://news.bbc.co.uk/1/hi/world/americas/4374288.stm).

treatment with a male air steward[23] or an army officer seeking to protect his or her privacy,[24] the principle of direct discrimination appears to provide an ideal route towards the abandonment of prejudicial and stereotypical thinking towards grounds such as race, sex and sexual orientation. Therefore a focused, individualistic human rights analysis is consistent with a 'prohibited factor', non-discrimination approach towards inclusion of equality grounds.

On this basis, it is possible to assemble a relatively 'long list' of equality grounds. Article 13 contains eight grounds. Article 21 of the Charter on Fundamental Rights sets out seventeen grounds. In 'prohibited factor' terms, the latter 'long list' is defensible in a 'constitutional' document such as the Charter. To pick up on the statutory objectives of British equality agencies, a focus of equality law must be 'the elimination of discrimination'.[25] But coupled with that objective in this context is the 'promotion of equality of opportunity'.[26] The former is a negative objective, the latter a positive one. It involves recognition of economic, social and cultural disadvantage and a determination to tackle it. In this sense, the primary focus of equality law can be perceived to be 'social inclusion'[27] but subject to latitude for 'variation' through respect for diversity.[28] Non-discrimination principles are usually, but not always, symmetric, in that they apply equally to women and men, black and ethnic minorities and whites, LGBs and straight people. There should not be reliance on a prohibited factor whether that person is white or black, male or female, straight or gay or lesbian. 'Promotion of equality' presupposes inequality. While constitutional regimes, and the human rights agenda underpinning them, can focus on non-discrimination, an equality law regime must give at least as much weight, if not more weight, to the promotion of equality of opportunity as to non-discrimination. Hence, in relation to a focus on the promotion of equality, far from disregarding the 'prohibited factor', the equality ground must be actively considered to alleviate the disadvantage which obstructs the achievement of equality. What may be a 'de jure' symmetrical regime for the purposes of non-discrimination becomes a 'de facto' asymmetrical regime, for the purposes of the promotion of equality,

---

[23] Case 43/75 *Defrenne* v. *SABENA* [1976] ECR 455.

[24] *Lustig-Prean and Beckett* v. *UK* (2000) 29 EHRR 548.

[25] See, for example, s. 8(1)(f) of the Equality Act 2006, in relation to the statutory duty of the Commission for Equality and Human Rights.

[26] See, for example, s. 8(1)(c) of the 2006 Act.

[27] H. Collins, 'Discrimination, Equality and Social Inclusion' (2003) 66 *MLR* 66 16.

[28] Section 8(1)(a) and (b) of the Equality Act 2006.

in that the primary, if not exclusive, focus of the regime is the disadvantaged group. Hence, although 'the promotion of equality of opportunity' is a natural development from 'the elimination of discrimination', there is also a tension between the two which can go to the heart of the rationale for an equality regime.

Indirect discrimination may initially be seen as an adjunct to direct discrimination, particularly if the 'apparently neutral' criterion is intentionally a surrogate for the prohibited factor. However, an indirect discrimination analysis requires a more proactive approach. All 'criteria, practices and provisions' have to be examined in order to establish whether a 'particular disadvantage' is being suffered. This is still technically a symmetrical analysis but the 'particular disadvantage' is almost inevitably disadvantage for those in a disadvantaged group. More obviously, 'positive action' presupposes disadvantage for which compensation can be made. At least in the context of disability, the 'reasonable accommodation' of a person's disability involves alleviation of the disadvantage which the disabled person is suffering.

Conflict between 'non-discrimination' and 'promotion of equality' is at its most acute if directly discriminatory measures are taken by way of 'positive action' in order to achieve 'equality' or as the 'justifiable' exercise of a 'genuine occupational qualification'. However, there is a vast range of 'positive inclusionary measures' which can be taken without direct reliance on otherwise 'prohibited factors'. Indeed, they may emerge out of an indirect discrimination analysis. They may even be targeted at the disadvantaged group and hence raise issues of indirect discrimination, or even direct discrimination, claims by the otherwise advantaged group. Nonetheless, a coherent and effective approach towards the alleviation of disadvantage will create significant tension between 'the elimination of discrimination' and 'the promotion of equality of opportunity'.[29]

It is arguable that, if an equality law regime was to be drawn up ab initio, it might be preferable to acknowledge this de facto asymmetry by restricting a longer list to issues immediately concerned with a 'prohibited factor' approach, most obviously, direct discrimination, harassment and genuine occupational requirements (GORs).[30] Issues of indirect discrimination,

---

[29] Compare D. Schiek, 'Broadening the Scope and the Norms of EU Gender Equality Law: Towards a Multidimensional Conception of Equality', (2005) 12 *MJP* 427 and E. Holmes, 'Anti-Discrimination Rights without Equality (2005) *MLR* 175.

[30] To this might be added 'extended' notions of direct discrimination, including 'surrogate' reasons which are inextricably related to the 'prohibited factor' and the intentional use of 'apparently neutral' criteria, which amounts to 'reliance' on the prohibited factor.

reasonable accommodation and positive action could hence be applied in a purely asymmetrical fashion. Of course, given the symmetrical nature of the EC equality law framework, this more rigorous distinction between symmetry and asymmetry is not sustainable. Nonetheless, it is suggested that, in cases of tension between 'the elimination of discrimination' and 'the promotion of equality of opportunity', at least a preference for, if not the pre-eminence of, the latter should be respected.

In this context, the inclusion of sexual orientation in Article 13 is both predictable but also problematic. It is predictable in light of the pre-implementation development of sexual orientation as an equality law ground in some Member States, namely Denmark, Finland, Ireland, Luxembourg, Spain, Sweden and the Netherlands,[31] the significant litigation both before the ECJ and the ECtHR and the close co-operation between EU level NGOs, including the International Lesbian and Gay Association (ILGA), in EU level negotiations on the Race and Framework Directives.[32] In this context, discrimination on grounds of a person's sexual orientation can be seen as 'an abuse of human dignity'. It is also the case that sexual orientation comfortably meets a 'disadvantaged group' analysis in that its inclusion, in a de facto sense, refers almost exclusively to LGBs, as opposed to straight people, as being subject to significant economic and social disadvantage as a result of their sexual orientation.

Nonetheless, there are problematic aspects to its inclusion. A common difficulty with both the Race and Framework Directives is the lack of definition of the equality grounds. Perhaps this is more acute in relation to the lack of definition of 'disability', where much dispute is likely over what amounts to 'disability' and what does not, and 'religion or belief', in relation to which there must be some controversy over the legitimate limits of 'religion or belief'. Even so, it might have been appropriate to make clear that 'sexual orientation' includes 'gay, lesbian, bisexual and straight sexual orientation', as in the British implementing legislation.[33] To the extent that 'sexual orientation' could be seen to include sadomasochism, necrophilia and paedophilia, there are no policy grounds, based on 'abuse of human

---

[31] Bell, *Anti-Discrimination Law*, p. 94.   [32] See Bell, *Anti-Discrimination Law*, ch. 4.

[33] Reg 2(1) of the Employment Equality (Sexual Orientation) Regulations 2003 defines 'sexual orientation' as follows: '(1) In these Regulations, "sexual orientation" means a sexual orientation towards – (a) persons of the same sex; (b) persons of the opposite sex; or (c) persons of the same sex and of the opposite sex'. Section 2(1) of the Employment Equality Act 1998–2004 (IRL) defines 'sexual orientation' as 'homosexual, heterosexual or bisexual orientation'.

dignity', and indeed wider considerations of the accepted criminality of such behaviour, upon which such orientations should be protected.

Despite the greater perceived legitimacy of LGB relationships, there are still significant reservations about homosexuality across European societies.[34] Some of these 'reservations' might be categorised as 'homophobic', most obviously in Eastern Europe.[35] This is not to deny that there is still significant experience of homophobia in Western Europe.[36] The most extreme manifestations may be tackled through hate crime legislation.[37] Clearly the harassment provisions of the Framework Directive are valuable in confronting homophobic behaviour in the workplace. Nonetheless, while there is little public sympathy for those who discriminate on grounds of sex, race or disability, there is clearly still a significant promotional role to be played in changing public attitudes towards LGB relationships. This is particularly difficult in the context of faith-based organisations. While there are potential conflicts between other equality grounds, the incompatibility between some religious beliefs and acceptance of LGB relationships is one of the most acute dilemmas confronting European and national equality law and policy.[38]

---

[34] A significant amount of data is available in K. Waaldijk, 'Combating sexual orientation discrimination in employment: legislation in 15 EU member states', vol 19: a comparative analysis at http://ec.europa.eu/employment_social/fundamental_rights/pdf/aneval/sexorcompan.pdf, in particular s. 19.1, and in the country reports upon which the comparative review is based at http://ec.europa.eu/employment_social/fundamental_rights/public/pubsg_en.htm#Sexual. See now C. Waaldijk and M. Bonini-Baraldi, *Sexual Orientation Discrimination in the European Union: national Laws and the Employment Equality Directive* (TMC Asser Press, 2006). There is also significant data on the ILGA-Europe website at, www.ilga-europe.org/, particularly country reports from Eastern Europe.

[35] For example in Latvia, 'The Siege of Riga' at www.ilga-europe.org/europe/guide/country_by_country/latvia/riga_pride_2006/the_siege_of_riga, in Poland, 'Human Rights Watch: Official Homophobia Threatens Basic Freedoms in Poland' at www.ilga-europe.org/europe/guide/country_by_country/poland/human_rights_watch_official_homophobia_threatens_basic_freedoms_in_poland and in Romania, 'Gay teens assaulted and fined by police in Romania' at www.ilga-europe.org/europe/guide/country_by_country/romania/gay_teens_assaulted_and_fined_by_police_in_romania.

[36] N. Jarman and A. Tennant, *An Acceptable Prejudice? Homophobic Violence and Harassment in Northern Ireland* (Institute for Conflict Research, 2003).

[37] For example, the Public Order (Northern Ireland) Order 1987 (as amended by the Criminal Justice (Northern Ireland) Order (No. 2) 2004) sets out a range of offences concerning incitement to hatred and arousal of fear, to include on grounds of sexual orientation.

[38] See, for example, the debates during the negotiations of the Framework Directive on a specific exception for faith-based organisations (now Art. 4(2) of the Directive) set out by Bell, *Anti-Discrimination Law*, at p. 117 and, more recently, the objections of the Christian Institute, an evangelic Christian organisation in the UK, to the extension of UK

Equality concepts

The Framework Directive sets out a range of equality concepts to tackle the lack of equal treatment on the specified grounds. In one sense, these concepts are a distillation of previous experience of EC sex equality law. However, the production of these Directives under the unanimity rules of Article 13 has resulted in compromises which potentially weaken the previous sex equality legal structure. On a positive note, both the Race and Framework Directives, and now the Equal Treatment Amendment Directive,[39] provide explicit definitions of direct and indirect discrimination, introduce definitions of harassment and reasonable accommodation, the latter only in relation to disability, and provide refined definitions of genuine occupational requirements and positive action. For example, the definitions of direct and indirect discrimination introduce qualifications which were not reflected in the previously understood definitions in the case law of the ECJ. Initially, Article 2.1 of the Framework Directive appears to repeat the original formulation of Article 2 of the Equal Treatment Directive 1976, which states:

> there shall be no discrimination whatsoever on grounds of sex either directly or indirectly by reference in particular to marital or family status.

However, Article 2.2 FEED goes on to set out more specific definitions of direct and indirect discrimination which arguably provide weaker protection than the direct and indirect discrimination concepts developed by the ECJ in its gender equality case law and which will, both on that account and in any event, provide particular challenges in relation to sexual orientation.

The focus of this section will be on direct discrimination and harassment as it is likely that, initially, most of the attention, and any consequent litigation, will concentrate on these principles. The introduction of a new equality ground inevitably involves a 'learning curve' in terms of the implications of the application of equality concepts.[40] Particularly in

---

sexual orientation discrimination law to the provisions of goods, facilities and services at www.christian.org.uk/soregs/sornewsletter_apr06.htm.

[39] Directive 2002/73/EC of the European Parliament and of the Council of 23 September 2002 amending Council Directive 76/207/EEC on the implementation of the principle of equal treatment for men and women as regards access to employment, vocational training and promotion, and working conditions.

[40] Indeed, it is arguable that EU sex equality law is still on a 'learning curve' thirty years after it first came to prominence. See T. Hervey, 'Editorial Thirty Years of EU Sex Equality Law: Looking Backwards, Looking Forwards' (2005) 12 *MJ* 307–325.

relation to sexual orientation, it might be anticipated that, at least in the short-term, these non-discrimination principles will be more significant than 'equality of opportunity' principles such as indirect discrimination and positive action. However, as EC sexual orientation discrimination law develops, these 'equality of opportunity' principles will take on greater significance.

Direct discrimination

Article 2.2.a of the Framework Directive provides:

> direct discrimination shall be taken to occur where one person is treated less favourably than another is, has been or would be treated in a comparable situation, on any of the grounds referred to in Article 1;

A point of divergence is that this definition introduces an explicitly comparative approach to the establishment of direct discrimination, on the model of British equality law. We have sought to establish above what the core definition of 'sexual orientation' does and does not involve. Inextricably tied into this consideration is the question of what 'on grounds of sexual orientation' means.

The case is not so complicated if an employer has directly relied on the worker's sexual orientation, e.g. if the worker 'comes out' as LGB or his/her sexual orientation becomes common knowledge. Given the phraseology, 'on any of the grounds referred to in Article 1', rather than the person's sexual orientation, this must also be the case that direct discrimination is established if the ground upon which the employer's 'less favourable treatment' is based is the worker's actual or perceived sexual orientation, or indeed, on grounds of association with LGBs.[41] It is clear from UK case law that the wider formulation encompasses discrimination by perception or association. For example, in *Zarcynska* v. *Levy*,[42] a barmaid succeeded in her race discrimination claim because she was dismissed for refusing to obey an instruction not to serve black customers. So also in Northern Ireland the Fair Employment Tribunal (FET) had no difficulty in concluding that discrimination against a Protestant because he was married to a Catholic was on grounds of religious belief, albeit the religious belief of the complainant's spouse.[43] Indeed, it would be perverse if three LGBs could bring a sexual orientation discrimination claim as result of being

---

[41] Bell, *op. cit.*, p. 115.   [42] [1978] IRLR 532 (EAT).
[43] *Meek* v. *Fire Authority for Northern Ireland* (FET, 22 July 1992).

expelled from a bar but a straight person who was thrown out, either for being perceived to be LGB or simply associating with LGBs, could not do so.[44]

However, discrimination against a 'practising' LGB moves the consideration into what may be described as the 'prohibited factor plus' scenario, as discussed above in relation to 'covering demands'. One controversy, apparent from the European Commission's first Explanatory Memorandum of the proposed Framework Directive, concerns whether there is any meaningful distinction between 'sexual orientation' and 'sexual behaviour'.[45] Certainly, this distinction, in the context of celibacy, may have some theological resonance but it is not sustainable to have a sexual orientation discrimination law regime which permits discrimination against those LGBs who practise certain sexual acts but does not permit discrimination against LGBs because of the sexual orientation which underpins those acts.

Discrimination is frequently on the basis of the 'core definition' but it can also occur on the basis of criteria which are so closely related to the prohibited factor that they amount to reliance on the prohibited factor itself. For example, if the perpetrator states, 'I did not sack for your religious beliefs, I sacked you because I saw you coming out of a church last Sunday', it is reasonable to conclude that religious observance is so closely allied to 'religious belief' that the action amounts to direct reliance upon it. In British equality law, *James v. Eastleigh Borough Council*[46] is frequently cited as authority for the objective, causation-based, 'but for' test. In that case, a council had restricted access to a leisure centre on the basis of state retiring ages, namely 60 for women and 65 for men. The majority in the House of Lords concluded that 'but for' J's sex, he would have gained admission to the leisure centre. On this basis, it can be concluded that 'but for' the person's religious beliefs, s/he would not have been observing them.

A more interesting, and potentially valuable, approach in the *James* case was set out by Lord Bridge when he stated that the 'state retiring

---

[44] See now the reference to the ECJ, Case C-303/06 *Coleman* (reference from Employment Tribunal, London), on discrimination on grounds of association with a disabled person.

[45] In the Commission's Communication on the proposed Framework Directive COM(1999) 566, it is stated, by way of explanation of the inclusion of 'sexual orientation' in Article 1: 'With regard to sexual orientation, a clear dividing line should be drawn between sexual orientation, which is covered by this proposal, and sexual behaviour, which is not.'

[46] [1990] 2 AC 765. The 'but for' test was initially enunciated a short time previously by Lord Goff in *R v. Birmingham City Council, ex parte EOC* [1989] AC 1155 (HL) and endorsed by the majority in *James*.

age' was a 'convenient shorthand expression'[47] for 'on grounds of sex'. On this basis, the 'prohibited factor plus' issue, on the limits of what is 'on grounds of sexual orientation', can be dealt with on the basis that some factors are so closely related to the 'prohibited factor' that they amount to 'surrogates' for it. Arguably, they are not even 'apparently neutral', within the context of indirect discrimination, because they are inextricably related to the prohibited factor. On this basis, 'religious observance' is a surrogate for 'religious belief' and 'sexual practices' is a surrogate for 'sexual orientation'. Indeed, it is this approach towards 'surrogate factors' which explains two of the Court's most dramatic judgments, P v. S[48] and Dekker.[49] In P v. S, despite a passing reference to a 'comparative' approach by the Court, comparing P with a man who had not undergone gender reassignment, the essence of the decision was that 'gender reassignment' was a surrogate for 'sex'. More obviously, Dekker was a case in which no attempt at comparison was made because only women could be pregnant. Hence, on this basis, the Court accepted that 'pregnancy' was a surrogate for 'sex'.

There are two implications for this inevitable use of a 'surrogate factor' approach to the 'prohibited factor plus' conundrum. First, not only must we establish the 'core definitions' for each of the EC equality law grounds, we must also establish what is the scope for surrogate factors, which amount to acting 'on grounds of' the prohibited factor. Indeed, the definition of indirect discrimination is of some assistance in determining where the line should be drawn between direct and indirect discrimination. If the criterion relied upon is 'apparently neutral', the matter should largely be treated as an indirect discrimination issue. But if the criterion is not apparently neutral, it should be treated as a surrogate factor. Hence, taking action against a person because of his or her sexual practices must surely be on grounds of his or her sexual orientation, unless the perpetrator can show that straight people are treated in the same way in relation to similar practices.

To consider another example, say a college lecturer sees a student leaving an almost exclusively gay club. In a class some days later, the lecturer makes sarcastic remarks about the student which could amount to harassment. Clearly, the lecturer's conduct is 'related to' the student's real or perceived sexual orientation.[50] However, if the lecturer improperly marks down the student's coursework, is the conduct 'on grounds

---

[47] At 764.   [48] Case C-13/94, [1996] ECR I-2143.   [49] [1990] ECR I-3941.
[50] See the definition of 'harassment' in Art. 2.3 FEED, discussed below.

of sexual orientation? Perhaps the fact that the Directive's definition of direct discrimination encompasses perceived sexual orientation and also association with those of a particular sexual orientation, the case can be argued that the lecturer's behaviour is a simpler case of direct discrimination on either basis. Nonetheless, in the same way in which issues of religious practice and religious manifestation are so closely related to 'religion or belief' as to arguably amount to surrogate factors, so also it can be argued that various manifestations of sexual orientation can also amount to surrogate factors.

This is not to deny that the issue of surrogate factors is a controversial one. We have already seen that the attempt, in *Grant*, to make sexual orientation a 'surrogate' for sex was unsuccessful. Certainly this discussion indicates that the addition of new grounds in the regime raises what may be unanticipated controversies. Given the rigorous approach towards GORs, an unanticipated extension of direct discrimination may make unlawful conduct which the legislator may well have not intended to be proscribed.[51] Added to these complications is the appreciation that the equality law regimes are symmetrical and hence that an extension of the direct discrimination concept may give protection in unanticipated circumstances to those in otherwise advantaged groups. The system would be brought into disrepute if, for example, a male employee could argue that the display of a calendar showing naked women was a manifestation of his straight sexual orientation, in the same way that an LGB worker may wish to argue that the wearing of a Rainbow badge was a manifestation of her sexual orientation. This example shows that the de jure symmetry of the equality law system may raise significant difficulties in a context in which the de facto objective of the system is to alleviate the disadvantages suffered by disadvantaged groups.

However, it would be highly regressive to retreat from the *Dekker* jurisprudence because it raises difficult problems in relation to other grounds. In this sense, it would be inappropriate to 'cordon off' sex equality law jurisprudence as it has a resonance for all other equality law grounds. However, as with the 'core definitions' themselves, it will ultimately be the Court of Justice which can authoritatively rule on these matters.

Another dimension to the 'prohibited factor plus' conundrum is the issue of the extent to which intentional indirect discrimination can

---

[51] There may be some room for the application of Art. 2.5 in these circumstances but that Article has its own limitations.

amount to direct reliance on the prohibited factor.[52] Say, for example, an employer introduces a new criterion into the essential criteria for promotion to a senior position. Perhaps, a certain period of experience or performance of certain functions is included. Of course, the criterion applies to all applicants for promotion. It is not a self-evident surrogate for sexual orientation. Nonetheless, it is clear that, although some straight employees cannot satisfy the new criterion, a particular LGB employee cannot satisfy it and indeed it is suspected that the criterion was put in place to prevent the LGB employee succeeding in the promotion exercise.

No doubt, even if indirect discrimination is argued, the employer will not be able to show a 'legitimate aim', in that its intentions were discriminatory. But it may be that the criterion is otherwise justifiable, in that the aim would otherwise be legitimate and the means are, in themselves, 'appropriate and necessary'. Indeed, it might be difficult for the LGB employee to show that s/he has suffered a 'particular disadvantage' compared to other applicants for promotion. Certainly, the revised definition of direct discrimination in the equality directives is not necessarily helpful in resolving this scenario. It is arguable that the LGB worker is being treated in exactly the same manner as comparable others, namely the straight employees who are also applying for promotion. This controversy goes to the heart of what the direct discrimination concept is about. It has been suggested earlier that the essence of direct discrimination is unlawful reliance on a prohibited factor. There can be little doubt, if proved, that the employer has relied upon the worker's sexual orientation in order to produce an 'apparently neutral' criterion which is directed against him or her. Given the insidious nature of the employer's conduct, it would appear that the equality law regime must be able to deal with such behaviour in a rigorous fashion. Hence, a claim of direct discrimination ought to be the appropriate vehicle for bringing the claim. The employer's conduct is clearly 'on grounds of sexual orientation'. It would have to be the case that the 'comparators' would be those who could satisfy the additional criteria. This is an example of a scenario in which a purely 'comparative' approach fails to identify what may be insidious forms of discrimination. It may well be that, particularly in relation to a ground such as sexual orientation that the regime must be vigilant over such

[52] See, for example, the discussion between Michael Rubenstein and Anthony Lester QC (as he then was), M. Rubenstein, 'The Equal Treatment Directive and UK Law', in C. McCrudden (ed.), *Women, Employment and European Equality Law* (Eclipse Publications, 1987), pp. 52–122, at p. 56, and fn 18a.

tactics.[53] Certainly the 'comparative' approach adopted in the revised direct discrimination definition does not contribute to this outcome.

Harassment

A clear advantage of the Race and Framework Directives is the inclusion of a definition of harassment. It has always been possible to construct a harassment case out of a direct discrimination comparison. Indeed, sexual harassment cases work on the presumption that a straight man would not harass a man in the manner in which he harasses a woman. Hence the inclusion of a harassment definition is particularly welcome in relation to sexual orientation, as it might be anticipated that many sexual orientation cases will be on this basis. Indeed, the Code of Practice on Sexual Harassment, issued by the European Commission in 1991,[54] identifies lesbians and gay men as potential victims of harassment and concludes: 'It is undeniable that harassment on grounds of sexual orientation undermines the dignity at work of those affected and it is impossible to regard such harassment as appropriate workplace behaviour.' Article 2.3 FEED provides:

> Harassment shall be deemed to be a form of discrimination within the meaning of paragraph 1, when unwanted conduct related to any of the grounds referred to in Article 1 takes place with the purpose or effect of violating the dignity of a person and of creating an intimidating, hostile, degrading, humiliating or offensive environment. In this context, the concept of harassment may be defined in accordance with the national laws and practice of the Member States.

There are three noteworthy aspects of this definition. First, we must consider the causal link between the conduct in question and each prohibited ground. This has been a significant point of analysis in relation to direct discrimination.[55] However, the causal link in relation to harassment is that the conduct must be 'related to any of the grounds referred to in Article 1', in this case sexual orientation. Whatever the controversy around

---

[53] See T. Tysome, 'Gay academics settle for wage "consolation prize"' *The Times Higher Educational Supplement* 26 May 2006, p. 56, discussing a glass ceiling in UK higher education depriving promotion to LGB academics.

[54] Annex to Commission Recommendation of 27 November 1991 on the protection of the dignity of women and men at work (92/131/EEC): 'Protecting the Dignity of Women and Men at Work A code of practice on measures to combat sexual harassment', Section 1: Introduction.

[55] See earlier discussion of *James* v. *Eastleigh Borough Council*.

'surrogate factors', such as sexual practices and manifestations of sexuality, in relation to direct discrimination, these are clearly 'related to' sexual orientation for the purposes of the definition of harassment. Indeed, given experience of 'disability-related' discrimination in UK law, any causal link between the conduct and sexual orientation will suffice.[56] Hence, in our earlier example, 'unwanted conduct' leading on from a lecturer seeing a student leave a gay nightclub will be 'related to' sexual orientation, whether or not it is 'on grounds of' sexual orientation.

Secondly, the definition precipitates a number of controversies surrounding the perspectives from which the alleged harassment should be judged. Clearly, the conduct must be 'unwanted', which must be judged purely from the perspective of the complainant. In relation to each equality ground, but particularly sexual orientation, discrimination law challenges stereotypes. Therefore conduct may be unwelcome to an LGB person even though this is not fully appreciated by a straight person. In this sense, harassment may be extremely serious at one end of the spectrum but be difficult to distinguish from 'banter' at the other end of the spectrum, between what is lawful or unlawful. If the 'purpose' of the conduct is to harass, as defined, then unlawful behaviour is established. Real difficulties arise where it is the 'effect' of the conduct which is at issue. Is a 'violation of dignity' to be judged purely from the perspective of the complainant? More particularly, from whose perspective should the creation of 'an intimidating, hostile, degrading, humiliating or offensive environment' be judged?

UK law has struck a balance between an objective and subjective approach to 'effect-based' harassment. Regulation 5(2) of the Employment Equality (Sexual Orientation) Regulations 2003 provides:

> Conduct shall be regarded as having the effect specified in paragraph (1)(a) or (b) only if, having regard to all the circumstances, including in particular the perception of B [the complainant], it should reasonably be considered as having that effect.

This formulation is now the subject of contention as some previous UK case law looked at 'unwanted conduct' primarily from the perspective of the complainant.[57] So also the European Commission's Sexual

---

[56] It should be noted that GB and NI implementation of 'harassment' in both directives is 'on grounds of' rather than 'related to' the prohibited grounds.

[57] See, for example, *Reed and Bull Information Systems Ltd* v. *Stedman* [1999] IRLR 299 (EAT).

Harassment Code of Practice,[58] defines sexual harassment from a subjective perspective:

> The essential characteristic of sexual harassment is that it is unwanted by the recipient, that it is for each individual to determine what behaviour is acceptable to them and what they regard as offensive. Sexual attention becomes sexual harassment if it is persisted in once it has been made clear that it is regarded by the recipient as offensive, although one incident of harassment may constitute sexual harassment if sufficiently serious.[59]

Once again, it is crucial to appreciate that discrimination law challenges stereotypes. Hence, the perspective of a member of a disadvantaged and socially excluded group is a vital component in this consideration. Nonetheless, although it is debatable whether there is any policy basis for the outcome, harassment, as with direct discrimination, is symmetrical and could be invoked by a straight or a religiously committed complainant against an LGB colleague or indeed by an LGB worker in relation to strongly held religious beliefs. It may be that a purely subjective approach, which is non-contentious in relation to many issues of gender and race, becomes contentious in relation to some of the wider categories of inequality such as religious belief or sexual orientation. What is a 'violation of dignity' and an 'offensive environment' for one person cannot necessarily be the basis for the serious outcome of a finding of harassment. It is therefore suggested that 'effect-based' harassment cannot be judged purely from the subjective perspective of the complainant and that some objective parameters should be placed around subjective assessments of the alleged harassment.[60]

The third issue which arises in relation to harassment concerns the type of environment which is being dissuaded and which is being encouraged and the interaction of the creation of that environment and a finding of 'violation of dignity'. A preliminary point on this issue is the contrast between the conjunctive approach towards 'violation of dignity' and an 'unacceptable' environment as set out in Article 2.3 FEED and the disjunctive approach adopted in UK law. This is in consequence of the approach in previous UK case law whereby either was considered to be a sufficient basis for a harassment claim.[61] It might be envisaged that a violation of dignity could be a 'one-off' incident, including physical assault, obscene

---

[58] See n. 54 above.   [59] See n. 54, Section 2: Definition.

[60] See reg. 5(2) of the (GB) Sexual Orientation Regulations 2003.

[61] UK case law on harassment is set out in C. Palmer, T. Gill, K. Monaghan, G. Moon, M. Stacey and A. McColgan (eds.), *Discrimination Law Handbook*, (Legal Action Group, 2007), ch. 8.

verbal abuse, etc. The creation of 'an intimidating, hostile, degrading, humiliating or offensive environment' might result from a single act but is more likely to involve a series of events culminating in the 'unacceptable' environment.

Paradoxically, 'violation of dignity' may be a less difficult hurdle for LGBs to satisfy than members of at least some other disadvantaged groups. Public policy now legitimises and encourages the full participation of otherwise excluded or disadvantaged groups from the workplace. Reliance on 'human dignity' as a keynote value in discrimination law is a significant element in understanding and applying direct discrimination and harassment. LGBs can rightly argue that exclusionary tactics or comments which reinforce homophobic stereotypes are a 'violation of dignity'.

Whatever the significance of 'violation of dignity' within the harassment definition, the core issue remains which scenarios will amount to an 'unacceptable' environment. Clearly, it is deeply disturbing to be subjected to an 'intimidating, hostile, degrading [or] humiliating' environment, although the inclusion of an 'offensive' environment, as indicated above, raises wider issues of objectivity and subjectivity. A crucial issue here is the extent to which an 'acceptable' environment should be 'neutral' and/or 'harmonious'. For example, there are some indications in the approach towards religious and political discrimination in Northern Ireland that workplaces should be 'neutral', in that workers should not be aware of the 'community background' of their co-workers.[62] So also, it is argued that workplaces should be 'secular'. However, this 'neutral' approach is difficult to maintain in relation to ethnic diversity. Hence, it may be more appropriate to consider a 'harmonious' environment in which some manifestations of religion, race and ethnic origin or sexual orientation are permissible but not others.[63] More broadly, this distinction between 'neutral' and 'harmonious' environments reflects the issue of striking a balance between social inclusion and 'respect for diversity'.

This is never an easy balance to strike. Indeed, from a legal perspective, permitting certain manifestations, for example, the wearing of a Rainbow badge by an LGB (or LGB-friendly) worker, may be offensive to some workers but its prohibition may be offensive to LGB (and LGB-friendly)

---

[62] In *Brennan* v. *Short Bros plc* (20 September 1995), the FET stated: 'A neutral working environment is one where employees can work without contemplating their own or any other person's religious beliefs or political opinion.'

[63] See, for example, Equality Commission for Northern Ireland, *Fair Employment Code of Practice*, where section 5.2.2 (www.equalityni.org) places a duty on employers to 'promote a good and harmonious working environment and atmosphere in which no worker feels under threat or intimidated because of his or her religious belief or political opinion'.

workers. More general prohibitions on various 'manifestations' may precipitate indirect discrimination claims by those who object to the prohibition. It is suggested that a 'harmonious' environment is a preferable policy objective. The danger of a 'neutral' environment is that members of excluded or disadvantaged groups are effectively expected to adhere to a majoritarian norm. 'Respect for diversity' must involve acceptance that women are not men, members of ethnic minorities are not white and gays and lesbians are not straight. Hence, some manifestations of difference ought to be celebrated, not repressed.

Indirect discrimination

Article 2.2(b) of the Framework Directive provides:

> indirect discrimination shall be taken to occur where an apparently neutral provision, criterion or practice would put persons having a particular religion or belief, a particular disability, a particular age, or a particular sexual orientation at a particular disadvantage compared with other persons unless:
> (i) that provision, criterion or practice is objectively justified by a legitimate aim and the means of achieving that aim are appropriate and necessary.

Of course, indirect discrimination is more directed at structural discrimination than behavioural discrimination. Indeed, given the 'apparently neutral' nature of the policies and practices under scrutiny, ensuring compliance with the indirect discrimination principle requires a form of equality audit in relation to all the relevant equality grounds.

It is significant that this definition, set out in all the EC equality directives, relies on a 'particular disadvantage' approach rather than a 'disproportionate effect' approach prevalent in the ECJ's case law on sex equality law. Although it is permissible to make use of statistics to establish a 'particular disadvantage', this is not essential.[64] Indeed, it is essential that there is an alternative means of identification of 'particular disadvantage' in relation to 'persons having . . . a particular sexual orientation', as there may well be no statistics on LGBs. The issue of monitoring on grounds of sexual orientation is a highly sensitive one. It is arguable that the collection of quantitative data is easier in relation to equality grounds which have a limited number of categories, such as sex or 'community background'

---

[64] Recital 15 of the FEED provides: 'Such rules may provide, in particular, for indirect discrimination to be established by any means including on the basis of statistical evidence.'

in Northern Ireland, or easily ascertainable such as 'age groups'. But it is significantly more difficult in relation to race discrimination where a significant range of racial and ethnic origins must be identified. So also there is a wide range of religious groups and many significantly different disabilities. There is a high degree of unlikelihood that the great majority of LGBs will be prepared to disclose their sexual orientation, even if protected by guarantees of confidentiality and there will be important privacy arguments under Article 8 ECHR and under data protection law. It is important to appreciate that data collection is merely the first stage of an equality audit. The data has to be analysed, 'particular disadvantages' diagnosed and remedial action taken.

Hence the 'particular disadvantage' approach allows for 'expert evidence' to be provided to the judicial process and also for 'judicial notice' to be taken of qualitative data on issues which may place disadvantaged groups 'at a particular disadvantage'. Indeed, equality audits must involve the collection of qualitative data as well as any available quantitative data. Quantitative data only indicates possible issues of discriminatory practices, which require analysis and diagnosis. Qualitative data, for example from LGB staff groups or trade union sections, LGB NGOs or trade unions, workers' representatives or work councils, is just as, if not more, susceptible to analysis and diagnosis. Although Article 13 FEED provides for social dialogue on FEED grounds, including sexual orientation and Article 14 FEED requires dialogue with NGOs, it is surprising that there is not a specific 'information and consultation' duty in relation to the achievement of the principle of equal treatment as there is for issues such as health and safety, collective redundancies, transfers of undertakings and now more generally on information and consultation in the labour market.

It is therefore essential that employers and providers of vocational training initiate systems of qualitative data collection to ensure that they are abiding by the indirect discrimination principle. At this early stage of the 'learning curve' on sexual orientation discrimination, attention will be focused, as stated above, on direct discrimination and harassment. But it will also be essential to consider indirect sexual orientation discrimination. For example, a requirement that the suitability of an applicant's 'partner' is considered as part of an appointment for or promotion to a position which involves 'social skills on behalf of the organisation' may well place LGBs 'at a particular disadvantage'. Requirements that a public house or guest house be managed by a 'married couple' (or even by civilly registered partners) could also be indirectly discriminatory.

Of course, any such potentially discriminatory policies are subject to objective justification. It is significant that the objective justification test in Article 2.2(b) is weaker than that articulated by the ECJ in at least some sex equality cases. The bedrock test in *Bilka-Kaufhaus*[65] was on the basis of a 'real need' on the part of the employer for a policy which had a 'disproportionate effect' on women. Admittedly, the Court itself diluted the *Bilka* test in welfare equality cases[66] and even in employment cases involving statutory schemes.[67] It may appear that this definition includes 'appropriate and necessary means' but it is important to the application of the test that the aim need only be 'legitimate'. For example, all the above named policies may well reflect 'legitimate' aims but not 'necessary' ones. There is a danger that a 'hierarchy of inequalities' might develop in that aims may be considered to be 'legitimate' in relation to policies which place LGBs at a particular disadvantage compared to other disadvantaged groups.

Nonetheless, the 'appropriate and necessary means' test remains a powerful one. It would be difficult to justify any of the above policies on this basis. The effect of each one could be mitigated or an alternative policy could be devised to achieve the aims of the policies. It seems clear that the Community legislator was wary of having a fully effective *Bilka* test of objective justification across the wider EC equality agenda. Although it may be some time before issues of indirect discrimination take on prominence in relation to sexual orientation, equality audits should be conducted across all the equality grounds as policies which may raise no issues in relation to other grounds may have pertinence for LGBs.

'Mainstreaming LGB equality'

A major focus of the equality debate for the past ten years has been the issue of complementing the 'rights based approach' to equality with a policy orientated approach, primarily in the public sector, whereby attempts are made to bring equality issues to the heart of the policy-making process.[68] One approach, exemplified by the statutory duty on public authorities in

---

[65] Case 170/84 *Bilka-Kaufhaus GmbH* v. *Weber Von Hartz* [1986] ECR 1607.

[66] Case C-444/93 *Megner & Scheffel* [1995] ECR I-4741.

[67] Case C-167/97 *R* v. *Secretary of State for Employment, ex parte Seymour-Smith* [1999] ECR I-623.

[68] For a recent commentary, see J. Shaw, 'Mainstreaming Equality and Diversity in EU Law and Policy', in J. Holder and C. O'Cinneide (eds.), *Current Legal Problems 2005* (Oxford University Press, 2006), pp. 255–312.

Northern Ireland,[69] is to develop an equality scheme on the basis of which all policies of the authority are 'screened' for possible adverse impact on any of the designated grounds and are then subjected to 'equality impact assessment' to establish if an adverse impact is being suffered in relation to existing policies or would be suffered by relation to proposed policies.

On the European level, the debate about a legal underpinning for mainstreaming has been somewhat curtailed by the stalling of the ratification of the European Constitution.[70] Art III-118 of the Draft Constitution provided 'In defining and implementing the policies and activities referred to in this Part, the Union shall aim to combat discrimination based on sex, racial or ethnic origin, religion or belief, disability, age or sexual orientation.' A more powerful provision is made for gender mainstreaming in Art III-116 which provided 'In all the activities referred to in this Part, the Union shall aim to eliminate inequalities, and to promote equality, between women and men.' These provisions set up the intriguing prospect of the mainstreaming of sexual orientation equality into European Union policy-making.

However, an element of gender mainstreaming now applies in the Amended Equal Treatment Directive, Article 1a of which states: 'Member States shall actively take into account the objective of equality between men and women when formulating and implementing laws, regulations, administrative provisions, policies and activities in the areas referred to in paragraph 1.' It is even arguable, as indicated above, that Articles 13 FEED (social dialogue) and 14 FEED (dialogue with NGOs) provide for an embryonic consultative model within which the mainstreaming of equality across the equality grounds could be conducted. Certainly national trade unions and LGB NGOs should seek to exploit Articles 13 and 14 to establish some form of mainstreaming agenda for sexual orientation equality.

The second point to make about the evolution of European-level processes of mainstreaming is that, to the extent upon which they rely on an equality impact assessment model, those subject to the directives, whether public or private, ought to be conducting equality audits on their policies in order to protect themselves from indirect discrimination cases. The outcome of that diagnostic process ought to be a conclusion upon 'adverse impact' or 'particular disadvantage' and consideration of how

[69] Section 75 of the Northern Ireland Act 1998 places a duty on designated public authorities carrying on functions in Northern Ireland to pay 'due regard' to the need to promote equality of opportunity on nine grounds, including sexual orientation.
[70] See M. Bell, 'Equality and the European Union Constitution', (2004) 33 *ILJ* 242.

the policies should be altered to mitigate the discriminatory effects of the policy or replaced by an alternative policy. It is perhaps a reflection on the opacity, at least hitherto, of the indirect discrimination principle, and its practical outworkings, that it is felt necessary to develop specific duties to achieve these outcomes. A final thought on mainstreaming is that these innovative, and potentially beneficial, processes should be seen, as referred to above, as being complementary to a 'rights based' approach. There is a danger that 'mainstreaming' might be perceived in some quarters as a replacement for a 'rights based' approach. As will be discussed below, access to justice, particularly by LGBs, is a complicated business but the pursuit of LGB rights and sexual orientation mainstreaming must complement each other in order that genuine equality of opportunity for LGBs can be successfully pursued.

Access to justice

It is tempting to relegate the 'Remedies and Enforcement' chapter of the Framework and other equality Directives to a footnote in consideration of them. 'Enforcement' might be seen as a technical matter for practising lawyers and of no real concern to a wider analysis of equality law. However, whatever the promotional value of equality legislation, unless it can be adequately, let alone effectively, enforced, it will have little practical impact. Indeed, it is better to have imperfect laws which are effectively enforced than perfect laws which are ineffectively enforced.

There has been little research into 'access to justice' issues on equality rights.[71] One example is the 'Utilisation of Sex Equality Litigation' project co-ordinated by Blom *et al.* in the mid-1990s.[72] This was an investigation into the utilisation of sex equality litigation across the then twelve Member State of the European Union. That report did consider aspects of the judicial process in each Member States and some of its conclusions are particularly pertinent to this paper. For example, the research concluded that more informal dispute resolution procedures such as the Dutch Equal Treatment Commission and the Irish system of equality

---

[71] See also, C. Tobler's report for the European Network of Legal Experts in the non-discrimination field, 'Remedies and Sanctions in EC non-discrimination law' (European Commission, 2005).

[72] J. Blom, B. Fitzpatrick, J. Gregory, R. Knegt and U. O'Hare *The Utilisation of Sex Equality Litigation in the Member States of the European Community* V/782/96-EN (Report to Equal Opportunities Unit of DG V of the Commission of the European Communities, 1996) p. 55.

officers, which predates the present Equality Tribunal, appeared to provide a more accessible quasi-judicial forum than traditional models. The
report also recommended systems of standing for equality agencies, trade
unions and NGOs to bring cases on behalf of or instead of individuals,
now reflected in Article 8 FEED and the creation of specialised agencies
to promote equality and assist individual litigants.

It is important to appreciate the differences between the practical realities of protecting rights across different equality grounds. Nonetheless,
the conclusion of the Utilisation Report was that, even twenty years into
the EU sex equality regime, sex equality litigation was absolutely low in
most Member States and relatively low, compared to other employment
law litigation, even in those Member States in which some sex equality
litigation was occurring.

Issues of access to rights for LGBs will, in many situations, be even
more acute than those confronting women seeking to protect their rights.
In many ways, the 'Enforcement' provisions of the Framework Directive,
as with other provisions of the Directives, reflect in legislative form the
jurisprudence of the Court of Justice on effective judicial process. However they also more widely reflect an awareness that, without effective
enforcement, the implementation of the Directives within the national
legal systems will not be genuinely effective at all.

The first issue obviously concerns access to justice for individual LGBs.
Article 9.1 FEED provides: 'Member States shall ensure that judicial and/or
administrative procedures, including where they deem it appropriate conciliation procedures, for the enforcement of obligations under this Directive are available to all persons who consider themselves wronged by failure
to apply the principle of equal treatment to them, even after the relationship in which the discrimination is alleged to have occurred has ended.'
Article 9.1 is a 'modernised' version of Article 6 ETD, upon which highly
significant ECJ case law is based.

In Case 222/84 *Johnston* v. *The Chief Constable of the Royal Ulster Constabulary*,[73] the Court effectively overturned a ministerial certificate pur-
porting, on grounds of national security, to prevent an Industrial Tribunal
in Northern Ireland from hearing a sex discrimination case. In a decisive
judgment, the Court concluded that Article 6 ETD articulated a wider
general principle of EC law, that of 'effective judicial protection', inspired
by Articles 6 (right to a fair trial) and 13 (effective remedies) ECHR. Given
the fundamental nature of the 'effective judicial protection' principle, it

---

[73] [1986] ECR I-1651.

must follow that it applies also to Article 9.1 FEED. One issue of particular pertinence for LGBs is the possibility of anonymity as an applicant
to courts and tribunals. Even those LGBs who are 'out' about their sexual
orientation may only be so in certain aspects of their lives, e.g. at work
but not to their families. Very many LGBs prefer to keep their sexual
orientation private either as a matter of choice or to protect themselves
from homophobia. In some Member States, for example Germany and the
Netherlands, anonymity in all legal proceedings is the norm but in others,
such as the UK and Ireland, the identification of parties to proceedings is
the norm in all but exceptional circumstances. Many LGBs will not contemplate protection of their rights without some guarantee of anonymity
within the judicial process. It is strongly arguable that the 'principle of
effective judicial protection' which underpins Article 9.1 requires sym-
pathetic consideration of requests for anonymity by LGB applicants who
invoke their rights under Article 9.1.

Even so, very many LGBs will be reluctant to litigate. Here Article 9.2
takes on potential significance. It provides: 'Member States shall ensure
that associations, organisations or other legal entities which have, in accordance with the criteria laid down by their national law, a legitimate interest
in ensuring that the provisions of this Directive are complied with, may
engage, either on behalf or in support of the complainant, with his or her
approval, in any judicial and/or administrative procedure provided for
the enforcement of obligations under this Directive.' Standing to bring
cases by associations and equality agencies was a key recommendation
of the Utilisation Report. This formulation begins to open up the wider
issue of the extent to which a 'public interest litigation' model should be
developed to enforce equality law, as it has been in environmental law
and consumer law. One analysis of Article 9.2 is that an LGB NGO would
be engaged 'in support of' a named complainant if the complainant was
bringing the case and the NGO was providing legal assistance. The NGO
would be engaged 'on behalf of' the complainant if it was bringing the
case but with the complainant's consent. The crucial ambiguity in Article
9.2 is the use of the word 'either'. Does this mean that the NGO should
be able to do either or does it mean that the Member State may allow for
either?

Unfortunately for access to justice objectives, the Preamble to the Directive is unhelpful. Recital 29 states: 'To provide a more effective level of
protection, associations or legal entities should also be empowered to
engage, *as the Member States so determine* [emphasis added], either on
behalf or in support of any victim, in proceedings, without prejudice

to national rules of procedure concerning representation and defence before the courts.' Once upon a time, preambles were purely explanatory. It is increasingly prevalent, and arguably inappropriate, for the Community legislator to include restrictive provisions in preambles which have a significant detrimental effect on the substantive provisions. Hence, the Court's choice of interpretation of what is meant by 'either' in Article 9.2 may be influenced by Recital 29. On the other hand, the principle of 'effective judicial protection' also applies to Article 9.2 and arguments can certainly be made that 'either' must be interpreted in the context of that fundamental principle also.

In any event, it is arguable that Article 9.2 should have gone further in that genuine public interest litigation ought not necessarily require named complainants at all. There are frequently issues of structural discrimination, particularly indirect discrimination in employers' policies etc., in which a named complainant is merely a necessary initiator of litigation in practice brought, as part of a litigation strategy, by a trade union, NGO or equality agency. Particularly where a potential complainant is LGB, but also in a wide range of scenarios across the equality grounds, it is unreasonable to expect a highly vulnerable member of the workforce or of society more generally to bring a case in their own name when the judicial process ought to provide a mechanism whereby equality agencies, trade unions and NGOs can bring cases in their own name. At this stage in the 'learning curve' of European sexual orientation discrimination law, most of the litigation will be issues such as direct discrimination and harassment, in which the personal testimony of the aggrieved LGB person will be central. Even in some of those cases, it would ease the personal pressures on an individual if an agency, trade union or NGO could bring the case in his or her name. Further up the 'learning curve', cases of structural discrimination will emerge and the need to have an effective system of access to justice for LGB NGOs, etc. will become more apparent.

One extra dimension to the Race Directive, unfortunately absent from the Framework Directive, is the provision for the establishment of specialised bodies. Article 13 REOD provides:

1. Member States shall designate a body or bodies for the promotion of equal treatment of all persons without discrimination on the grounds of racial or ethnic origin. These bodies may form part of agencies charged at national level with the defence of human rights or the safeguard of individuals' rights.

2. Member States shall ensure that the competences of these bodies include:

– without prejudice to the right of victims and of associations, organisations or other legal entities referred to in Article 7(2), providing independent assistance to victims of discrimination in pursuing their complaints
about discrimination,
– conducting independent surveys concerning discrimination,
– publishing independent reports and making recommendations on any
issue relating to such discrimination.

It is certainly true that many Member States, required to establish a specialised race body,[74] are either setting up specialised bodies across the
range of Article 13 grounds or extending the scope of pre-existing agencies. Given the range of issues which are specific to sexual orientation
discrimination, the vulnerability of many LGBs and the strength of homophobic attitudes, it is certainly to be hoped that as many Member States
as possible do extend the remit of their race and gender equality bodies
to include responsibility for sexual orientation discrimination.

The final significant element of enforcement is the question of effective
remedies. Article 17 FEED provides: 'Member States shall lay down the
rules on sanctions applicable to infringements of the national provisions
adopted pursuant to this Directive and shall take all measures necessary to
ensure that they are applied. The sanctions, which may comprise the payment of compensation to the victim, must be effective, proportionate and
dissuasive.' Once again, Article 17 is grounded in the case law of the Court,
most obviously Case 14/83 *von Colson* v. *Land Nordrhein-Westfalen*,[75] in
which the Court required Member States to have an effective system of
compensation for breaches of the equal treatment principle and Case C-
271/91 *Marshall (No. 2)*,[76] in which a maximum cap on compensation in
UK sex equality cases was held to be contrary to Article 6 ETD. While not
particular to issues of sexual orientation discrimination, the implications
of Article 17 are wide-ranging. For example, homophobic harassment
may inflict very significant non-pecuniary loss of an LGB victim. More
generally, it must be questioned whether a system based purely on compensation can ever be 'effective, proportionate and dissuasive' in situations in which it is a change in policies and practices which is required,
particularly where indirect discrimination is established.[77] Hence, it is
necessary to have some innovative thinking on more proactive remedies,

---

[74] And now a specialised gender body under Art. 11.1 of the Gender Goods and Services
Directive 2004.
[75] [1984] ECR 1891.   [76] [1993] ECR 893.
[77] Tobler refers on p. 42 to national laws in some Member States containing some interesting
elements 'relating in particular to innovative non-pecuniary remedies, the powers of the

such as court and tribunal orders on changes to policies and practices and the initiation of equality audits on the part of respondents found to have breached the equal treatment principle.

Conclusion

As stated in the introduction, it is necessary, when approaching new equality grounds, to take an integrated but differentiated approach, integrated in the sense that many of the practical implications of new grounds are common to those of pre-existing grounds, but also differentiated in that each new ground presents issues and controversies which are particular to that ground. Many of the issues raised in this paper are common to those which can be discussed in relation to sex equality, race equality, age equality, etc. However, there are particular issues surrounding the privacy and vulnerability of LGBs which provide particular challenges to the European and national legal systems. Of course, directives set down minimum standards but this has not deterred the Court of Justice in its sex equality case law from developing powerful concepts of equality and also effective mechanisms to encourage the enforcement of sex equality law. It is evident from the Court's judgment in *Mangold* that it intends to apply its jurisprudence on the fundamental nature of the equal treatment principle to all the Race and Framework Directive grounds.

Hence there is ample opportunity for those supporting and assisting LGBs in equality law litigation, and more generally in employment and training, to exploit the potential of the Framework Directive and the more general system of EC law principles in pursuing sexual orientation discrimination rights across the EU, thereby developing the process of 'mainstreaming' sexual orientation into the EU equality law agenda.

specialised administrative non-discrimination body, the range of ancillary administrative remedies, the use of punitive damages and the withdrawal of and exclusion from state benefits, in particular in the context of public procurement'. She concludes: 'However, in the case of most Member States greater efforts are needed in order to fully meet the requirements under EC law to impose a personal remedy of a judicial nature, and a remedy that is truly effective, proportionate and dissuasive.'

11

Conclusion

HELEN MEENAN[*]

Despite the immense and historic gains since the Treaty of Amsterdam, European equality law has been beset by the rhetoric and reality of a hierarchy of protected grounds that predates the incorporation of Article 13 into the EC Treaty. The equality hierarchy has been reinforced by the three Directives adopted under Article 13 EC.[1] However, the language of hierarchy conceals a number of underlying tensions. On the one hand there is the horizontal versus ground specific approach to non-discrimination and equality. On the other hand there is a combination of these two approaches, the idea that a common core of provisions should exist for all covered grounds with differentiation to adapt to the peculiarities of each ground. Another problem with the equality hierarchy is that it does not aid understanding of the differences between the grounds. This is so inter alia because no clear rationale has been given for the greater material and protective scope for sex and race. This volume has attempted to place the spotlight on the individual grounds against key contexts to see to what extent a greater understanding of the Article 13 Directives and their anti-discrimination grounds can be achieved. It has also attempted to move away from the equality hierarchy as the pre-eminent means of understanding the current state of equality law in the EU. Nonetheless some observations and conclusions on this paradigm are necessary to this process.

Thus, the Article 13 Directives reveal a hierarchy in two respects, in the material scope of the anti-discrimination grounds and in the level of protection they enjoy. The former concerns issues such as differentiated coverage in goods and services for race and gender and exemptions and justifications in respect of various grounds. The latter concerns issues

[*] I am grateful to Gerard Quinn for his very helpful comments.
[1] So argued by M. Bell, *Anti-Discrimination Law and the European Union* (Oxford University Press, 2002), p. 211.

such as the requirement of bodies for the promotion of equal treatment for some grounds. The pressing context in which the Race Directive was adopted justified racial and ethnic origin being the *first* ground to be protected. But there is no obvious reason why sex and race should be favoured above the other grounds contained in Article 13 in respect of either material scope or level of protection indefinitely. The fact that the requirement of an equality body to promote race or ethnic origin has proven so successful can only support this argument further.[2] Surely other victims of discrimination would also fear victimisation and be put off by the costs of litigation.[3]

There is also the perception of hierarchy to be addressed. Mark Bell's chapter is built on a critical assessment of all EU anti-racism strategies which reveals that softer law strategies in this field have been very slow moving and sometimes poorly developed. Thus an understanding of approaches that complement a legislative rights based approach is crucial to a more complete picture of protection. The existence of complementary or softer law approaches for different grounds reveals a different hierarchy altogether where disability ranks quite highly.

This volume reveals that a further tension exists between combating discrimination and promoting equality. Ann Numhauser-Henning sees these aims embodied differently in respect of the various Article 13 grounds. Arguably both aims are very highly developed in relation to gender in the EU which she argues as having made the shift to substantive equality. The law on sexual orientation by contrast is fundamentally different. While this volume makes a strong case for a promotional role to change public attitudes to lesbians, gays and bisexuals (LGBs) across the enlarged EU, this need is not reflected in current EU law and policy.

Equalising the hierarchy

If, as Barry Fitzpatrick maintains, the ECJ's decision in *Mangold* means all equal treatment principles manifested in the Race and Employment

---

[2] Commission 'Communication on the application of Directive 2000/43/EC', COM(2006) 643 final, p. 4. In February 2007, The European Commission commited itself to proposing new measures to prevent and combat discrimination outside the labour market for the other article 13 grounds, *Annual Policy Strategy for 2008*, COM (2007) 65 final. On 5 July 2007 it launched a public consultation as part of this process. The outcome of these initiatives cannot be predicted with any certainty at this stage.

[3] Barriers to litigation have been documented by a number of commentators including Bell, *Anti-Discrimination Law*, p. 49.

Directives are equally fundamental, this helps to give us ways of approaching the Article 13 grounds. Why should gender mainstreaming be present and so much more important than mainstreaming for the new equality grounds? Admittedly, the adoption of the EU's Constitutional Treaty would have gone a long way to making up the distance on this particular issue. The implied *equal status* of all the grounds thus erodes the foundations on which the hierarchy was constructed. So too will an approach based on multiple discrimination or inter-sectionality of the grounds. The equality hierarchy weakens the EU's ability to deal with multiple discrimination.[4] Yet even if all grounds are protected equally some more effective approach will be required to deal with multiple discrimination so that the combined, overlapping, cumulative or intersecting aspects of the discrimination are not merely dealt with separately. A multiple discrimination approach would sensitise us to the 'minority within the minority'[5] which may raise unique experiences of discrimination and unique access to justice issues. Looking at the impact of age and gender (if not also disability and gender)[6] on women alerts us to the complexities of the discrimination they face based on the interaction of these two grounds. Thus any perception that age discrimination law is the protectorate largely of middle-aged men is thus hugely damaging to an understanding of this field of law.

A third blow to the equality hierarchy may yet be inspired by the traditional methods of generating general principles in EC law, for instance, from the national laws of the Member States a number of which provide greater protection than the Article 13 Directives. McCrudden and Kountouros anticipate that 'increasingly, however, we can expect that domestic and EU legislation on discrimination will become less and less different, with each influencing the other'. It is important in light of *Mangold* to consider also the inspiration provided by conventions and international agreements which all Member States have signed. Do any of these conventions prohibit discrimination on the grounds of religion or belief, disability, age or sexual orientation in fields outside employment? The UN Convention on the Rights of Persons with Disabilities 2006, for one, covers a broad range of fields and services.[7] Given the EU's participation

---

[4] Bell, *Anti-Discrimination Law*, pp. 212–13.

[5] Timo Makkonen in Chapter 1 of this volume.

[6] Article 6 of the UN Convention on Persons with Disabilities 2006 deals with gender and disability.

[7] Note also the detailed extent to which it deals with children and women with disabilities in order to reach multiple discrimination.

in the drafting of this instrument, it is assumed that it will sign the Convention in due course.[8] So too will EU Member States. *Mangold* is a timely reminder that the Article 13 Directives operate in an environment rich in ECJ jurisprudence. Thus, these Directives may help to stimulate the ECJ in a field within which it has alternated between periods of confidence and reticence, notwithstanding the Court's judgment in *Chacon Navas*.

What the Directives have achieved

The fundamental and laudable achievement of the Directives has been the establishment of a common framework of important provisions across all grounds listed in Article 13, many of which enjoyed uneven protection, if any, in the Member States before the implementation of these instruments. The Directives then deviate beyond that common framework in both material and protective scope for different grounds. In constructing this framework the lawmakers adopted common definitions of key concepts such as direct and indirect discrimination, which build upon but diverge a little from those developed by the ECJ in relation to sex equality. Within this regime, indirect discrimination is also inspired by the ECJ's case law on the free movement of persons. These altered definitions have in turn inspired the amended Equal Treatment Directive, a non-Article 13 instrument, so that we now have a harmonised body of key concepts in European anti-discrimination law.

Some authors in this volume have questioned this development as weakening the definitions of direct and indirect discrimination as developed by the ECJ in relation to sex and whether this is a good thing for sex equality. By contrast the nature of the ground of sexual orientation has meant that it stands to gain a good deal from the redefinition of indirect discrimination. This is because the 'particular disadvantage' element permits but does not require statistical proof, which for reasons of privacy are less likely to be available for LGBs. So too is the inclusion of the definition of harassment particularly welcome for sexual orientation. One reason put forward for the threat of erosion of key concepts posed by their harmonisation is the now vast range of possibilities for objective

---

[8] The European Commission's presence throughout the negotiations and its role as a partner in the final session suggest that it might sign or ratify on behalf of the Institutions. The legal basis would be Art. 13 EC; if there are no reservations to Art. 32.1(a), the Commission's development aid budget would be covered by mainstreaming. Moreover, Article 4.1.(c) obliges States Parties 'to take into account the protection and promotion of the human rights of persons with disabilities in all policies and programmes'.

justification. If the traditional view is that direct discrimination can never be justified,[9] these Directives mark a significant point of departure for direct discrimination.[10]

Indirect discrimination has also been affected by these developments. In addition to a general possibility for objective justification, employers are obliged to provide reasonable accommodation for disabled persons to eliminate disadvantages caused by a given provision, criterion or practice. The concept of reasonable accommodation has found favour with some authors in this volume and elsewhere, as a concept that ought to be applied to age if not also to other grounds.[11] The highly individualised approach of reasonable accommodation as opposed to the more general approach of positive action would have particular advantages for age, as the ageing process is very highly individualised even among workers of the same age.[12] Gwyneth Pitt discusses the duty reasonably to accommodate the religious needs of employees in the US and in Canadian law and suggests that time off for religious observance is likely to arise as an indirect discrimination issue under the Employment Directive. However, some co-authors touch on the defence of 'disproportionate burden' in relation to the duty reasonably to accommodate an employee's disability. They consider it likely that economic and other costs will be taken into account in assessing whether the burden is disproportionate[13] and it would seem probable that a similar if not identical defence would accompany any extension of reasonable accommodation to other grounds.[14] But while there are many instances in which age and disability may overlap, a loss of capacity deriving from the ageing process may carry less weight if a firm's budget will only stretch to accommodating either disabled or ageing employees.

The redefined concept of indirect discrimination is generally viewed in a positive light for its capacity as a proactive measure. It is especially

---

[9] Ann Numhauser-Henning in Chapter 5 of this volume.

[10] Note Art. 6 of Employment Directive and Art. 4(5) of Directive 2004/113/EC. While not adopted under Art. 13 note also the possibility to justify direct discrimination under the Part-time and Fixed-term Work Directives.

[11] Interestingly, Flemish law requires reasonable accommodation on all grounds.

[12] French law allows family members to benefit from reasonable accommodation on the disability ground, providing a precedent for extending this obligation at national level. Note Gerard Quinn's discussion of reasonable accommodation in Chapter 8 of this volume.

[13] Article 5 and Recital 21 of the Employment Directive.

[14] Note also the final sentence of Art. 5 of the Employment Directive: 'This burden shall not be disproportionate when it is sufficiently remedied by measures existing within the framework of the disability policy of the Member State concerned.' Thus due account would have to be taken of relevant state aid measures, see Gerard Quinn, Chapter 8.

important for disability as it is the form which impacts most on disabled persons. However, the possibility of 'intentional indirect discrimination' has been raised in relation to both sexual orientation and disability. So too have doubts about the ability of either indirect discrimination or direct discrimination to deal with this situation. From the foregoing, three conclusions may be advanced, the adoption of modern EU anti-discrimination law may *depend* more than ever on the provision of objective justification for different treatment. Perhaps this may be explained by the spread of anti-discrimination law into new fields and new grounds, without wishing to disturb too many established customs and practices.[15] Moreover, the ECJ can expect to spend a good deal of its time with the issue of justification in all its guises. Finally, the nature of each ground and the particular issues facing it may mean that the anti-discrimination grounds have varying levels of attachment to the different key concepts of discrimination law at least at this early stage.

The issue of definition

One of the key issues to emerge from this volume is the absence of any definition in the Directives for the Article 13 grounds and the consensus that a definition may have been helpful to at least some of the grounds.[16] The lack of a definition is particularly acute for 'religion or belief', for several reasons. The challenges of disentangling discrimination based variously on grounds of race, religion, ethnicity and nationality have received attention in legal literature. Religion is capable of a number of meanings. Gwyneth Pitt concludes that it would be useful to expand race and ethnicity under the Race Directive to include 'religion as identity'. She also warns that it will be difficult to draw the boundaries of protected belief. Overall the ground of religion or belief appears to raise a considerable number of probable questions of interpretation.

It is very telling that the ECJ's first case on the ground of disability concerned the meaning of disability under the Employment Directive. The ruling in *Chacon Navas* includes what amounts to a brief definition of the concept of disability, which does not include 'sickness' under the Directive. The Court acknowledged that the Directive does not contain a definition of disability and does not refer to the laws of the Member States

---

[15] Quotas for disabled employees are a case in point but they may become questionable in time.
[16] Disability, race, religion and sexual orientation in particular.

for a definition.[17] The Court declined to consider that the general principle of non-discrimination should allow for the extension of an existing ground or the addition of a new ground by analogy.[18] From the point of view of the other grounds two aspects of this ruling may give cause for concern. An unduly narrow interpretation of an anti-discrimination ground limits the protectorate, may well have a greater impact on sub-groups and may fail to respond to pressing contexts.

This ruling jars with *Mangold*. It would have built on the significance of *Mangold* to have explored the reason why the general principle of non-discrimination is not to be of assistance here. All stakeholders need a rationale for these decisions otherwise the field risks becoming mired in confusion or subject to the application of new and distracting paradigms.[19] Apparently, cutting off the route of general principles as a means of adding new grounds of anti-discrimination is unpredictable. As a point of principle it is arguably more worrying than the limited meaning of disability which may evolve and influence the Court in time due to definitions of disability at national and international levels. But unlike *Mangold* a ground specifically named in Article 13 was not at issue in *Chacon Navas*. It would be a pity if *Chacon Navas* were to remain the final word (even for a time) on the issue of definition, or on the space for general principles.[20] McCrudden and Kountouros, writing[21] on the Court's declaration of the principle of non-discrimination on grounds of age, opine:

> This appears to create the possibility of the evolution of a body of EU non-discrimination law through direct application of the general principle of non-discrimination, if the ECJ is prepared to continue in the direction implied by [*Mangold*].

Despite the lack of a definition of age in the Employment Directive it seems clear that chronological age was the meaning of age that was intended by the Community legislature. This is due to the examples of potentially permissible differences in treatment contained in Article 6, especially references to minimum conditions of age and maximum recruitment ages. However, unless mandatory retirement ages start to

---

[17] *Chacon Navas*, Case C-13/05 [2006] ECR 1–6467, at paragraphs 39–42.
[18] Ibid., paragraphs 56–57.
[19] The equality hierarchy paradigm may serve as a warning here.
[20] The UN Treaty on the Rights of Persons with Disabilities now contains a definition of disability. However, the EU Presidency had acted in the negotiations as though no definition was needed for this non-discrimination treaty. Gerard Quinn, Chapter 8 discusses why the approach of the Canadian Supreme Court on definition is to be preferred.
[21] In Chapter 3 of this volume.

reflect the massive gains in human longevity whereby thirty years will have been added to the life span between 1950 and 2050, it will be difficult to adjust maximum recruitment ages, in particular. Allowing Member States to entrench age limits and apply them without distinction to the workforce arguably means that the Directive does not respond to the considerable physiological and functional heterogeneity of workers of all ages, especially older workers. Nor does it respond to the pressing context of demographic ageing, which affects the entire EU and will require many people to work for longer to help finance their extra years. It is interesting to note that the Employment Directive does not contain any reference to demographic change, which is acknowledged in some European policy documents as one of three main challenges now facing the EU.[22]

If the notion of reasonable accommodation for age is taken to include part-time work, this appears to produce an extraordinary range of added benefits for older workers in particular. However, care must be taken to avoid inter-generational conflict and to avoid measures in favour of older workers inadvertently triggering indirect age discrimination against other groups. It seems clear though that some such concessions for older workers are necessary to meet EU, national and individual challenges to population ageing. The balancing exercise requires skill, multi-ground and multi-age ownership of the opportunities and challenges of this demographic and social change. As age arguably possesses the greatest potential of all the Article 13 grounds to overlap with other grounds it ought to be explored for sub-groups, starting with gender to help ensure that law and policy meet their equality and anti-discrimination needs.

Discrimination on associative or perceived grounds, conflicts of rights and multiple discrimination

Robin Allen discusses the issue of associative or perceived grounds of discrimination as one of the issues that regrettably was not included in the Race and Employment Directives. His belief that this may yet prove to be a major issue across Europe appears prophetic in light of the preliminary reference to the ECJ in the *Coleman* case, involving the issue of discrimination and harassment on the ground of association with a disabled person. These forms of discrimination are treated differently in the EU Member States. While Robin Allen concludes that it seems likely the ECJ will

---

[22] For example, DG Employment and Social Affairs, 'Report of the High Level Group on the Future of Social Policy in an Enlarged Union', (2004), p. 7.

interpret the Race and Employment Directives to prohibit discrimination on associative or perceived grounds, the present lack of protection is out of step with some EU Member States[23] and third countries such as Canada.[24]

Notably absent from the Directives is the issue of how conflicts of rights are to be resolved. Barry Fitzpatrick describes the incompatibility between some religious beliefs and acceptance of LGB relationships as being 'one of the most acute dilemmas confronting European and national equality law and policy'.[25] Also absent is any legal framework for tackling multiple or inter-sectional discrimination. Yet multiple discrimination is likely to be a growing issue in the EU[26] and is arguably only beginning to receive modest attention from the European Commission. It also seems likely that some future consolidation (if not also modification) of the three separate Article 13 Directives would provide a more logical and necessary basis for taking multiple discrimination seriously.[27] That a coherent approach to multiple discrimination is necessary for the enlarged EU can be demonstrated not least by the multiple discrimination experienced by Roma and Roma women in particular. Indeed, Mark Bell considers that 'the entrenched inequality and exclusion of the Roma poses challenges for the limits of anti-discrimination legislation'.[28]

One problem facing an individual suffering from multiple discrimination is that they do not fit the 'where there is a right, there must be a remedy' system inherent in the EC Treaty.[29] There is no right not to be discriminated against on multiple grounds articulated in the EC Treaty or anti-discrimination Directives adopted thereunder. There is no general principle of non-discrimination on multiple grounds nor any EC principles governing how this issue ought to be handled judicially. Nonetheless, Tobler considers 'where Community law prohibits several different types of discrimination, some of which may be intrinsically linked, the issue of multiple discrimination is increasingly important'.[30] She also concludes that in order to be adequate and in line with the requirement of

---

[23] Most notably Ireland.   [24] Certainly in the case of perceived disability.
[25] In Chapter 10 of this volume.
[26] See inter alia H. Meenan's discussion of multiple discrimination between age and other grounds, 'Thinking outside the box: age and other grounds', in 8 *Contemporary Issues in Law* (2006/2007), pp. 80–96.
[27] Note Robin Allen's comments in Chapter 2 of this volume.
[28] In Chapter 6 of this volume.
[29] C. Tobler, *Remedies and Sanctions in EC non-discrimination Law*, (European Commission, 2005), pp. 4 and 14.
[30] Ibid., p. 34.

proportionality, remedies in multiple discrimination cases 'must reflect the multiple and thus aggravated nature of the discrimination'.[31] A large number of foreseeable issues thus await an individual litigant to champion them and the ECJ to pronounce on them. This depends on chance. An individual needs to bring the right case before a national court, which must then refer it to the ECJ. It may not be obvious to a victim of multiple discrimination that this is what they are experiencing.

European and international human rights instruments

EC equality directives have always been adopted against a rich background of national constitutional law, European and International human rights instruments. However, recent decisions in some other bodies have brought their anti-discrimination clauses to life and given them real effectiveness that is likely to increase their influence on the EU.[32] McCrudden and Kountouros sketch the differing approaches to equality and discrimination taken in human rights law. Perhaps the most influential of these to date is the ECHR. However, Article 14 ECHR has an idiosyncratic method of operation whereby the prohibition against discrimination is ancillary to a substantive right in the Convention. Moreover, the nature of the ECHR means ECtHR interpretations are less likely to be relevant for employment, which affects all Article 13 grounds. Religion or belief is the only Article 13 ground which is also a positive freedom in the ECHR.[33] Finally, a number of classifications have been ascribed to the non-discrimination grounds in Article 14 ECHR.[34]

Perhaps these factors help to explain why some chapters in this volume place different weights on the past and future influence of ECtHR jurisprudence. Thus ECtHR interpretations have been almost entirely positive for sexual orientation establishing significant human rights for this ground.[35] Religion or belief under the Employment Directive

---

[31] Ibid., pp. 4 and 34.

[32] The ESC is growing in importance and prominence in developing principles in the context of discrimination, as described by McCrudden and Kountouros, Chapter 3. Note especially *Autism-Europe* v. *France*, Complaint No. 13/2002, 4 November 2003.

[33] Article 9 ECHR.

[34] Terms such as 'choice' and 'non-choice' grounds and sensitive and non-sensitive grounds have evolved to describe and categorise them. For a commentary on these distinctions, see R. Wintemute, '"Within the ambit": How big is the "Gap" in Article 14 European Convention on Human Rights?' Part 1, (2004) 4 EHRLR, pp. 366–82 and Part 2, (2004) 5 EHRLR, pp. 484–99.

[35] Barry Fitzpatrick in Chapter 10.

raises some issues for which it might be prudent or appropriate not to follow ECtHR jurisprudence.[36] The judgments of the ECtHR on disability have been described as 'disappointing'.[37] The ECtHR's judgment in *DH v. Czech Republic* in 2006 found no proof of discrimination against Roma children in their segregation into special schools for children with learning disabilities. In doing so great weight was placed on the state's margin of appreciation in the education sphere.[38] This decision is very troubling for the enlarged EU where Roma issues are among the most acute challenges for anti-discrimination, equality and human rights law and policy. By contrast, the European Committee on Social Rights, another Council of Europe Treaty body, reached an entirely different decision in *Autism-Europe v. France* in 2004, where it decided that France's segregation of children with autism into segregated and unsuitable education violated the non-discrimination provision of the European Social Charter.[39] The increasingly strong position of the ECHR in the EC and EU Treaties, not to mention the future prospect of the EU acceding to this instrument, mean it is likely to continue to be an important influence on the ECJ. However, case law under the Article 13 Directives is also likely to generate issues, which are sufficiently differentiated from those under the ECHR to justify the ECJ taking a judicious approach to ECtHR jurisprudence where the legal and factual context so requires.

Above all it can be said that anti-discrimination has evolved into a mainstream human rights issue on EU, regional[40] and international planes.[41] The EU contributes to this development[42] and EC equality law is an inspiration for others in its own right. Community law on equality, especially sex equality, is now described as the most advanced of any jurisdiction in the world.[43] Moreover, it is now 'an acknowledged world leader'[44] in developing appropriate anti-discrimination law on disability in employment. Structurally, the Article 13 EC Directives have much to recommend them in contrast to regional human rights instruments. They apply to all EU Member States and to both public and private parties. Arguably the

---

[36] For example, Gwyneth Pitt's discussion in Chapter 7 on ECHR case law on proof of a particular religion or belief and manifestation of religion or belief.

[37] Gerard Quinn in an earlier draft of his contribution to this volume.

[38] Regrettably the question of education for children with disabilities was not considered as one that engaged rights rather it was a mere state policy.

[39] Article E.   [40] Speaking primarily of the Council of Europe.

[41] Note in particular the UN Treaty on Persons with Disabilities 2006.

[42] Such as the United Nations and the ILO.

[43] So stated in McCrudden and Kountouros in Chapter 3.

[44] Gerard Quinn in Chapter 8.

great degree of latitude left to States Parties to other instruments weakens their overall effectiveness. The extremely small number of ratifications of Protocol 12 to the ECHR, particularly by EU Member States detracts from its ability to act as a free-standing prohibition against discrimination. The choice left to States Parties to the Revised European Social Charter (ESCR) regarding which clauses to accept has a similar effect for those falling under its protection. Thus the universal application of EC non-discrimination instruments renders the basic right not to be discriminated against on the stated grounds universal.[45]

Nationality

Nationality continues to enjoy protection from discrimination in Article 12 EC and in free movement law. By contrast with the Article 13 grounds, it appears to operate in an almost exclusively non-discrimination domain. The exclusion of nationality from Article 13 means that it is kept apart from all other anti-discrimination grounds protected by EC law. This may be more difficult to defend in areas of multiple discrimination involving grounds of race, religion, ethnicity and nationality. The fact that the ground of nationality has no apparent role in the European Year of Equal Opportunities for All is significant. In addition to any gaps in protection from discrimination, this may well prove careless in light of ongoing tensions inspired by nationality within and outside EU borders.[46] Both sex and nationality anti-discrimination and equality laws have influenced the Article 13 Directives which have in turn influenced sex equality under Article 141 EC. However, there is no discernible impact by the Article 13 Directives on EC nationality discrimination law or free movement legislation. Is this good for the European Union? Certainly it would seem wise to conduct tailored research into the extent of nationality discrimination and multiple discrimination involving nationality in the EU, in order to answer this question. However, it is regrettable given its important (and continuing) role as the key which helped unlock the European project if it should be perceived as having less profile and less dynamism than the other EU anti-discrimination grounds.

---

[45] Notwithstanding arguments about the situation of third country nationals discussed in the introduction to this volume, the role of any exemptions and Art. 6 of the Employment Directive.

[46] For example, the activities of the British National Front, the French National Front Party and the Austrian Freedom Party.

The way forward?

There is a consensus in this volume (and elsewhere) that the Aristotelian concept of equality is not enough to challenge deep-rooted disadvantage and achieve far-reaching structural change where needed.[47] This shows the limits of the business case (economic rationality) as the principal foundation for non-discrimination law and of civil rights in tackling the causes rather than the symptoms of discrimination. Moreover, there is a need to anchor non-discrimination and equality in human rights principles like dignity. The Article 13 Directives contain three identifiable goals, economic, social and human rights, and thus in principle form a good starting point to the necessary approach. McCrudden and Kountouros advise that within such an approach, the promotion of equality requires other economic, social and supporting mechanisms in addition to legal provisions. They also warn against narrowing 'the equality discourse to only one, predominantly individualistic and economic-centred, meaning, but to acknowledge the diversity of meanings of the concept'. However, Ann Numhauser-Henning expresses the fear that 'an ever growing number of groups to be protected against discrimination will incline the notion of discrimination even closer to the Aristotelian concept of formal equal treatment as the least common denominator'. The necessary research outlined herein and a suitably responsive approach to different groups and sub-groups may help to achieve more substantive equal treatment for them. However, other grounds are currently quite a distance from the current proactive approach of sex equality.

Beyond anti-discrimination legislation many useful complementary approaches are contained in the Article 13 Directives or already existed in EC equality law but more may be needed to tackle complex issues. The picture is very mixed for these also. Comparisons of sex and race mainstreaming demonstrate an imbalance both in provision and in process. This partly reflects the fact that mainstreaming is a very broad concept and in future greater specificity of method and purpose would be desirable than appears to be the case for mainstreaming for race. Some grounds have been exposed for longer and to a greater extent to the Open Method of Co-ordination (OMC) than others have been, for example disability.[48] Mark Bell has recommended that the application of the OMC to

---

[47] Reflecting on the role of the non-discrimination principle in the ESCR Treaties is instructive as it is organically linked to more programmatic approaches in them.

[48] Which has featured in the European Employment Strategy and social inclusion strategy for a long time.

anti-discrimination policies should be examined.[49] This has much to recommend it in the field of positive action or contract compliance,[50] which would be especially valuable for disadvantage that can be said to be Community wide. While the Roma appear to have a universally difficult time throughout the EU further research could help to identify other groups and sub-groups for such a radical approach.

The softer elements of the Article 13 Directives should be seen as complementary to a right's based approach.[51] They apply to all of the Article 13 grounds while the hard law elements differ noticeably in material scope across the grounds. Such a variable rights-based approach is sitting on weak foundations. There may be a sound rationale why one or two grounds are the first to achieve protection in goods, facilities and services for instance but there is no discernible reason why they should remain 'first among equals' indefinitely. Pan-European research available on a vast range of age discrimination outside the field of employment suggests that age already fulfils the 'subsidiarity' requirements for the adoption of further legislation at EU level.[52] There may also be scope for relying on the traditional methods of creating general principles. A further argument for extending the material scope of all remaining grounds rests on a multiple discrimination and inter-sectional approach to the Article 13 grounds.[53] Serious and extensive research must be undertaken on the issue of multiple discrimination within the EU; this is one of the main unresolved issues. The simple fact is we do not know how to access justice on grounds of multiple or inter-sectional discrimination under the Directives and implementing legislation. Nor do we have much understanding of the scale of this problem and the range of interesting sub-groups that might be affected.

There is also a very strong sense in which the softer provisions of the Race and Employment Directives may not go far enough[54] or have not been relied on sufficiently since the implementation process. Preliminary

---

[49] M Bell, *Anti-Discrimination Law*, p. 215.   [50] Ibid., p. 216.

[51] Barry Fitzpatrick in Chapter 10.

[52] H. Meenan, 'Age Discrimination in Europe: A later bloomer or wall-flower', International Federation on Ageing Conference, Copenhagen, 30 May to 2 June 2006. Note, the European Commission's planned proposal to extend protection for the remaining Article 13 grounds beyond employment at note 2 above.

[53] There is considerable disadvantage faced by older ethnic patients in accessing healthcare services; see PRIAE at www.priae.org.

[54] Barry Fitzpatrick argues in Chapter 10 that Art. 9.2 should have gone further and not necessarily required a named complainant, bringing it closer to genuine public interest litigation.

research into the implementation of the age strand revealed that no Member State had announced an audit of existing legislation for age discrimination against Article 16 (compliance) of the Employment Directive.[55] This provision is one of the strengths of the Directive. Whatever research is conducted into multiple discrimination, equality strategies for all grounds ought to take into account different groups within them. This can only be adequately achieved through involving members of each ground if not also sub-groups, in the design and implementation of appropriate equality strategies. This is arguably facilitated by Articles 13 and 14 of the Employment Directive.

Four observations on the way ahead deserve to be reiterated here. Ann Numhauser-Henning highlights 'social inclusion', whether of women or the elderly, or of citizens of new Member States or the disabled, as a major concern for the future. While Robin Allen makes a compelling argument that if for no other reason than the implications of demographic change, the European Commission will have to revisit how rights for and action to secure substantive equality can be achieved. Israel Doron recommends that legal and policy discourse on equality need to be supported with empirical social and demographic data in order to connect equality to reality. He asserts that the power of 'equality' and non-discrimination as active social tools will eventually rest upon their ability to be sensitive to the diverse and complex interactions between the law and socio-economic changes in an enlarged EU. Finally, Mark Bell believes that the broader mandate of the Fundamental Rights Agency could be 'particularly valuable in addressing issues related to ethnic diversity, but which do not fit neatly within an "anti-discrimination" paradigm. . . . [and] . . . could facilitate a more comprehensive overview of the interaction between anti-discrimination, minority rights and human rights'. This new institution, properly planned and managed, has unexplored potential to support the covered grounds, human rights and equality in the EU.

It is apparent that an adequate, reflective and responsive approach is essential to combat discrimination and promote equality in a large and enlarging European Union. Subject to further research into the rich diversity generated by multiple discrimination, inter-sectional discrimination and nationality and obtaining good quality data across all grounds, it can be said that there is a reasonable range of tools already available in EC equality law and policy that ought to be fully utilised. While Robin Allen considers that the Employment and Race Directives have broadly

---

[55] AGE Analysis Report, 2004.

fulfilled the five conditions he proposed for effective anti-discrimination legislation at the Vienna Conference, additional approaches may prove necessary in time. Perhaps what is also needed now is a spilling over of existing strengths and good practice from the more advanced grounds in the softer areas of the equality regime, to all covered grounds. One thing, above all, is clear from this volume that the adoption of Article 13 and its Directives was only the beginning of an exciting and important new chapter in the history of equality and non-discrimination for the European Union. Another, as stated herein and recently by the European Commission, is that 'legislation alone is not enough to prevent discrimination and to promote equality'.[56] Much work remains to be done. The European Commission's plans announced in 2007, to extend protection beyond employment for the remaining Article 13 grounds, is an optimistic sign in relation to one notable gap in protection. However, even in this one respect, we cannot prejudge the outcome at this stage. It would also mitigate against justice and fairness if very many of the various outstanding issues revealed in this volume, were passively left for resolution by an over-worked European Court of Justice some day.

[56] Communication COM(2006) 643 final, p. 9.

INDEX